Medieval Armies and
Weapons in Western Europe

ALSO BY JEAN-DENIS G. G. LEPAGE

*Castles and Fortified Cities of
Medieval Europe: An Illustrated History*
(McFarland, 2002)

MEDIEVAL ARMIES AND WEAPONS IN WESTERN EUROPE

An Illustrated History

JEAN-DENIS G. G. LEPAGE

McFarland & Company, Inc., Publishers
Jefferson, North Carolina, and London

Acknowledgments

The author would like to thank
Jeannette à Stuling,
Eltjo de Lang and Ben Marcato,
Simone and Bernard Lepage,
Erik Karstel and Florence Rigal,
Anne Chauvel, Michèle Clermont,
Véronique Janty, and John Beauval.

LIBRARY OF CONGRESS CATALOGUING-IN-PUBLICATION DATA

Lepage, Jean-Denis.
Medieval armies and weapons in western Europe :
an illustrated history / Jean-Denis G. G. Lepage.
p.   cm.
Includes bibliographical references and index.

ISBN 978-0-7864-1772-8
illustrated case binding : 50# alkaline paper ∞

1. Military art and science — History — Medieval, 500–1500.
2. Military art and science — Europe, Western — History.
3. Military history, Medieval.
4. Military weapons — Europe — History — to 1500.
I. Title.
U37.L46 2005   355'.0094'0902 — dc22   2004013461

British Library cataloguing data are available

Cover image ©2005 Clipart.com

Manufactured in the United States of America

McFarland & Company, Inc., Publishers
Box 611, Jefferson, North Carolina 28640
www.mcfarlandpub.com

Contents

PART III. THE LATE MIDDLE AGES (14TH–15TH CENTURIES)

Introduction

Hundreds of years after the close of the Middle Ages, the period continues to exert a unique emotional power over Western culture. The attitude of Westerners is ambivalent but never detached. A governmental system that is disliked is termed "medieval," yet Westerners continue to be drawn to tales of King Arthur, Ivanhoe, and Robin Hood. The Middle Ages are considered a barbaric time, and yet they furnish enduring icons: the knight in shining armor, the idealized lady, and the king upon his throne. The perception many have of the Middle Ages is mythic rather than historical, but somehow the period remains in one's consciousness in a way that other historical periods do not. The medieval world is at times alien and remote, yet it always resonates within the psyche of Westerners. Such fascination is not an idle fancy.

In many respects, the Middle Ages represents the point of origin of modern Western culture based on three distinct cultural strands: the classical Mediterranean civilization of Greece and imperial Rome, the Byzantine and Jewish traditions imported from the Middle East with the advent of Christianity, and the "barbarian" culture of the German tribes from northern Europe. The Middle Ages cover about a millennium of human history—roughly speaking, from 500 to 1500. Medievalists commonly divide the Middle Ages into three periods, and this is how this book is designed: in three major parts following the chronology and describing the parallel evolution of warriors, weapons and armor, and warfare.

The Early Middle Ages began with the fall of the Western Roman Empire—not a single-date event but a long process of decline. For convenience we may place this era from the year 500 to the close of the 11th century.

This period was marked by migrations of whole tribes, a high incidence of warfare arising out of the lack of strong central governments, limited urban activities, and written culture in the hands of the monastic element of the Catholic Church.

The High or Central Middle Ages extended roughly from the 11th to the end of 13th century. It was the time of knights and chivalry, when Europe achieved a degree of political stability that permitted expeditions abroad (Crusades), a new flourishing of intellectual and economic life, a dramatic revival of urban activities, and an increasing sophistication in secular culture.

The Late Middle Ages, from the early 14th to the late 15th century, began with a series of catastrophes (Black Death and the Hundred Years' War) disrupting the traditional feudal structure. A number of developments in military techniques and technology undermined the supremacy of the knight. It was a period of transition characterized by a weakening of traditional power and an ongoing series of social and religious crises.

A work comprehensively covering so many years and so many regions would be too diffuse; therefore, this book will focus on the feudal heartland of Western Europe—sharing a more-or-less similar historical profile—including France, Great Britain, Germany, Italy, and the Iberian Peninsula. Some references will however be made to regions outside this core, such as the Greek-Byzantine Empire, Palestine, and Scandinavia, because of the influence they exercised at a certain time.

Success in war depends upon numerous factors. Questions of politics, strategy, and logistics all affect the outcome. But when it comes to combat on the actual battlefield, tactics are what count. There, the main factors of warfare are leadership, the use of ground, and weapons. The Middle Ages were not a period of unusually prolific advances in weapon design, and medieval soldiers went to war — broadly speaking — with the arms inherited from ancient antiquity.

A *weapon* is defined as "a material thing designed or used or usable as an instrument for inflicting bodily harm." If this definition stands in need of considerable revision today, it is accurate enough to apply to those weapons used during the Middle Ages: rather small things used by one individual against another. Weapons may be broadly categorized into two main classes: offensive and defensive weapons. As the names apply, the former are intended to strike and the latter to protect. Before the development of gunpowder, which totally changed warfare, the struggle between the two categories was fairly balanced, but there was always a competition between power and mobility, and protection from missiles and blows exemplified by the increasingly heavily-armored knight on his warhorse.

Throughout human history, humans have invested some of their highest craft and artistic skills in their weapons, equipment, and engines of war. Shields, blades, swords, and axes as well as armors could be so beautifully decorated by chiseling, embossing, and gilding that they became precious works of art which might give rise to aesthetic emotion. At the same time, weapons, their possession, and their legal or illegal use were (and still are) very hot issues. This book is not intended to deal with philosophical, moral, or legal considerations, as the focus is on medieval warriors and the historical and technical development of weaponry. But the reader may be reminded that all medieval weapons, primitive or elaborate, simple or ornamented, ugly or beautiful, were intended to *inflict harm*. Hooks, spikes, blades, and blunt items were meant to kill; they were designed to cut flesh, to smash brains, to tear muscles, and to shed blood.

Technical terminology in the Middle Ages tended to be fluid; standardization of language was limited and a tendency toward the use of localisms intensifies the difficulty of identifying authoritative terms for specific weapons. Specialized and foreign terms that are unlikely to be familiar to the ordinary reader are explained by the black-and-white illustrations within the text. As in my previous publications, the method adopted here relies thus on my own drawings, many of them specifically executed for this book. Like any technical subject, weapons and armies need to be translated into more digestible terms to be more widely understood.

My principal concern all along has been to synthesize the vast amount of existing information. There are indeed many outstanding books on the Middle Ages for children and plenty of advanced texts for history students, both offering a vivid look at warriors, weapons, and armors and providing details on medieval armies. My aim in writing this book is to provide an intermediate level. This work is oriented toward an introductory study rather than advanced research; it is a book that offers both a broad picture and informative details of medieval warriors, weapons, and warfare for readers who are not children but who are not familiar with the medieval world. In writing this book I have had to work in the shadow of many masterly historians, some of them listed in the bibliography. As with my other titles (e.g., *Castles and Fortified Cities of Medieval Europe*, published by McFarland in 2002), I have tried to offer here a historical and technical book that I would have wanted for myself.

— Jean-Denis G. G. Lepage
Groningen, Netherlands
Fall 2004

PART I

THE EARLY MIDDLE AGES
(6TH–11TH CENTURIES)

1

Late Romans, Germanic Invaders, and Byzantines

The End of the Western Roman Empire

The period roughly between the fall of Rome and the Frankish empire of Charlemagne is commonly called the Dark Age of European history. Throughout its long life, the Roman empire had been surrounded by "barbarians": wild Celts in Wales and Scotland, Germans in the heart of Europe, Persians in the east, and Arabs in the southeast. These barbarians had never been brought within the pale of Roman civilization. On the whole they were unsettled, townless, more or less nomadic, and frequently bellicose. The successive invaders followed, clashed with, and absorbed one another like the waves of a turbulent sea. The Romans drew a line fitted with fortifications (*limes*, plural *limites*) beyond which they did not venture and which were intended to repel the barbarians. Nevertheless the barbarians filtered in. As early as the 3rd century A.D., emperors and generals recruited bands of them to serve in the Roman armies. When their service was over, they would receive farmlands, settle down, and marry and mingle with the local population. By the 4th century a good many individuals of barbarian birth were even reaching high positions in the state and in the army. At the same time in the west, for reasons that are not fully understood, the activities of the Roman cities began to falter, commerce began to decay, local governments became paralyzed, taxes became more ruinous, and free farmers were bound to the soil. The army seated and unseated emperors; rival generals fought each other. Gradually the

western part of the Roman Empire fell into decrepitude and an internal barbarization so that the old line between Roman provinces and the barbarian world made less and less difference. The barbarians themselves, after centuries of relative stability, were pushed by other peoples from behind or were attracted by the sun and the wealth of Roman civilization. Rather suddenly whole tribes — including men, women, and children — began to move. Some of them sought peaceable access to the Roman empire; others came by force, plundering and killing as they went. As the Germanic barbarians broke through the frontiers of the empire, much tragedy, horror, suffering, despair, and despondency were brought to the people. It was the end of the Ancient world, and to many the future seemed hopeless.

In the 5th century, the Anglo-Saxons invaded Britain, the Franks overran Gaul, the Vandals reached as far as northern Africa, the Ostrogoths appeared in Asia Minor and in Italy, and the Visigoths lunged toward Constantinople, tore through Greece, sacked Rome itself in 410, and reached Spain. In 476 the last Roman emperor in the West was deposed by Odoaker, the chieftain of the Herulian tribe. This date is often held to mark the end of the Ancient time and the beginning of the Middle Ages in Europe. The unified world of Mediterranean civilization, as it existed under the Roman empire, broke apart into three segments. The first segment was the Eastern Greek or Byzantine Empire with its capital Constantinople. Representing the continuation of the Roman

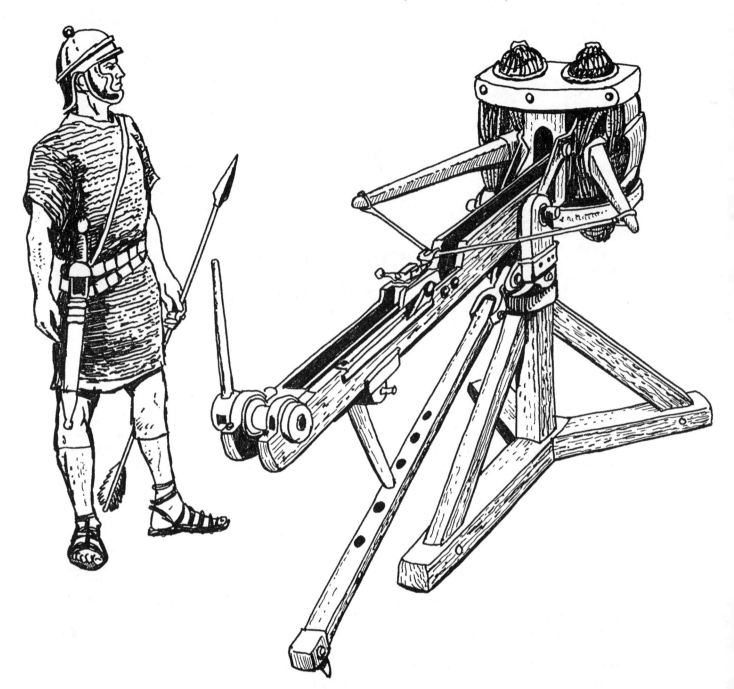

Roman Scorpio. The scorpio was a large crossbow that shot javelins. This type of primitive artillery equipped the Roman galleys, assault towers, and fortifications. It was also used as support artillery on the battlefield.

civilization, it was Christian in religion and culture and language. The second segment, the Muslim world, extended from Spain, North Africa, Syria, and the East. Arabic was its language, and Islam was its religion. The third segment, the chaotic Western Europe, where all central government had fallen to pieces, was the least promising. It was composed of what the Byzantines were unable to hold and what the Arabs could not conquer. It included many small barbarian kingdoms ruled by Germanic invaders. However, in the chaos which followed

the collapse of the Roman Empire, Western Europe slowly acquired an identity, made of three main influences: Roman, Christian, and German customs. The ancient civilization was partly preserved in the laws and institutions of the Roman heritage. Christianity — mainly in the form of monasticism — had widely spread and had become the uniting European faith, while the Germanic influence was to be a distinctive contribution to the making of Europe by bringing new customs and a dynamic civilization. Later, the continent discovered and developed a new form

Roman Centurion

Roman Soldier, about A.D. 350

of social organization—feudalism—which enabled it to confront and later to conquer its enemies, mainly the expansionist Islam.

The Late Roman Imperial Army

After the death of Septimius Severus (A.D. 146–211), the soldiers of the Roman army were indeed in charge of the situation. They made and unmade emperors capriciously, switching their support from candidate to candi-

date in return for promises of ever greater rewards. Any frontier commander who was able to persuade his army to support him in an assault on Italy could aspire to be emperor. Over and over again, pretenders marched on Rome and either murdered the reigning emperor or were themselves defeated and killed. The incessant civil wars naturally weakened the borders. Frankish tribes launched raids on the Rhineland, and Goths pressed on the Danube frontier.

The wars also had the effect of undermining the financial structures of the state. Each new emperor had to provide enormous bribes to satisfy the soldiers who had raised him to power. As the Roman Empire weakened, the sums swallowed up by its defense had been increasing steadily. The emperor Diocletian (284–305) and his immediate successors had doubled the size of the legions so that at the beginning of the 5th century the army numbered about half a million men. Given the population of the Empire — possibly 50 million — and its very extended and weak borders, this was not an excessively large number. But to the pay and provisioning of the soldiers had to be added the military supplies from the

Mauri Feroces. The "wild Moors" were North African light cavalrymen serving in the Roman army as auxiliaries.

elaborate system of governmental factories and the building and upkeep of the famous road network, together with the horses and vehicles for all overland transport as well as the building of frontier fortifications.

The weakening of the empire was particularly striking in view of the decadence of the Roman army, for indeed the greatest problem was to find enough recruits. At the beginning of the Christian era, the emperor Augustus had been able to recruit his main armies from Italy, for military service was then considered a honorable career. Every soldier became a Roman citizen, and at the end of his period of service he received a grant or money that enabled him to live decently as a respected veteran. During the second century A.D., when the people of Italy became unwilling to volunteer in sufficient numbers for the rigors of army life, the large-scale force that was needed to defend the borders was recruited principally from the Roman provincials to do garrison duty on the northern frontiers. That was not an inviting prospects for young men from the Mediterranean countries. At the same time it was not easy to recruit men locally at the frontiers for it was precisely in these areas of the empire that population was sparse and, in consequence, the great landowners of these parts were most unwilling to see their precious labor force recruited into the imperial army. Since the Roman government could not coerce the landowners, it fell back on recruiting into the legions the very barbarians from whom the empire had to be defended. The motto was "let barbarian fight barbarian," one under the Roman eagles, the other in his rustic skins. If peace could be bought by hiring soldiers, it was worth the price.

The barbarians on the Roman frontiers were not a monolithic force. They were quite used to fighting each other, and many were perfectly willing to serve in the Roman armies, especially as this involved the attractive offer of pay in the form of land inside the empire. As long as their numbers were not large, and as long as they were settled in small groups dispersed over large areas, the barbarians would eventually be Romanized and absorbed. But these conditions were precisely what the emperors did not manage to maintain. Some barbarians joined the Roman forces individually, but whole foreign tribes of warriors — with wives and children under the command of their own clan chieftains — were recruited as defenders of the empire. This service was recognized by a special agreement called *fœdus*: barbarian Alanni, Visigoths, Vandals, Franks, or Burgonds, authorized to settle inside the Empire, were called *feoderati* or federated people or simply allies. In exchange for their military service, they got lands, which they exploited, but they kept their language, customs, and hierarchy. Even though they were romanized in varying degrees, such troops had little instinctive attachment to the remote imperial government — they had never seen Rome or Italy.

Because the emperor was often merely a name to them, the feoderatis' loyalty came to be concentrated on their immediate commanders. By the beginning of the 5th century an alarming large part of the Roman army offices were sometimes filled by barbarians. During the minority of emperor Honorius (395–408), the effective control of the western half of the empire was already in the hands of a romanized Vandal, Stilicho, who held the title of *magister militum*, or commander-in-chief. Stilicho successfully defended Italy from two Gothic invasions. The Roman aristocracy, however, hated him and accused him of collusion with the invaders. True or not, the Roman troops murdered Stilicho's officers, and he was executed. His career shows the political and psychological strains created by the policy of employing barbarians in the defense of the empire.

The army, which was the pillar of the Roman society and the base of romanization, was germanized, mistrusted, and confined to the frontier zones in

Roman Cavalryman, 4th Century

limites (fortified lines) and lived on the margin of the society it was supposed to defend. The command was entrusted to *comes* (meaning "comrade" in classical Latin and later the basis for the words counts or earls) and *dux* (dukes). These high officers wanted a bodyguard of their own men –elite troops who could be relied on to deliver a charge in a wavering battle, to cover a retreat, or to provide personal protection in a period of disorder. These groups of soldiers could be large. Many were recruited from the lower classes, some were freed slaves, but all had some chance to become officers. There was nothing particularly honorable about their calling; they were more like a special class of servants. If they served their master faithfully they received food, clothing, a little pay, and, at times, a share in the spoils of war. But as a class they had no social standing and no political influence. These men fought — not for the Roman state — but because they had

a personal allegiance to a military leader. The notion of public state service disappeared, and a military regime existed based on the personal relations of men to men, which formed the premises of the future feudal system.

The efficiency and the military glory of Rome — still nearly intact in spite of the troubles of the 3rd century — disappeared after the reign of Constantine (306–337). It became then evident that if the Roman state was still effective in appearance, the power was completely in the hands of the barbarians warriors. Under the reign of Emperor Julian (361–363), the army was totally Germanized and later the writer and bishop Sidoinus Apollinarius (431–487) declared with sadness that it had become necessary to speak Germanic dialects to command the Roman soldiers garrisoned in Gaul. Roman armies at the close of the 5th century had ceased to be Roman. They were composed of barbarian contingents whose zeal and

Roman Armored Cavalryman, 4th Century

loyalty fluctuated alarmingly, and who were especially unreliable when they thought that they were on the losing side. The fine discipline and strict order of earlier and better days had fallen into contempt. In the long term, the expedient of employing barbarians was disastrous. Indeed, as long as the empire seemed unshakable and firm, the patchwork of Roman populations had a relative trust in the foreign defenders, but after the reign of Theodosius (379–395), mistrust and fear began to prevail. On the borders of the empire, the feoderati constituted important colonies and even small independent states within the large Roman state. In the second half of the 5th century, the feoderati — masters of the military power — watched over and held the emperors in Rome at their mercy. When these feoderati wanted to involve themselves in Roman politics, when they revolted, and when they marched into the Roman Empire, there was thus no — or very little — opposing force to drive them back.

Tactics and strategy were radically changed. The Roman legion underwent profound mutation and was divided in light infantry formations. In place of ten *cohortes* (troops), a legion was then formed of autonomous units called *numerus* — totaling each from 300 to 500 soldiers commanded by a *tribun*. By the time of Diocletian (284–305) the army was divided into two distinct forces. The *limitanei* were static militias tied to the frontiers who manned and guarded fortifications against raids from barbarians; the *exercitus comitanensis* were mobile forces located in strategic centers and which conducted the more serious campaigning. This two-fold policy was continued by Constantine (307–337) by increasing the cavalry for the mobile forces. The cavalry was much more suitable for mobile warfare against barbarian raiders. By that time, horsemen mounted bareback using a loose cloth as a saddle and a very primitive bit. Lacking stirrups, the cavalrymen were too easily unseated to make an effective charge, and their light javelins were difficult to use accurately. In spite of these technical limitations, the cavalry played an increasingly important role.

The good old Roman traditions had passed away; armaments had ceased to be uniform and standardized. As the need was for mobility, weapons and equipment tended to be lighter. They were modified and intermixed with Germanic-styled equipment and weapons. The *scutum* (large rectangular shield) was replaced by a round or oval light shield. The helmet tended to conform to that of the early Greeks, with a deep head piece furnished with a long, lowered visor or nasal. The body armor tended to be discarded or replaced with lighter armor. The *lorica* (heavy metal laminated breastplate protecting the trunk) was often replaced with the *squammata* (scale armor), a leather or linen tunic upon which overlapping scales of metal were sewn. *Hamata* (chain mail) was also introduced. The *pilum* (throwing spear) was partly abandoned for longer spears, pikes, and other pole weaponry. The short two-edged *gladius* sword was still in use but many other sorts of swords appeared, some with a long blade, and others like the *spatha*, were long single-edged swords. At the same time the number of archers was increased; the bow — with a range of about 100 meters — became more usual in the formation for both infantry and cavalry.

In the 4th century, the composition of the legion underwent another modification, becoming merely a single troop totaling some 800 to 1,200 soldiers which were supported by 500 mounted men. The infantry furnished a solid group of soldiers able to hold off the mounted barbarians, and the cavalry provided a mobile striking element. Cavalry began to count more and more, and in adapting their military organization to favor horsemen, the Roman had little choice. Desperately trying to repel mobile barbarian hordes from their frontiers, they gradually created more formations of cavalry and deemphasized the role of the traditional Roman infantry. The mounted combatant assumed a position of ascendancy, a position he retained for centuries. However, the barbarian horsemen proved superior in 378 at the battle of Andrinople when the Goth mounted men achieved an overwhelming victory over the Romans infantry. Using javelins and swords, their cavalry surprised the Roman army on the flank and drove it into confusion. The Roman infantry, unable to deploy properly, were massacred. This change was one of the most decisive features in warfare, and it announced the appearance of the armored horseman — the *miles*. This Latin term *miles* (plural *milites* from which the word military comes) was to be the word employed in the Middle Age for all combatants on horseback as well as for medieval knights.

The Huns

The Huns were a nomadic people who lived in the desolate Asian steppes of Mongolia. As they left no writings or inscriptions for historians and no artifacts for archaeologists, their previous history and wanderings on the extreme limits of the civilized world are still obscure. As true nomads, they probably herded cattle and sheep and lived in primitive wagons and tents. Their standard

Hunnic Horseman

of living was probably very low, but they were ferocious fighters and very good horsemen. They were so inseparable from their horses that a Roman writer called them "shaggy centaurs." The Huns' main weapons were spears, swords, and composite bows made of horn and wood. Their good mobility, superior fire power, unpredictable tactics, savagery, and frightening ugly appearance inspired terror and loathing among both Romans and Germans. They were short, had prominent cheek-bones, and were intensely hardy and unbridled in their cruelty.

Bands of Huns moved to Tibet, Mongolia, China, and India in the 4th century. The reasons for their westward march is quite unknown. After 375 their raids into Germany were terrible. They conquered the northern Danube region and formed a federation of clans and tribes under one king. The Huns swept into western Europe with a ferocity which has made their name symbolic of everything barbaric and cruel. So great was the terror they inspired, despite their relative small numbers, that their kings could compel the obedience of populations from the Caucasus to the Baltic Sea and blackmail the Byzantine emperor in Constantinople into paying large tributes. The primitive rule of the Huns was based on little more than terror and the personal renown of a successful leader and his henchmen.

The Hunnic expansion indeed had dramatic historical consequences as they profoundly disturbed the German tribes, putting them in a critical situation and pushing them westward into the Roman Empire. In 451 the Hunnic king Attila, leading some 70,000 warriors, crossed the Rhine and drove the terrified Germans before him into Gaul. Metz, Troyes, Paris, and Orleans were targets. In the summer of 451, the Huns were defeated by the Roman chief Aetius—allied to the federated Goths—on the Campus Mauriacus, the Catalaunian fields near Troyes in Champagne (France). Attila retreated, Gaul was saved, but the Western Roman Empire was badly crippled as the Huns made an attempt to raid Italy. They razed Aquileia, whose inhabitants took refuge on an island of the Rialto lagoon, the origin of Venice. Attila was advancing to Rome, and only plague in his army and his sudden death, in 453, saved the west from further devastation. His sons quarreled; the Hunnic Empire promptly collapsed, and the fearsome hordes fell back toward Hungaria and the region of the Sea of Azov. In the 5th century the Hunnic tribe Hephthalite launched raids into Turkestan, Iran, and India, where they were defeated. After this defeat the Huns totally disappeared.

The Germanic Invasions

Presumably, before they started migrating from their homelands in northern Europe, the Germanic peoples differed little from one another in either language and customs. There were however two main groups of peoples. The West Germans—Saxons, Suevi, Franks, and Alemanni—were probably peasants, living in permanent settlements and in villages of primitive wooden huts and supporting themselves by agriculture. The East Germans—Lombards, Vandals and Goths—were mainly nomadic horsemen and herdsmen. The Roman historian Publius Cornelius Tacitus (55–120 A.D.) described the Germans on the whole as tall men with red or blond hair and fierce blue eyes who were fond of war, feasting and wild drinking, and impatient of restraint of any kind and who had a strong love for freedom — or one may say license — which was to play an important part in the development of Western civilization. Nomadic or settled, all German tribes regarded war as a necessary welcome alternative to their pastoral or agricultural lives.

They had no temples or churches but worshiped and offered sacrifices to their numerous gods in sacred groves of trees. The main gods were Tiu, Wodan, Thor, and Freya, whose names survive in our days of the week, Tuesday, Wednesday, Thursday, and Friday. Once they had broken into the Roman Empire, the Germans converted to Christianity. Very little is known of these large-scale conversions or of the reasons for their rapid success, but progressively barbarian paganism slowly gave way to Christianity — either that of the classical Rome or diverging variations such the Arianism, a complex and controversial doctrine which considered Christ as not truly divine and which created an immense stir in the Church.

Their political institutions were rather primitive. There were different social classes among them: noblemen, free men, freed men, and slaves. Justice was administrated by popular courts, and laws were primarily devoted to supplying alternatives or private vengeance by means of oath-taking or various forms of violent ordeal. There was no central government, no sense of allegiance to a common state, but different clans were led by a chieftain. As reported by Tacitus, each tribe was governed by a chosen *rex* (king) who was more a *dux bellorum* (gang leader or a chieftain) with limited power than a proper sovereign. The emphasis was on companionship, and chiefs were chosen for strength and skill, not for their subtlety or political acumen. Cohesion of the tribe existed by bonds of tradition, by common upbringing between warriors, and was maintained by personal loyalties, ties of kinship, and devotion between the chief and his group of warriors.

War was the normal thread of every leader's career and the *raison d'être* of every position of authority. When a petty German kinglet was planning a military expedition, he issued a call to brave young men of good family in search of adventure. They swore to serve him faithfully in return for arms, food, clothes, and a share of the expected booty. This gang—both body-guards and army—was called *comitatus* (the group of companions themselves were called *comites*) by the Romans. In larger expeditions, several groups could be formed under the command of an elected chief. Tacitus also remarked that it was a foul disgrace to return alive from a battle in which the chief had been killed; it was a severe principle, involving a highly developed sense of duty with little regard for the self. Therefore, the Germanic armed retainers had a high social position. No leader had very many of these men, and he usually treated them with distinction; they were his companions rather than his servants, and they received presents rather than wages. They were, or could easily become, an aristocracy distinguished by birth or the great merit of their fathers. Relatively few in number, they had a great influence as guards of honor in peacetime and as elite soldiers in wartime. Their numbers and courage brought fame and glory to the leader in his own tribe and among neighboring people. Thus, long before the appearance of the knight proper, there had been an ancient tradition of a warrior elite whose idea of honorable conduct was bound up in a nexus of noble qualities such as courage, prowess, and devotion. The German loyalty of the fighting man to his leader, transmuted into the feudal relationship of vassalage, remained a basic bond of society all through the Middle Ages and particularly in the feudal period.

The barbarians' equipment for war is not very well known, and we cannot offer more than a few general statements. If we must believe Tacitus, their weapons and armor were simple and primitive. For defense they had only a circular or oblong shield made of wood, with a large and boldly projecting metal boss or umbo in the center; this was securely riveted and afforded a convenient and secure handle for holding the shield. They had neither breastplate nor helmet, but occasionally leaders and important warriors would be equipped with armor in Roman fashion — the spoils from some dead or defeated Romans. They went into action bareheaded, their bodies covered with some kind of vestment of linen, a tunic short in its skirt and tightly girded, or they wore skins or cloaks of woven cloth. Weapons included battle-axes and lances. Both these arms were made under several varieties of form and size with a dual purpose: fighting at close range or throwing. They seemed to have various sorts of sword. A short *swerd*, a longer *spatha*, and a one-edged *scramasax*. Their tactics was probably primitive and limited to deployment and a vigorous charge where personal courage and bravery played a central role.

The Germans constantly pressed against the Roman Empire's borders during the 3rd and 4th centuries. And, as previously mentioned, by the end of the 4th century the barbarian feoderati held the Roman frontiers against other barbarians. At times attackers would defeat the frontier guards and raid an imperial province, but eventually fresh mobile troops would arrive and drive them back. The gradual germanization of the western provinces of the empire and the romanization of the Germanic peoples could have led to a slow infiltration and the estab-

Visigoth Warrior, ca. 400

lishment of Germanic states. In fact the process was radically accelerated in about 400 A.D. by a new set of circumstances. Instead of launching mere raids, whole Germanic peoples began to migrate into the empire and to make permanent settlements. Very little is known why those people suddenly migrated. Perhaps it was the appearance of the terrifying Huns who set in motion this whole wave of migrations. Some barbarians came as suppliants, others as conquerors, but basically all of them came to stay. More than an invasion, it was a *Völkerwanderung* –a migration of people. By the end of the 5th century the Roman Empire in the West had ceased to exist as a political entity.

Visigoths

The Visigoths tried unsuccessfully to fight off the Huns, but outmaneuvered and defeated, they petitioned the emperor Valens (364–378) for permission to cross the Danube in 374 and settle in imperial territory. For the first time a whole tribe of barbarians—totaling probably some 70,000 people—had been admitted into the empire. Inevitably friction arose between guests and hosts. In 378 the Visigoths rebelled against the imperial authority and won a major battle at Adrianople, and for a moment the very existence of the Roman Empire seemed at stake. The situation was saved by the next emperor, Theodosius I (379–395), who restored order. The Visigoths were content then to revert to the status of feoderati. In 396 they rose again under their king Alaric, who ravaged Greece. In 402 Alaric led his warriors in an attack on Italy where he was repelled by the *magister militum*, the Vandal Stilicho. After Stilicho's death in 408, Alaric attacked Rome once again, captured the city, and looted it in 410. Alaric's successor, Ataulph, led the Visigoths into southern Gaul and defeated the Vandals in Spain.

Ostrogoth Chief, ca. 350

the Frankish Catholic king Clovis when he defeated the Visigoths in 507 at the battle of Vouillé near Poitiers (France). After this the Visigoths were driven out of Gaul into Spain. The Visigoth kingdom in Spain was finally destroyed by the Muhammadan invasion of 711.

Vandals

The Vandals were pressed by the Visigoths in Spain and migrated from there into North Africa in 429. Their chief, Gaiseric, created an independent state, built a powerful fleet, and harassed Sicily and southern Italy. In 455 the Vandals inflicted a terrible blow to the Romans; they looted the city of Rome. The successors of Ataulph created a great Visigothic kingdom that stretched from the Straight of Gibraltar to the river Loire in France. In 452, the last Roman army commander, Aetius, succeeded in making an alliance with the Visigoths and decisively defeated the Huns in the battle of the Catalaunian fields near Troyes in Champagne (France). In the conquered lands, the Visigoths formed an army of occupation living on the tribute of conquered populations, who outnumbered the occupiers many times over. The Visigoths were separated from their Catholic subjects not only by race and culture but also by religion, for they were Arians. Accordingly, the local people and their bishops welcomed

Ostrogoths

Under Hunnic pressure, the Ostrogoths had crossed the Danube in 453, threatened the Balkan province, and invaded Italy; in 489 their king, Theodoric, killed the usurper Odoaker and established himself as ruler of Italy. Theodoric was an intelligent man who understood the Roman tradition of orderly government. The whole apparatus of bureaucratic Roman administration survived in Italy, and the Ostrogoths' function was purely military. This system worked as long as the king lived, and after his death in 526 the Ostrogoth kingdom collapsed under the pressure of the Byzantine Empire in 552.

The Byzantine Empire

The Byzantine Empire was the eastern part of the Roman Empire with Byzance as its capital (later called Constantinople, today Istanbul). The Eastern Empire sur-

Byzantine Cavalryman

Byzantine Cataphract, 6th Century

vived the barbarian invasions, preserved some elements of the Roman classical civilization, and after the downfall of Rome determined the future course of history in Western Europe and had a decisive influence on Eastern Europe. The emperor Justinian — during his reign from 527 to 565 — sought to strengthen the Eastern Empire. He reorganized the state, regulated economics, codified the Roman law, strongly fortified and enriched his capital with splendid monuments (among them the cathedral Hagia Sophia) and launched great military campaigns to restore the Roman Empire in the Mediterranean world. Justinian's brilliant general Belisarius (ca. 500–565) drove

out the Vandals and regained for Byzance a large part of the former Roman possessions in North Africa. In 553 he led an expedition to Italy and expelled the Ostrogoths. However, another Germanic people, the Lombards, moved into Italy after 565 and conquered the whole north (now Lombardy) and Tuscany. In the east Justinian's successors conquered Syria in 613, Palestine in 614, Egypt in 619, and Persia in 627. However, the territories regained by the Byzantines were lost in the 7th century when they were conquered by the Arabs.

The Byzantine force was a progressive and sophisticated fighting machine in the early Middle Ages, and it consisted of three categories of troops. The first, the *numeri*, were regular imperial mounted troops and infantry. The second group, the *feodariti*, consisted of mercenary bands containing a variety of soldiers of fortune. The third category comprised the private armies of the individual Byzantine noblemen; called *bucellarii*, these troops usually swore an oath of allegiance to the emperor and to their immediate chieftain. On the whole the Byzantine army was well paid, carefully organized, diligently drilled, and thoroughly equipped. Its backbone was its heavy cavalry, which accounted for about half the total force. The Byzantine horseman wore a steel cap, a mail shirt reaching to his thighs, and metal gauntlets and shoes. One of his main arms was the bow; he was thus a mounted archer, capable of harassing a foe with arrows and overwhelming him by a charge with additional weapons such as a sword and lance. Thus he combined mobile shock power and mobile firepower. Stirrups may have come into use in a simple form as there is evidence of their use at the end of the 6th century in the *Art of War* of the Byzantine emperor Mauricius Tiberius.

The basic cavalry unit was the *bandon* or *tagma*, with an approximate strength of 300 horsemen commanded by an officer called a *tribune*. Several tagmas formed a larger formation called *moira* comprising 2,000 to 3,000 men under a *moirach*. These in turn were massed into a *meros* headed by a *merarch* or *stratelate*. The senior officer was the *strategos* (general), and his second in command was the *hypo-strategos* (lieutenant-general). Great use was made of flanking maneuvers, attacks on the enemy's rear positions, encirclements, and ambushes. The *Cataphracts* were the well-equipped, well-trained elite horsemen of general Belisarius. They—and their horses—were clothed entirely in scale armor. The

Greek Cheiroballista. The cheiroballista was a large crossbow which threw javelins and strong arrows.

helmet sometimes included a beautifully worked visor that covered the whole face and followed its contours to form a remarkable facemask. The riders were armed with bow, sword, and spear. The Byzantine cavalry was perfectly able to operate by itself without infantry support. Soldiers devoted all their time and strength to drills and fights, and they were well supplied with servants who set up camp, procured supplies, cooked, and cared for the horses. The Byzantine generals—like Belisarius—were often professional soldiers, not dashing amateurs like the warriors and their chiefs of Western Europe. They did not take unnecessary chances and never risked a battle without certainty of victory. The officers were nobles, the rank-and-file were small landholders.

The infantry was divided in two sorts. The light infantry included archers with bows that could outrange those borne by the horsemen and light-armored men armed with javelins, spears, and shields. The heavy infantry wore helmets, shirts of mail, and gauntlets; they carried shields and were armed with swords, lances, and impressive battle-axes—bladed on one side and spiked on the other—for hand-to-hand combat.

An artillery element accompanied the Byzantine army to battle. It was equipped with a catapult and ballista to hurl stones, arrows, or fireballs at the enemy. This sort of artillery contributed a lot to sieges. In the Mediterranean Sea the Byzantine fleet, composed of galleys and dromons, ruled the sea.

Byzantium remained for centuries a powerful state and the center of a brilliant culture which — although Christian — was much different from that of the medieval Western Europe. The two civilizations continued to influence each other throughout the Middle Ages. The strength of the Byzantine Empire depended not only on the efficiency of its military institutions, but also on the combined vitality of its political, economic, social, and cultural systems. By the 10th century, evidence of decay in administrative, economic, and military matters forecast the decline of the once powerful state. The most serious challenge developed in the East where the Muslim Seljuk Turks threatened Asia Minor. The Byzantine emperor was then forced to call for help to his "Christian cousins" of Western Europe, making the start of the Crusades.

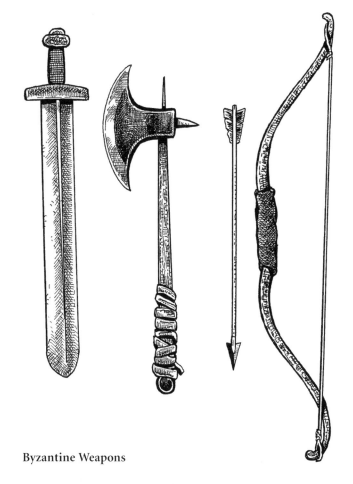

Byzantine Weapons

2

The Franks

The Merovingians

The Franks were originally a loose group of several Germanic tribes occupying the lands of the north bank of the Rhine stretching from Mayence to the North Sea. They had always successfully resisted the advance of the Romans in the 2nd and 3rd centuries and eventually began an aggressive migration southward which finally resulted in the submission of the modern countries of Holland, Belgium, and northern Germany. Many of them had freely enlisted in the Roman armies as allies and formed the bulwark between Gaul and the fierce barbarian hordes who finally poured down from the north. At the end of the Roman Empire, they invaded Gaul. They did not really migrate, rather they expanded, as they never lost touch with their original German homeland beyond the Rhine. Of the Germanic realms established on the ruins of the Western Roman Empire, the Frankish kingdom was the only one to remain. It gave birth to two important European nations: France and Germany. The modern name of France comes from the word *frank* (probably meaning "courageous" or "brave"), though the characteristics of the early Franks were indeed very far removed from those of the modern French people. Today Germany still has a province named Franconia, and several cities are called Frankfurt (the ford of the Franks).

The Merovingian dynasty was founded by a legendary warlord called Merowe whose successors, Childerik and Clovis, reconstituted a part of the former Western Roman Empire. The long Merovingian period —from 457 to 751— is rather obscure, because of the lack of reliable written documents, and very complex, because of the

decay of the Roman heritage and the growing Germanic and Catholic influences. The Merovingians began as a vigorous force that firmly established the Frankish domination.

The warlord Clovis, who ruled from 481 to 511, eliminated all his rivals, imposed himself as improvised king of all Franks, ousted the Gallo-Roman landowners who were the last remnants of the Roman Empire in Gaul, defeated other Germanic invaders such as the Alamani and the Visigoths, and conquered a large part of Gaul (today France) and large parts of western Germany. Clovis was a cunning leader who became a Christian, and his prodigious success was made possible with the support of the Catholic Church, which remained the only organized body in the general chaos. After the collapse of the Roman Empire, Christianity had been the strongest agent of "national" identity because Christian missionaries and monks, reforming abbots, and bishops transcended local rivalries. Regardless of class or regional differences, they united Europe into a Christian way of life which was distinguished from that pagans and heathens. Clovis's conversion to Roman Catholicism was indeed a clever move, allowing him to be regarded as a second Constantine and defender of the true faith. It is characteristic of the religious credulousness of the time that no one was in the least surprised at this curious deal between Christ and a military leader.

Clovis took over much of the Roman administration and established his capital in Paris; therefore, he is often considered — wrongly though — as the founder of France. Indeed after his death in 511, the Frankish realm was divided among his sons according to Germanic customs.

Early Franks with Scramasax and Battle-Axe

His successors took Burgundy, southern Germany, Saxony, and Bavaria. However Clovis's heritage was rapidly dismantled by severe family quarrels. The effective power of the Merovingian kings rested on tangible assets, and king Dagobert (reign 629–639) was the last Merovingian sovereign to wield effective power. The strong blood of Clovis had been diluted considerably and progressively, after many civil wars and fratricide struggles, and weakness appeared.

The Frankish realm was divided into four major parts: Aquitaine (southwest France), Burgundy (today called Bourgogne, but then spreading from Champagne to Provence including a part of Switzerland), Neustria (the nucleus of Clovis's domain in northern France with Paris as its capital), and Austrasia (eastern France and a part of western Germany including lands of the Rhine and Meuse with its capital city Metz). These territories—in which the Gallo-Frankish society survived in a viable fusion of Germanic and Roman traditions—asserted their right to be separate kingdoms even when subjected to one king. The great families of noblemen struggled with each other for power while the later Merovingian kings, feeble nonentities, were largely kept in seclusion on their own estates. Wars were numerous between those realms. In the 7th century the Merovingian kings had considerably lost their power, and the real authority was exercised by the *majordomus* (mayor of the palace). Originally a high domestic servant and a senior officer of the royal house, the mayor became a kind of prime minister who secured power for himself, his family, and his friends.

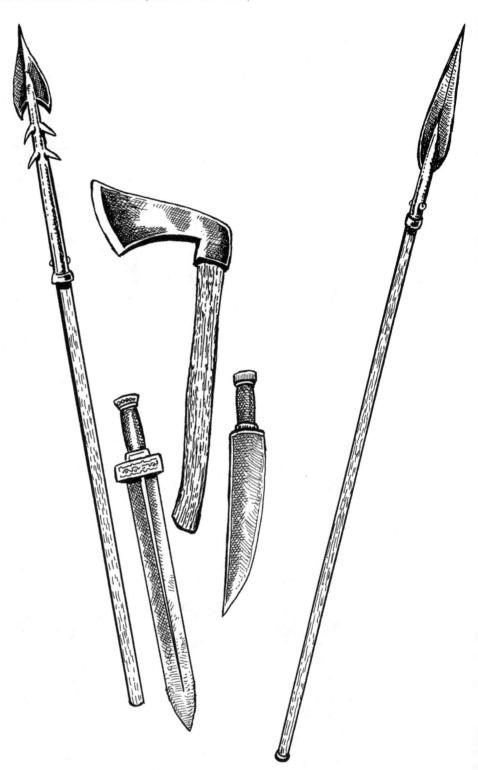

Merovingian Weapons. *From left to right:* Angon, sword, francisqua, scramasax, and framea.

The early Middle Ages were marked in the military field by the forgetting of the tactical sophistication of the Greeks and Romans and by the failure to make any significant technical improvements. The Merovingian army was composed of all Frankish free men who had to serve and to finance their own weapons and equipment. The warriors were not trained, their weaponry, as far as is known, was rudimentary, heteroclite, but however very costly. Weapons were indeed similar to these of the other barbarians. The richest of them wore an iron helmet and

Early Frank Warrior, ca. 400   Merovingian Warrior

a beastplate, but on the whole they had no armor — except that provided by looting Roman soldiers — as they appeared to have disdained any defense. The main bodily defense was a round or oval wooden shield in the barbarian fashion. In the shield was a boldly projecting umbo or boss. This kind of deep circular pan was made of iron and fixed to the front of the shield; its shape was that of an iron hat, and barbarian and Frankish bosses were at first thought to be helmets by early archaeolo-

gists. The device was securely riveted over a hole in the center, and thus the hollow under the face of the boss was open toward the reverse of the shield. Across this hollow there was a central bar offering a convenient and secure handle for holding the device.

However, the early Franks had several distinct offensive arms. The first of these was a heavy battle-axe to which they gave their name, the *francisqua*. This could be used in close combat but also hurled with tremendous force and devastating effect on the enemy — a hit could crush a shield and easily kill a man. Thus the North American Indian was unconsciously imitating the Franks when he dashed his deadly tomahawk with unerring dexterity against his enemy. The francisqua came in various forms. Some had a long and narrow blade, slightly curved on its exterior face and deeply hollowed in the interior. A variety of this sort included a kind of chisel on the other side of the haft, very like the blade of a carpenter's plane. Others were slightly hollowed, small and long in proportion to their size; others had a broad blade and a short handle. It is questionable whether the *bipennis*, the double-headed axe, ever found great favor with the Franks, although it has been attributed to them. The early Franks also fought with a lance called *framea*. This was a weapon chiefly associated with mounted men, and basically it did not differ in any essential points from that generally used by horsemen at the time. It was composed of a wooden shaft with a metal head inserted into a socket. The metal head assumed a variety of shapes: triangular, elongated, barbed, leaf- or lozenge-shaped.

The Franks also had various light javelins for throwing. One of these highly dangerous darts was called *angon*. Quite similar to the Roman pilum, it was a kind of harpoon — about six feet in length. It had a long, slender neck of iron fitted over a wood shaft. Near the point, it had two curved iron or small blades projecting on each side. The angon was a deadly weapon inflicting terrible wounds; when fixed in the flesh of the enemy it could be extracted only with great difficulty, suffering, and danger. The enemy could avert the blow with his shield, but if the angon remained fixed in his shield, the harpoon dragged along the ground, embarrassing, weakening, and depriving the enemy soldier of his defense. The early Franks had a one-edged — some twenty inches long — large knife called a *scramasax*. There was also a larger sword — about thirty or thirty-two inches — a privileged weapon generally reserved for the chiefs, those having an official position, and the elite of the soldiery. The scramasax had a flat, broad, straight, double-edged blade, sharp at the point. It had a very short cross-bar, a straight grip, and a small, slightly swelling pommel. The hilt could be decorated with inlaid work in copper, and the weapon was kept in a metal, wood, or leather scabbard. The early Franks battled mainly on foot, and only the chiefs and their richest warriors/bodyguards were mounted on horseback.

The Merovingian army was fully ruled by Germanic custom. More than an army, it was actually a gang of ill-organized warriors, certainly not numerous, with no discipline and rather poor efficiency, who were under the command of the king himself. In the second half of the 7th century command was often entrusted to high officers called *graven* (counts) and *herzogen* (dukes). The status of these warriors seemed to have varied directly with the degree of Roman influence in their territories. Where Roman traditions had been almost blotted out, the warriors held an honorable position and rapidly became an aristocracy. Where the Roman culture had left an indelible mark, the warriors were, at first, of lower rank, receiving not much more than food and clothing from their lords. However the status of the Frankish warrior improved steadily in the 7th and 8th centuries. This improvement was due in part to the extreme simplicity of Germanic government. No distinction was made between public and private services. The keeper of the leader's horse or the keeper of the chief's chamber could also be a member of the small group with whom the king took daily counsel. The armed retainer benefitted from his position as a member of the household. The army was not permanent but mobilized according to the need of a campaign.

The kingdoms were held together through the personal loyalty of warrior nobles to their king and the ability of the nobles to command the loyalty of their followers. There was no idea of loyalty to the state, to the Roman *res publica* (public affair) maintaining the public welfare. Merovingian and later Carolingian kings were essentially war leaders. The king and his officials were really a group of personal friends who were bound together by a special bond of loyalty, a Frankish version of the old German *comitatus*. When weak or unpopular kings were unable to retain loyalty, the counts tended to become rebellious or independent.

The southern border of the Merovingians kingdoms were threatened by a terrible enemy, the Islam conquerors appearing in the 8th century.

Islam

From an unlike land, the peninsula of Arabia, which had never exercised any influence on the history of the Western world, came a new religion and a new civilization in the 5th century. The prophet Muhammad (ca. 570–632) was born in the city of Mecca, and after having experienced revelations which he accepted as direct communications from Allah (God), he created in 622 a new monotheistic faith whose teaching was set down in the holy book, the *Qur'an* (Koran). Islam — based on Jewish, Christian, and local Arab traditions — recognizes the Bible as a holy text, and Muslim believers were (and are today) subjected to several main obligations: to believe that there is only one God and that Muhammad is His Prophet; to make daily ablutions and prayers facing Mecca; to make abstinence from alcohol and pork meat; to practice charity to the poor and hospitality to strangers;

once in a lifetime to go on pilgrimage to Mecca; and to observe a fasting period during Ramadan, the ninth month of the Muslim lunar year. In return for all this, the faithful were allowed four wives and the hope for a paradise in which they would lodge in pleasant mansions in the garden of Eden, and the thirsty would find rivers of milk and honey in the company of pretty dark-eyed *houris* (women). Since theirs was the only true religion, it was necessary to persuade nonbelievers of its merits also. Muslims were required to spread the will of Allah and fight and, if need be, die for the one and only true faith. For this purpose, Koranic theologists developed the notion of holy war or *jihad*. The Arab desert dwellers, who for centuries had loved to make war, now had a more noble reason to indulge their bellicose appetites, as they would be fighting not only for booty but to propagate the true religion.

The Muslim warriors—known as Saracens or Moors in southern Europe—were mainly horsemen. Bodily armor included a *Zirh* (shirt of chain mail), a tunic covered with metal scales, and a *hoqueton* (thick quilted jacket). On the whole the Saracens were loosely dressed with much less armor than their Christian mounted opponents. This made them more vulnerable in hand-to-hand combat but greatly increased their mobility. Head gear consisted of the traditional turban—a long strip of cloth wound round the head—and various forms of metal helmets, some with a spiky crest and additional plates protecting the face. Their shields were made of metal or wood, usually round with a spiky boss. They were armed with various forms of spears and *kilij* (swords), including the popular curved saber known as *scimitar*. They were experienced and skilled with the bow and played an important role as highly mobile archers on the battlefield. As the Koran forbade the use of human representations, weapons were decorated with beautiful geometrical patterns. Ornamentation also made use of the possibilities offered by the graceful curved Arabic language. On shields, swords, and banners, calligraphic inscriptions were displayed such as "Help Comes from God and Victory is Near" or "Ali is a Brave Soldier with His Sword Dulfekar" or "Have Faith in Allah and His Apostle," for example.

Driven by the ideal of jihad, the Arabs swept like an

Muslim Warrior

avalanche. The Islam expansion began immediately after the Prophet's death. By 732, just one-hundred years after the death of Muhammad, his followers had established a large empire with astonishing speed. Egypt, Tripolitania, Palestine, Syria, Mesopotamia, Persia, Afghanistan, North Africa, and Spain had all fallen to the Arabs in succession. No doubt, the enormous booty captured by the rapid campaigns was an equal incentive, both for the riches it provided for the warriors and as a sign that Allah was fulfilling the promises of His Prophet. The Caliphs ruled over half the known world and were eager to conquer the rest. The Arab Empire was based on great cities, and Arabic was used as the official language for administration and religion. There seemed to have been little destruction though, as Christians and Jews calmly accepted the new rulers who left them with their beliefs in exchange for taxes. Nonetheless, fanatical followers of the Prophet posed a grave threat to the Christian Franks. From North Africa the Muslim army — including large contingents of Berbers (early inhabitants of Northern Africa) — had invaded Spain in 711 and killed Roderick, the last king of the Visigoths. In the 720s, they penetrated into southern France and occupied Narbonne, which became a base for raiding the neighboring Frankish kingdom. When a raiding party sacked Bordeaux and was marching in a northern direction in 732, the Franks reacted. A Frankish army led by Charles Martel totally destroyed them in a battle fought somewhere between Tours and Poitiers.

The consequences of this victory were important. The advance of the Muslim Empire was halted, and Charles Martel gained such prestige and support as to make him a respected and permanent ruler. Militarily the battle of Poitiers marked the first significant triumph of the heavy armored cavalry. The Franks employed the tactic of charging their enemies in close formations of horsemen with spears bristling forward. When this terrifying onslaught had shattered the Muslim ranks, the Franks dispatched them with their swords. This was to become the main tactic on the battlefield for several hundreds years. The Arab defeat — it has been suggested — was also probably due to the fact that the Saracens were successful only in those sunny regions of the Mediterranean that were geographically and climatically reasonably similar to their own Arabian home.

The Carolingians

Charles Martel — the Hammer (about 685–741) — was the son of Pepin of Herstal and the majordomo of Austrasia and Neustria. His victory over the Muslims gave him enough power and prestige to unify the various tribes and provinces of the Franks into a credible kingdom. The period of Charles Martel was also important for the future development of feudal society. The Frankish kingdom was involved in many wars, and the kings were trying to increase the number of armed cavalrymen. When the Franks first began to use cavalry on a large scale, infantrymen were at a disadvantage before the horsemen who used the recently introduced stirrup; were protected by padded armor, helmet, and shield; and were armed with sword and lance. But this military equipment was extremely costly, and its effective use required continual practice. Skilled soldiers on horse had to be rich enough to buy the animal and the equipment and free of the need to work for their living. If the king was to have an army of mounted armored men, he would have to supply each of them with land and the labor to cultivate it. So the association of sworn vassalage and fief holding became a common practice. This was a difficult period for the Frankish kingdom facing the Muslim assaults from the south and unconverted Germans in the east. So great was the emergency that Charles the Hammer was obliged to requisition lands from the Church and used them as *precaria* (estates granted as a favor) to reward his warriors. In return they swore to fight for him on demand, equipped at their own cost with horses and weapons.

After the death of Charles the Hammer, his son Pepin the Short succeeded him as mayor of the palace and overthrew the last Merovingian king, Childerik III the Idle in 751. Within a period of about 300 years, the Franks had developed from a loose confederacy of Germanic invaders with mere tribal links into a fullfledged kingdom. They had experienced the development and the degeneration of the Merovingian dynastic royal line and replaced it with a most vigorous governing family. Cleverly, the cunning Pepin obtained the crown as king of the Franks by Pope Zacharias, making an illegal coup into a legitimate new dynasty called Carolingian after his father's name (*Carolus* is Latin for Charles). The first Carolingian king conquered a part of northern Italy from the Lombards in 756; those territories were yielded to the pope as a reward and formed the nucleus of the pontifical state. Pepin the Short continued the struggle against the Saracens, and he liberated the province of Septimania (today Languedoc in southern France) in 759 and repressed a revolt in Aquitaine from 761 to 768. On the death of Pepin the Short in 768, his kingdom was divided between his two sons, Louis and Charles. In 771 the younger brother Louis died, and Charles became the sole ruler of the Franks.

Charlemagne

Charles (who became known as Charlemagne from the Latin *Carolus Magnus*, for Charles the Great) was a remarkable man, a capable — if cruel — military leader, and a brilliant administrator. He was spectacularly successful in enlarging the Frankish realm. He had a keen interest in intellectual and cultural matters and promoted all branches of learning. He established schools and an embryonic of a university at his capital — Aachen in Germany — that attracted many scholars from Ireland, Northumbria, Spain, and Italy and was headed by the great teacher Alcuin of York. There many young men —

from rich noblemen to poor scholars—were educated at Charlemagne's expense to become themselves teachers, thus helping to spread the tradition of learning which developed later into the great universities of France (Paris and Montpellier), England (Oxford and Cambridge), and Italy (Padua and Bologna). Charlemagne worked closely with the Catholic Church in his attempt to spread Christianity by the sword and sponsored the building of churches and monasteries. As a reward for his efforts in defending Christ's faith, he was crowned emperor by Pope Leo III in 800 A.D.

The emperor organized new political and administrative structures in the large territories he ruled as shown by the *capitularies* (detailed letters of instruction and advice he send to his many vassals and officers). He moved about his realm from one royal estate to another; investigated the acts of his counts, dukes, and margraves; and send out *missi dominici* (agents) to give orders or hear complaints. The system of counties was essential to Frankish government, and a count could wield considerable power particularly in far-flung regions. However, even as powerful a man as Charlemagne found it difficult to follow up all the reports and complaints he received. A clever way to keep counts under control was to weaken their power by establishing rival authorities in each county. Charlemagne invested churchmen, abbots, and bishops, who received grants of immunity from him; placed them under direct imperial protection; and allowed them to rule their districts independently of the secular counts. In theory the system of counties was efficient and just. In practice it was prone to the limitations of travel, seasons, and the possibilities of corruption that were inevitable in such a vast empire. Throughout the Middle Ages, there were always acts of corruption, lobbying, and intrigues at the royal or ducal courts where opposing factions among the king's favorites and advisers sought power, influence, pension, wealth, and office for themselves, their relatives, and friends.

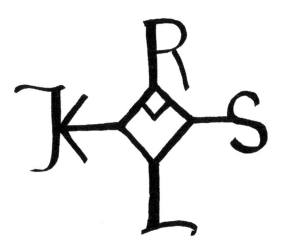

Charlemagne's Monogram (Carolus Magnus)

Carolingian Armies

According to the traditional Germanic custom, the Carolingian armed forces were raised for every campaign in spring and summer. Charlemagne, as Frankish warlord, had the right to call up all free men—up to the age of 60—for an expedition. Mustering was administrated by the counts. If anyone failed to attend the muster, heavy fines and punishment could be imposed, but the counts were frequently accused of bribery and coercion in the tally of the muster. The custom was to gather the army in spring, and it would remain active for three to six months. The army was mustered as late as May to allow snow to recede from remote areas and to have good and nutritious grass for the horses. Campaigning ceased for winter, although sieges could be maintained if required. Only the richest of the free men could be warriors because they had to finance their own weapons, military equipment, and servants. They got no pay but were rewarded by booty, land, and estates taken from the defeated enemies. The booty was divided among the troops as a fairly regular method of reward. The major part went to the nobility, of course, but every Frankish soldier could realize some spoil for himself by sacking a place or stripping the dead of the opposing forces on the battlefield.

The association of sworn vassalage and fief holding—fitting into an already existing pattern practiced in the time of Charles the Hammer—was continued and extended by Charlemagne. In a period of subsistence economy without money, and with rudimentary administrative structures, the easiest way to maintain a class of warrior was to lend or lease lands to dependants who in return gave military service. The *vassi dominici*—direct vassals of the king—were usually men of good family. Charlemagne relied heavily on their service for military purposes, but at the same time he did not want them to become too independent. Originally their status was insecure and unstable depending on the monarch's will. In the end the *vassi dominici* took roots in their counties, and eventually became castellans and important local rulers.

The total strength of the Carolingian army could not be numerous, probably a few thousands combatants. The huge figures given by the medieval chronicles describing thousands of valiant knights victorious over hundreds of thousands wicked enemies were written centuries afterward. They did not reflect reality but were intended to impress the reader by rhetorical, allegorical, and epic style.

Considering warfare, armament, and equipment, the period between the early Franks and the Frankish time of Charlemagne is difficult to fill in as written documents are scarce and figured monuments are altogether wanting. This is much to be regretted since it was an epoch in the history of arms and weapons when the ancient styles were gradually degenerating and new equipment appeared. How the changes occurred is difficult to say, but it is probable that the nations that the late Merovingians and the early Carolingians fought — the Saracens, the Lombards, the Aquitanians, and the Saxons — exercised some influence. A major change, in the military point of view of the greatest importance, was the introduction of a numerous cavalry. Charlemagne can certainly be credited with the development of the famous heavy cavalry of the Franks. The mounted warriors, the *milites*, who formed these elite troops were necessarily drawn from among the Frankish nobility and landed gentry as they had to be properly equipped for war and provide themselves — and their ser-vants and warriors — with horses and weapons. In addition, they had to bring supplies such as clothing and victuals for at least three months and various equipment such as tents, cooking instruments, spades, picks, iron-pointed stakes, and other things needed for a military campaign. The growing use of cavalry tended thus to exclude the poorer free men from fighting in full equipment because armament and equipment at the time of Charlemagne were rather costly. Estimates showed that a good war horse was worth twelve cows, a top-quality sword and its sheathe seven cows, an armored tunic ten cows, a lance and a shield two cows, and a good helmet between four and six cows.

Charlemagne was particularly well organized in terms of military logistics. Advance planning was carefully worked out, and supplies were often requisitioned the season before the start of the campaign. Charlemagne maintained supply depots with food, water, forage, and weapons during his Saxon wars in fortified garrisons at Herstelle, Eresburg, Buraburg, Fritzlar, and Paderborn. Mileage between depots was approximately one day's reasonable ride or two days if the pace were easy or being slowed by enemy harassment. Baggage and supply trains enabled the Frankish army to move without repeated foraging. Plundering was officially forbidden — not for any humanitarian reason but because it reduced the speed of the army. In practice, general looting occurred as a form of punishment for the rebels and the enemies. It could also be part of a vast and considered plan of devastation to crush the enemy's morale. Charlemagne employed extensive advance information, usually gathered by spies and considered before any expedition. This included details about the proposed territories for conquest, population, geography, methods of war, and patterns of life. This disciplined approach was very unusual for the time, and indeed, later medieval wars were conducted in a far more haphazard way.

Charlemagne's favorite tactic was to divide his forces into two or

Carolingian Spearman

Carolingian Horseman

more armies. This was intended to confuse the opponents, and when the Frankish forces reunited, they delivered a crushing attack upon the enemy. There are conflicting theories regarding the methods of combat used by the Frankish cavalry at the time of Charlemagne. Although mounted warriors had saddles and stirrups, it is not certain if they used these items to any great extent. Stirrups enabled a horseman to use his lance as a powerful stabbing weapon held much nearer to the blunt end clamped firmly against the body by the right arm, the "couched" tactic. Charlemagne's armies might have occasionally used this shock tactic of the heavy cavalry charging in close formations with spears and swords. However, records do not confirm that this tactic was widely used, and it seems that it was fully developed and employed with success later. Furthermore, if it is confirmed that Charlemagne's army counted as many horsemen as foot soldiers, it is not clear if they actually always fought from horseback or if they used the animal simply as a rapid transport. Undoubtedly, the tactics on the battlefield might have been without sophistication with possibly a barrage of archers, assaults either by foot or mounted soldiers, or perhaps cavalry charges followed by attacks from infantrymen. The time of Charlemagne was a transitional period in which military cavalry techniques were being tested.

Another evolution was the use of body armor. When the bareheaded early Franks from the time of Clovis disdained armor and relied only upon a shield as defense, the Carolingians of the time of Charlemagne made a wider use of armor. Charlemagne's soldiers—not only the richest of them—wore various forms of body protection. The jerkin, *byrnie*, or *brunia* was a leather-padded tunic more or less closely covered with small pieces of metal or thick scales of leather or horn sewn upon it. The armored jacket usually reached down to the thighs and had an opening at the front for convenient riding. There were various forms of helmets, notably a solid conical cap made of iron bands sometimes fitted with cheek guards and possibly ornate. To protect the legs, large leather bands, leather boots, or iron *bambergues* (leggings) were worn. The soldiers carried the traditional round or oval wooden shield with a metal boss in the center as an additional protective weapon.

If logistics, armor, and cavalry were increased, the offensive weapons of Charlemagne's time were on the whole much the same as those used by the early Franks, however with some improvements. The lance had usually a hilted blade fitted with lugs to prevent penetrating too deeply in the body of the enemy; the presence of this cross-piece implies the use of the weapons from horseback. Without the cross-piece the considerable force of the blow delivered by the mounted man might make it impossible to reclaim or pull back the blade from the enemy's body. The use of the long sword was developed and no longer reserved for chiefs as was the case in the previous Frankish period. The Carolingian warriors had a sword with usually a rounded end to the blade designed for cutting rather than stabbing. The popularity of the long sword tends to confirm the use of

Charlemagne's Guardsman

cavalry. On horseback, the long reach of the swordsman is supported by his horse, enabling him to use with great effect a weapon that might be cumbersome on foot. The early Frankish scramasax was still in used; with its single edge and thick heavy short blade, it could also be used as a bludgeon. Other weapons included the traditional Frankish battle-axes. The use of bow and arrow — discarded by the barbarian warriors — was revived by the time of Charlemagne. Many soldiers had a bow, arrows, and a spare bowstring as standard equipment, but there was not a separate force of specialized and skilled bowmen that used these as a collective weapon in their own right. Various forms of javelins and angons were used as throwing weapons. Therefore, Charlemagne's soldiers were skilled in all-round weaponry, able to fight both at a distance and at close quarters. From the equipment, we can see that the Frankish cavalryman was in the earliest stage of development into the armored knight of later centuries.

Charlemagne — as a Roman emperor — had his own bodyguards. These soldiers — selected from the best of his young noblemen — were distinct from other warriors. They formed a privileged body and were looked upon somewhat in the capacity of an imperial guard. They were provided with equipment which was a modified form of that worn by the Roman Praetorians. These elite troops wore an armored jacket, a circular shield, and a long sword, but instead of the true Roman globular helmet with neck and cheek guards, they wore a metal helmet of a triangular form with raised sides that was surmounted by a crest and a cluster of scrollwork.

Charlemagne's Conquests

Among the many achievements of Charlemagne, the most obvious was the extent of his conquest. The emperor was a capable and successful military leader who added vast territories to the Frankish kingdom that he had inherited. He launched about sixty military campaigns — half of which he directed in person — enlarging the Frankish kingdom into an empire which stretched northeastward to include Saxony, Bavaria, and Slavonic regions of the Drave and Elbe. Southward the empire reached to northern Spain and northern Italy, but Brittany and the British Isles remained out of his domination. Building on the military success of his forefathers Pepin and Charles Martel, Charlemagne was a famous conqueror. With the combination of superior numbers and their great skill, good weaponry, and reputation for savagery, the Franks overwhelmed most of their opponents. However there were

occasion in which they were defeated. In 778, on the return from a raid in northern Spain against the Muslims, Charlemagne's baggage train — commanded by Count Roland and full of looted goods — was ambushed by Basque bandits in the pass of Roncevalles in the Pyrenees. By the time Charlemagne arrived with reinforcements, all his rear guards had been slaughtered. Later this episode was immortalized in the great epic "song of deeds" the *Chanson de Roland*, which turned a defeat into a heroic victory. The length of the wars against the rebellious Saxons of northern Germany — who refused to be converted to Christianity — also showed the limit of the efficiency of Charlemagne's armies. Despite the consistent use of extreme violence, war lasted for about thirty years. Ultimately, the defeat and the conversion of the Saxons were achieved less by military victories than by terror actions, a harsh occupation, and atrocities such as the murder of thousands of prisoners and civilians.

The End of the Carolingian Empire

When Charlemagne died in 814, the Frankish kingdom had almost doubled in size. The empire created by Charlemagne did not form the basis for a united European state, a credible successor to the Western Roman Empire in which military power would support a strong central government. Nevertheless, Charlemagne's strong personality, energy, and ambitions made a lasting mark on European culture. During the succeeding centuries, the emperor was to be regarded as the ideal Christian sovereign, and he and some of his famous warriors were honored and celebrated in stories, legends, and art as models for the rapidly developing feudal society. After Charlemagne's death the unity of the empire was continued with difficulty by his son Louis the Pious (778–840). Louis's children and successors quarreled with each other as they were not pleased with the terms of the division. Further civil wars — aggravated by a series of invasions by Vikings, Saracens, and Magyars — ensured the gradual decline and the division of the Carolingian Empire. It was very seldom that the late Carolingian kings could get together an army in time to strike the new swift-moving raiders. The local authorities, lords, dukes, and counts took responsibility for self-defense. They rapidly regarded the territories they tried to protect as their personal properties. The people they attempted to defend gradually considered them as their real rulers instead of the distant and weakened king. This paved the way to a new organization of society called *feudalism.*

3

Vikings and Hungarians

The Vikings

The people we call Vikings lived in Scandinavia, that is, present-day Norway, Sweden, and Denmark. Scandinavia emerged from its prehistoric period in the 8th century. Although the three countries were linked together in many ways, each country was independent of the others. The Danes were politically the most advanced, and their kings dominated over large areas. The word *Viking* has never been satisfactorily explained. It might come from the Old Icelandic word *vik* which means "bay" or "creek," so a Viking would therefore be a pirate lurking with his ship in a bay. Some historians think the word comes from the Anglo-Saxon word *wic*, meaning "camp," so that a Viking would be a warrior. Other names were used to describe these particulars invaders such as Northmen, Normans, or simply foreigners; the Spanish Muslims' term was *al-Madjus* meaning "heathen wizards." Anyhow, the Vikings—who probably named themselves from the area in which they lived—were hunters, farmers, and fishermen living a hard and bleak life in mountainous, densely forested countries and islands with long, narrow inlets poorly suitable for farming.

Their society was organized in families and clans and headed by petty kings who were chosen from important families, but because any member of the clan could aspire to the kingship, succession disputes were common. Unsuccessful claimants often went into exile to pursue a career as a pirating Viking to win wealth and reputation and to make a fresh bid for the throne. The kings ruled over the *jarls* (noble landowners) and *karls* (rich free men and farmers) who ruled over free peasants and *thralls*

(slaves). Although the Vikings were fierce and quarrelsome they valued their freedom and believed in law and order; they had an assembly—called *Althing*—which was a parliament and partly a law court where they would debate matters of general interest and settle feuds and other disputes.

The Vikings lived in villages—fortified with earth walls, ditches, and stockades—in which stood long, rectangular wooden thatch-roofed houses. There were a few trading fortified towns, such as Kaupang in Norway, Birka in Sweden, or Hedeby in Denmark, which were populated by merchants, fishermen, and craftsmen.

They wore linen or woolen spun, woven, and dyed clothes, and they were great artists: They created beautiful designs, pictures, and bandlike animal patterns with complex rules of intertwinings, strapworks, interlacings, repetitions, and inversions which decorated their weapons, furniture, and houses. They worked equally well in wood, iron, horn, and ivory and made remarkable jewelry, such as brooches, bracelets, necklaces, armbands, and rings.

The Viking alphabet—called *runes* or *futhark*—was adapted from the Greek alphabet, and it was used, carved with a knife or chisel, on memorial stones. Since very few people could read and write, and since runes were mostly used for magic rituals and commemorative practices, the stories and legends of their heroes—called *sagas*—were not written down until the 13th century. Before that, sagas were passed from one generation to the next by word of mouth.

The Vikings had a polytheistic religion with terrible evil spirits and ruling divinities such as the upper-god of

Viking Karl

Viking Jarl

war Odin racing across the sky on his eight-legged horse called Sleipnir accompanied by his wolves Geri and Freki. Thor — armed with his huge stone hammer Mjollnir — was the god of wind, rain, thunder, and lightning riding across the stormy clouds in a huge chariot drawn by goats. Frey was the god of marriage and fertility. The religion had no clergy, churches, or temples, and Vikings probably worshiped their gods outdoors in nature. When a Viking warrior died, he was buried with great splendor. The richer the man, the more magnificent his grave. His body was dressed in his best clothes and jewelry and laid in his grave. Some rich and famous chiefs were buried in their ships. The man's tools, weapons and most precious possessions as well as food and drink were placed beside him in order to help him on his journey after death. The Vikings believed that as soon as the body was burned, the spirit went to Valhalla, the heaven where warriors where led by the Valkyries (women send by the upper-god Odin) and where they spent their time fighting, drinking, and feasting after life on earth.

As the Vikings have left fewer visible evidences than the Romans and the Greeks, graves and ship burials provide a great deal of information to archaeologists and historians about their lives, possessions, and way of living. Such a burial ship with its treasure — dating probably from 660 — was discovered at Sutton Hoo in Britain East Anglia. The ship contained various precious things and weapons including helmets, swords, shields, axes and javelins.

Viking Armor

Decorated Viking Axe Blade

Viking Swords 9th and 10th Centuries

Armor and Weapons

The Vikings were among the most successful warriors in history, although they were badly defeated by the Arabs, Anglo-Saxons, and Irish at various times. The Vikings were principally warriors on foot with primitive tactics consisting of following the gang leader into battle with individual, fearless, ruthless and ferocious bravery. They had an abundance of iron for their arms, and this made them fierce warriors with some of the best armor and weapons in Europe. They protected their bodies with tough leather tunics, fur coats, and occasionally with mail shirts which only the richest could afford; these were passed on from father to son. They wore conical helmets, sometimes decorated with horns but not the winged helmets that are often drawn by freakish artists. Some helmets could possibly be strengthened by a nose piece and a kind of mask protecting the wearer's eyes. The men carried large round shields made of wooden boards and painted and sometimes covered with leather; there was often a round metal casing (boss) in the middle protecting the hand. The most popular weapons were swords, spears, and axes. Their long swords were sharpened along both edges. The spears were of two types: light throwing spears and heavy thrusting ones. The battle-axes were fearsome, large weapons which could cut off an enemy's hands, feet, or head. As so often in human history, men invested some of their highest craft and artistic skills in their weapons and engines of war; therefore, the blades of swords and axes could be decorated. To do this, the blade was first heated over a fire until it was black; the design was cut into the surface with a sharp instrument; small pieces of bronze, brass, or silver were rubbed into the hot grooves until they stuck; the weapon was put back into the fire and polished with a long tool or a smooth steel; and this was repeated until the decoration shone. Fine weapons were greatly prized and handed down from father to son. Bows and arrows were sometimes used to shoot enemies at long range.

Viking Warrior

Viking Ships

Anyway, all this would have mattered little to the rest of Europe had it not been that the Vikings were also skilled carpenters, great ship builders, and audacious sailors. Although made of wood, some Viking ships have survived in a remarkable state of preservation because they were part of a ritual burial, and the earth in which they were interred had kept them in good condition. The most famous of the recovered vessels are those from the burial sites at Gokstad and Oseberg in Norway. Indeed, Viking ships were among the finest ever build. They were clinker built, which made the hull flexible enough to give against the waves and enabled sailing in very stormy seas. Clinker-built ships had overlapping planks which were

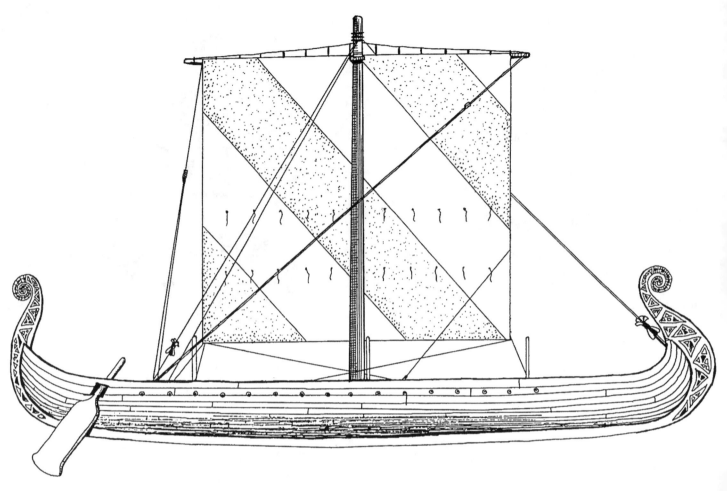

Viking Long Ship

lashed to a framework of ribs and cross beams; the joints were stuffed with rope to make them watertight.

There were several kinds for different uses, called *drakkar, karve, snekker, skeider,* or *knarr* according to size. One of the best known was the *langskip* (long ship), which was a canoelike ship with elegant lines allowing for great speed through the water. It was long (about 20 meters, or 65 feet) and rather narrow (about 5 meters, or 16 feet) and sat low on the water. The long ship had only one central mast and one large square sail, which was quite colorful — usually checkered or striped blue, red, or green. Each boat had a set of oars to port and starboard so as not to be totally reliant upon the wind in calm weather. The ship was steered by a large oar at the stern working as a rudder. The longship's arching prow and stern were often beautifully carved in the shape of savage animals — or frequently a dragon's head — which were covered in metal. Some rich men would even have them covered with gold and silver. These decorations flashed in the sun and were probably intended to impress enemies and to frighten off evil spirits. When the ship entered or left port, its sides were lined with gaily colored shields, which were removed when the ship put out to sea.

Viking ships had a low draft and could sail close to the coast and land on beaches or sail up rivers. From the end of the 8th century these vessels had been perfected to such a degree that they could sail on to the open ocean. The men on the voyage packed their belongings in a chest which was used as seat when rowing. They would take a few animals for food, a water supply, and a large amount of cargo.

The Viking merchant ship was different from the long ship. It was broader and deeper in the hull; its planks were often nailed — not lashed — to the frames. Such ships mainly used sail power for propulsion.

Viking Expansion

The Vikings enjoyed an overwhelming military advantage from a superiority in naval techniques, and by

Opposite: Knarr, Viking Cargo Ship

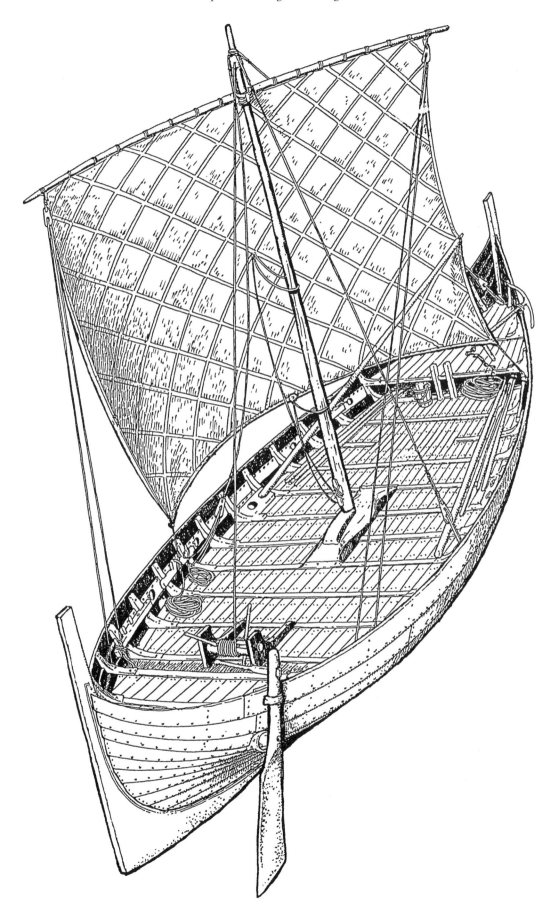

the end of the 8th century long voyages for trade but also aggressive looting raids began. The reasons for the Scandinavians' sudden outburst of hostile activity overseas are uncertain. The Viking expansion has been explained as being due, first, to over-population and the lack of new lands to bring under cultivation because the forests and mountains did not encourage the spreading of fresh settlements; besides, estates passed to the eldest son, leaving the younger ones to fend for themselves. Second, expansion may have been due to banishment of noble jarls to strengthen royal power. And lastly, it may have been caused by the simple lust for adventure and pillage, and as the geography of the region made its inhabitants a sea-faring race, it was quite natural that they should be attracted by the wealthy undefended lands around them.

Progressively, the Norwegians explored the northern Atlantic Ocean; they established trading settlements and permanent colonies in the Orkney Islands, Shetland Islands, Faroe Islands, Iceland, and Greenland. They even sailed to the North American coasts as far as Vinland (Newfoundland), Markland (Labrador), and Helluland (Baffin Island).

The Swedes developed important trading routes in the Baltic Sea, Courtland, and Ladoga. They set out southeastward with ships laden with furs, wax, honey, wood, and slaves up the rivers of northern Russia up to Novgorod, Gnezdovo, Kiev, the Dnieper River, and the Black Sea and sailed across as far as Constantinople in the Byzantine Empire.

Other Vikings made raiding expeditions, seizing plunder and abducting people to supply the wealthy Muslim kingdoms with goods and slaves. They sailed down the Volga River to the Caspian Sea as far as Baghdad, where they traded with Arab merchants from the Arabian Caliphate of Persia.

Further southwest — both in England and on the European continent — the Danes sailed to trade, but having been badly received, they launched deadly raids for loot. Their excellent ships with small drafts made them extremely stealthy, mobile, and almost unbeatable. They could strike when and where they wanted; they could sail deep inland on rivers, and they could quickly withdraw if they met a superior force. Before long the raiders — seizing horses — rode inland ravaging the countryside. Their immediate targets were monasteries and churches, such as the monastery of Lindisfarne in Northumbria which they sacked as early as 793 A.D. They are known to have landed in the Hebrides, on the north coast of Ireland, and on the southern shore of the Thames estuary between 787 and 795. From 799 onwards they sailed to the Dutch coasts, and in 809, the prosperous port of Dorestad in the Netherlands was attacked. Gaul was the next victim, and chronicles mention Viking aggressions in Rouen in 841

and Nantes in 844. The coasts of Spain and Portugal were targets in 844; Bordeaux was attacked in 848, and Paris was besieged in 845, 856, and 861. The Vikings passed the Straight of Gibraltar in 859 and spread murder and devastation in the Mediterranean coasts in Spain, southern France, and Italy. Other parties sailed the Rhine River in 885 and looted Nimegue, Cologne, and Bonn. In 886, a large fleet of Viking ships ransomed Paris, sailed further inland, and plundered the rich provinces of Champagne and Burgundy.

According to chronicles, everywhere they came, the Vikings would seek to surprise the place; then they slaughtered people, ransomed, looted, and burned villages and cities and even slew priests and plundered churches, monasteries, and abbeys because they were unscrupulous and devilishly pagan with a prehistoric background of countries untamed by Rome and Christianity. The ecclesiastical writers therefore viewed the pagan Scandinavians with special horror, and their chronicles have often the tendency to emphasize the cruelty of the invaders and to exaggerate their numbers and the devastation they caused. However, it is true that the ruthless Viking raiders were famed and feared throughout Europe; the sight of their ships sailing down the coast or up a river was dreaded by thousands of people.

The great age of the merciless Viking raiders lasted from the 9th to the 11th century. By the second half of the 9th century, the Viking raiders were better equipped, much more numerous, and better organized than they had been earlier, and they had permanent bases abroad which meant that they could winter and stay away from their native lands for years at a time if necessary. For example, the warlord Hastein — leader of a fleet of 62 ships — had a base in France, and between 859 and 862 he led a famous expedition. Hastein sailed to Spain where he was defeated by the Arabs; however, he managed to enter the Mediterranean sea and looted the coast of North Africa and Spain. He spent the winter on an island at the mouth of the Rhône River in southern France and sailed the following spring to Italy. He attacked the fortified city of Luna — which he thought to be Rome — but was repulsed because the Vikings had no siege machines. The cunning Hastein pretended to be dying and asked to be baptized by the priests of the city. His coffin was carried by his men to be buried in the town cemetery; once inside, Hastein suddenly leaped out of his grave, and his men drew their weapons and looted the town. Hastein returned later to his base in France laden with fame and treasure.

The Legacy of the Vikings

For many years people have regarded the Vikings as brutal barbarians who did nothing but loot and kill. This is partly true, but they did a great many constructive things as well. The Vikings were the first Europeans to sail far away on the oceans, some five hundred years before the Portuguese and the Spanish expeditions of the Renaissance. The Vikings have significantly influenced European history by turning men's mind against the Carolingian kings who failed to protect them and transferred their loyalty to those of the local magnates who did. In this way the Vikings greatly contributed to the collapse of the Carolingian Empire, and they unwillingly helped the growth of the territorial principalities and the establishment of the so-called feudalism. The way the invaders designed and built fortifications, notably the Norman *motte-and-baily castle* (a wooden dungeon on an artificial hill surrounded by earth walls, ditches, and stockades) played an important role in the early feudal time in France and England.

At first the Vikings made short raiding expeditions; later, however, they took to conquest and settlement. Gradually, many Scandinavian invaders settled in the lands they had attacked, and new political states were created. The Scandinavians became Christian, and — as they were flexible people and gifted state administrators with a special genius for adapting existing institutions to their own ends — they were quick to mix with the autochthonous population and to assimilate local languages, manners, and customs.

Norman adventurers played an important role in many areas. In southern Italy at the end of the 11th century; in 1059 the warlord Robert Guiscard drove the Saracens from Naples, became duke of Apulia and Calabria, and conquered Messina and Palermo in Sicily. In eastern Europe, Scandinavian adventurers, traders, and looters (called Varangians or Russians) mixed with Slav populations, set up their own principalities, and founded ruling dynasties in Kiev, Novgorod, Smolensk, and Moscow, creating the first Russian states. At the mouth of the Seine in France, the Vikings (called Northmen or Normans) had settled in 896, and in 911 their leader Hrolf (Rollo) was recognized as Duke of Normandy by the king of France, Charles the Simple (893–922). Normandy was to be a dukedom directly connected to the development of both France and England — notably after the decisive conquest of the British Isles by Duke of Normandy William in 1066.

The Hungarians

The Vikings were not the only raiders to bring danger to the Christian European lands in the 9th and 10th centuries. Between 850 and 890 the Pechenegs, a wild Turkish people, overran the country from the Don to the Sea of Azov. In doing so they disturbed the Magyars (today known as Hungarians). The origin of the Hungarians is quite doubtful. They were probably a Finno-Turkish collection of nomadic tribes, their language was Finno-Ugric, but a Turkish ruling class seemed to have dominated them and furnished their royal family. Obliged to flee southwest because of the Pechenegs' invasion, the Magyars tried to cross the Danube about 880, as the Goths had done before them. Repulsed by the Bulgars, they moved into Transylvania and from there, in 890, on to what is now called the Hungarian Plain from where they launched devastating expeditions.

The savagery of their raids once again brought Asiatic danger, forgotten for a century, to the lands of Western Europe. In 900, Hungarian raids pressed to the borders of Germany, then into Saxony and Bavaria. From 912 they advanced further still to Swabia, Thuringia, Lorraine, and even Burgundy in France, a few of them ventured as far as Nîmes and Narbonne in southern France. But soon the greatest attraction was Italy, a country in which petty princelings waged absurd, ferocious, internecine wars. The popes, quickly succeeding one another and often debauched, joined in the conflicts. Accordingly, the Magyars had little difficulties in crossing the Alps, and from 921 to 926 they were ravaging northern Italy and Tuscany. In 937 the Hungarians returned to Germany, and in 954, becoming reckless, they rode to the Rhine, crossed it, and raided Metz, Cambrai, Rheims, and Châlon.

Although their power had declined, they besieged Augsburg in 955. By that time the German emperor Otto I, the Great (936–973), had firmly established his power in Germany. Otto was able to muster a strong army and met the invaders by the river Lech. The battle of Lechfeld (10 August 955) lasted for ten hours, and the issue was in doubt to the end; finally, Otto won the day. The Hungarians fled in disorder and were pursued beyond Vienna and hacked to pieces. At a single encounter, the danger had been removed. There were to be no more Hungarian horsemen in Germany. The battle of the Lech stands out, not only because it reversed the flow of nomadic incursions into Europe but because it was one of the earliest examples, if not the first, of purely cavalry warfare in medieval western Europe.

The havoc wrought by the Hungarians can only be compared with that wrought earlier by the Huns. Harvests and farms were burned; cattle slaughtered; villages, houses, and churches left in cinders; and men were killed, children mutilated, and women raped and murdered. Only fortified towns and castles escaped their attention because the Hungarians had no siege machines.

The Magyars were not really numerous — probably not totaling more than 20,000 men on horse — so their military success can only be explained by the absence of a centralized power and the weakness, the division, and the ill-preparation of their opponents. Indeed, as soon as they confronted Otto's well-organized force, they were defeated in a single battle. Like the Huns, the Hungarians were skilled horsemen with a great mobility and flexible capability to maneuver on the field. Their main weapons were Turkish-like strong short bows, light throwing spears, war axes, and oriental-styled curved swords. They wore no armor but buffle tunics. Head gear consisted of felt hats or felt helmets reinforced with metal stripes. Their arsenal also included many weapons and other equipment captured from their defeated enemies.

In 970 the Hungarian chief Geza and 5,000 of his warriors were baptized, and the nomad raiders became settlers who established themselves in the Danube region. Geza's son Wajk was to become King Saint Stephen (997–1038), who created the Hungarian realm in 1001. Thereafter the Magyars ceased raiding and began to adapt to a European community.

**Hungarian Raider,
10th Century**

4

Anglo-Saxons and Normans in England

Anglo-Saxon Conquest

England had been conquered by Julius Caesar in 55 B.C. because the Celts of Britain supported the Celts of Gaul, but the north of Britain had never been pacified. The greatest trouble came from Caledonia (Scotland), Ireland, and Wales, whose populations had always successfully resisted the Roman legions. The Romans established a Romano-British culture, but even in the south, in the province of Kentium (today Kent) which they occupied, the romanization was superficial and the defenses weak. In the 4th century, the Angles, the Saxons, and the Jutes from Denmark and northern Germany took their ships and raided the coasts of England for a century. The Roman government appointed a special military officer, the count of the Saxon shore, to deal with them. Forts were build along the east coasts, and troops were brought from other parts of the empire to hold them.

About 410 A.D., as the Visigoths approached the Eternal City, all Roman permanent troops were withdrawn from Britain. The Roman retreat — which Emperor Honorius regarded as temporary — left England in quite a vulnerable position. As Anglo-Saxon-Jute deadly raids were increasing, the Romano-British called to Rome for help against the raiders, but no answer came as Rome itself fell to Germanic invaders. So the post–Roman history of the British Isles was in many crucial ways very different from that of the former Roman provinces on the continent.

About 450, all contact with Rome were broken, and the incursions had become a migration as the German Angles and Saxons continued to come — not any longer as plunderers — but as settlers. Among them there must also have been some Frisians from the northern Netherlands as the Frisian language — that is still spoken today — presents many similarities in both Dutch and English.

As the invaders expanded their conquest, conflicts with the local Celtic and Romano-Britons were inevitable. The Britons fought the German settlers as well as they could, but gradually they were compelled to retreat westward to the safety of the isle of Ireland and to get refuge in the mountain of what the Saxons named *Weallas* (Wales, meaning the land of the foreigners).

Very little is known about this long and stubbornly fought struggle. It is probable that during the many centuries of Roman occupation, many of the Celtic Britons had learned the method of warfare and the use of weapons of their conquerors as British natives were recruited for the local Roman legions. Consequently, we may fairly assume that the Romano-British fought against the Anglo-Saxons with a mixture of Celtic and Roman weapons such the *gladio* (short sword), spears, and javelin, such the *pilum*, and that a certain amount of Roman-styled armors protected them including breastplate and shield.

The rather shadowy time of Anglo-Saxon conquest forms a historical basis for numerous tales and legends. One of the Briton leaders in this period for which there are no writings was the prototype of the legendary King

Danish Warrior with Bipennis

Anglo-Saxon Warrior

Arthur, whose small force of well-disciplined armored knights inflicted some defeats on the advancing Anglo-Saxons. King Arthur and his Knights of the Round Table grew to a position of supremacy in the mythology of the

Middle Ages from very small and obscure beginnings. Arthur was a Briton *dux bellorum* (a war leader) in the 6th century A.D. who resisted the Saxon invaders in twelve great battles. Tales of the adventures of King Arthur —

immortalized by magical happenings and great military prowess — existed and circulated by word of mouth. The stories included Merlin the Magician; the seduction of Arthur's mother, Igerna, by his father Uther Pendragon; Arthur's marriage to Guinevere; accounts of his chief knights, Sir Gawain, Sir Kay, and Sir Bedivere; the treacherous Sir Mordred, who abducted Queen Guinevere and usurped the kingdom; and, after the final battle, Arthur's mysterious departure to the Isle of Avalon for the healing of his grievous wounds. The Arthurian romance was only written down in the 12th and 13th centuries. The tales of Sir Lancelot and the quest of the Holy Grail, and the popularity of the tale of Sir Tristan, paved the way for an enormous body of legends produced in every European country for the next five hundred years. Actually this literature gives more indications about the chivalric ideal of the 14th century than the reality of the mysterious Celtic world.

After the death of Arthur — presumably about 540 — the Germans triumphed and dominated what is now England and drove off most of the preexisting population. In the beginning of the 7th century, the Briton Celts held only the western fringe regions of Cornwall, Wales, and Cumberland while other Celts had settled in Armorica (French Bretagne or Brittany). The Angles and the Saxons extinguished virtually all traces of Roman civilization. They established a number of kingdoms, some of which still exist in county or regional names to this day: Essex, Sussex, Wessex, Middlesex, and East Anglia, for instance. The strength of the northern Germanic culture is still obvious today, notably in the days of the week which were named after Scandinavian gods. There is a proliferation of Danish names, for example those ending with -*by* and -*thorpe*, such as Grimsby and Althorpe, and many Scandinavian words have passed to the English language, such as *take, call,*

Anglo-Saxon Chief

window, *sky*, *ugly*, or *happy*. The ending -*ing* meant folk or family, thus Reading is the place of Rada's family and Hastings that of Hasta's clan. From this period, the 7th century, there is a large poem entitled *Beowulf*, written between 680 and 800, telling the exploits of a Scandinavian warrior mixing Christian values and pagan virtues.

One major innovation of the Anglo-Saxons to Britain was their military organization. Gone were the palmy days of a professional army. The early Anglo-Saxons settlers were joined in a levied armed force called *fyrd*. This was divided into two categories. The Great Fyrd was the levy *en masse*, no doubt mostly on foot with some wealthy enough to possess a horse. The Select Fyrd was drawn from the class of *thegns*, landholders with sufficient acreage to give them status in society.

It used to be generally accepted that Anglo-Saxon armies were infantry using horses for transport to battle, but fighting from horseback was unknown among them, even among the wealthy. As circumstances dictated, horses were used in offensive tactics.

Warriors were expected to use their weapons on behalf of their leader. It seems that the Saxons' chief weapon of offense was the spear, which was of two kinds: The longer lance — about nine or ten feet — was used by the cavalry and was often fitted with horizontal bar guards. The shorter spear partook of the dual nature of the lance and of the throwing javelin.

The sword — generally three feet long — was essentially a cavalry weapon reserved for noblemen. The earliest sword found in England had no *quillons*, or cross pieces, but merely a pommel, grip, and blade. The latter was 30 inches long and 2 inches wide at the hilt; it was straight, rounded at the point, and double-edged. Swords were provided with wooden scabbards covered with leather. Some had ornamental designs painted or stamped upon them and mountings of bronze or more costly metal. During the later Saxon occupation a cross piece was added to the

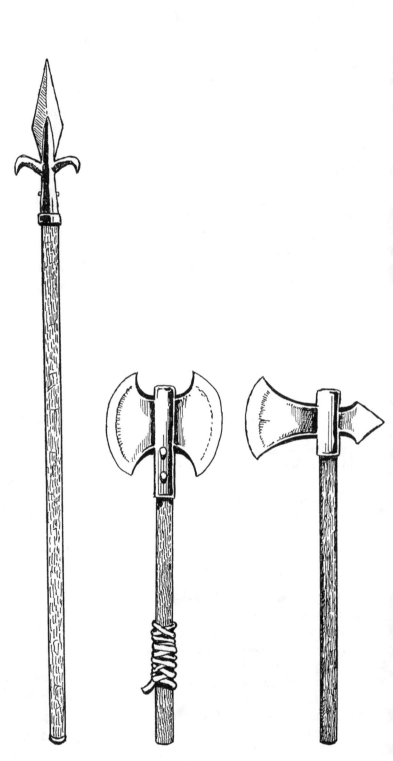

Danish Spears, Bipennis, and Battle-Axe

weapon; it became more acutely pointed, and the pommel occasionally showed signs of ornamentation. Some rich warriors of the fyrd would have had swords with hilts made of gold or silver, inlaid work, or a setting of precious stones.

The battle-axe was a distinctive and characteristic weapon of the northern nations. The Anglo-Saxons seemed to use three varieties: the taper, the broad, and the Danish-styled double axe or *bipennis* with two blades. Daggers and knives were in common use. They were of various sizes, the large ones being actually weapons; the smaller were used for domestic purpose. Mace, sling, and bow and arrow were not intensively used by the Anglo-Saxons; they were known but were individual, not universal, favorites.

Rather little is known about protective weapons such as helmets, shields, and armor. Maybe they were considered subsidiary or superfluous and essentially reserved for the rich leaders of the fyrd. However, as the Anglo-Saxon nation increased in prosperity, so the defensive devices were slowly added. The Saxon helmet was commonly of the Phrygian shape, but some evidence also showed combed hemispherical and conical helmets. These were composed of a framework of bronze or iron bands riveted together of which the principal and thickest band was the piece passing round the head making a sort of crest. Occasionally this band was lengthened at the front so as to form a piece protecting the face, known as a *nasal*, which became universal at the end of the 10th century. Upon this substructure a leather cap of varying form could be fixed, sometimes with ornamental additions in leather crowing it.

The Anglo-Saxon shield was probably made of lime wood covered with leather and was often round in shape, but at times oval and convex. The distinguishing characteristic of this defense was the central hollow projecting boss or umbo. About six inches in diameter, the umbo was riveted to the surface of the shield forming a grasp for the left hand. As it was often spiked, the shield was also used as an offensive weapon. The shield could be strengthened by strips of iron or bronze radiating from the umbo to the edges.

It is difficult to make authoritative statements about the body armor. It was probably a *byrnie* or *battle sark*, a coat made of hide or padded stuff. Also worn by the richest warriors was a tunic of woven material or leather covered with rings of iron or leather plates either cut into the form of scales and overlapping or square or oblong. The legs were either left bare or protected by leather bands. Toward the latter end of the Saxon period weapons and armor became almost identical with those in use on the

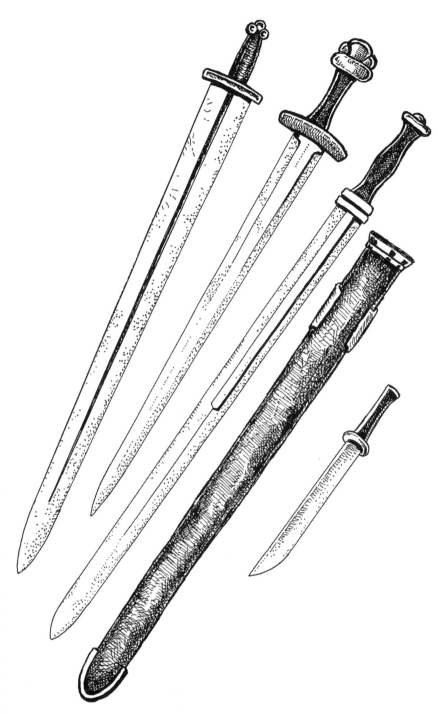

Saxon Swords, Scabbard, and Knife

continent, owing to the constant intercourse which occurred in the reign of Edward the Confessor, so that by the time of the Norman conquest in 1066, the differences in accouterments were simply small matters of detail.

The local Anglo-Saxon lords were at first little more than *aldermen* (tribal chiefs). Their authority was based partly on kinship but more on their reputation as war leaders and martial prowess. Gradually a class system was developed made up of petty kings, *earls* (lords), *house-*

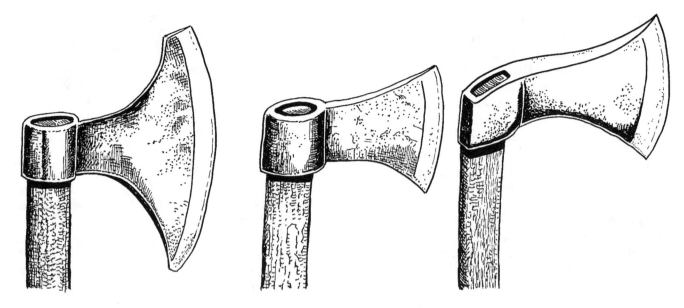

Anglo-Saxon and Danish Axe Blades

carles (soldiers), and workers on the land as well as a new class of clergymen.

Strangely the Christian religion adopted so late by the empire was one of Rome's few legacies to Britain. Although Christianity had disappeared from Anglo-Saxon England, it had not vanished from the British Isles. England was religiously reconquered and reconverted to Catholicism by Celtic Christian missionaries from Ireland. The English Church prospered extraordinarily, and in the 8th century it was the most vigorous church in northern Europe. Much of Germany was converted by English missionaries, and English clerks, such as Alcuin of York, were Charlemagne's principal assistants in educating the illiterate Franks.

Alfred and Knut

By the middle of the 7th century, the three largest and most powerful Anglo-Saxon kingdoms were those of Northumbria, Mercia, and Wessex. Toward the end of the 8th century, new raiders were tempted by Britain's wealth. Anglo-Saxon England was overrun by a vast Danish army that landed in East Anglia. The Viking Danes had been raiding eastern and north England for many years, but never before had they come in such numbers. In 867 they destroyed Northumbrian resistance, half of Mercia fell to them, and in 871 they launched themselves in full strength against the kingdom of Wessex. But when Alfred the Great (ca. 849–899) became king of Wessex in 878, the Vikings were repulsed. After a series of victorious campaigns, London was retaken, and the Danish invaders were checked. Alfred was strong enough to make a treaty

with the Vikings; the frontier between Scandinavian territory (the Danelaw) and Christian Anglo-Saxon land was settled by both sides in 886.

Alfred the Great was recognized as king by all of those dwelling in England in 892. At his court in Winchester, Alfred — who was as much a brave and skillful ruler as a poet and a literate thinker — drew up the first system of English laws. Alfred wrote the *Anglo-Saxon Chronicle*, the most important source, together with Bede's *Ecclesiastical History of the English People*, for understanding the period. The structure of authority consisted of *shires* (headed by *shire-reefs*, whence the term *sheriff*). These were divided in hundreds and boroughs. The whole realm used a uniform system of taxation and coinage, encouraging a sense of common identity in adversity.

England was prosperous and peaceful again after the troubles of the Viking invasions. Anglo-Saxon England exported to the continent woolen goods, cheese, pottery, and gold; it imported wine, fish, pepper, and jewelry. However, signs of weakness, disunion, and disorder appeared in the 950s under the reign of King Ethelred. Unfortunately for the kingdom of old England, the high quality of the rulers of the House of Wessex was not maintained, and when another great Danish invasion began at the end of the 10th century, no Alfred was there to hold them at bay.

About 980 the raids started again, but this time they were organized by Danish and Norwegian kings who had become powerful enough to prevent private initiatives of their subjects. The incursions were now on a much larger and more professional scale than the earlier ones. They were aimed at systematic conquest rather than private plunder. In 1016 a Danish Viking war leader named Knut

(955–1035, also written Knud, Cnut, or Canute) defeated Ethelred. Knut was an ambitious conqueror who by force of arms had become king of Denmark and Norway. England became thus a part of a large Scandinavian empire stretching over the whole lands around the North Sea. In England there seemed to have been a confusing resistance and several wars, but in the end the domination of Knut was rather well accepted as everyone feared disorder — and even a Danish king was better than no rule at all. The Danish dynasty ruled over England until 1042, and it was a period of significant change organizing a unified kingdom in reaction to the first Viking invasions and promulgating decrees regulating the Christian life. English, Danish, and Anglo-Danish peoples were not displeased with the rule of a powerful king who observed the separate customs of all his kingdom.

The military equipment of the Danes differed very little from that of the other Viking nations. A distinctive piece of armor protecting the chest was a broad collar encircling the neck, a pectoral or a gorget if it may be so termed, with depending pieces upon which were sewn flat rings, plates of metal or horn. Greaves were used to protect the lower legs, consisting of stout pieces of leather affixed after the form of shin pieces. These were probably made by boiling the leather and subsequently pressing it into shape. The Danish helmet in its early form was a close-fitting skull cap fitting well down into the back of the neck, sometimes with wings of metal imparting a highly ornamental aspect to the headpiece. Later a conical metal helmet with a knob upon the top was adopted and, in its fully developed state, fitted with a nasal. The shield was presumably round, and spears and swords with their ornamented scabbards were similar to those of the Anglo-Saxons. No single piece of Danish weaponry has been immortalized as a special significance with the exception of the battle-axe. The Danish axe was the famed bipennis, consisting of two axe blades of similar form on either side of the shaft, which latter in a few cases was furnished with a spike. A variation was furnished on one side with a diamond-pointed cutting blade in substitution for the axe blade. The axe could be used as a pole weapon for close combat or, if furnished with a shorter handle, could be hurled in a similar fashion to the Frankish francisca. After their settlement in England the Danes gradually adopted accouterments and weapons in imitation of the Saxons and the Normans until their equipment in the 11th century became in every respect a replica of those of the latter nations' weapons.

Norman Conquest

The union of Britain and Scandinavia was artificial. Knut's empire was so large that he was compelled to delegate authority to the increasingly powerful local Saxon earls who ruled their own regions without much royal interference — an early version of feudalism. Knut's followers lacked their father's authority, and in 1042 the independence of England and the House of Wessex were restored in the person of one of Ethelred's sons, Edward (ca. 1000–1066). Edward was nicknamed the Confessor, as he was more interested in religious than political matters. He encouraged the construction of churches all over his realm and started the construction of the Abbey of Westminster outside London. The traditional pattern of the English village, with its manor house and parish church, dates from this time.

One important fact was that Edward had spent almost all his life in the duchy of Normandy, on the other side of the Channel, as his mother was a daughter of the duke of Normandy. As stated previously, the Normans were children and grandchildren of Vikings who had settled in northern France in Normandy. This land was the strongest and the best organized province of France, and its people spoke French. They were Christian, but they were still well known for their fighting skills and ambition.

When the childless Edward died in 1066, the Saxon nobles chose one of them, Harold Godwinson, as a good choice for the throne of England. England was the richest country in Europe, and its throne was eagerly contested. Harold's right to the throne was challenged by the ambitious and aggressive Guillaume the Bastard, duke of Normandy. Guillaume (in English, William) had a vague legitimate right to the throne through his great aunt. His main claim was that Edward had — unsubstantially and verbally — promised it to him. The true reason was that the increase in population in his duchy created a land shortage and made his fief-hungry warrior class eager for the spoils of foreign venture.

Harold was faced by two dangers. In the north, Danish and Norwegian Vikings had not given up their claim to the crown of England, and a Scandinavian army headed by Harald Haardraad had landed and started an invasion. In September 1066, Harold had to march into Yorkshire to repel them. No sooner had he defeated the Danes at Stamford Bridge, seven miles from York, than he learned that Guillaume had used the opportunity to cross the channel and landed in Sussex, southern England, with a huge army. After their victorious campaign in the north, Harold's soldiers were tired but confident. The Saxon army marched south as fast as they could, and fresh troops were collected from the neighboring shires. Harold's soldiers were almost entirely infantrymen composed of poorly equipped levies of the Saxon *fyrd* — armed with kite-shaped shields and spears — and a few archers. His well-armed *husecarles* (professional soldiers) — numbering no more than 2,000 — formed the bulwark of his force. William's force was estimated at 800 ships and about 5,000 soldiers, including landless knights and adventurous mercenaries raised — with papal blessing — from France, Flanders, Brittany, and Normandy.

On October 14, 1066, Saxons and Normans met in a decisive battle near Hastings. Harold had established his army on an excellent defensive position atop a broad low mount called Senlac Hill. William opened the battle with a barrage by his archers followed by an assault of his infantry armed with swords and spears to weaken the English. As Harold's troops firmly held the hill, Guillaume ordered his archers not to shoot point blank but rather to use high-angle fire. A rain of projectiles fell upon the Saxons, and a chance arrow fatally struck King Harold in the eye. The main force, the Norman mounted knights, delivered the decisive blow; it took however several cavalry charges to dislodge them. The combination of events, and the exhaustion of a whole day's fighting broke up the Saxon army, and the Normans stormed Senlac Hill. The remaining Saxon forces surrendered or streamed back to the protection of the woods at the rear of the hill.

The success of William's knights at Hastings produced far-reaching consequences both in England and in the contemporary attitude toward the art of war. The successful defense of Harold's infantry force was largely overlooked, and Hastings was declared emphatic proof of the supremacy of cavalry. For nearly 300 years following the defeat of the Anglo-Saxons in 1066, European armies ignored the potential strength of disciplined massed infantry spearmen against knights. Giving due credit to the efficacy of mounted feudal knights, the pride of medieval cavalry obscured the more important and fundamental reason for Norman success at Hastings: the judicious combination of mobile cavalry and archers.

Norman England

After the victory of Hastings, Guillaume the Bastard — who was then called William the Conqueror — marched to London, which quickly gave in. He was crowned king of England in Edward the Confessor's new church of Westminster Abbey on Christmas Day 1066. A new period in the history of England had begun. After the coronation, the conquest continued, but it took William another five years to establish his power. The small Norman army — it was an army of occupation — marched criss-cross the country to subjugate the Anglo-Saxons, conquering villages and towns and crushing rebellion until 1070.

William organized his kingdom according to the feudal system which had already begun to develop in Western Europe. The Saxon earls, including bishops and abbots, were eliminated, forced into exile — some even killed. All were dispos-

Anglo-Saxon Foot Soldiers and Norman Horseman at the Battle of Hastings (after the Bayeux Tapestry)

The Norman Fleet Crossing the Channel in 1066 (after the Bayeux Tapestry)

Norman Horsemen Charging at the Battle of Hastings (after the Bayeux Tapestry)

sessed of their land; these estates were granted to William's warriors who had been instrumental in his victory. In return for these grants, the new ruling Norman aristocracy owed William mounted military service. The Normans constructed castles to guard and control a population that remained hostile — later illustrated by the legendary hero Robin Hood.

By 1150 there were approximately 1,200 castles in England. These were motte-and-bailey castles, composed of an earthen mount surrounded by a wooden fence and a ditch. In the 12th century, motte castles were gradually replaced by stone-built keeps such as Dover Castle or the White Tower in London. However, William was very careful in the way he gave land to his nobles. He granted separate small pieces in different parts of the country so that no noble could easily or quickly gather his fighting men to rebel against the crown, and he kept enough domains to himself to make sure he was the strongest of them all. William kept the Saxon system of sheriffs and

used these as a balance to local landowners. In 1086, William wanted to know how much was produced in his kingdom and thus how much tax he could demand. A survey was made, the *Domesday Book*, which gave historians an extraordinary amount of information about England at that time.

As a result of Norman administration, England was very different from the rest of Europe because it had one powerful royal family instead of a large number of powerful nobles. The unity of England was a sign of modernity, based on the models of imperial Rome and the Carolingian Empire. William — and the Norman kings after him — thought of England as their personal property. William and his successors controlled two large areas on both sides of the channel: Normandy, the family duchy, and England, conquered by force; this created an odd situation. As duke of Normandy he had to recognize the king of France as his lord, but as king of England he was sovereign with no lord above him. This situation was to create countless problems and numerous wars between France and England in the following centuries.

The Norman Army

No other army of the Early Middle Ages is so well known as William the Conqueror's force owing to a remarkable piece of art. The so-called *Tapestry of Bayeux* is a marvelous huge stretch of embroidery (about 70 meters or 230 feet long and 60 centimeters or 23 inches wide) commissioned by the Norman bishop of Bayeux and supposedly woven by queen Matilda and her hand-maidens but more probably of Anglo-Saxon workmanship. Anyway, whoever made it, the embroidery was completed within fifty years after the conquest, hence its reliability is undoubted in regard to its depiction of contemporaneous weapons, equipment, and armor. Whatever artistic imperfections may exist in it, they in no way affect its character for accuracy of representation. Thanks to short Latin texts and colorful scenes, we can follow the historical background represented with the grandeur, sense of inevitability, and absence of romanticism of a Greek tragedy. The importance of eating well is graphically illustrated: the Normans (referred to as Frenchmen) are shown seizing livestock, slaughtering it, roasting it on spits, and serving it at a banquet presided over by the bishop Odo of Bayeux. The embroidery gives in vivid, almost cartoon-style, numerous and accurate details about warfare in the end of the 11th century. The tapestry indicates the Normans' military professionalism. We can relive in detail the preparation of the campaign: trees being cut down and made into planks, well-designed Viking long ships being built and launched, the embarkment of troops and horses, the crossing of the English Channel, the disembarking of the troops ashore, the battle of Hastings where combatants both Anglo-Saxon and Norman are lively pictured. We can see how a motte-and-bailey castle is attacked with fire torches, and how cavalrymen and archers employ their arms. The lower border of the tapestry shows — among other interesting details — beheaded soldiers in horrible postures lying amid a litter of abandoned equipment, broken weapons, and dead horses as well as men stealing the armor and clothing of the dead, a common practice on battlefields through the centuries.

Norman Warrior with Hauberk

Norman Gambeson, 11th Century　　　Norman Foot Soldier with Wambey

A whole range of armor and weapons are also displayed with technical accuracy on the tapestry. A striking and recurrent feature are the groups of armored mounted soldiers with long shields brandishing spears or charging with lances on their warhorses, giving an impression of vigor and ferocity. The body armor depicted on the Bayeux Tapestry is of great interest due to its variety and complexity. There are examples of

Saxon-like byrnie and scale armor. The scales—sown on a leather or strong-material tunic named *hauberk*—were of various materials such as iron, bronze, leather, horn, or boiled leather. Also used were iron rings or discs of metal on leather or padded material with strips of leather sewn on between the rings. The hauberk reached usually down to the knee, and it had short sleeves that left the lower arm bare. The lower part of the hauberk was generally made to open up the front and at the back in order to afford convenience in riding. For foot soldiers no opening was necessary. A *gambeson* (or *wambey*) was a plain quilted defensive covering padded with a soft material such as wool, tow, or cloth which was enclosed between two layers of material and then sewn together. Although offering but little opposition to a lance-thrust, a quilted tunic was rather efficacious in warding off sword cuts or in stopping arrows that were not delivered at short range. Against the mace, or a stone from a sling, the padded material was of little use in preventing serious injury and bones from being broken. Under the gambeson or the hauberk a *camisia* was worn; that was a tunic reaching nearly to the knees and, as a rule, a little longer than the defensive garment. These bodily defenses with various styles of quilting and varieties of stuffing were in use for many centuries as the only defense worn by foot soldiers and as an undergarment later for armored knights.

Toward the end of the 11th century, the different distinct styles of armor became more numerous and were not as uniform as those at the time of the conquest in 1066. Hauberk could be *tegulated*, the square or oblong scales were overlapping like slates upon a roof. The coif or hood was generally a part of it, with only a small opening for the face. The legs were covered with leather bands or leather leggings (called *chausses*) that fastened down the back and sometimes were thickly covered with metal studs protecting the knees and shins of the wearer. The feet were protected by various forms of short leather boots. The helmets shown in the tapestry are the universal con-

Norman Tegulated Scale Armor, 12th Century

ical metal types furnished with a nasal to which was attached a cap or hood or camail of quilted material protecting the back and sides of the head and falling upon the shoulders. As a rule, this quilting was tied under the chin and continued over the head to protect the wearer from chafting of the helmet while at the same distributing the weight and bringing additional protection. The helmet with nasal and occasionally cheek and neck guards continued in use for centuries along with other new types.

The shield adopted by Norman cavalrymen was probably from Sicilian or Byzantine origin. Its length varied but may be taken as approximately four feet in height with a maximum width of two feet. It was kite shaped, either flat or round, so as to encircle the body to some extent. It guarded the body where it was the broadest, and by tapering downward it defended the left leg. It was made of wood covered with leather in addition to which extra bands of metal were fixed. It was always held in the left hand by a bar or strap near the inside upper portion. The shield of the foot soldier was generally smaller, kite-shaped or round, flat or bowed, with a Saxon-fashioned umbo. Off the battlefield, all shields could be suspended around the neck by a leather strap called a *guige*. Norman (and Anglo-Saxon) shields were often decorated with swirling shapes or fabulous beasts, though there is no evidence that these ornamentations were associated with specific knights or families in the heraldic sense.

The Norman lance was similar in length and structure to the Anglo-Saxon design. The iron head of the lance — riveted on the wooden shaft by a metal socket — was usually of the leaf/lozenge form and embellished with pennons. It was firmly held under the right arm to deliver a powerful blow when charging. Smaller spears and javelins were used to be thrown. The sword was essentially of the Scandinavian type, straight, long, double-edged, and slightly tapering toward the acute-angled point. It had straight quillons, a grip without swell, and a spherical-knobbed pommel. The scabbard was suspended upon the left side by a strong cord or a belt around the waist but occasionally was supported by the hauberk by being passed through a hole in the garment. The bow

was of very simple construction; the sharp arrowheads were made of iron and the quivers were without covers and at time slung upon the back. Some Norman and Anglo-Saxon soldiers were armed with a heavy wooden mace with a heart-shaped head. Scandinavian large axes were used with handles that were four or five feet in length. Mace, sword, and axe were used when the lance was broken, lost, or splintered and when all javelins and spears had been thrown.

Long after the conquest, during the 12th century, new weapons appeared chiefly for the use of foot soldiers adapted for rushing upon and disabling knights who had been unhorsed. The military pick, called *bisacuta, oucin,* or *besague* was a sharp *martel-de-fer* (war hammer) with one or two points fixed on a shaft designed to perforate the joints between the plates of the hauberk. For the same purpose there was a sharp dagger, named *cultellus*, occasionally the size of a short sword. For the purpose of fighting a mounted man, the *guisarme* or *bisarme* was introduced; this had a staff six or more feet in length and a metal head fixed on a riveted socket. It was composed of a blade edge for cutting, a sharp point for thrusting, and one or two rising hooks for warding off a blow by entangling another weapon. In its earliest form may to have been a combination of the scythe and the prong, and it was the forerunner of the later halberd. Various forms of axes, notably the bipennis, the Saxon double axe, were still in use as the weapons of the conquered Saxons and the Norman conquerors were rapidly mixed.

England played the most important part in the history of the British Isles, and Wales, but Ireland and Scotland had a different history. It took centuries before the four parts of Britain were united.

PART II

THE HIGH MIDDLE AGES
(11TH–13TH CENTURIES)

5

Feudal Lords

Nearly six hundred years elapsed between the first barbarian incursions in the 4th century and the end of the 10th century when the last of the invaders had been either assimilated or repulsed. The era of Scandinavian, Muslim, and Magyar invasions brought the collapse of Charlemagne's empire and marked the end of the period of transition from Carolingian to medieval civilization. Under the threat of external invasions, the people of western Europe displayed an extraordinary resilience and created the material and spiritual foundations for a new civilization — the feudal world characterized by the practice of fief holding.

Origin of Feudalism

Feudalism is a difficult term. It was invented in the 17th century by lawyers and antiquarians. The word was never used by the men of the Middle Age, so we cannot work out a definition from their statements. The word is derived from the Latin *feodum*, meaning a fief, an estate of land held by a lord in return for military service, hence the French *féodalité* and the slightly later English *feudalism*. The term "feudal system" is used to describe relationships among the ruling upper class. Feudalism is defined by Marc Bloch in his book *Feudal Society* as "a subjected peasantry; widespread use of the service tenement instead of a salary; the supremacy of a class of specialized warriors; ties of obedience and protection binding men to men." These fundamental features of European feudalism, in this wide sense, embraced all medieval societies between the 9th and the 12th centuries.

Feudalism as it developed in early medieval France was characterized by three main features. First, the fragmentation of political power and public authority. Second, the fragmented political power was in private hands and was treated as a private possession which could be divided among heirs, given as marriage portion, mortgaged, and bought and sold but also conquered or lost by war. Third, the armed forces were secured through individual and private agreements.

Feudalism was not new but evolved more or less naturally out of social conditions which had preexisted for hundreds of years in western Europe. It was a method of government emphasizing the distinction between the great lords who had extensive power, and the lesser vassals who at first were merely soldiers who rendered military service not because they were citizens of a state but because they — or their ancestors — had promised to give this service in return for certain benefits. Indeed, it was based on a fundamental two-way contract, protection in exchange for service. The tenant was a *vassal* of a lord (called a *suzerain*), and the vassal was bound to the lord by a special oath of loyalty, but the vassal was also a governor who exercised right of jurisdiction on his fief. This practice could be traced back to the time of the barbarian invasions of the western Roman Empire. The sworn loyalty binding a warrior to his chief was derived from the German *comitatus*, and conditional tenure of land in return for specified services came from late Roman land law. As already pointed out, an important period in this development was the reign of Charles Martel in the early 8th century, when the Franks first began to use military cavalry on a large scale. The result of this was the practice of the association of sworn vassalage and military service in exchange for fief holding that allowed the warrior caste to live without working.

The early practice of the feudal system presented some advantages but also serious drawbacks. What the suzerain saved in the expense of equipping and maintaining a professional soldier, he might lose in the amount of service rendered. A vassal who lived in the lord's household was always and immediately available for duty. This could not be true of a man living on his own estate. He had to have time for his own affairs, and he had to be given some advance warning before he could be called to arms. Some suzerains tried to avoid these inconveniences by giving their vassals only small holdings grouped around their own castles. Other lords gave estates only to their older and more experienced vassals while younger knights continued to live and serve in the household. Landless knights were still quite common as late as the 11th century, and they never disappeared.

A second decisive phase in the evolution of feudalism came during the collapse of Charlemagne's empire in the 9th and 10th centuries. The Viking, Muslim, and Magyar invasions and the continuous civil wars between the emperor's successors created a state of anarchy in which armed force was the only effective law. During the confusion of the 9th century, two processes contributed to the emergence of a new powerful class of feudal lords. On the one hand, there was a serious weakening of the centralized royal power and, thus, a constant alienation of royal rights. In other words, there was a political decentralization — a vacuum of power — and the rights of government were widely dispersed among the landholding class. On the other hand, there was a process of submission by lesser folk from below stimulated by the general disorder. War, brigandage, raids of pirates and looters, and the sheer difficulty of traveling over incredibly bad roads made people prefer a nearby ruler to a distant one. Ordinary peasants, farmers, and small landholders had to accept the military protection of more powerful men generating the manorial or seignorial system in which the local lord exchanged physical protection against a share of every type of produce raised by his tenants. In a primitive agrarian society — where virtually all wealth consisted of land and rural products produced in a system of autarchy, where there were no significant towns, and thus very limited trade — the tenant owed their lords a multitude of rents in kind. In addition — as central power had disappeared — the lord had the right of jurisdiction, controlling both the persons and their properties. There was no uniform law, and very little in the way of legal redress for common people wronged by their lords.

As a result, during the 9th century there developed a hierarchy of suzerains and vassals. Simple lords and poor knights who had just enough land and peasant labor to support them and their families were the vassals of a larger landholder who, in turn, would be the vassal of a still mightier man, perhaps a baron or a viscount. These landholders were the vassals of a greater count, of a duke, or of the king himself. The political structure took then the form of a great pyramid, with the king at the top and the ordinary man at the bottom. The possessors of political and military power at each level of the pyramid naturally wanted to mold the society to fit their own needs. They manipulated the economy so they got the greatest share of production. They developed a class structure which gave them the highest position. As wealthy consumers, they influenced writers and artists. They established standards to which the whole society had to conform. The descendants of the warrior class were a few hundred families constantly intermarrying and constantly reinforced by fresh recruits. With the blessing of the Church, the feudal society was codified and divided in three classes: the clergymen, who prayed and took care for the spiritual well-being of the people; the aristocratic noblesse, who fought to defend and protect the community; and the common people, who worked the land to provide food for everyone. Feudalism was the cornerstone of medieval society, but the status of the vassal evolved differently in each European country, and patterns varied from region to region. Roughly speaking, the feudal organization was in real effect from the decay of the Carolingian empire in the 9th century until the end of the 12th century. The aristocratic rulers were to retain the landed dominance of Europe until the 16th century and political dominance until the 18th century (in France until the Revolution of 1789). Traces — at least of social prestige — remain until our own day as some aspects are still alive in the royal dynasties of northern Europe and, more particularly, in Great Britain.

Heredity of Fiefs

During the period in which the feudal hierarchy was taking form — that is, during and after the collapse of the Carolingian empire — the relationship between suzerains and vassals underwent profound changes. Fiefs were originally granted to a local lord by a greater overlord for the local's lifetime in return for service to the crown and were supposed to revert to the crown or the authority on the local lord's death. Vassals came to be obsessed with the problem of strengthening their hereditary right in their estates, to change the precarious possession into something more like private ownership. As the central power decreased, most suzerains succeeded in transforming the fief from a revocable — or at best a lifetime — grant into

Charlemagne Receiving the Oath of Fidelity and Homage from One of His Barons (after the 14th Century Chroniques de Saint Denis)

a hereditary one. The basic reason for this development must have been the extreme difficulty of preventing an adult son of a vassal from taking over the family estate. There was a shortage of trained warriors throughout northern Europe, and any lord who did not bind his vassals to him by largesse found it hard to retain their loyalty. A vassal who wanted to create his own dynasty was less likely to desert if he could be assured that his estates would legally go to his heirs. It is impossible to reconstruct this process in detail, but it was clear that by the 10th century most fiefs were hereditary. The system of inheritance was one of *primogeniture*, that is, the eldest son inherited his father's land. Dividing the inheritance between children proved impractical since it meant

smaller subdivisions of land which ultimately were insufficient to support the rank of ruler. Younger sons had to make a career in the Church or seek their fortunes as freelance knights.

Feudal Obligations

As long as land holding was a revocable grant, the obligations of the vassal were determined by the suzerain's will. But when the fief became transformed into hereditary private property, these obligations were governed by mutual contract. Feudalism grew up in a haphazard fashion, and it is important to bear in mind that the "feudal system" was anything but systematic. Jurisdiction, customs, services, and rules varied from fief to fief. There was thus absolutely no uniform pattern of organization. Moreover, the "system" was complicated by particular situations, preexisting local conditions, survival of old traditions, and ancient Roman or Germanic laws. Indeed the Middle Age was a period of *more majorum* in which the authority of custom was very great and men were inclined to do what their predecessors had done. This being understood, there were, however, certain customs and obligations which were common practices of feudal society all over western Europe.

Personal duties and mutual obligations played a vital part in the feudal relationship. First of all, vassals and suzerains had to be loyal to each other. The basic purpose of the feudal relationship was cooperation in war. The suzerain had to protect his vassal's fief from all foes outside the lord's estate. He was bound to do justice to his vassals in his court and to respect their family and personal interests. The vassal was required to be a trained warrior, capable of turning out, ready and equipped, to fight when summoned by his overlord from whom he held his land. If the vassal had a large holding, his obligation would extend to the provision of a number of knights and trained fighting men in addition to himself; the wealthier he was, the larger, better equipped, and more highly skilled had to be the force he had to provide. As a rule, a period of forty days a year —called *ost*— was the common maximum time a vassal had to serve at his own cost in an offensive war. If the lord's estate was invaded, the vassals had to fight until the enemy was driven back. The vassal had the duty of acting as a member of the garrison of the lord's castle; this castle-guard duty differed greatly from fief to fief, likely as a rule limited to thirty or forty days per year. The vassal had to attend the lord's court when summoned for a variety of purpose. There — together with other vassals and the lord's officers— he was expected to give honest advice and counsel about any question of interest to the fief as a whole, such as discussing welfare, choosing a wife for the lord or his son or a husband for his daughter, departing to crusade, waging a war on a neighbor, etc… Another obligation of the vassal was the *aid*, which included raising money to pay for the lord's ransom if he was captured and contributing to the cost of the crusade and of the castle etc. The vassal also had the duty of offering hospitality to the lord. The personal relationship between the vassal and the lord was symbolized by an oath of allegiance. This was inaugurated in a solemn and public ceremony known as *homage*, (from the French *homme*, meaning "man"). The suppliant would kneel, bareheaded and weaponless before his lord, place his hands between the hands of his suzerain in token of his obedience and the lord's protection, then swear — usually on a relic — to serve the lord with loyalty and declared his intention aloud: "Sire, I become your man."

The "system" was particularly complicated as a vassal could swear homage to one or more lords, resulting in a source of considerable confusion, especially when two overlords were at war with one another. To counteract this problem, the solution of *liege homage* was devised. A vassal holding several fiefs would choose one — usually the lord from whom he held the most land — as his especial lord and swear a specific oath to serve him in preference to the others. But if the liege homage was a revival and a reinforcement of personal ties, it soon was debased in much the same way as simple vassalage before it. There was another tie which united the members of the feudal hierarchy: Family and marriage connection played a vital part in procuring the advancement of individuals, cementing an alliance, strengthening political ties, and building the wealth of a dynasty. Heiresses were sought after since they could bring additions to their husbands' estates. Relatives could usually be relied on to combine against the outside world. But brothers or cousins might also quarrel bitterly and even wage war against one another.

In theory, feudalism was a cluster of personal institutions that furnished a means for the peaceful settlement of all disputes. It was meant to be a way of organizing life in a region, and it functioned as a structure of local government. Each link of the feudal chain made an oath to the effect that tenure of land was conditioned on the service rendered. Any subordinate who abused his power could be punished by his immediate superior, the lord from whom he held his fief. The system of oath was supposed to enable a well-regulated kingdom to mobilize an efficient fighting force against a common enemy for the protection of society.

Needless to say, this concept of the delegation of political power and solidarity suffered sharp breaks in the chain of command. Actually — as the whole point was to maintain a class of professional warriors and privileged rulers— the practice was never applied *ad litteram*, it did not follow theory very closely. In practice — where the authority of the monarchy was weak — kings had to give a very free hand to their deputies. This meant that the great nobles, counts, and dukes who possessed large territories did owe fidelity, but at most it was only a vague obligation to be helpful and often only a promise not to harm the superior. These nobles had great political authority and military power and could mobilize efficient groups of fighters against anyone harming them or trying to reduce their power. They could maintain their total independence — even at times against the king. A count's holding could usually be seized only at the price of war.

Among the aristocracy, war was an instrument of policy, a test of manhood, and the greatest pleasure in life. Subsequently, private wars on a local scale between vassals of the same lord or between vassals and lords were numerous.

Peace and Truce of God

During the local wars opposing the early medieval ruling class, church properties were not always spared, and the peasantry suffered a lot. This state of disorder and uncertainty annoyed the Church, and two ecclesiastical decrees — enacted between 990 and 1048 — were launched to counteract and control the violence of the European knights. The *Peace of God* was supposed to protect noncombatants (peasants, merchants, women, children, priests, and clerks), and it prohibited certain acts such as destroying vineyards, mills, and, of course, churches. The *Truce of God* was aimed at preventing hostilities at certain times (Fridays, Sundays, holy days, and during the major religious feasts such as Christmas and Easter). The laws marked the beginning of a period which saw the Church claiming to assert temporal as well as spiritual authority as put forward by Pope Gregory VII (1020–1085). Warriors and rulers, said Gregory, were the "vassals of Saint Peter," and if the interests of the Church conflicted with the interests of the secular lords, it was a ruler's duty to obey the Church first and foremost. Although the penalty for breaking the laws was excommunication, the feudal warriors regarded the legislation as unwarrantable interference in their own affair. It is, of course, impossible to measure the effects of those ecclesiastical initiatives, but they certainly played a part in reducing the devastations and atrocities of the medieval upper class whose whole ethos was rooted in selfishness and love of fighting.

Another important influence on warrior behavior in the 12th century came from the increasing importance of the cult of Jesus' mother, the Holy Virgin Mary, which promoted the respect due to the ladies in feudal society. This gave birth to the so-called courtly love, in which women were treated with greater consideration. However, it must be pointed out that the change in behavior, smoothing of brutality, improvement of manners, and development of morality and respect shown to women were probably important but still only comparative. Many knights and landowners remained unscrupulous looters, murderers, and rapists; prostitutes and illegitimate mistresses still swarmed in their castles; and no noble blushed because of his bastards. However, both Peace and Truce of God reached a peak with the First Crusade in 1095.

Castellany

In theory the whole feudal pyramid of loyalty culminated in the king. But as the kings — until the 12th century — were rather weak powerless rulers, political power was based almost entirely on force of arms. Anyone prestigious enough to gain followers, able to build a castle, and rich enough to garrison it could create his independent state and concentrate in his own hands military, political, juridical, and economic power within his tiny kingdom. Moreover, the holder of a court of justice gained both authority and income as fines paid by offenders went into his coffer. The working unit of government became thus the castellany — the land near enough to a castle that it could be protected, policed, and administrated by the lord of the castle. In the 10th century, most castles were motte-and-baily fortresses. Based on a Viking/Norman design these were made by digging a ditch and piling the dirt into an artificial *motte* or mound. The edge of the ditch and the top of the mound were fortified with wooden palisades. On the summit of the mound inside the stockade stood a wooden tower which was the residence of the lord and his household. At the foot of the motte there

Saint Theodorius. Theodorius is here depicted as a man-of-arms (after a statue from the gate of the cathedral of Chartres).

Motte-and-Bailey Castle

were shallower and narrower ditches and stockades enclosing a *bailey*, an area which was a small village with houses and workshops for the lord's servants as well as stables and other outbuildings. In case of danger the baily served as a place of refuge for the lord's subjects from the neighborhood: the peasants, their families, and stock.

Siege warfare was then quite primitive. The besiegers could make a blockade all around the castle and wait until the hungry and discouraged assieged would surrender. But if attrition did not work, the attacking party would assault the place. The ditches could be crossed, the palisades scaled. After having conquered the bailey, the aggressors would attack the tower on the motte, breaking the palisade with a battering ram, setting the tower on fire, and launching an assault.

Very few people could read, and as the only artificial light available was from smoky torches, the lord was likely to go to bed right after darkness set in. In peacetime, the

feudal lord at home got up at dawn, heard mass in his chapel, and got the daily business done with his officials. Some rich lords might hold many estates a considerable distance apart. If so, they might live in different houses at different times, traveling from manor to manor to ensure that their lordship was recognized and respected; they might also grant a manor with estate in fief to loyal subvassals.

A king, a duke, a count, or any mighty lord would have a household, a court, and various officials to assist him in ruling. The same men who ministered to the domestic needs of the household conducted the business of the fief and participated in warfare. The provost superintended the demesne and collected taxes and dues. In England the Anglo-Saxons kings appointed a *shire-reeve* or sheriff, a removable agent in each county. The chaplain heard confession and said mass in the chapel. Since the chaplain was a clerk, he did not fight, and, as he was often literate, he held the lord's written records. In time he was called *chancellor* and had other clerks under him who served as chaplains and secretaries. The chamberlain looked after the bed chamber, watched over the lord's valuables, jewels, and clothes as well as archives and charters, and he generally controlled access to the lord. The constable and the marshal were military officers that commanded the soldiers, were responsible for armor and weapons, and saw to the horses and, as such, had a high status in the feudal demesnes showing the importance of horses. The steward was the head of the administration; he was also responsible for the provisioning of the household. The steward was assisted by the butler, who procured the wine, and the dispenser, who supervised the issuance of wine.

Entertainment included solid meals and drinking and possibly more refined shows with minstrels displaying varied talents, storytellers with magnificent tales, tumblers, and dancing bears. Hunting and hawking were the feudal ruler caste's main pleasure, and the hunting grounds were guarded with jealousy against the depredations of poachers. Penalties for catching reserved animals— such as a deer — were severe and included flaying, mutilation, and even hanging. Hunting was regarded as a sign of great courage and an opportunity to exercise healthiness, knightly qualities, and a display of skill besides providing a valuable addition to the medieval diet. The *chasse-à-courre* consisted of pursuing on horseback stags, wild boars, deer, and wild cats with the help of a pack of hounddogs. Animals were put to death with spears or swords. Troublesome animals were also hunted — as much for pleasure as for the necessary extermination — including wolves, bears, lynx, elk, aurochs, and bison, which terrorized peasants, ruined their crops, and decimated their cattle. Wild animals could be hunted with bows and arrows. Game birds were hunted by hawking with a trained falcon. It developed into a great art, falconry. Hawks and falcons were valuable and sometimes given as prestigious gifts.

Needless to say the feudal ruler of the 10th, 11th, and early 12th centuries were no model of refinement and gentleness. There was little or no legal restraint on their personal behavior. Castle could be full of mistresses and prostitutes, heavy drinking and rough conduct were common, and servants— and even wives and children —could be beaten, sometimes with savagery. The feudal caste was quite religious though. They accepted without question the basic teaching of the Church, followed the observance, heard mass, and gave alms and donations. However, repentance and atonement were far easier than virtue. Some rich counts or dukes founded religious houses and abbeys; many went on long pilgrimages; some departed to the crusade in the Holy Land. But — on the whole —

faith did not seem to interfere with personal conduct. Along with fair rulers, noble gentlemen, and generous lords, there were bad knights, blood-thirsty perverts, and wicked men who terrorized helpless peasants, dishonored ladies, and even desecrated churches. There were countless robber barons, ruthless freebooters, and unscrupulous mercenaries who brought knighthood and nobility into disrepute.

Principalities

Extreme political fragmentation did not occur everywhere, nor did castellanies develop in the same way and in the same form. In some parts of Europe, larger units— principalities— were established.

In northern France, where feudalism originated, the inability of the later Carolingians to provide more than the semblance of protection against the Northmen led to the decentralization of effective central power on to the allegedly subordinate counts; the companions of the old Germanic warrior bands settled in hereditary, and so virtually independent fiefs such as Hainault, Anjou, Flanders, Burgundy, Brittany, and many others developed. The relative weakness of the French kings until the 12th century meant that royal vassals were conveniently able to forget any claims from the kings. These territorial units had castellanies, but these were closely controlled by the counts.

The duchy of Normandy — created by descendants of the Vikings in the 10th century — did not break apart in castellanies but stayed held together by a vigorous line of dukes ruling the duchy on one side of the Channel and a royal dynasty ruling in England on the other side. England, because it was a relative small country, could be governed like one of the most cohesive continental principalities. The Norse invasions of the 9th and 10th centuries led the Saxon kings to supplement the *fyrd*, the obligation of all free men to bear arms, but it was the Norman conquest of 1066 which placed all land at the disposal of the crown, thus making possible a centralized feudal state. As previously noted, the first Norman king — William the Conqueror (1027–1087) — divided the lands among his vassals as a reward for their military help in defeating the Anglo-Saxons, but he created a strong centralized state and retained effective administrative control throughout his realm through the channel of his appointed sheriffs. Only in frontier districts near the uncontrolled Wales and Scotland were the vassals more independent, and their independence continued to plague the kings of England well into the 15th century.

Northern France preserved some aspects of the early Germanic kingdoms characterized by the survival of public courts, the existence of important landholders who did not take any feudal oath, the precarious position of vassals, and the strength of powerful dukes and counts to reassign great command. But these older political forms showed no great vitality, and political fragmentation was proceeding rapidly in these areas as well. In southern France the counts and dukes of Provence, Aquitaine, and Toulouse had their own strongholds and did not acknowledge any submission to the king of northern France but created their own particular Occitan civilization.

In Italy, where the power of towns and the importance of trade increased steadily after the 10th century, feudalism never worked very well. Urban communities survived among the rural noblesse, impervious to the feudalism spread by the Carolingians from Lombardy in the north and later by the Normans from the south. Towns could govern and merchants, landowners, townsmen, and peasants all took arms when threatened by the Magyars and Muslim raids. Cities were defended by their own citizen militias. The conflicts between popes and German emperors at the end of the 11th century polarized Italian society in a continuous feud which divided city against city and family against family in endless civil wars that provided a paradise for the freelance soldier of fortune.

In southern Europe the position was far more complex because of the continuous warfare against the Moors in Spain and southern Italy, but there too local rulers were independent. In Spain — where war was constant against the Moors — the arrogant independence of the Castillian nobility (the very name of the land — the "country of castles" — is expressive) was notorious throughout Europe. In Catalonia, the counts of Barcelona were able to impose subordination on their distant vassals and, supported by a fanatically militant Church, pushed on with the *Reconquista* of central Spain from the Moors at a more rapid pace.

In Germany the tribes of Saxony, Franconia, and Swabia remained a free peasantry fighting on foot with axe and spears until the Ottonian dynasty was established as successor of the Carolingians. In the Rhine valley, feudalism developed as intensively as it did in northern France, and the mystic of *Rittertum* (knighthood) was very strong. The growth of feudalism helped build up principalities, duchies, and margravates which became hereditary possessions of certain families. Even if the emperors of Germany attempted to reduce their power by using any opportunities to split off portions of their territories, the princes of the German principalities remained a very powerful group with direct administrative authority, controlling great military forces, and many of them were independent rulers. As a result, the state — until the end of the 19th century — in Germany grew out of the principalities and not out of the German kingdom.

6

Knights and Chivalry

Origins of Knighthood

The society of early medieval Europe was engaged in a continual struggle for survival against hostile forces. Successive waves of Barbarian tribes displaced from their own homelands by invasion or in search of new more fruitful land made the 8th, 9th, and 10th centuries a time of instability and violence under the constant threat of destruction. The idea of the knight as protector of society developed in response to these pressures. It was not in the Roman world that the medieval knight had its origins. The Roman *equester ordo* (order of horsemen), descended from the mounted troops of the Republic, had become a class of wealthy financiers and administrators whose military connections were entirely dissolved. The roots of the knight of the Middle Ages—as previously pointed out—are to be found in the Germanic tradition. Curiously—whereas the French word *chevalier*, German *Ritter*, Dutch *ridder*, or Spanish *caballero* translate the meaning of horseman exactly—the English language has simply the word *knight* which comes from the German *Knecht* meaning "retainer," "groom" or "servant." However, these words are modern, and in the Middle Ages, the mounted warrior was always referred to as *miles* (plural *milites*).

In the confusing period following the break-up of the Carolingian Empire, war leaders, lords, vassals, dukes, counts, and kings badly needed soldiers and recruited them without worrying about their social origins. *Audaces fortuna juvat*, so a young peasant who was physically fit with an adventurous and ambitious spirit and who proved to be a skilled horseman and a good soldier could easily become a *miles*. He was under his lord's protection and in turn furthered the latter's interests—if need be—with arms. In the first period of feudalism, the line between free peasant and knight was not sharply drawn. A poor knight might be no wealthier than a rich peasant. Both had a relatively low social status; both might hold the same amount of land with a few serfs working for them. A knight could also be of noble descent, being a cadet who had to make a living as a freelance soldier.

Gradually the knight became a professional soldier who was better off than the great mass of the population. As an expert fighting man, he was better fed, better housed, and treated with more consideration than peasants. Knights formed a social group of specially trained and specially rewarded armed retainers, but they still had little political power. They could settle minor squabbles, such as fights among villagers and disputes over peasant holdings or labor service, but any serious matters would go to the court of the local superior lord.

Progressively knights ceased to be primarily soldiers and gained a greater influence by participating in the administration of the courts of the lords. Lords were either too busy or too important to manage alone their domains. It was politically unwise to assume full responsibility and socially degrading not to be surrounded by respectful subordinates. These conditions created opportunities for competent knights to be promoted to officers. One was noble *ipso facto* by blood and birth, but one became a knight after years of training and by a ceremony allowing the entrance into the warrior order. Gradually *milites* could pass their occupation and title on to their sons. The recruitment—open to all in the early time—became exclusively restricted to sons of knights,

Quintain

and the role of warrior became hereditary. This transition took place largely in the late 10th and early 11th century. Equipment for mounted warfare was expensive, and only those who were prosperous enough could afford it. Furthermore the right to bear full arms was restricted to them only. The new class was a compound of men whose families were well-established without being noble, and of a few newcomers whose knighthood had been granted as a reward for great deeds of arms.

By 1100 knights had become an essential group in most feudal courts, the lords regularly asked their advice — particularly in the important military aspect of feudalism. The knights had ceased to be mere soldiers, they were recognized as especially privileged class of elite horsemen. The distinction between knights and the older nobility — whose roots went back to the Merovingian time and even early Germanic princely families — progressively blurred. This process is rather obscure, but even if squires and knights lacked high birth and noble ancestors, they became part of the nobility who claimed special status by virtue of their descent. Knights and squires remained soldiers, but they became as privileged as the rulers and, like them, were exempt from taxation. In the long run, some of these members from the caste of warriors acquired the necessary military resources—castles and a band of armed men — to become themselves minor lords. Although poor landless knights were common figures throughout the

Middle Ages, they merged within the ruling noble class as the lowest ranks of the aristocracy under the marquis, the baron, and the viscount. Knighthood became entirely a matter of membership of an order with a specific and costly ceremony as its distinguished mark.

Training of Candidate Knights

The noble feudal male had one primary function in society: fighting. His education and his way of life were programmed for this task. Major factors affecting the development of knighthood were the new developments in military technology and tactics which occurred in the second half of the 11th century. These were related to the use of the lance by the mounted warrior. Stirrups were introduced by contact with the barbarian horsemen — such as the Magyars of Hungary — and were in use by the 9th century. Stirrups enabled the man on a horse to have much greater control over the animal and much greater stability in the saddle. In the late 11th century developed the tactic of charge with "couched" lance — that was holding the weapon much nearer to the blunt end, clamped against the body by the right arm. This method — already known in the time of Charlemagne — became the standard technique of medieval cavalry. During centuries the only fighting man of consequence, the only *miles* who

Squire Taking Care of the Horse (after Herman Huppen)

counted, was the mounted warrior whose military dominance led to political control. The skill and training required to operate this kind of tactic successfully was considerable. To learn to hold the heavy lance steady while wearing armor and helmet and controlling a galloping horse required a great deal of practice. The knight had to be accustomed to the handling of many other weapons, such as the sword, axe, war hammer, and mace. He had to be a good horseman as well. In short, he had to be a professional.

Adubment in the 13th Century (after Matthew Paris)

It was thus customary for young boys of good birth to start their military training very young. At the age of seven he became a *damoiseau* or *varlet* (page) and would be fostered out to received his education at some friendly court, usually that of his father's lord or of a relative. Under the lord's tutelage, the young boy provided service in exchange for his instruction. For some years—together with the sons of other knights—he would be a domestic serving the lady of the castle and acquiring some non-military talents such as playing a musical instrument or singing. At this stage—like the youngest boys at a public school—his status was menial, and he could be ordered by other members of the household, sent on errands, or given cleaning tasks. He would learn the history of his lineage, the rudiments of heraldry, the epic stories and legends about the great heroes of the past, and a few prayers in Latin, but very few medieval noble men could read and write. Another and less pleasant form of fostering for a noble child was to be given as a hostage to a lord in dispute with his father as a guarantee of good behavior. Such hostages were usually well treated, but occasionally they were placed in grave danger.

At the age of fourteen the cadet would graduate to the next stage and become a *scutarius* or *escuyer* (squire) this term meaning originally the carrier of the knight's shield. The squire had certain specific duties to perform such as serving his lord at table, taking care of the horses, and in particular being responsible for assisting the knight with his armor and weapons. For more menial sorts of service, squires relied on ordinary servants; they also had to learn good manners, the finer aspects of courtly life, and the skill of hunting.

Physical fitness was essential for warriors. Apprentice-knights and squires had to develop strength and skills through everyday practice. They would gradually be hardened to the wearing of armor—which could weigh about 22 kilograms (50 pounds)—and trained in horse riding and in the use of various weaponry on foot and on horseback. They trained individually practicing the so-called "quintain," hitting targets with a lance carried at a run, and if the horseman misjudged his timing, the pivoting quintain would inflict him a blow and even knock him on his horse's rump. Apprentices also trained together thwacking each other with swords and shields. This helped to reinforce the knights' sense of brotherhood, prowess, and professional solidarity.

Military leadership was considered the aristocratic's natural prerogative, and the knight's military training, combat experience, and social authority suited him to the task. Squires and knights had special chambers set apart

Adubment on the Battle Field (after a 14th Century Arthurian Romance)

for their use, since it would have been inappropriate for aristocrats to mix with ordinary soldiers. Class distinction between officers and soldiers is still fundamental to the organization of modern armies, and fraternization is frowned upon to this day.

Adubment

When the candidate knight was about twenty — and considered adequately prepared physically and mentally — he would be solemnly and publicly made a knight. If he did not have enough income to maintain the status of knight, the squire might remain a bachelor for several years or even not be knighted at all. There was plenty of honorable employment for well-brought-up young men at courts and castles throughout Europe. Good squires were valued, and those of an intellectual bent could become heralds, writers, and administrators.

A ceremony — the *adubment* — marked the entrance of the young man in a new "state" — the order of chivalry.

The roots of adubment lay in the initiation ritual by which Germanic primitive societies marked the coming of age of adolescence, the token of maturity of young males of the tribe who were then given the right to bear arms for the first time. In its simplest form — before the development of extravagant chivalrous institutions — the ceremony of knighting consisted of the simple words "Be thou a knight!" accompanied by a light blow either with the hand or the sword. There were many variations of the rite, such as putting on one's armor, kneeling before the master (the lord who trained him), and — a constant and essential act in the ceremony — receiving the *colée* a blow on the head or the flat of the officiant's sword on the shoulder. The origin of the traditional and symbolic *colée* is quite mysterious, and its meaning uncertain. It is possible that it is related to the blow given to free slaves and to an obscure Germanic custom of striking the witnesses to a legal act to make them remember the occasion — perhaps also to wake them up? Gradually the ceremony became more elaborate and came to acquire a broader significance.

Under the influence of the Church, which increased between the 9th and 10th centuries, the adubment took on a more moral and religious overtone. It became a religious ceremony and a highly sophisticated ritual accompanied by great pomp and expense. As the Middle Ages had few written records, ceremonies including commitment such as marriage and adubment were celebrated in the presence of witnesses: suzerain, family, relatives, friends and companions, clergymen, noble neighbors and allies and, eventually, common people of the fief. The ceremony often included a preparation in the form of a symbolic purifying bath, the dressing in a white robe, and a night of prayer in a chapel. The next morning, the ritual took place in the hall or in the chapel of the castle. Knighthood was conferred to the young man by another knight or — preferably a distinguished and prestigious one — or even by the king.

The ritual began with the traditional colée on the neck or the flat of a sword on the kneeling candidate. The knight was kissed and solemnly admonished about the duties he had to perform with faith, loyalty, and devoutness. Then he was presented his weapons, armor, surcoat, banner, and shield — which were blessed by a chaplain, possibly a bishop. Spurs were fixed to the heels, and his sword was girded around his waist. The ceremony was generally followed by celebrations, a feast, and the practice of "military games" such as a tournament and joust.

Circumstances did not always permit the ceremony to be conducted in its full magnificence. Some young men were hastily mass-knighted on the eve of a battle or before assaulting a fortress, and in this case the ritual was shortened and did not entail vast costs. This was a cheap manner of boosting morale and motivation to fight. Knighting could also occur *after* the battle, as a reward for those who had "won their spurs" by gallant achievements and great deeds of bravery. Coronations of kings and pilgrimage to the Holy Sepulcher in Jerusalem in the company of important rulers were frequently occasions for mass knighting.

Once knighted the young feudal male received a military promotion: he was then a privileged member of an elite caste, and he was part of a brotherhood, of a great international noble association. If he were a younger son, he might enter military service in a lord's household where he would be much better paid than a common soldier; he could officially lead and command a group of warriors; he was less likely to have difficulty in raising a ransom and was certainly in little danger of being killed out of hand instead of being taken prisoner. He also received a social promotion: He had to abstain from the cultivation of land, from the care of animals (except his horses), and from trade in commodities, and he should not manage the business of other people nor engage in civil duties. If he were an eldest son inheriting an estate, he could become a vassal, do homage, and possibly rule his fief.

Chivalry

The early Catholic Church's attitude to war and violence was clear: "Thou shalt not kill." So killing people, even in battle, was homicide, a break of God's rule and a major sin, and no Christian could excuse its consequences. The first Christians were convinced pacifists. In the 5th century, the theologian Saint Augustine (354–430) evolved the concept of "just" war, and the religious authorities recognized that there were circumstances in which homicide was excusable in Christian duty. *Lato sensu*, broadly speaking, "just wars" were those waged on the authority of a lawful superior in a righteous cause. The Church — as early as the time of the first Merovingian kings — accepted and blessed the warrior class; it could hardly do otherwise since they were fighting to defend Christendom against the incursions of heathen Muslims, and later the pagan Magyars and Norsemen. So in war against the pagan no holds were barred, and knights indeed could gain remission from their sins by waging war.

When the barbarian raids ebbed, the Church attempted to bring the conduct of war and Christian morality into some kind of focus. The progressive establishment of the feudal system gave rise to endless disputes and, in default, of a clear system of law and law enforcement; rulers were likely to vindicate their right by battle. The modern attitude is to regard peace as normal, war as the exception and as immoral and evil. The medieval attitude was quite different. Knights and rulers regarded war as the normal state of mankind, partly through dim memories of days when this had been true (in the time of the Muslim, Magyar, and Norse incursions) and their service as defenders of society had been essential and partly because war was so strongly in their financial interest. At the most abstract level — that of the lawyers and theorists — war was part of the established order of things. However, that Christians should fight each other was deplorable, and the Church deplored it regularly.

Over a long period the Church tried to control the often destructive energy of the knights and the abuses of the ruling class by legislature and prohibition (Peace and Truce of God), by directing martial energies to ecclesiastical ends (such as the Crusades), and by taking over the pagan ritual and ceremonies of knighthood. Through these edicts, the Church began to recognize the increasing social and political importance of the fighting class. The consolidation and extension of ecclesiastical power during the 11th and 12th centuries affected all parts of feudal society including the knightly class. Knighthood was a way of life sanctioned and civilized by the ceremonies of the Church until it was almost indistinguishable from the ecclesiastical orders of the monasteries. As a matter of fact, clergymen and warriors were close to each other as, respectively, rulers of the spiritual and material worlds. The important officers of the Church (abbots, bishops, and popes) were always drawn from the ruling class, the warrior caste, and landholders. No matter how bitter the quarrels between individual prelates and lords might be, both privileged classes always cooperated to maintain their dominance, and they always united against the threat of a popular social insurrection.

The Church was deeply involved in local, provincial and national government, and its influence over the daily life of every member of medieval society was enormous. The Church offered honorable careers for younger superfluous sons of landholding families. The Church itself was deeply involved *in temporalibus*, in the material world, as popes were worldly monarchs and as many abbeys and monasteries were feudal landlords ruling over large estates. Popes, bishops and abbots happily assumed military obligations with the fiefs of lands granted them by the kings they crowned, and seldom showed much reluctance about bearing arms to defend and even increase their worldly privileges and territorial properties. Until the new atmosphere of the Reformation and the heat of greater religious issues which moved and divided Christianity in the 16th century, luxury and even license prevailed in the papal and episcopal courts.

Out of two separate ideas (one pagan and the other Christian), the Germanic tradition of honor and the growing influence of Christianity, emerged the concept of chivalry, a noble and all-embracing ethic. The ideal of chivalry formed one of the brightest threads in the rich tapestry of medieval life. The status of chivalry distinguished the knight from his contemporaries, but it created obligations. The Church's concern with the ethics of knighthood and the rise of the crusading ideal lent color to the argument that knighthood was intended as the secular arm of the Church. Thus the first stage of honorable achievement was to defend the faith and protect the Holy Church and, second, to serve loyally one's lord at home and on the battlefield. Other duties were to defend and protect the weak, including women, widows, and children, and to pursue criminals and bring them to justice. But honor meant more than courage and skill. The knight had to be *sans peur* (without fear) but also *sans reproche* (without reproach). The concept of chivalry developed a code of a sophisticated system of values such as personal integrity and the practice of knightly virtues such as generosity, compassion, a free and frank spirit, and courtli-

ness especially to women. A knight had to hold an untarnished personal reputation and, *potius mori quam foedari*, would rather die than dishonor himself. His honor was holy. Honor was the shrine at which the knight worshiped. It implied renown, good conduct, and the world's approval. There were cases for exclusion from the order: perjurers and those who had broken their word of honor, usurers, and those who married beneath their station, for example. The knight had never to be satisfied with what he had done but should always wish to achieve more. It was considered a good thing for a knight to be in love as *omniat vincit amor*, love would spur him to yet higher achievement. A knight had to be modest about his achievements and — if successful — he would be wise to attribute this to the aid of God and the Holy Virgin who would reward him with eternal rest in paradise. Chivalry acquired a holy patron in Saint George, a 4th century Christian martyr, legendary prince of Cappadocia, often represented slaying a dragon. The archangel Saint Michaël, chief of the heavenly militia protecting Israel according to the prophet Daniel (Daniel, X: 13) also played a major role in the ethos of chivalry.

The realities of war, ideals of the Church, pride of noble families, records of the heralds, and researches of the lawyers all contributed to give the cult of chivalry an ardent following. Hundreds of poems and epic *chansons de geste* (songs of romantic adventures) were written to describe the heroic deeds of ideal knights and their obligations as shown in the following extract of the *Romance of the Rose* written about 1237 by Guillaume de Lorris.

> But be thou careful to possess
> Thy soul in gentleness and grace
> Kindly of heart and bright of face
> Towards all men, be they great or small
> Watch well thy lips, that they may be
> Never stained with ill-timed ribaldry
>
> Have special care
> To honor dames as thou dost fare
> Thy worldly ways, and shouldst thou hear
> Calumnious speech of them, no fear
> Have thou to bid men hold their peace
> Let him who would in love succeed
> To courteous world wed noble deed.

Until today, the enthusiasm and fascination about medieval knights gave birth to familiar and heroic figures such as *Quentin Durward* and *Ivanhoe* created by the British novelist Sir Walter Scott (1771–1832). The chivalrous ideal as portrayed in literature was of course only one side of the coin. In the practice, knights and feudal rulers only heeded the Church's injunctions which related specifically to them and their violent activities when it suited them to do so. They saw themselves as working in their own way for God's purpose. They were infused in many ways with strong religious sentiments, but these were always subordinated to ultimately secular goals. Chivalry was a way of life, a form of behavior according to a certain code of conduct, but it became a golden and fictitious glamour, a sunset glow from a consciously disappearing society seen through the distorting lenses of troubadors' legends, songs, and stories. All too often knights—instead of being unselfish defenders—were greedy predators and wicked aggressors. They had a strong and stubborn tradition of independence from authority aggravated by their arrogance and the persistence of the idea of private war as a legal right. As soon as central power diminished, the old Germanic instinct for plunder and rapine reappeared among some of them. And—of course—human nature being what it is, far from the ideas of chivalry defined by the Church, and in contradiction with the sophistication mandated by courtly courtesy, it was not uncommon for knights to abandon themselves to all sort of disorders like drunkenness, libertinism, adultery, and even rape, theft, and murder. Chivalry cast a golden spell over the black harshness of war, an illusion in which the knights themselves believed but which was, nonetheless, unreal. Beneath the high idealism of chivalrous honor, war continued much as before, as cruel, atrocious, and pointless as ever.

Tournaments and Jousts

For all his involvements with higher ideals, the knight remained first and foremost a warrior. As there were no military colleges, young knights acquired the skills of fighting in two main ways: in real warfare and in the practice of arms off the battlefield. Young warriors were encouraged to go abroad individually or in small groups, to serve in foreign wars or crusades in Palestine against the Turks, in Spain against the Moors, or in Prussia to combat with the Teutonic Knights against the pagans. On these remote fronts, there was always a shortage of men-of-arms, and knights from all over Europe, wishing to gain a reputation and experience in warfare, traveled to take part in these conflict as freelance soldiers. This policy was actively encouraged by the Church. In the course of these operations, a young knight might find himself engaged in many different kinds of warfare: pitched battles were comparatively infrequent, much more common were sieges and raids in enemy territory with the expectation of booty taken from the enemy.

The other way for a knight to learn the basic skills of his trade was through military games, known as tournaments and jousts. Training for war had existed since

time immemorial, but when the conduct of war played so important a part in European society, training came to occupy a quite exceptional place. And in the absence of a central organization with the means to supervise such training, it developed a formal outline of its own: the tournament. It is hardly possible to overestimate the importance of tournaments to the culture of the Middle Ages. The ancient Greek and Roman worlds had known nothing like them. The Greek Olympics were purely sportive meetings and by no means related to the military. Gladiator combats in ancient Rome were also exploitation of physical skill and courage for entertainment, but the bloody circus fights were primitive elements in social life intended first and foremost to control and entertain by thrill and blood the idle free population. Medieval tournaments—although spectators of all classes were present—were rather different in essence as they were primarily mock battles organized for the enjoyment of the participants.

The origin of tournaments is quite unknown, but it seems that they would be related to military games and mock fights opposing early Germanic warriors on horseback. As well as hunting, Charlemagne's court practiced war games showing military skills among the Franks. The precursor to the later tournaments seems to have been held at Worms in 842 on the occasion of a meeting between Franks and German knights; the game took the form of simulated charges, retreats, and counter-charges, with lances swinging in so disciplined a way that no one got hurt. Although the first great tournament of which we have reliable record is that held at Würzburg (Germany) in 1127, the first tournaments took place in France as reflected by the early name for such events: *conflictus Gallicus* (French battles). *Tournament* comes from the French word "*tournois*" (coming itself from the verb *tournoyer* meaning "to turn around"). A knight who did not go on crusade had little hope of seeing more than intermittent war, so tournaments became fashionable and popular in the beginning of the 12th century. Their purpose seemed to be a substitute for private wars created by enthusiast knights themselves, as the Crusades were an alternative for the very dedicated, the very rich, or the very pious, and as private wars and large-scale warfare in Europe were increasingly outlawed by strong rulers and thus became rare.

In their early days tournaments were fairly unregulated free-for-alls and little different from a real battle. Such semifriendly battles were organized by some great lords on a certain day and at a certain place. Messengers would be sent all over the country, and on the appointed day the knights would gather and form two parties. The battle had only a few rules: it lasted for a prescribed time limit (a part of one day) and could range over a wide space, though those who wished to please the ladies probably tried to display their courage and skill within the ladies' view. The tournament proper was a disorganized *mêlée*, a mock battle in which the two teams would charge, attack, turn, and fight each other in a crude and rough fight. Real war weapons were used as in a regular battle, only there was no purpose beyond amusement and personal benefit. The aim was to take as many prisoners as possible from the opposing side, and those defeated would pay a ransom or would have to give horses, weapons, and armors to the victors. Naturally, bellicose and hot-blooded knights were prone to lose their temper. The frenzied and confusing battle could rapidly degenerate into a more dangerous brawl, and men were severely wounded or even killed.

Later in the 13th century, tournaments were more regulated, and weapons were blunted to reduce casualties. The fighting space was a *list*, enclosed by barriers, and there were refuges where the knights could prepare themselves and retreat to rest. In Germany, Burgundy, and Italy, many nobles lived in the towns, and urban tournaments — held on the central square — were popular. There was also mock fights, particularly popular in Spain and Italy in the 15th century, called *pas d'armes*, that simulated siege warfare. These were fought between two teams; one being the *tenants* (holding a bridge or a tower) and the other *venants* (coming to attack the position). Another form very popular in Germany in the late 15th century was the *Kolbenturnier*, in which heavy wooden maces were used by horsemen to demolish the opponent's crest on top of the helmet.

Ecclesiastical authorities were strongly opposed to the practice of tournaments. By 1130 Pope Innocent II preached that crusades were a better means of employing exuberance than these wanton fatal affairs. The prohibition was officially — but vainly — repeated many times, notably in 1139, 1148, 1163, and 1179. The Church argued that simulated battles disturbed the peace and that they were occasions encouraging pride and violence, and it deplored that they too often ended in drinking bouts. In 1288 at the Fair of Boston (England), two gangs of tourneying knights got so carried away that half the town was ravaged, thus providing an excuse for renewed protests against tournaments. In addition the Church added that this pastime could be very expensive not only to organize but in the results; unlucky tourneying knights could waste their revenues, even to the point of complete ruin, in order to pay ransoms and replace lost horses, weapons, and armor. The Church's official disapproval of the violent games was maintained throughout the Middle Ages. The thunder of popes and bishops was regularly renewed and fulminated in threats, edicts, and anathemas. However, one prohibition was respected, that against clergy taking part in martial games as ecclesiastics were not supposed to harm Christians and shed blood. Although the clergy succeeded to some extend in taking over the ritual of dubbing to knighthood, and in getting tournament competitors to fight with blunted weapons to reduce casualties, its efforts to ban totally the martial games were unsuccessful. Even kings and princes organized and participated in tournaments, and even the noble Crusaders organized them, notably at Antioch in 1156. Tournaments were too central and too important to the ethos of knighthood to be prohibited. They provided a prestigious arena for the display of all important knightly virtues and a showcase for knightly qualities. They were a crucial training ground for warfare. Young knights could practice handling their horses and weapons, tactics of attack and defense, coordinating their actions with a team of companions. The battles were also a way of recruiting. They offered an opportunity to win praise and glory, and talented knights could be remarked and could find employment with great lords.

Politically, tournaments could be used for the settling of scores. When the knights of two hostile lords met in the lists, the tournaments could — and often did — become a real war in miniature and a substitute for local baronial wars. Political authorities had mixed feelings about tournaments. On one hand, powerful counts and dukes, kings and emperors were often enthusiastic tourneyers themselves as the battles were instruments of princely prestige, but on the other hand too many of their good fighters got injured or killed in pointless combats. Indeed tournaments could affect the course of political events through the accidental death of important persons. King Philippe II August of France (reign 1060–1108) enjoined his sons not to take part in tournaments. Political authorities did not try to ban tournaments (as did the Church), but instead attempted to make a profit out of the knights' favorite activity. Some cunning kings in need of money for crusading and wars created a tax on tourneying. King Richard I of England (the Lion Heart who reigned from 1189 to 1199) was the first to create a system of licensed tournaments in August 1194. Illicit tournaments were an element of struggle for political power and became associated with revolt against the crown's authority. They were repressed by force and punished by heavy fines — another way to fill the king's coffer.

Tournaments remained in practice well into the 13th century. Originally they had few limitations and few rules, boundaries, referees, or judges. But by the end of the 12th century owing to the development of heraldry — and possibly to the pressure of the Church and that of royal authority — the event became more civilized. Structuralization and signs of control, restrictions, and limitations appeared. The heralds announced the place and date,

Jousting Knights about 1320 (after Codex Balduini Trevirensis)

prizes were awarded by consensus of either the competitors or spectators, the number of competitors were gradually reduced in each battle to avoid too great confusion, foul blows were forbidden, unfair behavior was banned, and weapons were blunted and limited to the sword and lance. The events became less a battle than a sportive encounter and an entertainment. Tournaments were then regarded as a highly enjoyable sport, and successful knights acquired something of the aura that sportsmen have today. For young knights in search of renown and profit, tournaments could be a possible source of income. A successful tourneyer could gain a formidable reputation but also make a comfortable living by obtaining wealth through rewards, gifts, sums of money, and booty such as valuable horses, costly armor, and weapons of the vanquished.

By the end of the 12th century, the first jousts were recorded. These may have started as a reaction against the chance and brute force which decided the fortunes of the collective tournament. The *joust* was a duel between two mounted armored challengers armed with lance and charging and attempting to unseat each other. As the prime objective was to unseat one's opponent, jousting became rather divorced from the practical side of war. It was a highly esteemed supplementary exercise though, which permitted the opportunity for personal glory. It was the show of gallantry and the display of skill. When fighting man-to-man, skill was more important than endurance, and individual skill was all that mattered. In addition, a joust had the advantage of being less dangerous than a tournament.

With the rise of the courtly philosophy and idealized chivalry, clear rules were decreed. Tournaments and jousts were strictly reserved for noblemen and knights and excluded those who had criminal records, were guilty of unchivalrous behavior, had repeated gossip about ladies, had deserted their lord in battle, had destroyed vineyards and cornfields etc. Scoring was introduced, implying the presence of officials to record and supervise the actual events. The encounter was regulated by heralds who presented rules which were ritually observed. Each knight challenged another, and the jousts were fought between challenger and defendant. Negotiations were made to discuss the requirements as well as details of the prizes and rewards offered.

By the end of the 12th century the ideas of courtly love were adapted to the circumstances of jousts, and the romantic ideals of the poets began to be reflected in real life. Personal honor, individual glory, and the lady's love were now the spurs for the events. Jousts were usually fought with *armes courtoises* (arms considerations), implying that weapons were rebated: swords had both edges blunted and a rounded end instead of a sharp point, and lances were deprived of a point. Exceptionally, *armes à outrance* (excessive arms) could be used. In that case weapons were not blunted, and the encounter was a thrilling demonstration for knights skilled enough to use such dangerous weapons with a minimum of injury to each other. Weapons that were not blunted could also be used to fight a genuinely hostile duel perhaps over a point of honor; the duel for honor survived until the 19th century as an institution.

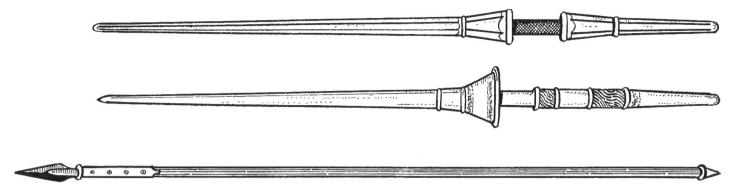

Lances Used in Jousts. The lance was the main weapon used in a joust. It was about twelve feet in length and averaged three inches in diameter, being thicker toward the butt end and tapering toward the point, and often fitted with a conical guard protecting the hand and arm.

As the years passed, more and more aids were allowed that kept the participant in the saddle, such as bootlike stirrups and a high pommel on the saddle. Man and horse were almost inseparable, and only the breaking of the lance was possible. Techniques within the lists became a complex art, with distinct runs calling for very good horsemanship. This led to the development of special heavy armors designed solely for tournaments and jousts for both men and animals in the later Middle Ages when the armored knight became a primitive form of our modern tank. The costs, too, grew to huge proportions as the expense of equipment, armor, and weapons increased and as the pageantry and pomp involved grew more elaborate. By the 14th century, tournaments and jousts became a very expensive hobby for the select few who could afford them.

Unhorsing and breaking lances remained the most impressive and most spectacular feat, but when the competitors wanted to prolong the issue, the sword came into play. Duels on horseback were sometimes followed by man-to-man sword fights on foot — a rather crude form of fencing match — and another forum to display spectacular bravado, strength, and skill. In the early 14th century, jousting was firmly established through Europe as part of the sport. Even during the Hundred Years' War, when a truce or a lull in the fighting occurred tournaments were organized to occupy the interval, continuing the war in another guise.

Even with regulations, limitations, fair-play behavior, blunted weapons, and special equipment, tournaments and jousts were dangerous amusements, foolhardy sports that could have fatal results. Serious injuries were frequent, and many deadly incidents occurred. Geoffrey of Brittany was tramped to death in 1186. Leopold VI of Austria was killed in a tournament in 1194. Three successive earls of Salisbury died in the early 13th century. Count Floris III of Holland in 1223, Floris IV in 1234, the margrave of Brandenburg in 1268, and Johannes I of Brabant in 1294 were other distinguished victims. The most spectacular accident was the death of King Henri II of France (in 1559) when a splinter from the constable of Montgomery's lance penetrated his visor and damaged the monarch's eye and brain.

By the middle of the 15th century, tournaments and jousts ceased to play any part in politics but were purely a sport, a social diversion, mundane feasts, and formal social events where knights enjoyed spectators and ladies witnessing their triumphs. Tournaments were inevitable for state occasions such as at a coronation of a new king, marriage of a prince, knighting, celebration of victory, and feasts. They were an important social aspect for the "jet setters" of the time. The feast was a kind of joyful festival of chivalry and always a colorful social gathering. Participants prepared for the games for months and events could last for days. They were generally held on a Monday so they could possibly continue until Thursday without interruption, as Friday, Saturday, and Sunday were subjected to the *treuga Dei* (Truce of God), an agreement obtained by the Church in the 11th century whereby no fighting would take place from Thursday evening to Monday morning.

The first morning began with a ceremonial display and official presentation of arms and the competitors. After these elaborate preliminaries, the climax came in the afternoon when the aristocratic knights fought on horseback and on foot before cheering crowds, noble ladies, and important rulers sitting in highly decorated stands richly draped and covered with flags and banners waving in the wind. The fighting area was usually about 200 by 160 feet surrounded by a stout fence six feet high. For the joust — toward the middle of the 15th century — a tilt was placed, a wooden barrier dividing the lists in the middle. To separate the combatants and force them to ride in a parallel course to avoid incidental or intentional collision of both charging mounted challengers. The place had entrances and exit points with outer spaces serving

Dueling Knights (after a Middle Ages Miniature) ca. 1280

as refuges where squires and knights could prepare themselves before the encounter and nurse their wounds after it. At the appointed hour of ending, at dusk or later if the lists were lit with flames, the heralds would sound retreat, and in the evening the best performances in the lists that day were solemnly and publicly awarded with great pomp. Prizes varied but could be of considerable value such as horses, weapons, sums of money, jewels etc. After this, details of the jousting to be held on the following day were announced, and the teams were arranged. The night con-

cluded with merrymaking, elaborate social festivities, music and dance, and joyous banquets, after which the company said their farewells before dispersing for a well-earned night's sleep.

The apogee of tournaments and jousts was in the late 14th and early 15th centuries. Even if earlier ages had been more enthusiastic and more attentive to what actually happened in the lists, it was at this time that such activities were most highly regarded and most splendid.

Various Forms of Crosses in Heraldry

Various Coats of Arms

Heraldry

Heraldry — the art of armorial bearing — played a vital role in the developing ethos of chivalry. In its origins heraldry was practical because it was important at tournaments and essential in battle to be able to recognize who was, and who was not, on your side. When armor evolved to the stage when a warrior was completely encased in mail from head to foot and wore a helmet which concealed his face, the only way to recognize him was by the particular signs and colors regularly worn on his shield. It is reported that at the siege of Gerberoi in 1079, Robert of Normandy wounded his father William in the arm, unhorsed him, killed his horse, and prepared to kill his opponent only only to recognize him at the last moment by his father's voice, after which Robert presented his excuses. It is generally accepted that during the period of the First Crusade, about 1100, knights began to wear distinguishing marks of one kind or another. Such marks were either painted on their shields or in the form

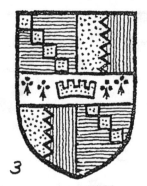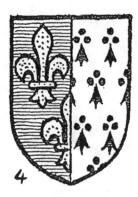

City Coats of Arms. 1. Ypres, Belgium; 2. Cologne, Germany; 3. Birmingham, England; 4. Brest, France.

Various Forms of Flowers in Heraldry. 1. Tudor rose; 2. fleur-de-lis (coat of arms of Lille, France, ca. 1199); 3. fleur-de-lis, symbol of virginity; 4. coat of arms of Eton College, Buckinghamshire, England; 5. German fleur-de-lis, 16th century; 6. coat of arms of Florence, Italy.

Various Forms of Eagles in Heraldry. 1. coat of arms of Montbrisson, France, ca. 1300; 2. coat of arms of Wijnbergen, Netherlands, ca. 1270; 3. coat of arms of Bellenville, ca. 1364; 4. coat of arms of Richard of Blankenberg, ca. 1361; 5. eagle of Poland, 14th century; 6. coat of arms of Emperor Frederick I Barbarossa, 12th century.

Castles in Heraldry. *Left:* coat of arms of Castile, Spain; *center:* coat of arms of Salzburg, Austria; *right:* coat of arms of Dublin, Ireland.

of an effigy attached to the top of the helmet. The name *Plantagenêt* (the dynasty from French Angevine origin that reigned in England from 1154 to 1485) seems to come from a broom or crest that the count of Anjou, Geoffrey V le Bel (1113–1151), had fixed on his helmet as a sign of recognition. It is however worth noting that the use of some form of distinctive colored signs decorating shields, helmets, banners and flags was a practice widely used by the ancient Roman, Greek, and Celtic warriors. Heraldry was thus the continuation of a known

Rhodes, Saint John Gate. The armorials of the Knights Hospitaler is carved in stone above the gate.

The Duke of Brittany (after "Le Livre des Tournois du Roi René," first half of the 15th century). Both man and horse wear a surcoat bearing the arms of Brittany.

practice, and its revival can also be attributed to the taste of noblemen for bright colors.

In the early days, heraldry was rather simple, of a single color with a simple device, such as the three leopards of Anjou, the black eagle of Germany, the three lions of England, the fleur-de-lis of France, but during the 12th century the practice became widespread and developed fixed rules. Heraldry includes tinctures which are denoted metals, colors, and furs. The two metals are silver (white)

and gold (yellow). The colors are gules (red), azure (blue), sable (black), and vert (green) to which were later added purpure (dark purple), murrey (blood red), bleu céleste (light blue), and tenné (tawny orange). The furs are ermine (black spots on white), counter-ermine (white spots on black), erminois (black spots on gold), and vair (small symbolic squirrel pellets, alternatively white and blue). As printing has always been costly in 1638, a herald named Pietra Santa designed a pattern made of dots, lines, and hatches to indicate the colors in black-and-white.

The core of heraldry is the shield, which can have various forms and can be edged, divided, or quartered in many fashions. The field—the background of the shield—may be plain, patterned (checkered), semy (strewn with little figures) or divided by a line or lines which may be embattled (crenellated or notched), wavy, or indented (zigzag). The right side of the shield is called *dexter* and the left *sinister*. The top area of the field is the *chief* and the bottom the *base*. The top center is the *honor point*, the middle center the *fess point*, and the base center the *nombril point*. The surface of the shield is decorated with a wide variety of charges (symbols, pictures, and pictograms) including ordinary geometrical shapes such as the pale (a broad vertical stripe), the fess (a horizontal strip) and the bend (a diagonal strip). Charges also include a large number of crosses (such as the Latin, Greek, Saint Anthony's tau, dappled, fleur-de-lis, or Maltese cross), people (such as a king, warrior, or monk), parts of the human body (hand, arm, head, face, or heart), as well as Christian symbols and saints (such as Holy Mary with child Jesus, Christ on a cross, Saint Andrew with his cross, Saint Christopher carrying Jesus safely, Saint Martin sharing his coat, Saint Peter with the keys to heaven, Saint George slaying a dragon, the Agus Dei, the Lamb of God, cherubim, seraphim, and angel). Animals are also widely used as charges. The most popular are the lion (in standing or lying position) and the eagle (generally with spread wings), but the hawk, hound, squirrel, wolf, salamander, bear, wild swine, beaver, horse, goat, ox, and deer as well as various kinds of fish and small birds were used. Fabulous creatures are also used: the two-headed eagle, the dragon (a monstrous fire-spitting reptile with batlike wings), the griffon (with a lion body and the head of a hawk), the opinicus (a griffon with wings), Pegasus (a winged flying horse), the unicorn (a horse with a horn on the forehead), the phoenix (firebird), the centaur (the bust of a man on a horse body), the siren (a woman with the lower body as a fish), the triton (a man with the lower body as a fish), the harpy (a woman with wings and the lower body as a bird), the chimera (a woman with arms as a lion, lower body as a goat, and with a snake tail). Also used are stars with different shapes and branches as well as a crescent moon, sun with beams, and various sorts of trees and flowers (such as a fleur-de-lis, daisy, shamrock, or oak leaf). Towers, castles, crenels, gates, bridges, churches, houses—more or less stylized—as well as boats, anchors, domestic objects (such as a knife, key, hammer, glove, or bell) and weapons (such as a sword, halberd, battle-axe, or bow and crossbow) are often displayed.

The shield may be surmounted by a crest modeled

Seal of the Association of the German Merchants from Gotland, ca. 1291.

onto the helmet (emerging in the late 14th century) and a crown—both indicating the rank of the bearer. The frame may be held by supporters: ladies, a pair of giants, animals, or angels. It can be decorated with a wreath and foliage or covered by a mantle or a chapeau (a crimson cap turned up with ermine). The arms may also include a scroll displaying a short text, a motto, or a device—often, but not always, in French or Latin. Until today the Dutch family of Oranje-Nassau's device is "Je Maintiendrai!" (I will uphold), that of the British royal family is "Honni soit qui mal y pense" (Shamed be he who thinks evil of it).

From the shield, heraldry was repeated in many symbols, shapes and forms, devices, and colors and ornaments on the helmet's crest, the surcoat, and horse's caparison (ornamental covering); it appeared upon servants' liveries; it was carved above castle doors, abbey gates, and hatchments (a tablet with a dead person's armorial bearings placed on a house or tombstone). Signs of heraldry were also displayed on vexillogical emblems such as a flag, ensign, oriflamme, pennon, guidon, standard, or banner. These items were composed of a haft and a piece of colored cloth in various sizes, shapes, and forms: triangular, square, or rectangular and with pointed ends or roundish straps. Waving in the wind, they added a touch of gaiety to the austere clank of armor. Flags also symbolized hierarchy and command. They served to identify the bearers, were used as a rally point in the heat of battle.

Their numbers could impress the enemy, and they brightened camps, tournaments, and towns. Flags waved upon the highest tower of the castle indicating the presence of the ruler, and they were set up on the walls of a fortress and taken by force as a sign of victory. The Church provided armies with sacred banners bearing a saint's image, which often became the subject of miraculous tales.

Armorial coats were also shown on wax seals, engraved stamps which closed, secured, and authenticated letters and official documents. Coats of arms could be inherited, granted by a prince, or captured. They were sometimes changed for various reasons. For example, augmentations were additions to arms to commemorate and often reward doughty actions. Marshaling was shown when a married man impaled (joined) the coat-of-arms of his wife by placing the two coats side by side on a shield. Quartering was used to divide the shield into four or more parts by horizontal and vertical lines to accommodate the requisite number of inherited coats.

There evolved thus a specialist of coats-of-arms, blazoning and armorials—the herald. Originally the heralds were officers charged with carrying messages to and from the commanders of opposing armies. They made royal proclamations and arranged ceremonies, and they could also be used as diplomats for negotiations and—in this case—were protected by a status of neutrality. Gradually their task was to conduct tournaments—by proclaiming the place and date, presenting the competitors to the spectators, recognizing the doers of deeds of prowess, and presenting prizes and rewards to the victors. Heralds were not only important at tournaments for organizing the events, but at war they played an important role for identifying the enemies on the battlefield and—being usually experienced men of war—for giving tactical advice. They were recognizable by a special *tabard*, an official cape with the arms of their lord emblazoned on it. Increasingly—as the question of armorial bearings became more involved and more important—it was a part of their business to keep records of arms, to know exactly when and how a family had come by its arms and to prevent the assumption of arms by those who had no right to them. Heralds wrote and illustrated books showing shields with heraldic devices together with the names of their owners and gave detailed explanations, regulations, and restrictions.

By the 15th century, heraldry was no longer needed as identification in war. Designs became more intricate and developed into a highly complex science requiring years of training and extensive learning. In answer to a query, the herald could reel off the arms of any noble family, the origin and significance of the arms, the history of the family, its genealogy, and any particular noteworthy deeds performed by any members of the lineage. Heralds and their encyclopedic knowledge provided a way of codifying knights' honor and that of their families. Therefore the position of herald grew to be one of great distinction, and they became highly regarded officers and valued members of the medieval society.

To "bear arms," that is, to have a crest on one's helmet and symbols on one's shield that were instantly recognizable in the heat of battle, became in European society for a thousand years the symbol of the nobility of the hereditary caste of rulers and warriors. Heraldry was also used by nonnoble entities such as craft guilds and corporate bodies, free towns, religious orders, lay associations, and common families for reasons of prestige and identification. In spite of a common thought, heraldry—even today—is not reserved to nobility but is open to all. Anyone is allowed to design a shield, a blason, an armorial, or a coat-of-arms, provided the rules of the art are respected and nothing encroaches on or usurps existing heraldry.

Seal of Sir Thomas de Beauchamp, ca. 1344

7

Knight's War Equipment

In the military sense, technology is the application of science to war. However, even before the expansion of science in our modern times, man coupled deduction with intuition to produce weapons. The idea that drove the Swiss to revive the ancient Macedonian pike was impelled by the same spirit that produced the nuclear weapon: the desire to gain advantage over one's opponent. As a tank, the medieval mounted knight was the combination of striking power and range (provided by his offensive weapons and, more particularly, his lance), protection (provided by armor, helmet, and shield) and speed (provided by the power of his horse).

Offensive Weapons

Lances

The lance was the knight's favorite offensive weapon. Range came from the length of the lance, and this was the weapon with which a knight would make contact with the enemy. It was a wooden spear about nine to eleven feet long with a sharp metal point at the end. Originally the lance was intended to be thrown (from the French verb *lancer*), but it was gradually used to charge. This was done in conjunction with the use of stirrups and a saddle with a raised and reinforced back which prevented the knight being thrust backward off his horse by the impact when he struck his target. The "couched" technique (holding the lance tightly under the right arm) enabled the knight to deliver an enormously powerful blow to his opponent because the lance, held in this rigid

fashion, had the collective momentum of the man and the charging horse behind it and speed was converted into shock. Horsemen had an advantage over soldiers fighting on foot, and a whole line of knights charging en masse with lances tucked hard under their arms in this manner was, at first, unstoppable. However, there was a danger that the lance would stick in the target and break or twist the knight from his saddle. This was averted by adding a small cross bar, or pennant, just behind the point of the lance to stop the point from penetrating too deeply into the enemy's body. The pennant could also have the form of a small flag that could be used as identification and as a rallying point in the heat of battle. Once combat was joined at close quarters, lances were useless, and other weapons were drawn.

Swords

The knight's favorite weapon was the sword. His life and fortune often depended on the power of his sword. As early as the Merovingian time, smiths were so skilled that they could apply new techniques to work metal, such as soldering, brazing, and hammering, allowing them to manufacture blades that were both resilient and flexible. The medieval sword was the noble weapon par excellence. It was held in greatest honor as the symbol of independence and of the virtue of a warrior. The sword was the very weapon of the knight; its employ was forbidden for the base-born, except in the defense of the lordly castle.

From the 10th to the 13th century, the typical knightly sword weighted about two-and-a-half to three-and-a-half pounds and had a blade a bit over thirty inches

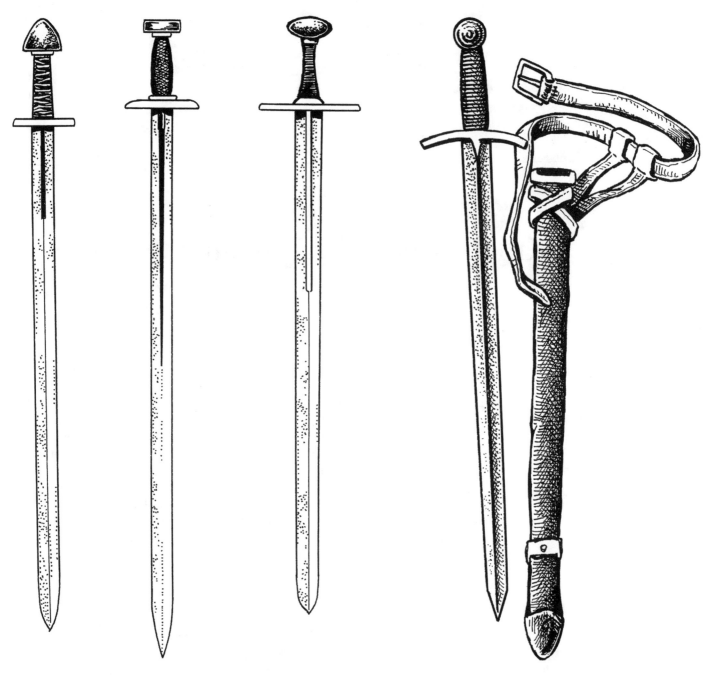

Various European Swords, 12th–13th Centuries   **Sword and Scabbard**

long. To counterbalance the weight of the blade, the sword had a weighted pommel at the end of the grip, in various shapes disk- or brazil nut–shaped or a ball or oval. The grip was often made of wood covered with leather. The hand of the warrior was protected by a cross guard composed of two projecting quillons. The blade was double edged, designed for *taille* (slashing and cutting), and ended with a sharp point used for *estoc* (thrusting). The blade was stout because combat was a rugged contest of crushing blows in which a man's superiority depended on the quality of his weapon. Under its own impetus,

coupled with the weight of the man holding it, the cutting power of the sword was such that it could cleave clean through helmet and skull right down to the shoulders. Exhumed graves have revealed men who had been sliced open from shoulder to thigh bone or who had lost whole arms or even, in some cases, both legs from a scything blow aimed at the knees.

The sword was always held in the right hand (the left one holding the shield); it was kept in a metal or leather sheath which was fixed on the waist belt. Nothing was too good for the sword; the most precious materials were used to decorate it, and the finest artists worked on it. Some blades were inlaid with decoration and inscription which concealed religious or even cabalistic invocation, for example *NED* which stood for "Nomine Eterni Dei." The scabbard could also be enriched by various decoration and ornament depending on the owner's wealth.

The sword had a very strong, sacred, and sentimental value. It was the symbol of the division between ruler and ruled, between knight and commoner, between cavalry and infantry. In feudal times the possession of arms and armor made one man the master of many, for the commoners at first had no effective weapons and no right and means of acquiring them. It was not uncommon for an old knight to demand to be buried with his sword which—it was then believed—had a soul. Certain swords were legendary and held to have magic powers and extraordinary strength. They had names such as Hrunting (belonging to Beowulf), Durendal (Knight Roland), Mulager (Knight Ganelon), Almace (Bishop of Reims Turpin), Joyeuse (Emperor Charlemagne), Excalibur (King Arthur), or Balmung (hero Siegfried). The sword—because of its shape evoking Christ's cross—had a highly symbolic religious value too. The two edges of the sword showed that the knight was supposed to be the bulwark of medieval society against disorder and evil and served both God and the people, and its sharp point showed that all had to obey him.

The sword was a fairly handy weapon, and a well-trained swordsman could handle it with grace and skill. Its handling became codified as a noble and refined art, fencing. This art was taught by a specialist called the *maître-d'armes* (master of arms). One of the first books on that subject was an illustrated manuscript written by Hans Talhoffer published at Nuremberg in 1467.

Daggers

The dagger or poniard is a sword reduced to the size of a big knife between 30 and 50 centimeters (about 11 to 20 inches). It formed the additional and obligatory complement to the equipment of the knight, the man-at-arms, and the simple brigand. Daggers were kept in a metal or leather sheath and were used for the everyday life but also as war or assassination weapons. They were worn in various positions: conspicuously on the waist belt

Various Forms of Daggers. *From left to right:* dagger, ca. 1250; ballock or kidney dagger, ca. 1400; French ear-dagger, ca. 1400; German Hauswehr peasant dagger, ca. 1450; Italian stiletto, ca. 1500.

but also hidden at the back, under the sleeve, or inside the boots. Daggers and poniards were used often as last resort to cut, stab, or throw. They came in different forms, types, shapes, and sizes for various functions with numerous names such as *cinquedea, baselard, main-gauche, coutelas, langue de bœuf, bastardeau, badelaire, malchus, coutil, braquemart, miséricorde, stiletto, dagasse, anelace,* and many others.

Axes

The ordinary axe—used by carpenters, lumberjacks, and anyone else who wanted to cut wood—had been turned into a war weapon since the beginning of mankind. In the Middle Ages it existed in numerous types with many names from a small hatchet to the huge Viking battle-axe or that of the Franks, the francisqua. It could be used either to chop the enemy to pieces or to throw. Axes were still used as weapons of war as late as the 18th century; the Hussars (originally Hungarian mercenaries serving in western armies) used it to cut off the heads of their enemies.

Shock Weapons

Additional offensive weapons were those used not to cut but to deliver powerful crushing blows, taking advantage of the weakness of mail protecting against impact. Shock weapons were probably the oldest forms of weaponry used by mankind commencing in the Stone Age and not discarded until the 16th century. They originated from primitive items such a big animal bone, a strong piece of wood, or a sharp stone. Those used in the Middle Ages originated from the tools used by peasants and craftsmen such as the mace, the hammer, or the axe. Tools were adapted to warfare for both foot soldiers and horsemen. They were made larger, thicker, harder, and more efficient by means of various aggressive additions such as hooks and spikes. Numerous, diversified, and terribly efficient, shock weapons enabled the user to break a shield, knock off a helmet, tear off a mail coat or smash armor. They had wooden handles (which could be reinforced with spiked metal strips) or an all-metal hafts which could be fitted with leather bands for a secure grip in the hand. A *dragonne*, a leather loop or a chain fixed at the end of the handle, was often passed around the wrist in order to avoid to lose the weapon in combat.

The *mace*—in the form of a thick piece of wood, a beetle, a club, or an animal's bone—was probably the most primitive item of weaponry ever used by mankind. In the Greek antique mythology, it was already the weapon used by Heracles (Hercules in Roman mythology), the heroic son of Zeus and Alcmene, famous for his twelve "labors" against evil. In the early Middle Ages, the mace was a primitive piece of wood, a simple club with its end weighted and studded with sharp nails and spikes. Gradually it became an elaborate weapon,

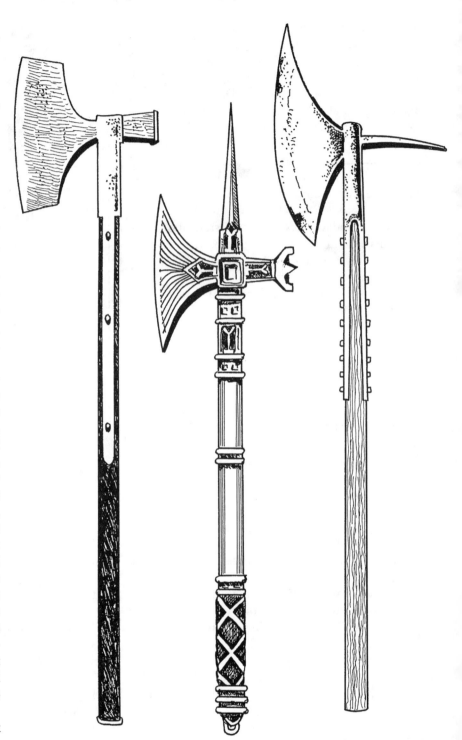

Various Forms of Battle-Axes, 13th and 14th Centuries

often all metal, with a heavy, round, spiked head; a spiky, ribbed head; or a ball with sharp flanges radiating and surrounding a central head. The heavy mace was sometimes furnished with a spike as a prolongation of the shaft. The other end, the grip and eventually the hand guard, was often decorated. It was the only weapon officially allowed by the Church to be used by clergymen and

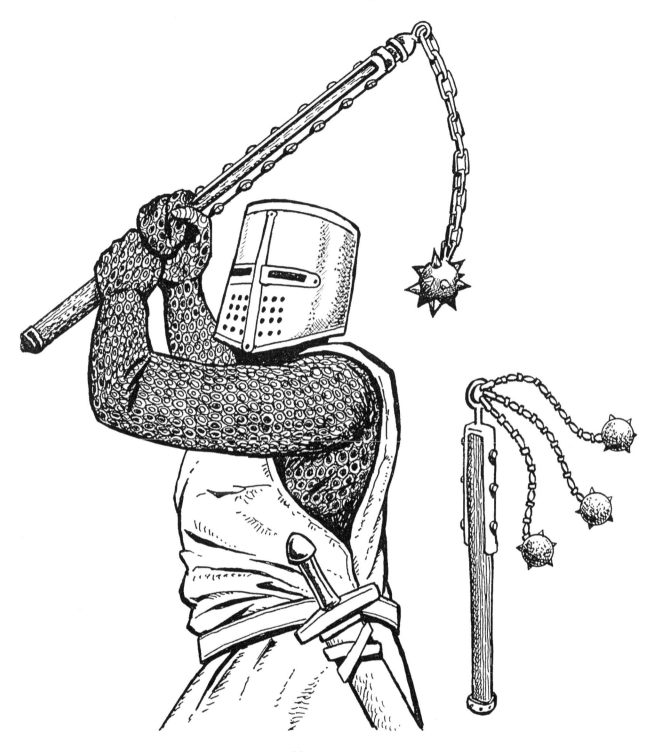

Morgenster

military-minded clerics, as the scriptures did not permit them to shed blood of Christian people, but —curiously— there was no restriction respecting the knocking down and the dashing out of brains! At the battle of Bouvines in 1214 the bishop of Beauvais captured the Earl of Salisbury by stunning him with a mace.

There were naturally different shapes and sizes with various names such as *morgenster* (morning star), *chandelier*, *plançon*, and others. The *morgenster* could also be fixed on a long pole and was known as an infantry weapon under the highly ironic name of *goedendag* (good morning). The *war flail* was also a kind of mace. Named *fléau d'armes*, *goupillon*, *aspergillum* or —more often— *holy water sprinkler* (ironically because of its resemblance with

Various Forms of Maces   **Various Forms of War Hammers**

the brush used by clergymen to sprinkle), it was composed of one heavy spiked ball attached to a chain fixed on a short handle. There was also a variation fixed on a long pole and a short version including three studded balls. In all cases, the flail worked as a leather strap for chastising children. The impact of the shock was increased by the centrifugal force.

The mace-of-arm became a symbolical weapon of command and a ceremonial item for the king's bodyguards, high royal dignitaries, municipal magistrates, aldermen, and deputy majors. The *sceptre*, the rod forming a symbol of sovereignty, was actually a kind of richly decorated small mace. Even today, the stick carried by the master of a military or marching band is a kind a long ornamented mace. The mace can also be traced today in the policeman's bludgeon and rubber truncheon.

The *war hammer* was another shock weapon. It obviously originated from the ordinary civilian mallet or maul. It was usually larger and heavier than the common tool and fitted with a sharper hook. The general form was a plain hammerhead projection designed to perforate the joints between the plates of the armor, balanced by a pick or blade upon the opposite side. In a few examples the shaft was prolonged into a spike. It had many designations too, such as *maillot* (mallet, which gave the name to the *maillotins*, Parisian bourgeois in rebellion against King Charles VI in 1381). Other names were *military pick, martel-de-fer, bisacuta, bec-de-corbin* (raven's beak), or *bec-de-faucon* (hawk's bill). As a weapon of war, it was very popular in the 14th and 15th century. In the 15th century, war hammers were fitted to long shafts and were known as *Luzern-hammer* (originating from the Swiss city of the same name).

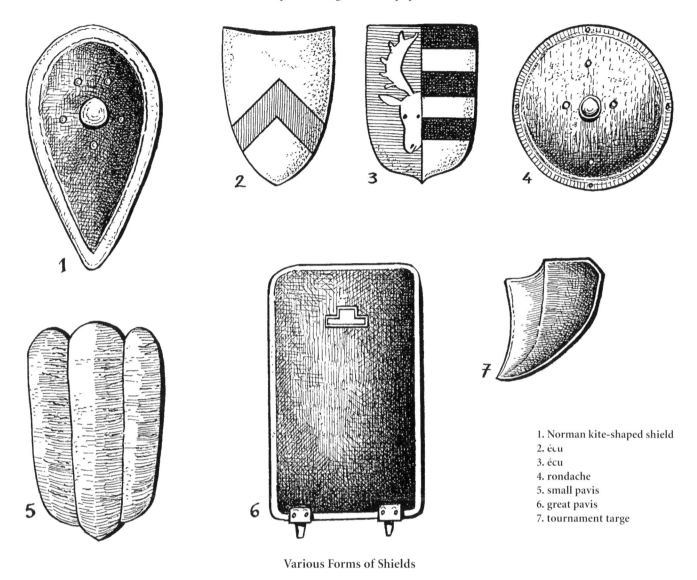

1. Norman kite-shaped shield
2. écu
3. écu
4. rondache
5. small pavis
6. great pavis
7. tournament targe

Various Forms of Shields

Defensive Equipment

There was little point in arming a soldier with an offensive weapon unless he survived to use it and was therefore given some protection. Defensive devices were an important part of soldiers' equipment since the earliest days of warfare and the combination of shield, helmet, and armor originated from the ancient time. The oldest surviving illustration of armored warriors — the Standard of Ur — dates from 3500 B.C. Defensive weapons were passive; they were intended to protect against enemy blows and to ward off projectiles. There were three main forms; those held or carried by hand (shield), those worn as head gear (helmets), and these worn as body protection (armor). Their evolution was directly related to the improvement of offensive weapons. Defensive weapons too reflected the ethics of chivalrous behavior. Each part of the armor was sanctified and worked to the symbolic ideals of chivalry: helm, hauberk, and shield were intended to safeguard the Church, defend the people, repulse evil, and drive back enemies.

An important point should be stressed: There was never any one style of armor or of weapon that was at any time universally used. The military uniform was unknown to medieval warriors; there were no official regulations regarding weapons. Styles came and went according to need and wealth of the warrior as much as to fashion, and different countries had very different designs with different names for similar items. However the use of a kite-shaped shield, coat of mail, and helmet with nasal (all items in various forms, shapes, sizes and quality) was an international style of war gear worn by almost all European knights of the 11th and 12th centuries.

Shields

The shield was a plate carried for defense. This portable protection was made of various materials: hide,

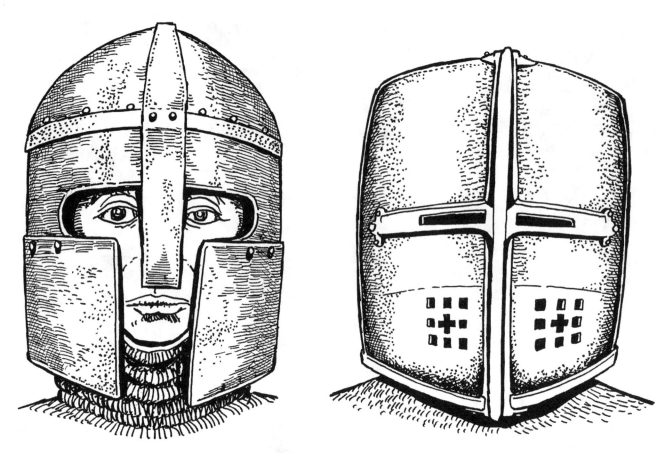

Evolution of the Closed Helmet

brushwood, wood, metal, or various combinations of these or wood with metal reinforcement. The shield was composed of a plate and an umbo (projection or knob) for holding it. It was always carried on the left arm, and while marching, it was carried on the back by means of a *guige* (strap). Dimensions, weight, forms and sizes varied widely according to time, place, and cultural influence. As previously discussed, warriors of the early periods used round and kite-shaped shields, sometimes referred to as a Norman shield — though they were probably of Byzantine origin. In the 12th century, the increasing protection given by chain mail allowed a reduction in size and weight of shields. Kite-shaped as well as circular and rectangular shields did not disappear though, but a smaller shield — called *écu* (from the Latin *scutum*) — was introduced. The écu was usually heart-shaped or triangular and cut off in a straight line at the top, a shape which remained in vogue for centuries. It was about one meter (about 40 inches) in length, enabling the protection of the face, breast, and belly. The surface of the shield was obviously an invitation to decoration. The ancient Greeks and the Gallic tribes decorated them with warlike symbols intended to impress their enemies. The Roman shields were decorated with their own legion emblems. In the High Middle Ages, the shield became the symbol

of chivalry and gave its shape to the *blason*, the coat of arms displaying the heraldry. With the appearance of firearms, the shield became totally useless, and it was completely discarded for centuries. However the shield reappeared in the second half of the 20th century to be a part of the equipment of police forces specializing in controlling urban riots.

Helmets

The head required the most protection because of its importance and vulnerability. Helmets, defensive head-coverings, existed in numerous shapes, forms, sizes, and degrees of protection. Military technology was evolving slowly during the Middle Ages, and during the early period a knight's equipment remained relatively constant. Early medieval helmets — originating from the Byzantine Empire — were conical caps made of metal, bronze, or iron framework and were lined with plates of bronze or iron. The best and strongest were forged out of a single piece of iron. This helmet, also known as *Sprangenhelm*, was widely used by the Franks, the Northmen, and all other European warriors. It was highly efficient by providing maximum deflection for any blow aimed at the head. For more comfort, the innermost layer of the head

1. cervelière
2. conical helmet with ear guards
3. conical helmet with nasal
4. pot helmet with face guard
5. Phrygian-styled helmet

Various Forms of Helmets, 11th–12th Centuries

protection consisted of a quilted or padded coif or cap secured in place by ties under the chin. A helmet protected principally the skull, but various elements were added such as a bar projecting downward in front of the face called a *nasal*. The nasal protected eyes, nose, and forehead against a swinging sword cut against the face.

From the simple conical helmet there developed more elaborate face plates that eventually covered the face, and side plates were sometimes added to protect the cheeks. One of these richly ornamented helmets with face protection has been discovered at Sutton Hoo in East Anglia (Britain) dating from about 660 as part of a treasure found inside a Viking long ship. Another popular helmet—from about 1200 onward—worn by all ranks was the *cervelière*; this was a simple half-globed, close-fitting helmet made of metal usually worn under the hauberk's coif or over a leather protective hood.

In the 12th and 13th centuries, it became common to wear a large cylindrical "barrel" helmet or pot helmet also known as a *heaume*. The pot helmet covered the entire head including the face, with *occularia* (one or, more commonly, two horizontal slits at eye level for

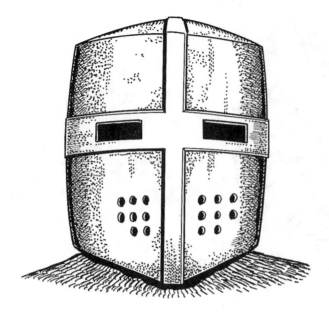

Closed Heaume. *Left:* front view; *right:* cross-section showing padded cap.

vision) and a *vantail* (a perforation or grille of breathing holes in the area of the mouth and nostrils). Here again, many shapes existed. It could be flat-topped, round-topped, or like a sugarloaf. It was generally made of metal plates riveted together, and some with a movable vantail. The heaume added to protection and could impress enemies and noncombatants, but it increased weight (between 1.7 kilograms and 3.5 kilograms or 3.7 and 7.7 pounds), which rested on the shoulder. It fitted on over the top of the chain mail coif, and an arming cap (made of a roll of padding) was introduced about 1200; this helped to protect the head and held it in position. The closed heaume considerably reduced sight, impeded mobility, and complicated breathing. Eye slits and ventilation holes were probably far from efficient, and anyone can imagine what it must have been like inside a closed metal canister after several hours of battle. Therefore, the heaume was never constantly worn; it was either hung at the saddle or carried by the squire when not in use. Helmets were usually painted with bright colors and decorated with plumes and feathers to impress the enemies and help distinguish the leader in the heat of battle. After 1150 the top of the heaume could be decorated with a crest or a comb.

Armor and Tunics

Armor's first purpose was to protect the knight against his enemy in battle. But it was also more than just protection against the most violent aspect of his lifestyle;

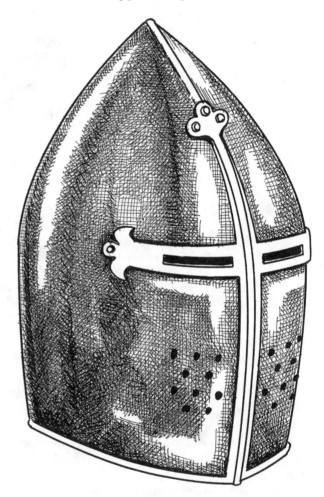

English Closed Heaume, 13th Century

Interlinked Chain Mail

it was intimately connected with his status as part of a military and social elite. Quality and craftsmanship were valued almost as much as efficiency. From the earliest days of the Middle Ages, armor was expensive and represented both a major capital investment and another opportunity to indulge the knightly love of finery. It became noticeably subject to the need to display wealth and to keep up with the latest civilian fashion. A good coat of mail could last its owner a lifetime with obviously repair after battle and regular good maintenance. From the 10th to the 13th centuries there was no uniformity; however, protective dress for body covering consisted mainly of mail. Although several kinds of plate armor were known in the ancient world and were widely used by the Greeks and the Romans, plate armor appeared to have largely been discarded in Western Europe. Broadly speaking, the period approximately from 1180 to 1250 was the "age of mail." The term *mail* comes from the Latin *macula* meaning "net." It was employed by the Romans as a body armor called *lorica hamata*. The medieval coat of mail was called *hauberk, jaseran, byrnie,* or *brunie*. It was composed of a tightly packed surface of small forged-steel rings, each interlocking with several of

Knight with Scale Armor, ca. 990

its neighbors in each direction and riveted shut for added strength. Mail armor was by no means easy to manufacture; it was an immense labor involving the forging of thousands of wire rings, which had then to be beaten flat with holes drilled into each end, and rivets added. For

Various Forms of Body Protection. *From left to right:* Aketon, hauberk, haubergon, and jaseran.

additional strength, mail coats were sometimes constructed from patches of four links to one. They were then further riveted, welded, or soldered, and various parts were strengthened even further by doubling or even tripling the rings. It was a tedious, time-consuming job to produce since every ring had to be woven individually into the coat or each link had to be individually riveted and connected. The armorer manipulated the wires with pliers and hammered the rivet on a small anvil.

An alternative method of protection was scale armor, consisting of many rows of overlapping scales (made of metal or thick leather) secured by sewing or riveting on the surface to a tough lining. In lamellar armor this process was improved; the scales were pierced along the edges and laced together with thongs. For hundreds of years these basic types of armor in many variations provided the protection for the armies of the world — that is for those who could afford armor, for it has always been costly.

A coat of mail reached from neck to knee like an overcoat, with a slit from hem to crotch in front and back,

allowing the bearer to sit on his horse. The sleeves of the hauberk might only come down to the elbow, but the tendency was to extend them right down to the wrists. Later a knight's hands were protected with mail mittens built into the hauberk with slits at the wrists that allowed him to free his hands when needed. The hauberk also included a coif of mail, a close-fitting full hood, sometimes called *camail*, attached to it covered the entire head, leaving only the face exposed. On his legs the man of war wore long stockings or leggings of mail protecting everything from his feet to his thighs. Feet were covered by strong and thick shoes made of mail with a leather sole. A coat of mail was an expensive item of equipment and, after the sword and the horse, the knight's most valuable possession.

The hauberk's structure permitted some ventilation, allowed some freedom of movement, and was comparatively light (between 15 and 20 kilograms, or 33 and 44 pounds). However, because of the weight of the fabric padding coupled with the even greater weight of the mail, it was hardly possible to take more than a wide swinging cut with the sword arm. Furthermore, as the arm rose, the mail collected in folds at the elbow. At the same time the action of raising the arm inevitably dragged upward the section of mail between the armpit and the waist. What with its weight, its heat, and its restrictions on fighting movements, chain mail can only be said to have justified its use in a purely defensive capacity. Mail had further drawbacks. It was difficult to keep clean and free from rust as its maximum surface was exposed to atmospheric oxidation; it could be kept clean by the simple method of scrubbing it with fine sand. It was particularly good at resisting the bite of the sword's edge, but it offered somewhat less protection against the crushing force of a blow of the point, and it could be penetrated by the highly concentrated power of the lance's point or that of a crossbow bolt. The force of blows could sever the links and drive the sharp-ended pieces of metal wire into the body of the wearer and producing fairly serious wounds. Therefore, underneath the hauberk the warrior wore a padded cloth tunic called an *aketon*, or acton, or haqueton, or hoqueton, that provided some of the impact absorption that the mail lacked. The aketon took its name from the Arabic

al-qutn from which the word *cotton* is also derived. This padded undergarment made wearing mail tolerable to the skin by preventing severe bruising. When one reflects on the high temperatures that are common in southern Europe and in Palestine in the summer months, one can only marvel at the physical resilience that enabled armored warriors and Crusaders to campaign on horseback under the scorching sun in thick quilted garments covered with heavy chain mail, coif, and helmet and carrying a shield and weapons. Mailed, scaled, or lamellar armors were — of course — worn only infrequently for exercises, parade, tournament, or war. They were kept in a saddlebag and donned in a hurry if the knight ran into trouble.

In early days only wealthier warriors were able to afford mail, the lesser ranks being protected by leather or quilted jackets. The knight's subalterns, squires, infantrymen, and others often wore the *haubergon* and the *jaseran*, which were shorter forms of the hauberk slightly longer than jacket length. The *brigandine* (literally meaning armor for brigand) and the German *Kettenhemd* were similar short coats of mail with an interlining of row upon row of small overlapping plates secured by exposed rivets; these protected only the bust but could be worn without much discomfort. Another protective device was a waistcoat of *cuir bouilli*, which was made of leather boiled and pressed and made additionally stiff with wax. This evolved later to become the all-metal cuirasse (cuirass or breastplate).

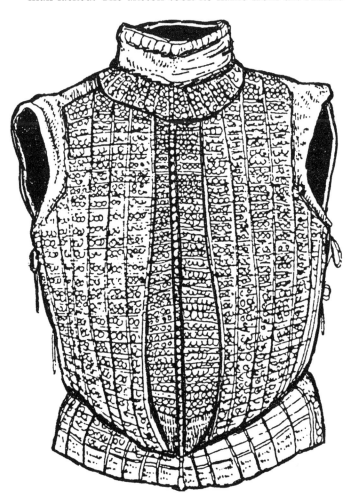

Brigandine or Kettenhemd

Surcoats

In the 12th century, knights often covered their armor with a surcoat. This was a loose-fitting, sleeveless jacket reaching to the ankle or to the knee. Called a *tabard*, *surcotte*, surcoat, or coat of arms, this long flowing gown was split up in front and back for convenience in riding, it was tightened at the waist by the belt supporting the sword. The surcoat was probably created for some form of fashion, and it served various purposes. It was an additional protection against sword cuts as the folds in the material reduced somehow the direct force of the blow. It also protected the chain mail from rain and sunshine. But probably the chief reason was that the surcoat, just like the shield, was a surface that allowed the display of decorations and heraldry emblems. The emblem identified the wearer and often saved his life, for it informed his enemies who he was and if he was of a rank that could afford to pay a ransom. Surcoats were made of various materials, according to the taste and means of the wearer: canvas, linen, or even silk embroidered with gold and sometimes decorated with precious stones for the richest. Surcoats were popular and were soon adopted as ornamental and bright-colored distinguishing marks, adding a touch of gaiety to the austere clank of metal. In

Knight with Surcoat and Mantle   **Knight with Surcoat**

addition — in cold conditions — a large loose-fitting mantle could be worn.

Speed and Mobility: The Horse

Horses were essential to medieval society. Destriers, coursers, rounceys, palfreys and packhorses all had their place in the service of the Middle Ages warriors. The knight's speed and mobility on the horse had to be balanced against the weight necessary to bear an increasing heavy load. The knight who rode horseback grew heavier and heavier as his personal armor increased in size and weight. With the evolution of armor for both men and mounts, the burden borne by each individual beast was enormous. The development of heavier, stronger horses was essential to take the weight of the heavy panoply of mail. So horses were specially bred for their carrying and staying power and the momentum they could engender in the charge. Consequently, the native beauty, grace, and elegance of the horse were often sacrificed to the qualities of power and endurance.

A knight's warhorse—often called a *destrier*—was in a very real sense an extension of his courage, ferocity, and arrogance. The horse was also symbolic of power, majesty, grace, and beauty, and there was a definite love of this animal in the medieval world, especially and obviously among the ruling class and the knights. The horse gave the knight not only a physically high position but also a spiritual one. The horse that carried him represented the people and the Church whom he had to defend, but who also had the duty of supporting him and giving him the wherewithal for an honorable life. Knights and lords felt themselves judged by the quality, beauty, and number of their horses. A horse was thus considered one of a knight's most prized possessions, a valued partner on whose skill much of a knight's safety and success depended.

Horses were usually divided into four categories: cold-blooded (referring to animals for draft service); hot-blooded (horses of Oriental ancestry); Oriental (such as Arabian, Akhal Teke, Turkoman, or Berber); warm-blooded (a cross of hot and cold, and/or cold and Oriental ancestry). Breeding, trading, and mustering quality horses was obviously a flourishing business, and riding a horse became an art called "equitation." Many medieval monarchs and dukes were practical men and aware of the importance of breeding stock and of adding to their own stables. If they spent a great deal of money on buying animals for transport, tournament, and military use, it was not an uncommon custom for those rulers to pass acts to prohibit the export of good, strong, muscular horses from their kingdoms and duchies. Warhorses were regarded in much the same way as weapons, and their falling into enemy hands was to be avoided. Unlike weapons though, it took many years to

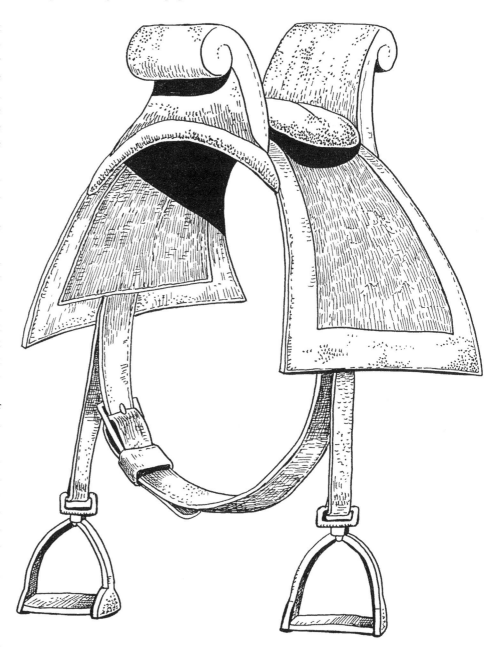

Saddle

produce a good warhorse. Horses and men were kept fit both physically and mentality by exercise, hunting, and tourneying.

Equipment

In antiquity, riding was either done bareback or with a blanket. This developed into using a stuffed pad, and it is generally accepted that some of the tribes in Gaul possessed saddles of a kind in about 100–200 A.D. The medieval saddle became more like a high armchair with a pommel to the front and a cantle behind. Despite the shock of a knight's own charge and the blows of his adversaries, this saddle design made it much more difficult to be unseated in battle. Securing the saddle was often by means of a girth attached by a buckle around the lower part of the barrel (the animal's body). Occasionally a double girth was used for additional security: In a violent situation, as in combat, for example, air intake could suddenly expand the horse's rib cage causing a buckle to rip through leather, and safety depended on the extra girth secured with a flat knot. In addition, to counteract the tendency to slide back, breast collars were often used to secure the saddle.

Stirrups—probably invented in China in the 4th century—were used in the Byzantine Empire at the end of the 6th century. They came to use in Western Europe by the 8th century, and by the 10th century they were normal pieces of the riding equipment. Stirrups were an essential element of the horseman's equipment that reduced the rider's discomfort and enabled a knight to retain his seat against the shock of a lance's impact. With the aid of stirrups, the mounted warrior could virtually stand up, lean his whole weight forward, and thrust with his legs. There was no room for riding with bent knee. The relatively short seats and forward placement of the stirrups forced the horseman into that position. Stirrups gave the rider much better balance and opened the way

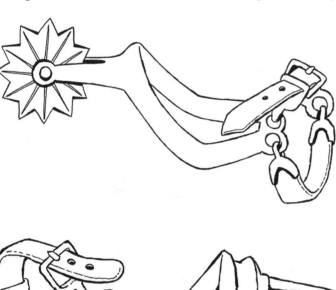

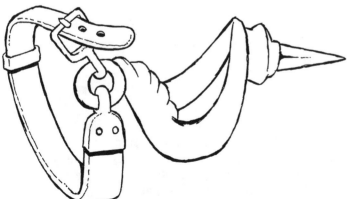

Spurs. *Top:* rowel spur; *bottom:* prick-spur.

for the development of the heavy lance used held resting tightly under his arm. The additional force of his horse's impetus could be brought behind his lance delivering a formidable blow. The full force of the lance used as a battering ram replaced the tactics of throwing a lighter javelin. The shape of stirrups varied a lot, including triangular, round, and rectangular forms. In the Late Middle Ages they tended to be heavier, with a box-like shape.

Spurs, attached to the rider's heels, came in a great variety of styles. In the 11th and 12th centuries they often had four tiny prongs just like a little fork; although sharp, the prongs could not penetrate further than the surface of the skin. Another model—lozenge-shaped—was very sharp, but its shape prevented deep entry into the horse's side. A 14th century model was usually rather long with a free-moving rowel, or wheel.

Medieval bits continued the evolution of types existing in the ancient world. Similar bits are used today but with improvements and an amelioration of severity. There were two basic designs. Snaffle bits were used on horses that were easier to control or when an instant response was not required. Curb bits were potentially harsher to enforce rapid control on the animal.

In the 9th century, the horse's capacity was greatly improved by the introduction of shoeing, thus protecting the animal's hooves from splitting, cracking, laminae deterioration, and sole bruising. This was done by blacksmiths or horseshoers, though the correct term was *farrier*. The horseman's equipment was the object of particular attention. It was manufactured with good materials, and reins, saddles, bits, stirrups, and spurs could be decorated with elaborate ornamentations with precious leather, silk, velvet, gilding, carving, etc.

Care

In age when armies had no or very few logistics, feeding horses could present some problems. It has been estimated that horses used in warfare in early medieval Europe would eat 10 kilograms (22 pounds) of food a day, half grain and half long feed (hay/grass). March grass, even if it were available, had little food value; May and June were when grazing was thickest and most nutritious, so campaigns could be launched only in spring and summer when grass was abundant. A huge amount of forage was thus needed for warhorses, riding horses, and pack animals—the latter group probably outnumbering the total of the first two. Even more important was the need for water and, not often considered, for salt, which was vital in hot climates where sweating caused heavy salt and trace-element losses. Warhorses suffered even more in the hot arid conditions encountered in southern Europe and in Palestine during the Crusades. When water and food, particularly the former, were found, horses tended to gorge themselves and perish. Deaths from gorging were due to colic and possibly crippling laminitis.

As veterinary science was primitive, fatal diseases were frequent, and not all young stock reached mount-riding age. Added to that, the campaigning, bad weather, and injuries from natural or war hazards took their toll. Regardless of their carrying capacity and speed, horses always were afflicted by fundamental weaknesses which restricted their military use: They were big targets, easily frightened, and difficult to protect. They were finicky, requiring three regular meals and at least eight hours rest if they were to maintain their condition and resist disease. Therefore, the animals demanded specialized manpower to be fed daily, watered, cleaned, and exercised; their harnesses and equipment had to be maintained; there had to be a constant backup for health checks and veterinary care.

Caparison

Standards

A suitable horse should be tough, sound, reasonably speedy, and not too coarse. It should have good teeth, special reference being made to avoidance of "parrot mouth." The facial plane should be straight, the forehead broad, ears long, fine, and erect. The neck should be long with an open gullet, and it should be set on well into the shoulder without coarseness. The barrel should also be fine with a long underline. The chest should be broad; the loins short-coupled. Limbs should be substantial; the shins should be smooth, and there should be an absence of hair on the lower limbs. Hooves should be black, hard, and long, and the sole should be round. The tail should be either long or with a short dock. Colors preferred were bay, dun, or ash gray with black points—showing hard and tough animals—followed by cream and chestnut, while piebalds were rather disliked.

Horses were valuable booty and were offered as a gift to reward or guarantee loyalty, great deeds of gallantry, and other acts of bravery. In 1173 Count Raymond of Toulouse did homage to King Henry of England promising to supply one hundred soldiers for forty days' annual service plus paying an annual tribute of forty very valuable horses—probably a considerable drain on his resources either from his own stud farms or as direct purchases from horse dealers. According to the medieval "macho" spirit, no knight would ever accept a ride on a gelded animal. Castrated horses (hongres), mules, and donkeys were reserved for women, merchants, peasants, and prelates.

Armor

The High Middle Ages knight was a fully armed, fully armored, and fully mobile fighting machine, but the most vulnerable point of this moving fortress was the horse itself. Opponents often shot deliberately with arrows and threw javelins at the animal's vital spots and thus broke the cohesion of the opposing party. Horse defenses were not of comparatively late introduction; as a matter of fact, as early as the 12th century horse armor became a crucial need.

To some extent, armor for horses followed the fashion of the rider. In early times, horse armor consisted of mail similar in structure to the knight's hauberk. This could then be covered with a large, loose-fitting cloth called a *caparison*—a counterpart of the knight's surcoat often in the same color and pattern and displaying armorials.

With the development of plate armor in the 13th century, armorers provided better—but much more expensive—protective equipment. The accouterments of the knight's warhorse had the general name of *barding* and came in use about the middle of the 13th century. It was composed of a mix of chain mail and various plates

1. chamfron
2. crinet
3. peytral
4. flanchard
5. culière or crupper

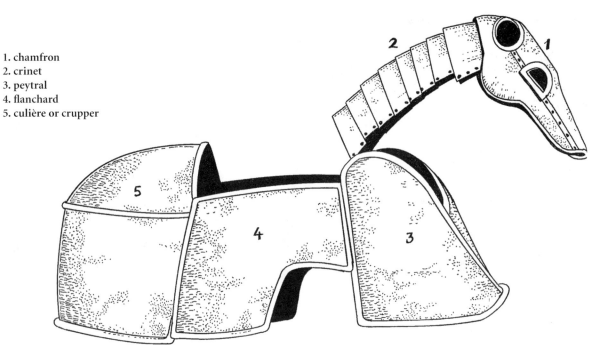

Horse Barding

Fully Armored Horse

fixed by straps and buckles. In its fully developed form, the barding included a series of metal plates closely adapted to the horse's anatomy. A bard called a *chamfron* protected the head of the animal with ear and eye guards; the chamfron could be decorated and fitted with a spike which could be used as a weapon and which increased the terrible aspect of the horse looking like some kind of metallic unicorn. A cervical *crinet*— made of a series of articulated lames of plates or plates and chain mail — protected the neck. A *peytral* covered the chest, *flanchards* the flanks, and a *culière* the crupper. Though laminated plates could cover the legs of the horse, these parts of the animal were very difficult to protect if the horse was to retain its complete mobility; the legs often remained bare and, therefore, crucially vulnerable.

As with the armor for men, horse bards were often decorated with engraving and etching. The weight of armor (excluding that of the armored knight) could reach a total of fifty to seventy pounds. The appearance of firearms in warfare made this cumbersome and heavy load useless and obsolete. Horse armor was abandoned in the 16th century for fighting purpose, though it was continued for jousting.

8

Infantrymen

Infantry

The term *infantry* seems to come from the Latin *infante* and Italian *infanti* meaning "young man" or "lad." This body was composed of foot soldiers who—on the whole—were despised by the aristocratic mounted men-of-war. Rather little attention was paid to them in the medieval literature, so information about these second-class soldiers is much less plentiful than about knights. Prior to the 14th century, common soldiers figure but little, if at all, in the military imagery. However, knights never fought without the support of infantry, and usually a medieval army was composed of mixed horsemen and soldiers on foot, with proportions ranging from one knight to four footmen, up to one mounted man to eight infantrymen. Infantrymen obviously formed the bulk of the garrison force manning castles, and their role on the medieval battlefields was probably largely underestimated. The bearing of arms among peasants was strictly restricted in peacetime, as the aristocracy feared the use of violence against them. But—in time of war—infantrymen were an assemblage of serfs, peasants, and dependants who were impressed into the armed force, led to war by their feudal lords, and placed under the authority of a constable, sergeant, or squire. Some of them were professionals—equipped by their masters—and were recruited from the landless peasantry or urban laboring classes and among adventurers. When weapons were not provided by their master, their equipment was simple, as the mean of each man would permit.

There were many forms of swords used by foot soldiers. The *falchion* was often used by English archers; it had a blade that was wide at the point; the edge was curved and convex, and the back concave. The *cultellus* was a short sword especially designed for use by foot soldiers when rushing upon knights who had been dismounted or for close encounters of infantry against infantry. The *scimitar*—of Arabian origin and rather popular because of the Crusades—had a blade that was curved at the back with a cusp at the point; it often had a finger guard added by prolonging one side of the crosspiece and turning inward to join the pommel. Various forms of knife, dagger, mace, and war hammer—similar to those of the knights—were also popular weapons among infantrymen.

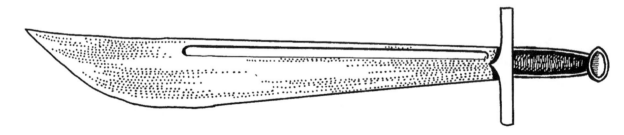

English Falchion, ca. 1270

100

Various Infantry Hand Weapons. These were on the whole the same as those used by the mounted knight and included the mace, war flail, war hammer, battle-axe, and dagger.

Foot soldiers were always much less armored than the knights. Instead of a mail hauberk and later scale and plate armor, they might wear whatever pieces or fragments of pieces of armor they had obtained either from the wreck of a field of battle or from any other sources; they also gladly assumed any garments that they might be able to add to their scanty armory such as a simple padded aketon, a quilted tunic, or a leather coat reinforced with metal disks. Many soldiers simply wore their civilian clothes. Bands of leather could be worn around the throat as a gorget. Legs could be enclosed in leather chausses protected by metal studs or by leather bands or not protected at all allowing however a great freedom of movement. Infantrymen wore a simple conical Sprangenhelm helmet with nasal or a *chapel de fer* or *Eisenhut*, a broad-brimmed kettle hat. In many cases, the helmet was not solid metal but made of hardened leather reinforced by iron ribs, and anyway many of them fought bareheaded. As protection they would have a shield; this would have various forms, but it was generally a circular *rondache* or

Infantry Armor. *From left to right:* broigne, a kind of scale armor; cuirasse, made of metal or boiled leather protecting the chest and with metal strips protecting the waist; brigandine, a short chain-mail jacket; gorget, suspended by a chain around the neck protecting the chest.

buckler made of wood and reinforced with nails and metal strips. Another form of shield used by soldiers on foot was the *pavis* which drew its name from the city of Pavia in Italy where it appeared in the 13th century; the small pavis was oval or rectangular. Each man was armed in accordance with his own taste. Next to daggers, swords, battle-axes, and maces, the infantrymen's favorite weapons were pole weapons and long-range weapons.

Pole Weapons

Pole or staff weapons — sometimes called hast-weapons from the Latin word *hasta* meaning spear — were used by mounted men in the form of the lance and javelin, but many other pole weapons existed especially designed for infantrymen. Many of these weapons descended from agricultural implements, such as the billhook or scythe, and others from the spear used since the dawn of history for both warfare and hunting. They were all composed of a long staff with various length (usually about 1.7 meters, or 67 inches), but the boar spear was only 1.3 meters (51 inches) long, and the pike could be as long as 6 meters (almost 20 feet). The shaft was often made of ash, hornbeam, or yoke elm, as those types of wood provided a flexible and hard material but were also considered in the Middle Ages as being symbolically mannish, noble, and warlike. A socket — holding a metal part in the form of blades, hooks, and spikes — was fixed at one end of the pole. Metal strips were often fixed along the shaft (sometimes as much as 20 feet long, though usually 10 feet), and they acted as a steady reinforcement for the point and protection against sword or axe cuts. Staff weapons were rather cheap to manufacture since they required little

Decorated Blade of a Ceremonial Fauchard, 1694. This highly ornamental weapon equipped the guards of Emperor Joseph I of Germany (1705–1711).

metal and were simple to make without the skills of a real armorer. They were however very specialized and — being rather heavy and cumbersome — they required the use of both hands; this meant that foot soldiers had to fight in close team, those carrying a shield protecting their companions armed with pole weapons who held mounted men at a distance.

Staff weapons came in numerous sizes and shapes and had many names. Technical terminology in the Middle Ages tended to be extremely fluid, standardization of language was limited, and the tendency toward using localisms intensifies the difficulty of identifying authoritative terms for specific weapons. Pole weapons formed a very large group which were constantly in evolution; there were many hybrids, and their classification is sometimes difficult according to types, land of origin, and times when they were used. They were decisive for the organization of troops on foot. Long and strong enough, and put in good hands, they could repulse the charge of the mounted men and allow soldiers on foot to attack knights with success. Pole weapons could also be fitted with bells to frighten horses, a fact which emphasized very well the general style of warfare in which soldiers on foot and mounted knights continually strove to outdo each other. Pole weapons lost a great deal of their efficiency when firearms appeared in the end of the 15th century. However, they did not disappear overnight, and many were still in use until the 18th century as symbols of authority or command weapons for infantry officers. By the 16th century, pole arms had been raised to the nobility, as objects of ceremonial use bearing heraldic arms and often sumptuously decorated.

The *military fork* was simply a military development of the parallel agricultural implement. It appeared as early as the 11th century and was not entirely discarded until the end of the 17th century. The fork was usually of simple construction with two prongs. Some models were more elaborate and had two or even three prongs of deliberately unequal length with hooks and sometimes barbs added to pull a horseman down. It could also be used in siege warfare to hold or repulse an assaulting ladder or to move fascines (a cylindrical bundle of brushwood used

to fill ditches for example). Some could be made with long shafts and prominent hooks to dislodge defenders from walls (as in the scaling fork).

The *trinquebasson* was simply a peasant's bill hook, a crescent-shaped blade sharpened on the inside and fixed on a long shaft. It could also be fitted with a projecting spike.

The war scythe was simply a military adaptation of the peasant's scythe. Forks, scythes and axes were heteroclite, improvised, and favorite peasants' weapons when they departed for a Crusade, revolted against their lords, or defended their villages against a gang of bandits. They were popularly known as "brown bills" as such improvised weapons were often rusty.

The *fauchard* was a development of the scythe for war. It was a large razor blade fixed to the end of a staff. It existed — as early as the 12th century — in various modifications named *couteau de brèche* or *couse* or *glaive* (in this case having the cutting edge upon the convex instead of the concave curve of the blade). This family of weapons — sometimes named by the generic term of *bill* — were popular particularly in Flanders and Germany. Bills were of a truly formidable character in close fight and rightly considered almost too cruel to be used in Christian warfare. They were widely used all over Europe and did not become obsolete until the beginning of the 17th century. From the 15th to the 17th century, principally in Italy — and, more particularly, in Venice — the fauchard was used as a parade weapon by the Doge's guards. It had a richly decorated blade which could be of impressive and terrifying size.

The somewhat uncommon *bardiche* was of northeastern European and Russian origin. Already known and used by the ancient Egyptians, it was a sort of pole axe or a large fauchard so heavy that it needed two attaching points to secure it to the staff.

The *guisarme* was an elaborate, dangerous, and efficient weapon of war. Although heavy and cumbersome, it was one of the most popular weapons used by medieval foot soldiers. Probably originating from the peasant's bill hook, it was used to great effect for thrusting and cutting; it could inflict terrible wounds as it was a kind of primitive halberd which allowed various modifications. At its full development in the 14th century, it combined a broad curving razor-like cutting blade ending in a hook, a thrusting point, one or more projecting spikes or hooks sticking out at the top and to the rear, or spurs and a sharp cross guard on the base of the blade for specialist purposes: Knights could be hooked from their mounts with the spike, stabbed with the point, and then sliced or chopped with the blade. The guisarme could also be used in naval warfare for boarding an enemy ship. The rather broad blade lent itself to elaborate ornamentation, and many examples of Late Middle Ages and Renaissance — both for use at parade and war — are on exhibit as splendid specimens of the art of the engraver.

The *vouge* or *guvia* — originating in Switzerland — was in use from the 12th to the 14th century. It was a long, simple, practical, and cheap weapon composed of a strong staff having at its extremity a rondel and a sharp knife or dagger. Men armed with it were sometimes called *vougiers*, foot soldiers specially trained to repulse horse-

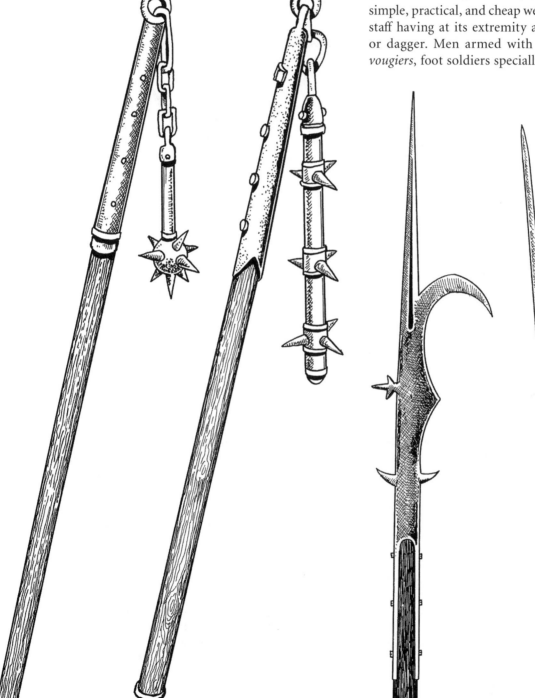

Holy Water Sprinklers (War Flails)   **Two Forms of Guisarme**

men. The blade was used to administer the *coup de grace* to unhorsed knights. *Vouge* was also a generic term for other weapons of this kind called *bisacuta*, *oucin*, and *besaque*, all of which were types of sharp blades or picks used to pierce the hauberk and the joints between armored plates worn by horsemen.

The short *bear spear* was used for both hunting and war. Generally 1.2 meters, about 47 inches, long, it was equipped with two side lugs or wings to prevent the sharp blade from penetrating too deeply into the body of the enemy (or that of the animal).

The *goedendag* or *plançon des Flandres* originated from north Germany and Flanders. It was the infantry version of the knight's short *morgenstern*, the spiked mace eventually fitted with a thrusting point. A variations was the *holy water sprinkler*, a kind of flail composed of a strong, long pole with a staple at the end to which a chain was attached. The chain terminated in one or more heavy studded and spiked balls; a variant form had the chain supporting a wooden or iron flail sprouting spikes.

The *langue de bœuf*, or *ox tongue*, was a kind of broad, long, double-edged blade of various shapes and sizes fixed on a staff. It had many variations, some in the form of a large knife, a huge dagger, or a sword. It could be fitted with hooks forming a cross guard at the base of the blade, becoming later the so-called "partisan."

The *partisan* or *pertuisane* was extensively used in France and Italy; it was introduced in England in the middle of the 14th century and later in Germany and Spain. It consisted of a long double-edged blade, wide at the base, where it was provided with projections of various forms— hooked, crescent, and other — and tapering to a point. It was always symmetrical, both sides balancing in form. A derivative of the partisan was the *spontoon*, which had a long shaft with a leaf-shaped head, the latter having, as a rule, a cross guard beneath it. The spontoon — often with a decorated blade — was carried until the 18th century as a command weapon by infantry officers.

Another variation was the *runka* composed of three blades. The side blades resembled the wings of a bat. In French it was called *chauve-souris*.

The *corsesque*, probably originating in Corsica or Italy, was another derivative in which the lateral projections gave the appearance of a trident with a graceful outline while at the same time increasing the efficiency of the weapon. It was in wide use among foot soldiers at the time of the wars in Italy at the end of the 15th century and in the 16th century a favorite weapon for German infantrymen.

The *gouge* included a sharp central spearhead with a cross guard at the base of the blade.

The *roncone* (also called *ranseur*) had the two side hooks pointing downward.

French Infantry Officer with Spontoon (Beginning of the 18th Century)

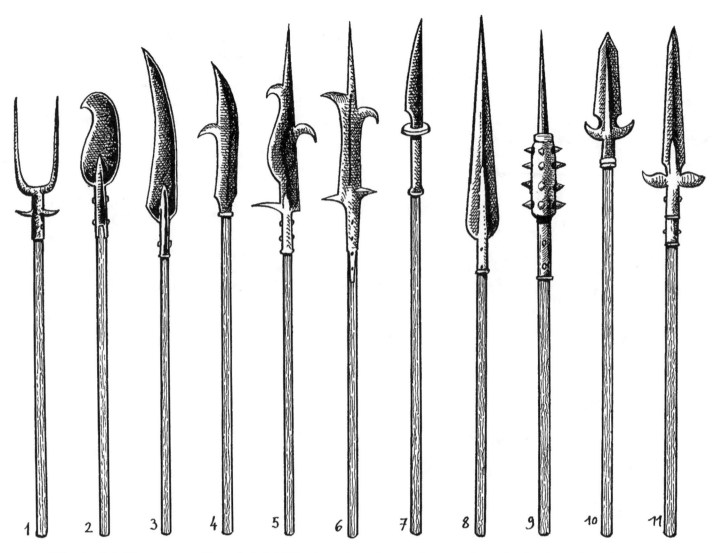

Offensive Pole Weapons. 1. military fork; **2.** bill hook or trinquebasson; **3.** war scythe; **4.** fauchard; **5** and **6.** guisarme; **7.** vouge; **8.** ox tongue; **9.** goedendag or plançon; **10** and **11.** partisan.

The pole-axe—found in many forms—was a long-shafted fighting axe, the infantry version of the knight's short battle-axe. Originally a northern European weapon—known in Germany as *Kriegshippe*—it consisted of a simple axe blade balanced by a spike on its reverse.

The *halberd* was a logical development of the battle-axe. It was certainly the most elaborate and famous pole weapon. Originating in Switzerland and Germany, the halberd drew its name from the old German words *Halm* (shaft) and *Barte* (axe). It consisted basically of a shaft fitted with a sharp axe blade, balanced by a sharp pick on its reverse, with the head of the shaft terminating in a long vicious spike. It existed in endless variations. Its blade could be lengthened, broadened, or flattened; it could be square, curved, circular, beak-shaped, straight, or crescent-shaped. The spike underwent many changes, broadening or flattening, occasionally became lance-shaped or falcon-beaked, while the pointed head devel-

oped into a thin, long spike or a short double-edged sword blade. More than any other staff weapon, the form of the axe blade was an invitation to ornamentation, and many were elaborately cusped, pierced, or carved with beautiful decorations. Some halberds, made especially for parade purposes, exhibited a remarkable wealth of decoration. Halberds were not introduced extensively into England and France until as late as the 14th century, but they were widely used everywhere. The halberd was replaced as an infantry weapon when the pike came into favor. Richly decorated halberds with elegant and graceful outlines were used as command weapons for officers in the 17th and 18th centuries, and they are still used today as parade weapons for special ceremonies.

The *pike* was the "bayonet" of the Middle Ages and disappeared at a comparatively recent date. It was a very old weapon used by the Greek phalanx by the time of Alexander the Great. Toward the close of the 12th cen-

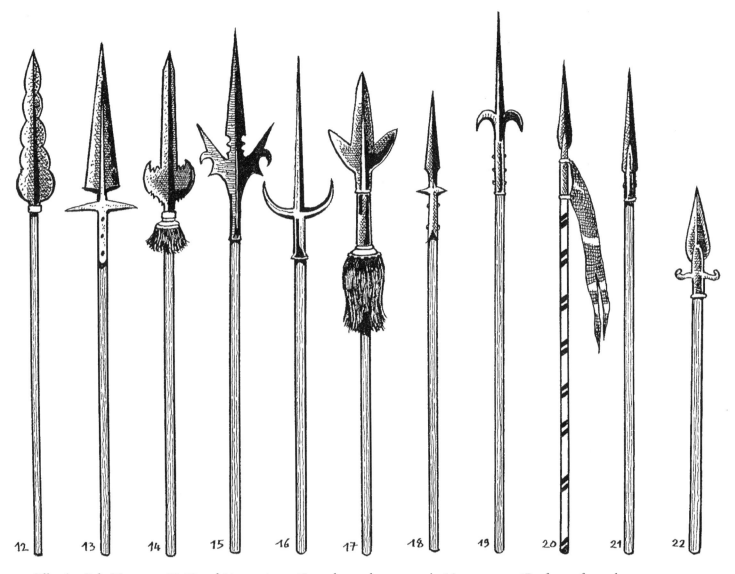

Offensive Pole Weapons. 12, 13 and 14. spontoon; 15. runka or chauve-souris; 16. corsesque; 17. a form of parade corsesque; 18. gouge; 19. roncone; 20 and 21. spear; 22. boar spear.

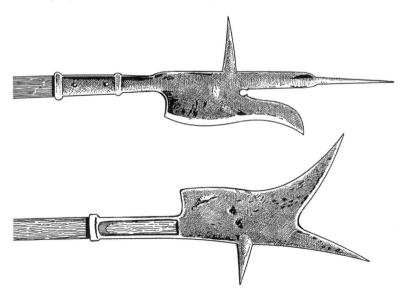

tury, the use of the pike was revived to counter cavalry charges, and the weapon remained in use in various forms as late as the beginning of the 18th century, when it was replaced by the flint musket fitted with a bayonet. A pike consisted of a long, narrow, steel spearhead fixed to a very long wooden shaft (up to 5 meters and even 7 meters, about 16 or 23 feet respectively), often reinforced with strips of metal to render it immune from sword cuts. The butt end of the pike was commonly fitted with an iron shoe which could be grounded to take the shock of the horsemen' charge. Heavy and cumbersome, the pike was a poor individual weapon, but it was intended to be

Left: Early Forms of Halberd (Ending with the 13th Century)

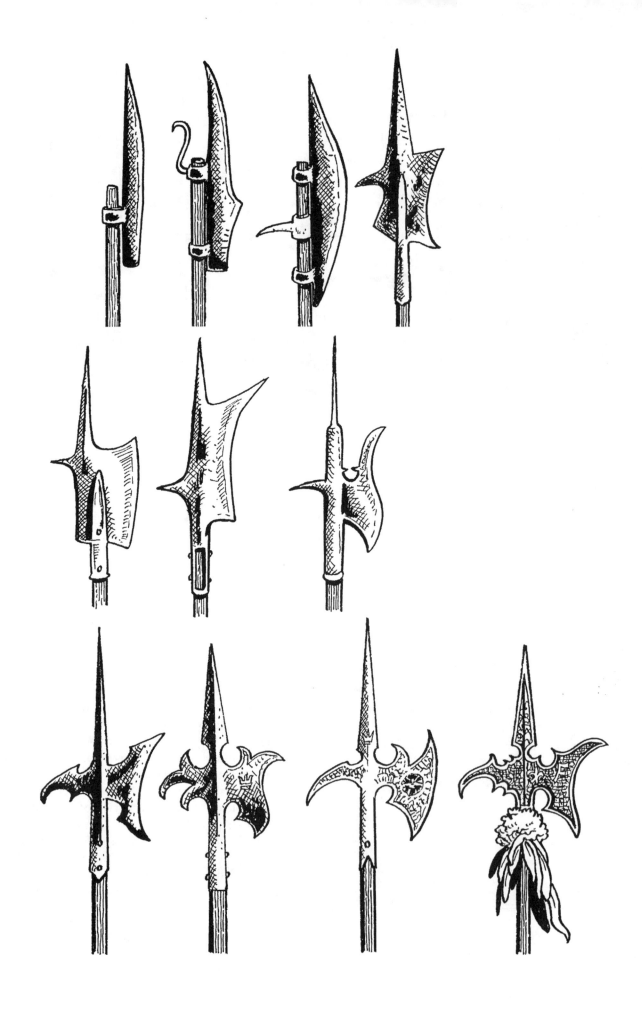

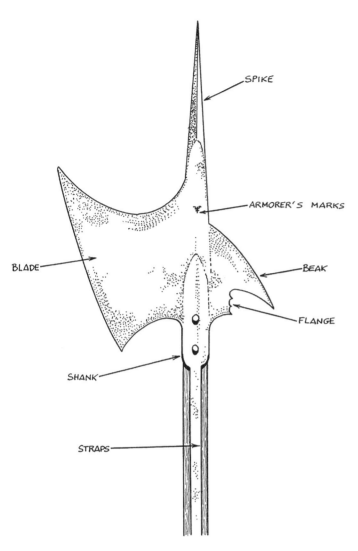

Parts of a Halberd Head

SPIKE

ARMORER'S MARKS

BLADE

BEAK

FLANGE

SHANK

STRAPS

Fustibal

collectively used by a dense and compact group of pike-men forming an impenetrable hedgehog.

Long-Range Weapons

Offensive throwing weapons were used both for hunting and warfare since the early days of mankind. As the name implies, long-range weapons served to launch a missile toward a target at some distance with the intention to hit, wound, or knock out without hand-to-hand combat. In principle, any projectile (a stone, for example) could be thrown at an enemy, but certain weapons were designed specifically for this purpose.

Long-range weapons can be divided in two main categories. First, there were those thrown purely by using the human muscular force, thus they had to be light. They included a whole range of spear-styled weapons (a pole with one end fitted with a sharp point) such as the javelin, Roman pilum, lance, Frankish angon, assegai, or dart. Certain axes and knives were specially designed both to strike and to be thrown. The main drawback of this kind

Opposite: Evolution of the Halberd from the 13th to the 16th Century

Slinger   **Archer, 12th Century**

of weapon was that they could be used only once with dangerous result if the thrower missed his target. Furthermore, the enemy could pick them up and throw them back. Secondly, there were throwing weapons using muscular strength with the aid of a launching device. It was one step forward to grasp a weapon in the hand, another to throw it, but the effect became greater when further impetus was provided by some sort of launching device.

Slings had been used since the earliest time by the Assyrians and the Romans. For example, one of the most famous and oldest incidents in which a sling proved its worth was the single-handed combat between the Israelite

David and the Philistine Goliath, set against each other to decide the outcome of the general battle in front of their respective armies. The giant Goliath, protected by armor and wielding a sword, proved no match for the sling-stone of young David which struck Goliath between the eyes and knocked him down. The humble slingers were valuable missile men in the Middle Ages, capable of discharging a hail of bullets or stones with considerable accuracy and in rapid volleys. The slingers were usually accustomed to their weapon since childhood; they were often peasants who needed to protect their livestock against wild animals with a cheap weapon.

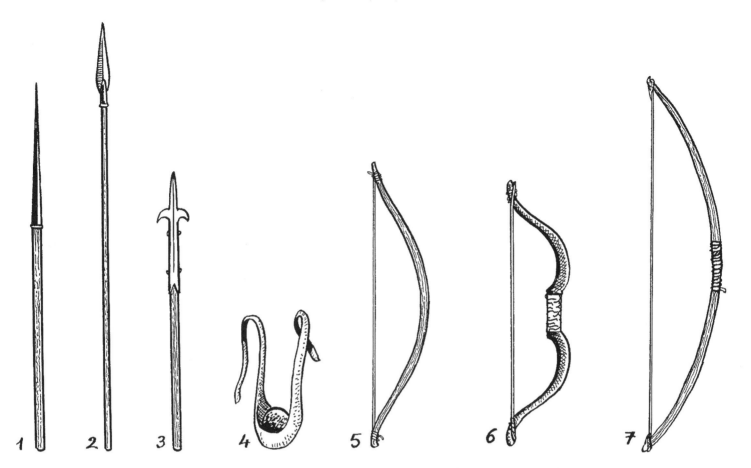

Various Throwing Weapons. 1. dart or pilum; 2. javelin; 3. Frankish angon; 4. sling; 5. bow; 6. Turkish bow; 7. English long bow.

In its simplest form, the sling was a strip of leather folded over so that the thrower held the two ends. The sling was then swung round in the hand several times to gain momentum until at the right moment one end of it was released and the projectile hurled out. Ammunition was readily available and free — stones of all sizes were valuable projectiles; more elaborately, metal balls could be used. A sling was effective as a lethal weapon up to a distance of about 25 yards, although admittedly less effective than an arrow. The sling was improved during the Middle Ages. The staff sling or *fustibal* was a sling attached to the end of a pole; the momentum attained by the sweeping arc of the pole gave the projectile great additional power and range.

The combination of bow and arrow was known as early as the Neolithic period, and late Stone Age men used it for hunting and warfare. The bow was efficient, accurate, rather easy to employ, and cheap to manufacture as its simplest form included only a curved piece of flexible wood and a string. The bow was used by ancient warriors (Sumerians, Assyrians, and Egyptians) but the Greeks, Gauls, and Romans did not make a wide use of it. In Europe the bow was revived as a weapon of war by the

time of Charlemagne. The primitive design made of a stave of wood was improved. A more elaborate design, the composite bow, was usually made of several different materials glued together, such as wood, horn, and animal sinew to increase flexibility and power. Operated by a skilled archer, the bow could range up to 200 meters, or about 656 feet, with a rate of fire of about ten arrows a minute.

Before the 14th century the ordinary bow was rather weak against an armored target; the archer could only deliver as much power as he could bring to bear by drawing the string with his arms and shoulders while trying to aim the arrow at the same time. But in the 14th century the archer first stepped into prominent notice, and the efficacy of his weapon, the most deadly that the art of man devised until the introduction of gunpowder, came to be fully recognized. The 14th century showed the fullest development of the bow, and the archer attained the height of his importance notably in the English armies. The English cultivated a strong archery armed with the so-called long bow and were able to draw sufficient strength to pose a threat to the armored knight. Before that, however, bowmen played an important role on many

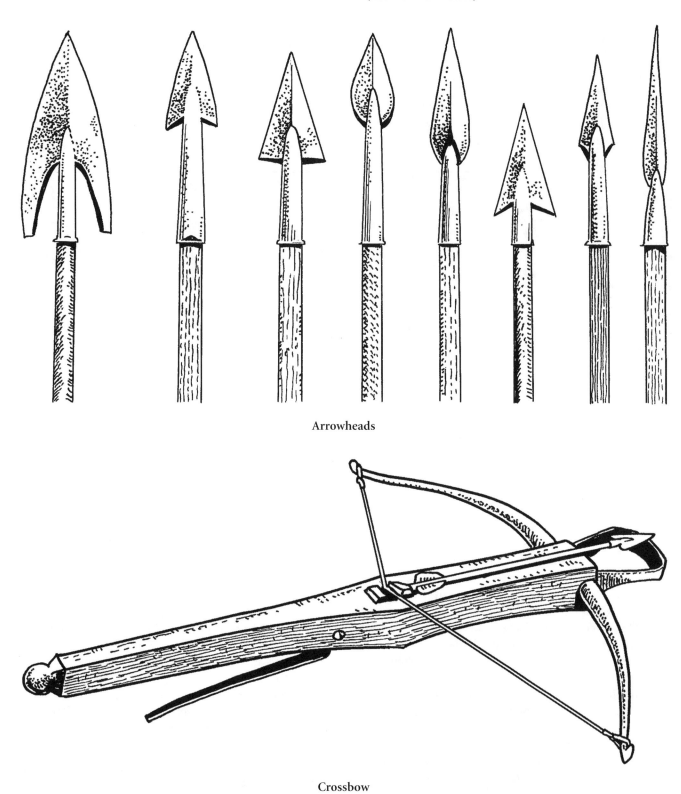

Arrowheads

Crossbow

battlefields. The victory of Hastings in 1066 was won by the combination of Norman archers and cavalrymen as the famous Bayeux tapestry so vividly shows. During the Crusades, the Christian forces were confronted with the remarkable Turkish archers using a strong accolade-shaped bow which could be lethal to a range of 250 meters, or about 273 yards.

Arrows were made by fletchers. They were about 90 centimeters (35 inches) long, fitted with feathers for a better stability and ending with a sharp metal point. The

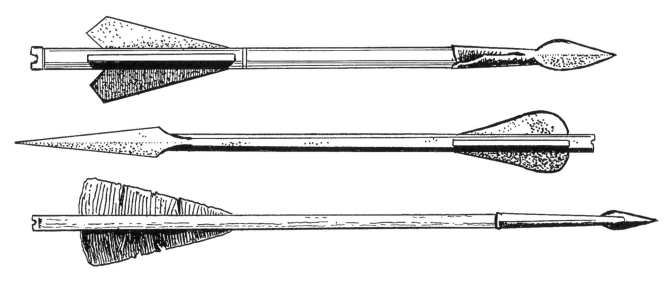

Crossbow Bolts

earliest arrowheads were made of flint or stone bound tightly to a wooden shaft fitted with feathers. They were carried in a quiver, a wooden or leather elongated pouch, sometimes named *carquois*, held by a bandolier. They could also be bound together in a sheaf and so suspended from the waist belt. Arrows were shot either by grazing fire (that was, by aiming directly at the target) or in parabolic fire (indirectly, with a curved trajectory). In battle it was not important to aim at a particular target; hundreds of arrows falling onto a host of men and horses were always bound to hit somebody, and horses were particularly vulnerable because they were maddened by the slightest wound and could not be controlled. In siege warfare, the archer acted as a sniper shooting from the walls of a besieged castle. Arrows could be impregnated with incendiary material which set ablaze houses with thatched roofs and wooden siege engines. The archer's lower left arm was often protected against the blow of the string by a piece of leather or a metal bracelet (a manicle), and his right hand was often protected by a leather glove.

The crossbow originated in the East. It was known, in a modified form, to the Romans. Its other name, *arbalest*, came from the Latin *arcu*, a bow, and *ballista*, throwing machine. Although the crossbow seems to have been known as early as the 4th century in Europe, its main use was as a hunting weapon, and it was not until the 12th century that it was recognized as a major military weapon. It was revived in north Italy and became a specialty of the Genoese. The crossbow was so deadly that the Church opposed to its use. In 1139, the council of Lateran, presided over by Pope Innocent II (pontificate from

Right: Crossbowman Loading with a Hook, ca. 1200. The weapon is spanned with the help of a hook fitted on the man's belt and by pushing with the leg and leaning back.

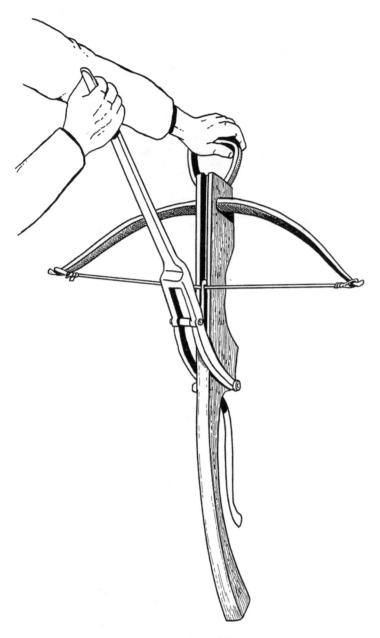

Crossbow with Goat's Foot Loading System

1130 to 1143), banned the crossbow as a barbarous weapon forbidden use against fellow Christians but freely allowed against the infidel Muslims. The ban was confirmed by Pope Innocent III (pontificate from 1198 to 1216), but it was a vain condemnation as the crossbow was far too useful a machine to ignore. The devastating weapon was rapidly adopted by all belligerents, and during the Crusades the use of crossbows was advocated. During the Third Crusade, Richard Lion Heart of England's victory at Arsuf in 1191 was greatly assisted by the chaos caused among the Muslims from his crossbowmen.

The crossbow was a powerful arm which increased the archer's power by separating the processes of draw-

ing and shooting. It was composed of a short cross arm mounted on a stock with a groove cut along the stock to guide the missile and a trigger by which to release it. The earliest crossbows were made of wood and could be loaded, or spanned, rather easily by hand. The arbalester used his legs to assist his arms in the task; the feet were placed on either side of the bow or in an iron stirrup fixed on the end of the stock. A hooked strap, attached to the girdle, was often employed, and the bow was spanned by straightening the body.

When strong and more effective steel crossbows was introduced by the end of the 13th century, various mechanical spanning devices made their appearance for bending the bow and drawing up the bowstring. A simple and quick loading device was the *gaffle* or bender, usually called the "goat's foot"; this was a double lever consisting of two pieces articulating together. The smaller piece was divided into two distinct parts, each of which terminated in a catch; one of these engaged with the bowstring and the other upon points on either side of the stroke. The longer arm of the lever was drawn back, and the catch with the bowstring followed it until, being brought up sufficiently into position, the string was caught by the notch and remained secure until discharged.

The wheel and ratchet — also called a *cranequin* — was an apparatus affixed to the bow stock behind the trigger by a stout cord which passed round the stock and held the mechanism firmly. It consisted of a flat, circular, iron case which contained in its outer periphery a small toothed wheel which could be turned by a long handle. Passing through the circular case and engaging with the small wheel was a straight ratchet with one side cogged: This ratchet had a catch at the end remote from the case which engaged with the bowstring. By merely turning the handle and revolving the wheel the ratchet was wound through the case, thus drawing back the string to its resting place. The apparatus was then detached and hung at the belt of the crossbowman until wanted again.

Another mechanism was the *moulinet-and-pulleys* system. A piece of iron bent into the form of a stirrup was affixed to the stock (adjacent to the bow in this case), similar to that of the hand-crossbow for the insertion of the left foot so as to gain the largest amount of steadiness and purchase. At the butt end of the stock, against the man's body, a system of fixed pulleys, having cords running over another system of free pulleys, was firmly affixed by the insertion of the butt into a socket. The free-pulley system had a catch attached to it which engaged with the cord of the bow: By winding up the fixed system with a small windlass having a handle on either side, the free system approached the butt, bringing with it the string of the bow, which after a time was duly caught in the notch provided for it.

Whatever method was used, when the cross-bow was bent, the man laid the projectile (quarrel or bolt) in its proper place in the guiding groove cut along the stock and the weapon was ready for aiming and firing. The crossbow shot a small — about ten inches long — metal arrow known as a bolt or quarrel. It was generally terminated in a four-sided pyramidal head, or pile, which occasionally was feathered with wood or brass causing the projectile to rotate upon its axis for accuracy. The quarrel was expensive to manufacture, but it was lethal between 150 to 250 yards and still effective at 300 yards to the extend of piercing armor with comparative ease. There were also very small crossbows that could be hidden in the sleeve of a coat, and that could be used for assassination, close-range combat, or self-defense.

The crossbow was rather expensive to manufacture and maintain, but its principal weakness in battle was its rate of fire. It was a slow, tedious, and vulnerable job to rewind the crossbow. It took much longer to reload it than a normal bow, and the reloading crossbowman had to stand upright and was, therefore, fully exposed to enemy fire during the operation. Where a trained ordinary archer could easily shoot ten arrows a minute, only two shots a minute would be a good rate of fire for a crossbowman, though this could be improved by using one shooter and one or more loaders. The crossbow was therefore a better arm for using in the defense of a castle than on the open battlefield.

In siege warfare, crossbowmen were used by both sides, acting as snipers and aiming and shooting at particular targets. The crossbow was a powerful and comparatively accurate weapon — well adapted to sniper fire — as it was held up to the cheek and aimed very much like a modern rifle. It was the ideal weapon for the ordinary soldier because it enabled a common man to knock down a soldier — even a mounted noble knight — anonymously from a safe distance. One of the great advantages of the crossbow was that its use did not require much training, nor intellect, nor the keen judgment and considerable strength needed by the archer.

In the 15th century crossbowmen were often protected by a large shield called a *great pavis*; this was rectangular in outline, convex in form, and rather heavy. It was about 1.2 meters (about 47 inches) long, thus almost covering entirely the person; it was carried by an auxiliary soldier called *pavisier*. Its main purpose was to shelter the vulnerable, upright crossbowman while he was

Loading a Crossbow with the Pulleys System

reloading and firing his weapon. The great pavis was fitted with two iron points enabling it to be set up into the ground; so a rank of standing great pavises formed a *mantlet*, a screening wall, an entrenchment used by knights and other soldiers during both siege and battle as a protection against hostile archers. The pavis was also used to deck the crenels of a fortress as an expression of resistance.

Firing the Crossbow

Self-protection against bow and crossbow was necessary, but it inevitably turned the cavalry into a much heavier and less flexible fighting machine; it also made war more expensive. However, both weapons became outdated when small firearms were developed. The bow and crossbow were replaced in the 16th century by the arquebus and the musket. Today bow and crossbow are still used as skill and sport weapons.

There was no question of the knights adopting either bow or crossbow for their own use. Apart from the difficulty of handling these weapons on horseback by a heavily armored man, they were both supporting weapons which required an offensive squadron to press home the advantage. Knights hated archers and arbalesters who dislodged them from their position as the mainstay of the army and had thus a strong disdain for such servile weapons used by "cowards who were afraid to approach them" but shot from a safe distance. Archers and crossbowmen were specialists who had a better standing than the common footmen, and they received thus higher wages. By the 13th century the crossbowmen of France and Spain — some organized in light mounted units — were an important branch of the army and were recognized as such, while the 14th century saw the supremacy of the English bowmen. The Genoese were famous both for manufacturing and using the crossbow. They were hired by European monarchs, but the cost of employing them was accordingly high in the early 14th century, and like all mercenaries, their loyalty was uncertain.

Manufacture of Weapons

Medieval military equipment was particularly diversified. It was manufactured by specialists called armorers and furbishers, working with skill on iron and steel. In the Early Middle Ages — as society was organized in quasi-autarchy — each village and castle had its own blacksmith who manufactured, repaired, and maintained tools, weapons, and armor. In the 13th century the armorer's craft moved from the local workers, who were little more than skilled blacksmiths, to the great international centers. The

The bow and the crossbow were silent weapons. They could be employed for a surprise action, an ambush, or an assassination. On the battlefields and at sieges their deadly effect were fully recognized and feared, and both weapons were the reason why knights had to be more and more armored. The deadly effect of arrows and quarrels resulted in the abandonment of chain mail and the gradual adoption of full plate armor for knights and horses.

armorers established themselves by that time and dominated the trade.

Some cities developed weapon industries with a local, regional, and even international renown. In France the best weapons were manufactured at Lyon, Tours, Paris, Angers, Arbois, Bayeux, Coutances, and Cambrai. The most famous production centers made a huge business and exported throughout Europe: Basel, Luzerne, and Zurich in Switzerland; Toledo in Spain; Greenwich in England; Brescia, Milan, Mantova, and Padova in Italy; and Passau, Cologne, Solingen, Nuremberg, Augsbourg, and Innsbruck in the German Empire. In the Middle East the main centers producing weapons and armors were Khorasan, Isphahan, and Damascus. Some workshops could be specialized for making only blades, or only armors or crossbows, and all had their own trademarks which authenticated provenance and quality.

In arms and armors the use of leather was normally restricted to the manufacture of sword scabbards. But some pieces of early plate armor were made of leather, as were some later examples of scale armor. There were leather shields, the leather applied as a tooled and embossed covering to a stout wooden foundation. The term *cuir bouilli* (boiled leather) was usually applied to work of this character. It seems likely that the leather was first rendered soft and supple by boiling water or by a hot solution of oil or wax. It was then modeled in relief, and the design was outlined with a heated tool, becoming hard and rigid when dry.

Medieval armorers were remarkable craftsmen who produced equipment of high quality. Most of the production was made for warfare, but a certain number of weapons and armors were especially made

Decorated Blades of Pole Weapons. *Left:* **Blade of a spear of the guards of Emperor Ferdinand I, ca. 1558.** *Center:* **Blade of a spontoon carried by guards of France's Louis XIV, representing figures of Apollo and Hercules, ca. 1675.** *Right:* **German halberd decorated by Hans Polhaimer the Younger, ca. 1563.**

for important personalities and were genuine pieces of art. The preoccupation of men with the lusts of life and the terrors of death was reflected not only in the sculptures, paintings, and engravings of the time but also in the form of decoration on weapons and armors. Throughout human history, men invested some of their highest craft and artistic skills in their weapons, equipment, and engines of war. Shields, blades, swords, and axes as well as armors could be so beautifully decorated by chiseling, carving, embossing, etching, gilding, bejeweling, and engraving that they became precious works of art which might give rise to a real aesthetic emotion. Some of this artwork was actually used in war; others were given as gifts and only worn at parades.

Engraving was a difficult process involving the incising of lines of the design with a *burin*—a sharply pointed light chisel. The less laborious work of etching became increasingly popular with two available methods. The first was to cover the whole of the surface with a protective coating which was then scratched by a needle along the

Armorers at Work in Augsburg in 1515 (after Hans Burgkmair)

Sforza, the leader of a new regime, excused him from paying taxes. In 1491, the armorers of Milan celebrated the wedding of Lodovico Sforza by lining their street with effigies of mounted warriors clad entirely with mail and damascened steel. It was a magnificent display of the product which salesmen from Milan sold in every court in Europe.

In a world where weapons and armor were very expensive, people were motivated to make the fullest possible use of manufactured wares. Old weapons were not casually discarded. If they reached the end of their usefulness to a rich owner but were still functional, they were sold (or given as a gift) to someone further down the social scale and mended as necessary. When a weapon or a piece of armor was too worn or too damaged to serve its purpose, the expensive and rare metal might be recycled.

lines of the required design, and then using acid to imprint it into the metal. In the second method the design was painted with the protective medium, leaving the background to be etched away. The latter method was popularized by the German school of etchers who employed backgrounds filled with small dots.

To acquire such armor, rich knights, dukes, princes, and kings were willing to pay a high price and to travel far to one of the towns that grew famous for the skill of their armorers. In the 15th and 16th centuries, the greatest center of armor making in Europe was Milan. It was said that the craftsmen of that city could outfit an army in a few days. It is a fact that they armed the kings of France and Spain, the dukes of Italy, and many others. To the ablest Milanese armorers, the Missaglia and Negroni for example, came renown, fortune, and royal commissions. Tomasso Missaglia was knighted by the duke Filippo Maria Visconti in 1435; fifteen years later Francesco

As with all other medieval crafts, the armorers and weapon makers were organized in guild. The guild was a social fellowship, an association of craftsmen practicing the same activity. It had its own structures with rules governing the practice and customs as to the tradesmen's right and responsibilities. The fellowship was headed by an elected guild master assisted by a body of jurors who helped adjudicate matters; control quality; regulate prices, terms of competition, training of apprentices, tradesmen's work schedules and all other aspects of the business. The armorer and blacksmith guilds were the most highly regarded and also the most strictly regulated among the trades since their products were so important for the community of the warrior/rulers. No trade was allowed to work at night—for fire security in a world when light always meant flame — except those of the bakers and armorers.

9

Land Warfare

Number of Fighting Forces

If we must believe the *Chroniques* written by the French poet Jean Froissart (1333–1400), medieval war was dominated by knights, sole protagonists deciding the outcome of the day in a series of charges; deaths were rare but heroic; the war was "clean" and similar to an exciting chivalrous game fought between gentlemen, as it were, a kind of elegant tournament for real. In the chronicles, *chansons de geste* (songs of romantic adventures), and manuscripts with illuminated initials and intricate borders, the line between a romantic dream world and the military reality was always indistinct. The lordly audiences who listened to romantic songs and the few who read epic poems wanted to be entertained and thrilled; they were not particularly concerned whether the story was historically true or not. Critical examination of history was very rarely part of medieval thinking. In fact medieval warfare was a much rougher and bloodier business than Froissart would have us believe. There is nothing quite so difficult to portray accurately as complex medieval warfare.

First of all, figures given by contemporary sources regarding the numbers of combatants were invariably exaggerated or even products of chroniclers' imaginations. For instance, at the battle of Bouvines in 1214, chroniclers record up to 9,000 knights and 50,000 infantrymen in the French army of Philippe Auguste, when the royal account gives the real figure as being a little over one-tenth of these. The opposing side—composed of a combined Anglo-Angevin and German Imperial army—would have totaled nearly a quarter of a million men according to the same chroniclers; the real figure was probably not more than 10,000 men. Reliable estimates of army sizes are impossible until the 12th century. When numbers can once again be reckoned, the medieval army appears to have been a force of between 7,000 and 10,000 men, though there is no definite instance of the latter number being engaged in a single battle. Thus—with the exception of the Crusades and the Hundred Years' War, during which huge armies of coalesced allied realms were raised—medieval armies were never numerous. For the siege of Jerusalem in 1099, the coalition armies probably ranged from 1,200 to 1,300 cavalrymen out of a total strength of 12,000 men. When the French king Philippe Auguste went on crusade in 1198, he disposed of a force including 650 mounted men and 1,300 infantrymen. In 1248, when King Louis IX of France led the Seventh Crusade, he had 12,000 soldiers on foot and some 2,500 knights. In addition, the armies were always accompanied by noncombatant craftsmen, clerks, and camp followers. Knights and professional soldiers sometimes took their wives and children with them. These were exceptionally large armies raised by very wealthy monarchs, but on the whole the armies levied by smaller rulers never involved more than a few thousand men, very often merely a few hundred. Today such establishments correspond to the size of battalion and division, but in the Middle Ages these numbers were important.

Various Forms of War

Wars ranged from local confrontations between competing lords to international large-scale conflicts such as the Hundred Years' War. If a knight were a baron—a lord holding a fief and a castle — he would fight to keep his vassals in hand and to gain what he could from his neighbors. If he were a simple knight he would follow his lord to battle or on crusade hoping to get his share of glory and booty. War was dangerous because it could result in death, severe wound, mutilation, or amputation. Nevertheless, it was considered a delightful sport, a justification of the privileged status of the feudal rulers, and a right used to defend one's honor and property. There were, however, some actions that were "done" and "not done" between knights. There was a kind of unspoken code of behavior dictated less by humanitarianism than by making things more "pleasant" between rivals who — sometimes — saw each other more as colleagues than enemies. These "rules" did not apply to foot soldiers, civilians, and common people, who were despised and often treated with indifference, cruelty, and ruthlessness.

Behind honor and glamour, war was commercialized. It could be a profitable business by selling expensive safe-conducts through the controled territories, extorting peasants, plundering villages, looting merchants, and sacking a town as well as by the chance of capturing a fellow knight and holding him for ransom. Ransom and extortion of money from the common folk, as well as booty, were always agreeable bonuses, but for a growing number of feudal belligerents, this unchivalrous business became the major object of their aggressive activity as the profits of a campaign might make their fortunes. The sword was a means of making one's future, and those who did not perish by it in this dangerous process might amass great wealth. Even within the strict framework of feudalism and its oath of allegiance, in spite of the Church's efforts to limit violence, and in spite of the supposed chivalrous honor, war could be a thoroughly mercenary occupation for the ruling class. The line between fighter and robber, warrior and brigand, or soldier and thief was never clearly drawn.

Under the influence of the Church, a distinction was made between various forms of war. Private war of opposing individuals and local rulers (who were originally established to protect the people from the Vikings and the Magyars) developed into a feudal selfish aristocracy. War between local lords was considered a perfectly normal method of settling a dispute. It was supposed to be waged with as little damage as possible to the general community. A local ruler might kill his adversary in battle but not burn or despoil his property. But in practice it was the noncombatants who suffered most — the urban bourgeois whose trade was disturbed and the peasants whose crops and cattle were either destroyed or looted. Gradually, as the central power was more or less restored, devastating private wars were outlawed.

Public wars were conducted by princes. In public war the limits were broader. *Gloria Victis*! Prisoners could be taken and held for ransom. The property of the defeated enemy was lawful booty, but ecclesiastics and their possessions were exempt — at least in theory — from looting and pillage. Large-scale destruction, pillage, and burning, however, may have seemed wanton and merely designed to demoralized the population, but heavy contributions could be levied on the people. Devastation was part of the normal business of a war in enemy territory. A public war could become an open war in which quarter and ransoms were allowed.

There was a yet more terrible form of war — commonly seen in siege warfare — when the besieged refused to surrender when summoned: This was *guerre mortelle*, or mortal war, in which no quarter was to be given and not only the property but the lives of the vanquished were at the total mercy of the victor. In public war and mortal war, the right of totally exterminating the enemy was fortunately not always applied, but drastic measures of retaliation could be expected from the victors.

The holy war — widely encouraged by the Church — was that conducted against pagans and Muslims in the Crusades. Here the greatest cruelty and ruthlessness were allowed and resulted in the butchery of prisoners and even the extermination of civilian populations.

By the 14th century the laws and limitations on the conduct of war were elaborate, much written about, and fairly uniform throughout western Christendom.

Pitched Battle

Knights played an important role in battle, and from the 10th century to a large part of the 13th century, they reigned supreme. Medieval warfare was characterized by duels between horsemen with infantry support, and the spectacle of two armies meeting in a full-scale charge was soon to become the climax of pitched battles in the Middle Ages. However, the idea of medieval tactics as consisting of vast mêlées or charges by heavily armed knights, invariably on horseback, captures the imagination all too easily. This is an oversimplification; each pitched battle was totally different from another by the number of forces engaged, maneuvers during the battle, and skill of the leaders, for example. This being understood, there were, however, a certain number of basic dispositions that remained the same throughout the Middle Ages. Because the charge of mounted men was only possible on a large, flat, dry, and bare space, the choice of a suitable battlefield — possibly a plain — was often agreed to by both sides before the confrontation. Surprising the enemy by swift action or ambushing him was of course also possible.

A Knight's Team, Called a Lance or a Banner

Both armies established their camps where they could rest before the battle. The modern concept of logistics and administration developed, in the last centuries, into one of the dominant factors of warfare. It includes the functions of supply, transport, evacuation and hospitalization, and the capacity of supporting military forces in campaign. None or very little of this existed in the Middle Ages.

An average medieval army on the march was composed of numerous, ponderous, and heteroclite vehicles and carts mainly drawn by donkeys and oxen; for quicker haulage purposes packhorses were also used. The odd convoy moved with slowness and difficulty on unpaved roads which turned into quagmires when it rained and dusty tracks in hot weather. Carts and chariots were reserved to carry the noblemen's luggage and the heavy war equipment. Soldiers had to walk along for miles, escorting the long and slow column and carrying their weapons and own implements. Cavalrymen formed groups of scouts in the van, flank and rear guards.

Modern army supply services did not exit, but at the beginning of the Hundred Year' War, some merchants were commissioned to provide supplies for the troops. Named "vitailleurs," they quickly came to light as profiteers and swindlers. The term *vitailleur* was later applied to captains charged with providing supplies for sea fleets and eventually became a synonym of pirates in the Baltic Sea (Vitaliebrudern or Vitalian Brothers). On the whole, the art of logistics had disappeared after the fall of the western Roman Empire. The supply of the medieval army in campaign was thus completely improvised. Soldiers had to shift for themselves and live off the land. Marauding and pillaging the countryside, friend or foe, was the only way to survive.

The army on the march was followed by noncombatant personnel including clerks, saddle makers, carpenters, blacksmiths and farriers, surgeon-barbers, and other craftsmen needed for the purpose of war and daily life of a community. The wives of professional soldiers could be useful as sewers, vivandières, and washerwomen. This "logistical" personnel included ambulant merchants and traders but also prostitutes — a fixed institution in every army — as well as beggars, tramps, and thieves who took advantage of the confusion to loot with impunity. The passage of such an army, lacking true and effective cohesion, was always a calamity for the local countryside population because the notion of indemnifying civilian victims of war was totally unknown.

Before a battle, soldiers heard mass, armies were blessed by their respective clergymen, and prayers for victory were said. It was not uncommon that saints' relics were carried with the troops. In theory, clergymen were not permitted to take part in combat as the Church forbade them to shed the blood of Christians. But in practice, it was not uncommon to see a bishop temporarily exchanging his miter for a helmet and his crook for a lance. The mentality of the Middle Ages was indeed complex as material, even materialistic, motives were not infrequently interwoven with religious and idealistic feelings. Before a battle, young squires were knighted, and the leader might speak to his troops to boost morale and courage after which the forces were deployed on the battlefield. It could occur that two leaders would fight in a duel before their troops.

For an extended campaign, a knight needed some assistance. More than one horse was necessary, and the knight needed help in manipulating and carrying his

Sergeant à Cheval

cheval, lightly armored horseman to scout and skirmish for him; and perhaps one or more foot soldiers to stand guard. So the lone knight expanded to a fighting team of half a dozen men — in some case more — like the crew of some enormous battle tank. By the 10th century, the whole apparatus became very expensive indeed, and the management of war was a business for wealthy specialists. A knight with his team was called a lance or a banner. More of these units together — say about thirty to forty groups — formed a *bataille* (this term later became *battalion*, indicating an infantry unit composed of companies and platoons). The mounted batailles formed the main attacking force with infantry as supporting and defensive troops.

Before the 12th century, the infantry force was rather small and despised. If the armed force had archers, the battle would commence with a preliminary volley of arrows. Skirmishes could be launched between outriders, while the opposing forces maneuvered and each tried to persuade the other side to charge. A first charge of knights rarely succeeded, and if the enemy could be persuaded to commit himself too heavily to his initial effort, the chances of an effective counterstroke before he could recover were increased. Many battles were lost by an impulsive opening attack by overeager knights. As always in warfare, an initial success brought over-confidence, and it could be followed by a disastrous enemy counterreaction. The mounted men could also try to outflank their enemy, and it was naturally desirable for the leaders to hold troops in reserve to reinforce the weaken-

growing number of impediments such as his lance, sword, helmet, and shield. At the very least he needed a shield bearer, the *escuyer* (esquire). Probably he also had one or more grooms for the horses; one or more *sergeants à* ing ranks, to launch a decisive charge, or to place a force in ambush if a feign retreat were to be used.

The clash of the charging armored combatants rapidly developed in numerous duels into a confused

An Episode of the Battle of Hastings, 1066 (after the Bayeux Tapestry)

mêlée. When lances were broken, knights fought with their other weapons: sword, axe, hammer, and mace. Tactics on the battlefield could not be other than primitive. It was of course difficult (if not impossible) to make complicated maneuvers and large movements as the leader (who might be the king, duke, or count himself) was at the head of his troops. Charging and fighting with them, the leader had no or little prepared plans, no general view over the battlefield and could not give tactical orders. During the battle the chief probably had difficulty imposing discipline on his young and foolhardy knights. Discipline was indeed the weakest point of the medieval army, especially of the young and boisterous knights. The emphasis on individual glory was so strong that even experienced men of war were often unable to argue reasonably against it. Personal courage and undisciplined impetuousness sometimes brought disaster on an entire army by hot-headed knights disobeying specific orders. Many of them did not always understand the tactical necessity of a cautious retreat that allowed to regroup forces and relaunch a successful counterattack. Instead, they fought on and on with energy and courage in pointless situations. They often urged charges against unfavorable odds or against strong positions because they were eager for bravado and glory. Knights—on the whole—were very courageous soldiers but very poor strategists.

Of course not all mounted men were stupid and suicidal, many had an idea of discipline and of its importance on the battlefield. They stayed in close formation with their companions, using their shields as cover, then charged, retreated, regrouped, and reattacked when ordered to do so. The crucial problem of discipline depended largely on the leader who could (or could not) instill its value to his troops.

The clash of two charging bodies of knights was probably the most awe-inspiring sight the battlefields of Europe had ever seen. However, even in the heyday of the knight, cavalrymen were not always used as mounted troops. There are numerous examples of battles fought by dismounted cavalry. For example, during the battle of Crécy in 1346, the English knights dismounted and fought on foot with the support of archers. This tactics was also employed by Bertrand du Guesclin at the battle of Cocherel in 1364. The same happened at the battles of Roosebecke in 1382 and Agincourt in 1415. To explain the superiority of cavalry forces whether mounted or dismounted, we must return to a simple explanation: mounted troops usually arrived in better condition on the battlefield than infantrymen who had walked for miles. The role of infantry during those days before the 13th century was modest and secondary. Infantrymen were auxiliaries. They were charged to guard the camp, horses, and transport vehicles. If thrown into the battle, foot soldiers could only hope to cut the horse from under the knight; they had no hope of standing against the irresistible charge of armored knights. In every way the knight dominated his surroundings, roaming where he liked, and killing when he felt inclined. Foot soldiers were highly despised, and a saying of the time was that a "hundred horsemen are worth a thousand footmen."

Pitch Battle (after the 15th Century Chroniques de Charlemagne)

Medieval combatants were not spurred by a national idea or a patriotic ideal. They were motivated to fight by fun and passion; by the desire of prowess; by loyalty to defend the private interests of family, clan, or one's lord; or by fanatical religious zeal during the Crusades. Nationalism, that is, the feeling of belonging to a community larger than one's village, fief, province, or region, was unknown. In France, for example, patriotism seemed to appear with the heroine Jeanne d'Arc (1412–1431). Patriotism and nationalism were vague and confusing principles for the common man. Such notions as citizenship, patriotism, and sacrifice for the nation actually arose only by the time of the French Revolution in 1789 and were fully exploited by Napoleon in the period 1799–1815.

A battle never lasted for very long, perhaps a few hours, a part of a day, or a whole day. If delivered in a disciplined, united manner, the knights' charge could shatter the enemy ranks and have a decisive effect on the outcome of the battle. Much depended on individual factors, such as physical fitness, audacity, and bravery, on the hand-to-hand fighting following the charge. Prowess played a central role, but pugnacity was not enough when outnumbered. Mounted knights were always vulnerable to archers though, and once the horse had been felled — either temporarily bowled over, injured, or killed — the unhorsed knight had small chance of surviving except through surrender. Gradually one side or the other took the upper hand.

The luckiest of the defeated withdrew to safety, the less fortunate surrendered and were taken prisoner. Chivalrous behavior, the sense of honor — popularized by the literature of courtesy — provoked acts of bravery and gestures of gallantry in conformity with the ideal of the knightly code. But — as we already know — these virtues only applied to the knights, combatants of the same social world, and noble warriors who considered the opponent as a colleague or a brother-in-arms. Against common people, foot soldiers, and civilians, knights often behaved with savagery and showed no or little mercy. The numerous acts and laws of the Church that tried to humanize war showed that the execution of nonnoble prisoners, carnages, massacres, mutilation, devastation of villages, pillage of cities, and rape of women were not exceptional atrocities.

In conclusion, large encounters — costly in human lives — were rather rare. Warfare in the Middle Ages was — on the whole — much less spectacular than it has been long thought. More than pitched battles, it consisted of local wars, limited conflicts, short operations, hit-and-run raids, ambushes, skirmishes, and small-scale sieges with a rather limited number of combatants. It must be kept in mind that the considered period lasted for a thousand years, and accordingly, moments of peace and relative quiet periods were numerous. Frequency and intensity of war are difficult to measure as they varied considerably in time and space. Medieval wars — as other

Fighting Knights (after Lives of the Two Offas by Matthew Paris)

wars elsewhere and in other times—were cruel, hard, ruthless, and pointless, Europe suffered many dark and disastrous periods, notably in the 9th, 10th, and 14th centuries. But we—who have witnessed and experienced industrial conflict, general mobilization, total war, mass extermination, genocide, and nuclear fire—can easily imagine how rudimentary and small-scale medieval warfare might have been. It is very questionable to assert that the Middle Ages on the whole was more violent than any other period of history. Proportionally, how barbarous was improvised medieval warfare compared to the massacres during the wars of religion in the 16th century, the killings of the time of Louis XIV, the Napoleonic butcheries, the harshness of the American Civil War, and the two horrifying recoils of civilization during the two World Wars in the first half of the 20th century?

Ransom

The uncertainty of the fate of common people contrasted sharply with the treatment of noble prisoners. To be captured was no dishonor when a knight had fought bravely. Chivalry became a question of business, and cap-

tives of any standing were rarely killed because of the very lucrative system of ransom. The custom of ransoming and extorting goes back to classical times. It was in some degree forgotten during the 9th and 10th centuries, and the practice was revived in the 11th century. As ransoming grew, the agreement came to imply slightly more than merely buying one's way out of imprisonment. The prisoner had to be protected from other members of the opposing army, and he could not be severely treated while detained. Irons were permitted but very rarely used. However these conditions were by no means universal; the Germans and the Spanish had a bad reputation for their treatment of prisoners. Hostages (relatives, wives, or children) could be detained while the captive was released to gather the ransom for his liberty. On the whole, there was a tacit understanding that a ransom should be related to the prisoner's rank and wealth and that it should not ruin him financially to such an extent that he could no longer live the lifestyle of a nobleman.

Occasionally royal ransoms reached huge proportions, as was true of the French king Jean II Le Bon captured by the English at the battle of Poitiers in 1356. King Richard I of England was captured in 1193 by the archduke Leopold of Austria and had to pay 150,000 marks, a colossal sum by the standard of the time. Taken prisoner at the battle of Agincourt in 1415, the royal prince Charles d'Orléans languished for twenty-five years in the White Tower of London—bewailing his lost youth in some of the loveliest of French poetry—before his ransom was raised. Great captains were also highly valued. When Bertrand du Guesclin was taken prisoner by the English Black Prince, the prince asked him what ransom he ought to pay. Du Guesclin named the impossible figure of 100,000 francs, at which the prince remitted half of it and sent him to raise the remainder. The sum was paid by the king of France. When François I of France was captured at the battle of Pavia in 1525, his ransom became a state affair costing huge sums to the realm. The business of ransom—especially at national level—was very unpopular because it was the common people who had to pay by means of extra taxes. At the very humblest end of the scale, a sum of a few crowns might well suffice if the prisoner were a mere man-at-arms, or the captor might settle for a suit of armor or a horse.

Dead, Wounded, and Invalids

After the battle, the dead were stripped of their possessions (weapons, armor, money, dress, jewels etc.), and the loot was divided among the victors. Common people and horses were hastily buried in mass graves. The dead bodies of important noblemen were either brought back to their fiefs or buried in the nearest church, abbey, or monastery. Certain heroic defuncts and nobles of high lineage were given grandiose funerals. When constable Bertrand du Guesclin died in 1380, he was so prestigious that he was granted the honor of being buried in the necropolis of the kings of France in the basilica of Saint-Denis near Paris.

After a single battle, the war could be over, and the fate of a whole nation could be sealed as happened after the battle of Hastings in 1066. When peace was restored, the small number of belligerents engaged in the conflict did not cause regrading and social problems. The warrior-rulers returned to their fiefs covered with booty and glory, and the mobilized foot soldiers returned to their fields and workshops. In the 15th century, however, the growing number of mercenaries who had no other occupation than war became a huge social problem. Without employment, they roamed the land, plundering and pillaging as they went.

As for the wounded soldier—if he was not dispatched or abandoned to his fate—he was nursed by physicians with a rudimentary knowledge. Medieval medicine could be appallingly primitive and must have killed more often than it cured. The practice of medicine and surgery had been developed in antiquity by scientists such as Hippocrates, Celsius (during the reign of Emperor Augustus), and Galen (in the 2nd century A.D.), but most of this knowledge was forgotten. Contact with the Arab world during the Crusades might have brought some improvement since methods of Arab doctors from the 8th century, such as Avicenna and Razes, were much more advanced than the crude methods of the Franks. Western European art of healing was nonetheless much in its infancy.

There was a certain knowledge of medicinal herbs as illustrated by the Augustine monk Strabo who, between 839 and 849, had written a manual called *De Medicina Praecepta Saluberrima*. Herbal recipes of considerable sophistication existed to cure simple ailments, but they could do nothing against serious wounds and epidemics. Medieval medical care was limited to empirical knowledge without any notion of anatomy and physiology. Pharmacopoeial and medical treatments were elementary—even freakish—and were ordered by whimsical and ignorant physicians. With no understanding of the need for cleanliness, there was a fatal lack of care for hygiene. Surgical operations were often inefficient, and a benign wound would often fester with lethal result, like the arrow wound which killed King Richard Lionheart of England in 1199.

Medical operations and amputations were made by tradesmen, surgeons, and barbers. Scholar/physicians only made philosophical speculations or described the wound or sickness in pedantic and turgid Latin terms; they made diagnoses and gave prescriptions but disdained touching the patient. The actual preparation of medicine was the work of the apothecary. Drastic remedies were required to try to save a limb threatened by gangrene, such as cauterizing it with hot irons. There were several academies of medicine, in Salerno (Italy) as well as in Chartres and Montpellier (France), which produced scholars. If the physician and the surgeon had not killed him, a wounded helpless soldier could turn to quack remedies of a charlatan or magical, astrological practices and good-luck charms of a medicine man or witch doctor. Those practitioners of folk medicine were sometimes efficient because their practice was also based on experience and good sense. Prayers might have helped too as the highly religious spirited men of the Middle Ages considered that suffering, sickness, or wounds were the will of God and He, only, might cure them. However, it was only by the time of the Renaissance that serious research and experimentation about blood circulation, wounds caused by firearms, and amputations were made, resulting in significant improvement of medical care owing to the works of the French surgeon Ambroise Paré (ca.1509–1590) and, later, the English physiologist William Harvey

(1578–1657). Before that, any wounded man survived more because of luck and his individual physical robustness and lust for life than through medical attention.

The main soldier killer was sickness due to lack of hygiene, harshness of military life conditions, profound medical ignorance, and promiscuity in unhealthy conditions in camps, towns, and castles. Heat and the often unsuitable food that soldiers scavenged to supplement their meager rations contributed to the swift spread of dysentery and typhus, known in the Middle Ages as "the plague" (from the Latin *plaga*, blow) or "flux." Diseases depleted whole armies when pestilence raged through a camp. Plagues, infectious fevers, contagious afflictions and epidemics decimated whole populations. By the Renaissance a new venereal disease appeared, *syphilis* (originally called "French sickness" by the Italians and "Italian disease" by the French), which killed more soldiers than died in battles. Until decisive medical progress was made in the second half of the 19th century, epidemics were more lethal than wars.

During centuries, nothing was done regarding invalid soldiers and veterans. Crippled and old combatants, as well as their wives and children, were abandoned to their unfortunate fate. Widows and orphans of dead soldiers were also forsaken as pensions and indemnities were not obligations but only compensations that were obtained through a sense of willingness and favor. The luckiest among these waifs and strays might be assisted by family or friends or by charitable Christian institutions, but most of these poor souls miserably survived as ragged beggars or petty thieves. In France for example, it was only during Henri IV's reign (from 1589 to 1610) that a small effort was made to comfort, house, dress, and feed veterans and crippled soldiers. The *Maison de la Charité Chrétienne* (Home of Christian Charity) was founded in 1596. This institution was the fore-runner of the *Hôtel des Invalides* (Hotel of Invalids) created in Paris in 1674 by Louis XIV, at the instigation of Vauban and Louvois.

Writings about Medieval Warfare

Chivalry drew its inspiration from the heroes of the romances and *chansons de geste*. These poetic epic works rooted firmly in the world around them, but the military historical truth was subject to the vagaries of the poet's imagination. As the concept of chivalry grew more complex, Charlemagne and his heroic paladins and King Arthur and his Knights of the Round Table were replaced by men inspired by new ideas, men offering a more human and practical example to the aspiring knight. Gradually, poetry was supplemented by prose. A new form of writing became popular and played an important part in the cult of chivalry: the heroic biography written by men who had witnessed the events and people they described. These works were intended to entertain but also to give instruction and advice.

The biography of *William Marshal*, written in French in the 1220s by an unknown squire, gave the portrait of a knight-errant in the late 12th century; the book described the exciting and adventurous life of a hero of the hour mixing chivalrous romance and actual life. Trained as a squire in the Tancarville family in Normandy, William fought in France and later went on a pilgrimage to Jerusalem. He was a knight-errant pledging himself to superhuman quest, and he stood as a focus of loyalty and honor in terms of European chivalry, medieval custom, and feudal law. Marshal died about 1219 and was a symbol of chivalrous idealism. The *History of the Kings of Britain* was written in about 1135 by Geoffrey of Monmouth. The *Tournois de Chauvency* (Tournament of Chauvency), written by the minstrel Jacques Bretel, described a tournament of 1285. Geoffroi de Charny — a distinguished French knight whose career was at its zenith in the 1350s — wrote a manual of knighthood, the *Livre de Chevalerie*. The *Poem of the Black Prince* was written in about 1385 by Chandos Herald. The *Biography of Bertrand du Guesclin* from the 14th century was a rather realistic portrait of a poor knight who — owing to his military genius, courage, and feats of arms — earned the post of constable of France. The *Victorious Knight*, a biography of Don Pero Nino of Castile — a renowned soldier and a skilled jouster — was written about 1449. The life of *Chevalier Pierre Terrail Seigneur de Bayart* (1476–1524), written by his loyal servitor Jacques de Mailles, described the career of one of the best French men of war from the time of King François I of France.

There were obviously no military academies in the Middle Ages, and training for war was practiced either at the tournament or on the battlefield. The common idea that there was no military art at all, no collective organization, and no elaborate tactics is not totally true. Though very limited, modest, and primitive (as illiteracy was wide-spread even within the ruling class), there was however some theoretical thought and attention given to the problems of warfare. The thinking behind the development of warfare was greatly influenced by examples from classical antiquity, particularly Roman. Many rulers and men of war were aware of and admired the successes and victorious deeds of the great soldiers of history such as Alexander the Great, Hannibal, Pompey, Julius Caesar or — more recently — Charlemagne. History and military authors of ancient times were useful for their didactic value. The need to apply discipline, which owed much to Roman tradition — as well as the revival of the Aristotelian idea that any society should be ready to defend itself —

lay at the root of medieval thinking. Some literature existed based upon the appreciation of the military values of Rome. There were a few copies of the *Stratagemata* (Strategy) of Sextus Julius Frontinus and of Caesar's *De Bello Gallico* (Wars in Gaul). Vegetius's work *Epitoma de re Militari* (*Concerning Military Matters*) remained, a millenium after its publication in the 4th century, the most-cited work on military art. It was translated into French in 1284 and was the inspiration for many books, treatises, and manuals written on that subject.

One of the most popular treatise about the codification of chivalry was *Parzifal* (name of a knight) written between 1198 and 1210 by the German knight-poet Wolfram von Eschenbach (1170–1220). Another was the *Libre del Ordre de Cavayleria* (Book of the Order of Chivalry) written in 1275 by the Spanish theologian and poet Ramon Lull (1235–1315).

The three major military orders, Templars, Hospitalers. and Teutonics, had their *regula* (rule) written down. They issued precise regulations—not only about the behavior and conduct of the knight-monks in peacetime—but also how they were to wage war. Strict orders were observed concerning how to organize a campaign, manage supplies, ride horses, march in column, set up camps, maneuver, fight and retreat in battle, and treat prisoners and many other rules.

In the second half of the 13th century, King Alfonso X of Castile published *Siete Partidas* (The Seven Parts) and Gile of Rome wrote *De Regimine Principum* (The Mirror of Princes), both works about warfare. The *Tree of Battles* was written by the lawyer Honoré Bonet toward the end of the 13th century. Bonet attempted to define in legal terms what constituted knightly proper behavior in war. The author was also concerned about developing practical guidelines for soldiers' pay, fixing and paying ransoms (which should be set according to the captive's wealth), determining compensation for horses and armor or health lost while on campaign, and dividing booty.

Bonet also stressed the importance of discipline and cohesion of an army.

The *Livre des Faits d'Armes et de Chevalerie* (Book of Book of Deeds of Arm and Chivalry) on military strategy, conduct of war, and law was written about 1410—and, worthy of mention—by a woman, the Venetian poetress Christina of Pisan. It was translated into English by William Caxton as *The Book of Fayttes of Armes and of Chivalrye* and published in England in 1490.

As early as the end of the 13th century, a Franciscan friar, Fidencio of Padova, in his book *Liber Recuperationis Terre Sancte* (Reconquest of the Holy Land), advocated the creation of a large phalanx armed with pikes—an Ancient Greek tactic later revived by the Swiss mountainers. Jean de Bueil wrote a military treatise in 1466, *Le Jouvencel* (the "Young" or the "Young One"). Alain de Chartier published in the 15th century, the *Bréviaire des Nobles* (The Noblemen's Breviary) in which he painted a realistic picture of warfare and tournaments.

At the beginning of the 14th century, the Venetian thinker Torsello in his book *Liber Secretorum Fidelium Crucis*, wrote about siege machines and made the first military maps. Military cartography was developed in Italy about 1540 with various maps indicating roads, rivers and bridges, fortified cities, and fortresses as well as the distances between these strategic points.

It is true that those manuals were not numerous and that their theoretical reflection reached very few people indeed — we must repeat it — as illiteracy was widespread. Nonetheless, they emphasized basic standards which led to a greater efficiency. As a result there were examples of well-prepared campaigns, orderly battles, well-disciplined charges, and cleverly executed maneuvers. Besides, siege warfare and the art of fortification became complex, sophisticated military activities done by specialists. They spurred imagination, stimulated technical research, and encouraged innovations.

10

Siege and Naval Warfare

Siege Warfare

Each period of history has had its sieges, some short, some protracted, many bloody, and a few civilized. The history of siege warfare is as old as the existence of cities. More than by pitched battles, which were on the whole rather few, medieval warfare was dominated by siege. It could not be otherwise as the fortified castle was the basic and central point of feudal life as much politically as militarily and economically. Battles—when they occurred at all—were often merely subsidiary to the major business of investing and relieving fortresses. With the development of strategic fortification, the capture of castles by siege became an increasingly common military objective. A whole system of tactics and technology grew up around the needs of the besiegers and the besieged. This was already true in the 11th and 12th centuries and became more particularly a central focus in the 13th and 14th centuries, when medieval military architecture reached its apogee.

The primitive motte-and-bailey castles of the Early Middle Ages—made of earth walls and wooden palisades—had been superseded by huge fortresses that usually included a high and powerful dungeon (also named *keep*) with thick walls made of stone. The keep was generally surrounded by an outer stone wall, high enough to discourage escalade. The outer wall itself was reinforced by powerful and high corner towers and wall turrets. The entrance to the castle—the weakest point in a fortress—was protected by a strong gatehouse including two towers, a retractable drawbridge, and a portcullis made of oak plates with metal for lowering across the gateway. All this was defended by well-placed and well-protected observation and combat emplacements in the tower; the walls were crenelated with a parapet and a wallwalk on top. Towers and walls were punctuated with narrow loopholes from which the defenders could fire bow and crossbow while offering the smallest target possible to the attacker. And—very often—the whole castle was hemmed by a deep and wide moat that could possibly be filled with water for additional defense.

The garrison of the castle was generally not numerous and would be very much smaller than the attacker's army. Some English castles—Bodiam in Sussex and Harlech in North Wales, for example—were designed to be held by as few as 30 to 50 soldiers. More often however, one could expect a garrison of perhaps 30 or 40 archers and twice that number of men-at-arms. The huge castle of Dover (Great Britain) called for a garrison of 832 soldiers based on the ratio of three men to every two battlements on the outer wall, but during the siege of 1216, it was manned by 140 knights plus an unknown number of ordinary soldiers for a total of probably not much more than 500 men. If they had water, supplies, and ammunition in sufficient quantity, a small and determined garrison could resist for quite a while. The attackers of such a fortress would number in the hundreds and possibly thousands.

Sieges were the main ingredient of any campaign in the Middle Ages, and the real object of military maneuvers was a kind of chessboard tactic to deprive the enemy of his strongholds and hence of control of the countryside. The purpose of a siege was not necessarily the destruction of the besieged. The aim could be to bring a

rebellious vassal back to submission or to obtain political and economical compromise. Entrenched behind high, thick, strong stone walls, defenders were — in theory — in an advantageous and superior position. However, history showed that reputed inexpugnable fortresses, defended by regiments, could fall at the blast of a single trumpet. On the other hand, some modest fortified places garrisoned by a handful of half-starving men resisted for months to a whole army. Indeed, high walls were not sufficient to stop enemies; the outcome of a siege depended for a great deal on many factors such as physical courage, individual bravery, logistical preparation, morale determination, and pugnacity on both sides. Weather conditions also played an important role; if it rained, camps and roads became impracticle mud pools, bows and hurling machines were useless, and morale collapsed. Medieval wars only took place in spring and summer.

The besiegers disposed of several means to achieve the seizure of a fortified place. They could impose capitulation by displaying their force and threatening terrible retaliation (pillage, fire, rape, and general massacre). They might profit from internal quarrels among the defenders and negotiate various advantages with the ones against the others. They could use guile and treachery by infiltrating parties disguised as merchants, pilgrims, traders, or travelers in need of assistance; once inside, the friendly posing party would open the gate to admit hidden armed comrades waiting outside. Traitors could be paid to do the same. The besiegers could also launch a surprise attack or a discreet assault at the end of the night when guards were tired after a long watch. So, owing to intimidation, menace, negotiation, ruse, treachery, corruption, or surprise, the operation could be quickly concluded. But if these means failed, the besiegers were obliged to take the place by force with methods originating from ancient Middle East, Greek, and Roman siege craft. The medieval fortress owed its strength not only to its construction, but also to the feeble nature of the attacking methods of the period.

Overcoming a fortress was slow, difficult, and costly. A military siege was a large-scale undertaking demanding time, comprehensive logistics, and considerable organization. The attacking party had to have soldiers, engineers and workers, ammunition, machines, tools, accommodations, and water and food supplies. Besides, armies of the Middle Age were very slow to move and mobile only for short periods. Vassals were available for forty days a year for the *ost* (military service). The success of a siege was largely due to the skills of specialists in siege craft and the use of mercenaries who were prepared to sit out a long siege, unlike the feudal levies (vassals and peasants/soldiers mobilized by the suzerain) who became impatient and were liable to go home at the end of their allotted time regardless of the state of the campaign. As can be easily imagined, the length of time that a siege could last varied enormously.

Blockade

The first stage of the siege was the establishment of a hermetical blockade intended to isolate the place and cut all communication and supply lines. Patrols of mounted men initially surrounded the place and cut it off from the outside world by the simple expedient of seizing all roads, bridges, waterways, and villages in the vicinity. At this stage the would-be besiegers were rather vulnerable, for they were thinly spread and were trying to control a fair amount of territory with comparatively few troops. One spirited counterattack here by the defenders could cause untold havoc for the attackers, who did not have anything like the numbers necessary to resist a concerted assault on them. Before the arrival of the main army, there could be skirmishes, hit-and-run raids, and even battles. Once the attacker's army had successfully completed the task of blockading the target, the blockade resulted in a war of attrition. The besiegers waited until the besieged were worn out and exhausted by hunger, isolation, sickness, and discouragement. It was consequently important for the encircled garrison to dispose of sufficient supplies and to have reliable allies coming to their rescue. Clearly, allies were of crucial importance to the beleaguered. Should the defender's relieving army be victorious, then the siege was doubtless lifted, but should the besieger's army win the day then the fate of the garrison was indeed sealed.

In the limited space offered by the castle and its walled bailey, peasants and noncombatants of the neigh-

Opposite: Schematic View of a 14th Century Castle. Such a castle was characterized by height and verticality. (1) Ditch (possibly filled with water) creating an inaccessible zone around the fortress. (2) Gatehouse with portcullis (a large iron or wooden grating used to block the passage when released vertically) and drawbridge (provided with a raising-and-lowering mechanism to hinder or enable passage). (3) Tower, projecting combat emplacement also used as lodging and storage place. (4) Wall, also called "curtain." (5) Wallwalk protected by a creneled breastwork on top of the wall. (6) Hoarding, also called "brattice," a wooden balcony fitted with apertures through which the defenders could throw down missiles on enemies. (7) Postern, or sallyport, a secondary access. (8) Pepperpot turret, a small watchtower or lookout post. (9) Bailey, the open courtyard with chapel, well, stables, and other lodging and service buildings. (10) Dungeon, or keep, the most powerful tower of the castle and the dwelling place of the lord.

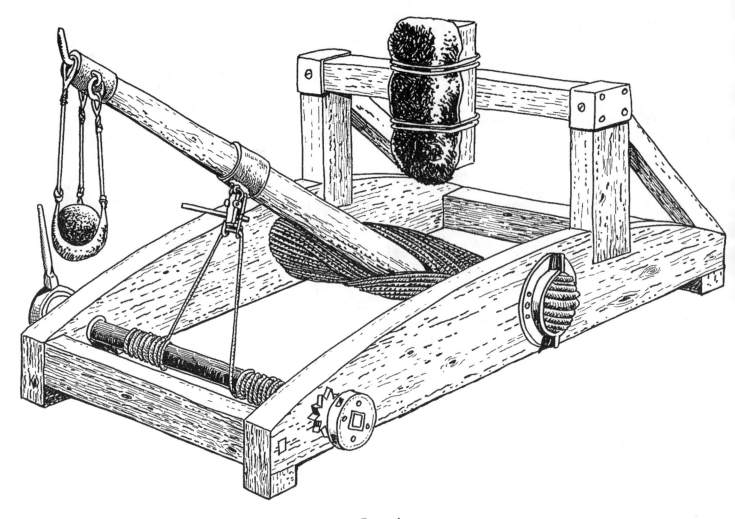

Catapult

borhood were temporarily refuged; they participated actively in the defense or at least tried not to be a hindrance. They could be an irritant to the garrison and were a constant drain on supplies. If the siege lasted long, supplies had to be rationed. A knight would be allocated a particular amount of food, a fighting man a slightly smaller amount, male civilians still less, with women and children the smallest amount. As reserves dwindled, all manner of problems set in. Some ghastly stories are well-known of beleaguered garrisons eating their own horses and then cats, dogs, and rats. In some cases, when supplies were running out and when the garrison refused to surrender, "useless mouths" (women, children, and the elderly) were expelled from the castle.

Siege is indeed a harsh word, certainly less resounding than *battle* because the word *battle* is unchained violence and the uncertainty of fortune — just like a siege — but the latter possesses another element in the exasperation of time going by without one's being able to placate this violence, to solve this uncertainty. *Siege* implies the slow death of people in cities, streets, and houses made for peaceful everyday life. The siege is therefore often connected with the suffering of civilians rather than the sacrifice of soldiers. On the other hand, citizens of a beleaguered town or the garrison of a besieged castle were not the only ones to suffer pain and hunger. The local countryside doubtless was often scoured clean and empty by "scorched earth" devastation, by the defenders prior to them retreating behind their walls, making the maintenance of the besiegers that much more difficult.

Ideally, the attacker's lines would totally encircle the object of their attention, but due to physical limitations, sometimes this was not possible. The presence of water was often a problem. When the defender's position was on the bank of a river, then the river itself had to be blockaded to deny its use to those defenders and whoever wanted to come to their rescue. When there was a larger expanse of water involved, the attackers had to patrol with warships to seal off the intended target or else be prepared to live with the fact that the defenders would retain the ability to resupply themselves by virtue of their access to the sea or river in question. The attrition siege was thus based on patience, watchfulness, logistics, and time.

The attacking force would be much less comfortably stationed than the besieged. The besiegers had to be accommodated in one or more temporary camps providing living quarters and some sort of military base. The appearance of such a camp had the gaily colored flags, banners, and tents of the kings, dukes, or counts. The senior noblemen's quarters were often luxurious with their shields, banners, and flags displayed as recognition. Around them there were the somewhat less spectacular temporary canvas homes housing the greater part of the army. It was doubtless a place of great activity with workshops where fletchers made arrows and carpenters built the assault engines, stables where grooms attended to horses, the comings and goings of wagons full of supplies, the marching of soldiers, and women and servants preparing meals. There was always the danger of running short of food, and camp conditions could become unsanitary. Unhealthy food and poor sanitation could result in outbreak of devastating diseases. Stores (food, hay, ammunition, and water), brought with the army or plundered from the neighborhood, and were also kept in large tents. It was not until the 17th century that military camps for armies in campaign were formally and orderly designed. Medieval camps were informal and arranged without great order and poor accommodation. Moreover, it was difficult to sustain the morale of the troops, who—idle and bored—frequently deserted during long periods of inaction.

It was of course important to establish sentry points both to guard the camp and to keep a watchful eye on the activities of the defenders. If the siege was to last long it was necessary to protect the camps by field fortifications (obstacles, moats, earth entrenchments, and palisades) to repulse counterattacks launched by the beleaguered garrison. A *sortie* or a *sally* was a brusk operation carried out by the defenders who took advantage of the besiegers' off-guard moments. Such a venture had various purposes. The beleaguered garrison could simply intend to create a little havoc in the enemy lines; they rushed out, struck, and inflicted as much damage as possible to the attacker's camp, then returned within the castle walls before the attackers could react. The sally could also be launched in coordination with a relieving, army and the purpose of the action was to break the blockade and lift the siege. When the supplies of the besieged ran out, when the garrison's hopes were dashed, the raid had the sole purpose of securing food stuffs. Of course, there was always the chance that the members of the sortie—delighted by their success or perhaps with their bloodlust up—might stay out too long. Then the besieger's force would quickly converge on the place of the attack, and the sortie party could

be repulsed or overwhelmed. Surprise counterattacks were psychologically quite important for the morale and tactically might turn the tide of the siege by breaking the blockade and disorganizing and driving the besiegers back.

Siege Artillery

The pressure on the besieged was increased by archers and crossbowmen deployed behind mantlets and pavis (wooden protective screens) shooting arrows and bolts, some incendiary—fire constituted a very real hazard to the defenders whose houses within the castle or the town were often made of wood with thatched roofs. Even more devastating were the bombardments effected by siege artillery machines, the word *artillery*—in its primary and true meaning—denotes every variety of hurling or launching machine. Those primitive forms of artillery, already employed in the ancient times and revived during the Crusades, were called engines. They were designed, built, and used by specialists called *ingeniatores* (whence the word *engineer*). These men were not regarded as proper soldiers, and, for centuries, they were hired civilian specialized carpenters and lumberjacks. In Britain, it was not until 1856 that the Royal Engineers were formed into a single military unit including soldiers and officers, engineers, sappers, and miners.

The *ballista* or *springal* was effectively a giant crossbow; it had an arm which was forced by tension and—when released—shot a missile generally in the form of a dart or a spear.

The catapult was an ancient hurling machine which was first recorded to be used by the tyrant Dionysus I of Syracuse in 400 B.C. The catapult was a nevroballistic or torsion weapon relying for propellant power on twisting and releasing an elastic material. It was composed of a solid timber framework holding a pivoted arm tightly strained on a rotating roller fitted on a tensile material such as twisted rope or horsehair or sinew. The arm was winched down, and the missile was then loaded in a kind of spoon or a sling. A system allowed it to unlock the mobile arm which, owing to the tension of the rope, was released up with great strength; the rotating upright movement of the arm was brought to an abrupt vertical stop against a solid crossbeam fitted with a padded cushion resulting in the projectile being propelled in high, curving trajectory. By angling the whole machine or changing the angle of the crossbar, the trajectory of the missile could be altered. There was also a variant that worked with a large bow rather similar to a ballista.

The *trebuchet* (also called a *magonel*)—probably introduced during the Crusades—was another hurling machine. The principle of the trebuchet was quite sim-

Trebuchet Being Winched Down

ple. The propellant energy was provided by a solid, heavy weight of several tons (a wooden box or container filled with earth and stones); this counterpoise was fixed to the short arm of a huge pivoted beam resting on a solid framework. The long arm was winched down to the ground, and the missile was loaded in a sling placed at its end. The loading procedure could take some time, needing a large crew to winch the arm down. When the arm was released, it went up violently under the weight of the counterpoise, the sling opened by centrifugal force, and the missile was then flung through the air with a high parabolic trajectory.

Projectiles launched by catapults and trebuchets were mainly stones or rocks which killed men, crushed brattices, staggered merlons, punched walls, collapsed towers, and destroyed houses and huts. Catapults and trebuchets were also used for psychological and primitive chemical and bacteriological warfare. One launched pots of tar,

quicklime, powdered sulphur, and Greek fire — an evil mix of oil, pitch, quicklime, and sulphur. These projectiles shattered on impact, sending their burning contents flying in all directions, setting ablaze wooden houses and huts in castles and baileys and towns, and blinding the soldiers on the battlements. Medical experts of those days were not fully cognizant of the means by which disease was spread, but they knew it had something to do with dead and rotting flesh. Accordingly, the decomposing corpses of men and animals were among the projectiles. As already pointed out, diseases were important factors; until the second half of the 19th century, more soldiers died of sickness than by fighting. Excrement, trash, and garbage were also thrown with the intention of humiliating the opponent and poisoning his wells. It is recorded that on at least one occasion, beehives were similarly employed. More cruelly, the defenders' morale could be attacked by parading the captive survivors of a relief party in full view of the garrison, then killing them and hurling their heads into the besieged place; a variation was to speed the living prisoners on their way to their intended destination by catapult. Such drastic actions were intended to frighten and demoralize the defending party, but they were generally a last resort, a recognized and effective method of shortening a siege.

Hurling machines existed in numerous variations in shape, strength, and size, with many appellations such as the *balist, mangonneau, bricole, couillard,* or *perrier,* for example. The high curve trajectory of these weapons, hurling over walls, made them the ancestors of howitzers and mortars. The range of those siege engines was extremely various, depending on solidity, structure, weight of projectile, length of mobile arm, tension given to twisted rope, and so on. Experiments made in the 19th century with reconstructed machines indicated a range up to 450 meters (about 492 yards). Loading those devices took some time, so the rate of fire was low. Accuracy was rather hazardous, though some trebuchets were precise owing to the counterweight being slid up and down the short arm to vary the range. Their use was just as effective for defenders and for attackers. When both sides were armed with such weapons, the result was an artillery duel, and the issue of the siege could depend on who had the heaviest weapons and who aimed the best. Missiles of the

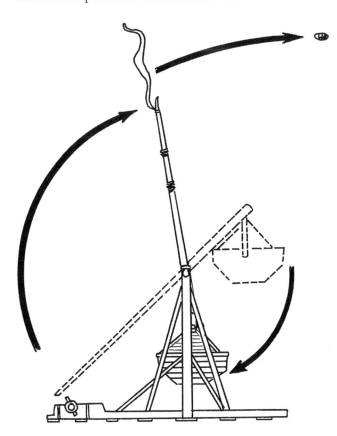

How the Trebuchet Worked

besieged could create considerable disruption in the camp of the attacking party, on grouped soldiers, on mobile wickerwork shields, and on assault towers. But trebuchets and catapults were useful against large stationary targets, and their inaccuracy increased terror and fright among the defenders. Indeed, even if the impact was unknown, damage was a certainty. The main targets of those hurling machines were thus dwellings inside the defenses rather than the defenses themselves, but it is certain they contributed their fair share in demolishing stone walls and towers. Catapults and trebuchets were deterrent weapons too, their menacing deployment was sometimes enough to decide the besieged to surrender.

Catapults and trebuchets were very strongly built because they were submitted to heavy mechanical forces. They were movable, transported piecemeal and reassembled on the spot. They could also be constructed on the site of the siege itself with timber collected in a nearby forest. It is very difficult to quantify the time needed to build such machines, but assuming a team of about twenty men — possibly two master carpenters and eighteen laborers/workmen —could build a catapult in two days, a trebuchet in a week, and an assaulting tower in two weeks. Once the engines had been built, they were moved to the spot from which they would fire, so some draft teams of men, horses, mules, or oxen were needed. Hurling machines were gradually superseded and permanently replaced by heavy firearms (siege guns and mortars) during the second half of the 15th century.

Breach

Blockade and bombardment were preparatory actions; they preceded the most important and most dangerous phases of the siege — the making of a breach and the assault. These phases of the siege were highly hazardous because the attackers were in a disadvantageous position, so repeated calls for negotiation and surrender were made. If such actions were refused, the siege continued. The main offensive was always directed toward a weak point of the defense: a low wall, a rampart deprived of ditch, a tower of small dimensions, or a ill-defendable suburb in a town, for example. When the assailant disposed of numerous troops, the main attack was completed by diversions on other points in order to oblige the defenders to scatter their forces. A decisive assault could be done in two main ways: either by assaulting the top of the wall or by making a breach.

Assaulting the top of the wall could be achieved by throwing grab-dredgers fitted with a rope or by using scale ladders. Anyone can imagine the chance taken by an armored man climbing a 10 meters (about 393 feet) high unsteady ladder holding a sword and a shield under a hail of projectiles: arrows, stones, darts, and spears. However, tales of cascades of smelted metal or boiling oil cast down by defenders must be discounted as untrue or exceptional: These materials were too expensive and too difficult to manipulate in combat conditions from a narrow wall-walk. Other burning materials were probably dropped over battlements down on the attackers to inflict serious burns and set the assault machine afire. These included hot water, burning straw, red-hot sand, and — when available — quicklime and "Greek fire" (probably made of sulphur, naphtha and quicklime) which burned on water, was very difficult to put out, had an intense heat, and stuck to whatever it touched. If the ladder was not repulsed, the attacker was very vulnerable while ascending and when he reached the top of the parapet.

A much safer method of assaulting the top of the wall was by means of a *beffroy* or *belfry*. Used in the ancient times, called *helepole* by the Ancient Greek, the *belfry* was a mobile wooden assault tower as high as the wall to be conquered, which could be two or three-stories high. The tower consisted of a strong timber frame mounted on wheels or on large wooden rollers. It was moved by means of capstans, pulleys and ropes maneuvered and winched (or simply pushed) by a party of men. The tower was rolled close to the wall; it was fitted with ladders permitting the assaulting party to climb in safety. The summit included a platform where a group of archers could shoot at the defenders; the platform also included a sort of drawbridge which was dropped allowing attackers to set foot on the parapet for a hand-to-hand combat with the defenders. Because the belfry was made of timber, it was vulnerable to fire; therefore, it was covered on its front and sides with wet rawhides or turf to resist incendiary projectiles thrown by the besieged. The utilization of this machine was very slow. The belfry was built on the spot, which meant that the attackers had to have timber, building materials, and skilled carpenters to erect the device. A steady track had to be made for moving the cumbersome and clumsy machine into position, and it rolled with great difficulty. Sometimes they had to fill in a deep ditch, an operation that required a large party of men working while under a rain of projectiles. In addition, the preparation of the track clearly revealed the intention of the besiegers and the point where the assault was going to take place, giving the besieged time to reinforce the very point of attack.

On one occasion an assault tower was used in a very particular way. During the wars between the German Empire and the free cities of Italy, at Crema in 1159, Emperor Friedrich I Barbarossa (1122–1190) was so irri-

tated by the losses suffered by his troops that he decided to bring the matter to an issue by breaking the will of the defenders. He ordered that eight hostages from Crema be tied to a belfry. It was a cruel retaliation because if the defenders of the city struck at the tower, they would kill their fellow citizens. When the assaulting tower was moved to the walls, loaded with warriors who were using the defenseless bodies as shields, the hostages encouraged the defenders to kill them to save the city. This heroic deed alas did not prevent Crema from being conquered in January 1160. After six month of siege, the city was taken by famine, and Barbarossa ordered the slaughter of the inhabitants, the destruction of the walls, and the burning of the houses. So died, after six centuries of life, one of the most lively communities in Italy.

Assaulting by making a breach consisted of destroying a portion of the defensive wall. To do so, the attackers could use a mine. This technique required skilled specialists. Special units of experienced miners and engineers would select the weakest spot, dig an underground gallery under the wall, and hollow out a space by removing masonry. As the tunnel progressed, its sides and roof were supported with wooden timbers to prevent the entire operation from prematurely crashing down on the unfortunate tunnelers. Once the required length of tunnel had been achieved, the excavation was packed with combustible material — cotton, straw brushwood, and others, packed with pig fat or petroleum. This was then set fire after the men had scrambled to safety. The wooden props, now the only means of support for the undermined section of the defenses, would burn away, and the wall above, bereft of support, would collapse.

Undermining was a long, arduous, and dangerous operation. It was not always successful and, obviously, not always possible if the castle was built on marshy or wet ground or on solid rock or if its foundations were particularly strong. Many castles were built on rock to preclude the possibility of demolition by mining. The great advantage of the mine was discretion. The defenders did not suspect its existence, and if they did, it was difficult for them to know its precise position. The attacker — if he had sufficient men — could dig more than one tunnel, but it took a long time.

To detect mining, the defenders established an *écoute* (listening post). They placed bowls of water at suspected sites so the surface of the water would reveal the slightest vibrations. When the mine had been detected and discovered, the besieged reacted by digging a countermine tunnel. When a mine and a countermine met, a grim skirmish, a dangerous and dreadful underground hand-to-hand combat ensued. The defenders could also try to

Opposite: Belfry

Mine

drive the intruders off by fire and flood, or they could fill up the tunnel by throwing stones, rubble, and other material. Another rather more exotic method of defeating tunnelers was for the defenders to unleash wild animals (dogs, cats, and, when available, rats, wolves, and bears). One can imagine the panic caused by the rapid advance of angry, confused and perhaps hungry animals as they rushed along the dark and narrow tunnel.

Mining was one of the oldest method of attacking a stronghold. Maybe this manner was used by Joshua to take Jericho in the end of the 13th century B.C. The walls "came tumbling down" probably more from a mine than from the sound of divine trumpets.

Another means of making a breach was sapping: Stones at the base of the wall were individually picked off, dislodged, or torn out until the wall collapsed. Sapping too was a very dangerous operation because the defenders dropped stones, threw down incendiary materials and spears, and shot down arrows on the exposed sappers. In reaction, a cat was constructed; a cat (also

called "penthouse," "rat," "chasteil" or "tortoise" from the Roman *testudo*) was a stout, strong movable timber gallery covered with a solid sloping roof. This shelter was intended to protect sappers, miners, or men attempting to fill a ditch. Just like the belfry, the wooden cat was vulnerable to fire and riveted with rawhide, sacks, or wet turf.

Another ancient method of making a breach was using a battering ram. In its simplest form the ram could be a tree trunk. It could also be more elaborate in the form of a strong beam without or, more often, with a metal point at one end, often in the form of a ram, adopted doubtless in consequence of the natural habit of this animal to butt with its head and horns. Known and used by the ancient warriors, the beam was maneuvered by a party of men giving a backward-and-forward movement against a gate or a masonry wall. The violent shocks worked by direct percussion but also by vibrations which loosened the stones. The defenders' reaction consisted of interposing a bunch of hay or hanging down big wads of

Battering Ram

padding between the wall and the metal head to absorb the force of the blows. They could also try to deviate the ram by catching its end with a rope fitted with a slip knot or gripping the ram head with long pincers to deaden the blows. And, of course, they riddled the attackers with various missiles. Therefore, rammers were protected by a sort of penthouse or cat in which the battering ram was suspended from the roof by means of solid ropes or chains. This provided not only protection but gave considerable momentum and thus increased the effectiveness of the battering operation.

Obviously, assaulting using ladder, belfry, undermining, sapping, or ramming was very difficult — even impossible — if the fortress was surrounded by a broad ditch filled with water. The only means left for the attackers then were to ferry assaulting troops by boat, or to construct an improvised bridge or a kind of dike across the wet moat with fascine, earth, brushwood, tree trunks, or whatever materials they could find. Another method was to get rid of the water by digging a deviation canal which left the defenders high and dry.

Ram Protected by a Cat. For the convenience of showing the inside of the device, the left side of the cat has been cut away.

Assault on a Fortress (after Tschachtlan Berner Chronik, 1470)

Assault

Ordinary knights were likely to see more of sieges than of battles in their military careers. Siege warfare, with its digging, sapping, mining, engineering, and complicated machineries, was an art which lay outside the knights' ken. It was the engineers who made the preparative work. The knights regarded themselves too noble to participate in such low activities. They often found the long inactivity of the siege irksome and sought diversions to while away the time. Challenges between garrison and besiegers were possibly organized, usually for a skirmish, a contest, or even a joust or a tournament *à outrance*. One of the most famous of siege combat was that of the *Combat des Trente* (Battle of the Thirty). This joust to the death took place during the siege of the castle of Josselin (Brittany, France) in 1351 and opposed thirty men on each side, the French knights defending the castle under command of Jean de Montfort to the English besiegers headed by Bemborough.

It was only when a breach was practicable or a siege tower built, that the knights would see action at last. The width of the breach varied with the method used to bring it about, and as soon as the breach appeared, the defenders did do their utmost to fill it with debris and all types of obstacles available. The frontal assault in the breach was launched by soldiers and knights, and it was regarded as a great honor to be among the first into a beleaguered fortress so many volunteered for this honor. The assaulting party — if they survived the fight — were rewarded. At the siege of Acre (Palestine) in 1189, the English king Richard I Lion Heart offered a gold piece to any man who would bring him back a stone from the walls of the city.

An assault was a confused and bloody hand-to-hand battle. It was a crucial confrontation for both parties and the turning point of the siege. Individual factors, such as physical fitness and bravery, played a central role, but pugnacity was not enough against greater numbers. A repulsed assault generally cost a lot of casualties; it could become a harrowing defeat that loosened all the bonds of discipline, generating fear and spirit of *sauve qui peut* (run for your life!) and resulting in a rabbling retreat. If the assaulting parties succeeded in penetrating the castle or the town, they would rush and fight their way to the gate to open the doors for their companions. Combat could continue, however, if the defenders had hastily built a *retirade*, another improvised defensive wall behind the breach to prolong the resistance. The defenders could also withdraw behind a second line of defense in the castle keep or in the urban citadel.

Aftermath of a Siege

A successful assault often resulted in pillage, rape, destruction, fire, and massacre. To avoid this terrible predicament, the defenders often chose to pay a ransom or negotiated an honorable capitulation before things really got that bad. The fate of a fortress taken by force was uncertain, and it greatly depended upon circumstances which were dictated by the mercy of the victors. The garrison might be taken prisoner; the people and the goods respected. But the place might also be sacked, women raped, and the garrison killed. At the siege of Calais in 1347, after eleven months of resistance the town was obliged to surrender to the king of England, Edward III; six bourgeois of the town accepted to be taken hostage, and the king wanted to hang them as retaliation. They were finally pardoned because of the kindness of the queen, who begged her royal husband for mercy. In some extreme case — as happened in the siege of Jerusalem in 1099 — the entire population was butchered including women and children. It was agreed — according to the principle of *guerre mortelle* (mortal combat) — that the responsibility for such outcomes lay squarely with the commander who, by failing to yield when summoned, brought their fate down on them. However, the victor was expected to uphold the standards of chivalry, but it

is an open question as to how far the leader should try to restrain his men.

Sacking an assaulted town or a castle taken by force was too often a convenient way to pay mercenaries and to obtain wealth, supplies, and goods. Spoils of war were deducted from pay, so a rich haul of booty might well prove to be nothing more than wages. Large-scale plundering and ghastly atrocities could be done in the heat of the moment as retaliation for the stubborn resistance of the fortress. Looting could also be systematically done because the defeated technically forfeited their goods for having rebelled against their lawful lord. The spoils were usually practically arranged and divided in a fixed proportion: one-third for the soldiers, one-third to the commanders, and one-third to the crown.

The Siege of Lisbon, 1147

In 1147, in an attempt to establish a worthy capital for his territory in Portugal, Alfonso Henriques I solicited the aid of an army of Crusaders who were on their way to the Holy Land during the Second Crusade. On June 16, 1147, the army — composed of about 30,000 English, Flemish, Norman, Frisian, and German troops — besieged the beautiful and flourishing city of Lisbon. No sooner had the Crusaders pitched their camp around the city walls than quarrels arose among them about the division of the expected booty. After a difficult negotiation with Alfonso, an agreement was reached, and the Moorish garrison was summoned to surrender. When they refused, the English seized a suburb, and a sortie launched by the besieged caused considerable damage to the attackers. In the meantime, the Normans and Germans had constructed several catapults with which they bombarded the city. As the siege went on, in Lisbon the scarcity of food made itself dramatically felt; the stench of corpses increased along with hunger, and the danger of an epidemic became menacing. At the end of September a confrontation took place when a mine gallery being dug by the Germans opened into a Saracen countermine, with disastrous results for the latter. The digging continued, and on October 17 a section of wall crashed. The Crusaders assaulted the breach but were met by the Moors who, fighting with courage and desperation, managed to repulse them. On the other side of the city, the attackers had built and put in position a large assault tower. The pressure on the exhausted garrison was so great that they decided to surrender. They negotiated to pay a huge ransom in exchange for respect of goods and people. This was agreed upon, and on October 23, 1147, King Alfonso, preceded by the archbishop of Braga, entered Lisbon. The solemnity of the moment and the seriousness of the agreement were however disturbed by the Flemish and the German knights

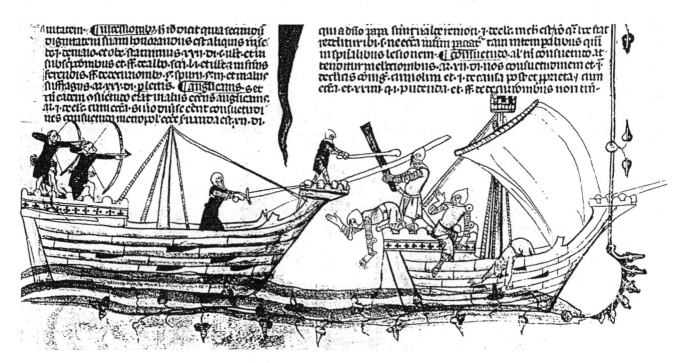

Sea Battle. A dramatic portrayal of a sea battle from an early 14th century manuscript clearly shows the functions of the forecastle and aftcastle as platforms for the fighting men.

who—in violation of the pact—entered the city and abandoned themselves to pillage and massacre of indescribable violence.

The Siege of Château-Gaillard, 1204

Château-Gaillard (originally called La Roche Gaillarde) was erected on a spur of the dominating river Seine near Rouen (Normandy, France). The huge castle was constructed in an astonishing short time from 1196 to 1198 by order of the duke of Normandy and king of England, Richard Lion Heart. Château-Gaillard was composed of four main parts. A huge four-story, almond-shaped dungeon with walls 5 meters (about 16 feet) thick reinforced with buttresses was crowned with crenelation and machicolation. The dungeon was hemmed with an elliptical-shaped skirt with living accommodations, moat, a gatehouse, and a drawbridge. The skirt was enclosed by a low enclosure flanked with towers including various service buildings. Finally, a huge triangular outwork was built including five towers, a moat, and another drawbridge. Château-Gaillard was considered impregnable, but it was, however, taken by the king of France, Philippe Auguste, after a six-month siege in 1204 through various tactics in siege warfare.

The French royal army first established a blockade around the place, but knowing that the besieged had supplies for two years, an attrition siege was out of question. In the first phase, catapults and trebuchets were used for a bombardment while miners dug a tunnel under the outwork, which was taken. The second phase of the siege was marked by luck and guile; the drain of a latrine was discovered, and a party of audacious soldiers scaled the wall of the outer enclosure. They reached a window in the chapel and succeeded in lowering the drawbridge to admit the rest of the besieging force. The bailey was then taken while the defenders took refuge in the dungeon. The final phase reverted to military means; after a combination of concentrated fire of catapult and mining, a breach was made in the shirt, and the dungeon was successfully assaulted. The seizure of Château-Gaillard resulted in the annexation of Rouen and Normandy. The castle was demolished by King Henri IV at the end of the 16th century, but its ruins and vestiges are particularly imposing today.

It is important not to overestimate the spectacular and dramatic aspects of siege warfare as just described. They were rarely pursued with such energy. Sieges were not all that frequent, and many were unsuccessful. It was rather unusual for a major town or an important castle to be taken by assault. Most fortresses fell by intrigue or attrition rather than through open warfare. It must be kept in mind that medieval armies were heterogeneous, temporarily raised, not very mobile, and never numerous. The attackers did not generally dispose of enough time to lead an attrition operation, had only a few hurling machines or none at all, and did not always have enough troops. Only the large conflicts which involved

Cargo Ship, 13th Century (after B. Langdström)

realms, large duchies, or coalitions— such as the wars opposing the French Capetian kings to the English Plantagenet sovereigns, the Crusade against the Albigenses, the Reconquista in Spain, the Crusades in Palestine, and the conflicts during the Hundred Years' War — saw the deployment of huge armies and exceptional operations. If siege warfare was comparatively common, large-scale siege warfare was exceptional for practical reasons: lack of time, combatants, and military means.

Naval Warfare

Sea battles— such as the battle of Sluis in June 1340 — were extremely rare in the Middle Ages. With the exception of Venice, it was not until the 16th century that states began to invest in permanent navies. However, naval war-

fare was characterized by smuggling and piracy, which were large-scale activities. We have already pointed out the important role played by the Vikings at the end of the Carolingian empire. At all periods, waters were infested by pirates. In the Northern Sea in the 13th and 14th centuries the Vitalie Brothers operated from Mecklenburg. In the Mediterranean Sea, the Saracens from northern Africa were a constant threat as early as the 9th century. Maritime insecurity in the Mediterranean Sea lasted until as late as 1830. A lot of ships were used in the Middle Ages, but basically there were two main categories: sailing merchantmen and galleys.

Merchantmen

Ships of the Middle Ages drew their inspiration from the Viking long ship. The Viking-styled long ship was

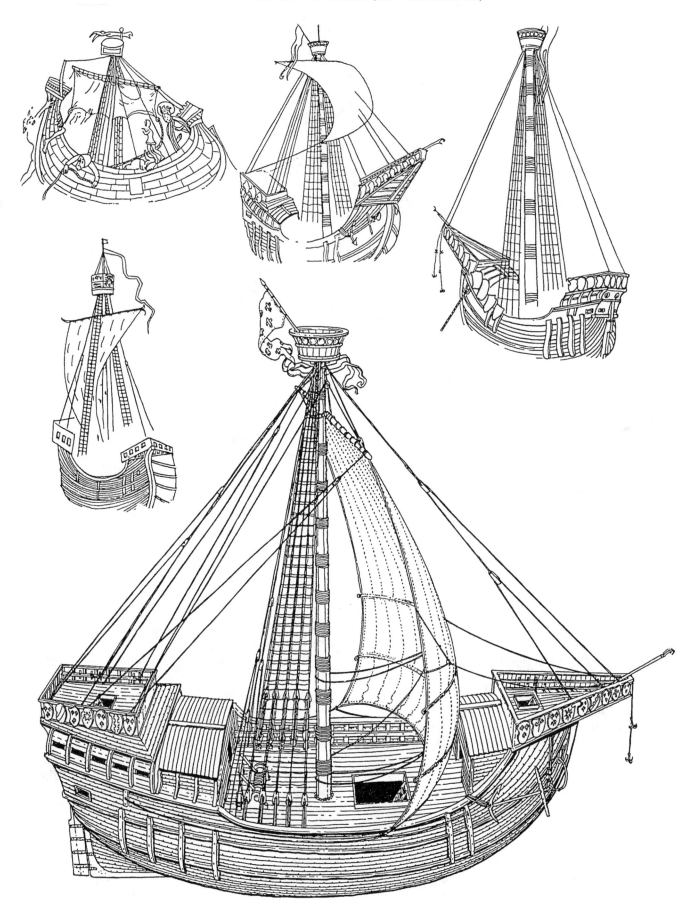

Opposite and above: Various Forms of Round Ship (after B. Langdström)

A Galley (after Furttenbach)

commonly used throughout the Middle Ages for various purposes such as medium cargo carrier, warship, or pirate vessel. Characteristic was clinker construction made of overlapping planks. She was swift, high-prowed, and easily maneuvered and moved by oars or by a large square sail. From this design evolved numerous types such as the northern *curragh* and *knorr*.

Merchantmen or "round ships" from their shape — something like a half walnut — were designed for carrying capacity and, since they needed capacious stowage above all, they were entirely dependant on sails for their moving power. They were beamy, high-sided, and driven by square sails or a combination of square sails and lateens. The square sail had reefpoints to furl the sail; mast shrouds had ladder-like lines for climbing. Until the invention of the gaff rig centuries later, the lateen was the most efficient sail for almost all purposes. It required little manpower to hoist and set, was quite efficient for windward work with the two main lateens boomed out on opposing sides (goose-winged), and provided a well-balanced sail area for down-wind work. When tacking

the wind does not push the sail, but the airflow on the outside of the sail's curved surface pulls the sail and hence the ship forward. It is basically the same principle as the airflow over curved wings lifts a modern airplane. Round ships were rather good sea boats but were cumbersome to handle and comparatively unmaneuverable. Unless flying with a fair wind astern, they were no match for an attacking galley and rather difficult to use for maritime fighting.

A variant of the round ship was the northern *kogge* or *cog* — probably invented by the Frisians from the Netherlands at the end of the 12th century. The cog too existed in various sizes and capacities. She had one or more masts with square sails, could be as long as 30 meters (98 feet), and 7 meters (about 23 feet) broad, and could carry up to 300 tons. An important technical improvement was the center rudder which was introduced probably in the 12th century and became standard of all ships.

During the Crusades, sea travel was greatly intensified, and new and larger ships were required. Half way between a merchantman and a galley came the *galleass*, a hybrid cargo-carrying ship dependant upon both sail and oar power and a thoroughly seaworthy vessel. A large galleas of the Venetian type — which carried the Crusaders to the Levant and brought Indian spices back to Italy — might be as long as 55 meters (180 feet), although other types were usually shorter than this. *Dromons*, *naves*, and *hurks* were some kinds of galleasses for cargo. Shipping horses required special boats. In Byzantine writing they were referred to as *triremes* and *chelandia*, in Muslim works as *tarida* and *usari*, and in Christian sources as *huissiers*, *salandria* or *uscerii*. These highly specialized boats were fitted with large doors in the stern and had ramps for easily loading and unloading the animals. Onboard stabling arrangements included mangers, stall rails, bedding of esparto grass, and rope and ringbolts to secure the horses.

Merchant ships were primarily intended for transport, but for defense purposes high wooden fore and stern castles furnished with crenels were built at each end. These raised castles were also (wrongly) thought to give ships greater stability in heavy seas. On top of the mast there was an observation and combat post, the crow's nest. From these high-leveled combat emplacements, soldiers could throw down javelins and spears while archers and crossbowmen could fire down on the decks of their enemies and, if need be, on their own decks if it were boarded.

War at sea was a fierce and brutish business with little skill or subtlety; it was, indeed, nothing more than an extension of war at land. The object of battle was to disable and weaken the enemy ship and to soften up the enemy from a short distance with bow and crossbow; the second act was to get close to the opponent with grapnels and board the ship. The final and determinant action was a hand-to-hand assault to overwhelm the crew with the same weapons as those used in land warfare. For mutual protection two or more ships were sometimes lashed together to form a kind of more-or-less precarious stronghold in a furious mêlée. Ports were the places where fleets tended to gather, and where they could be destroyed. So naval actions normally took place near the coast, in shallow waters rather than out at sea. The capture of ports situated on estuaries gave the chance to control access to rivers and the possibility to ship men, supplies, and other heavy equipment such as siege engines, further into the country.

Galleys

The most effective warship — as it had been throughout antiquity and as it lasted until the 17th century — was the oared galley. For both Christians and Muslims, that was the best ship that adapted to the specific conditions of the Mediterranean Sea with its very small tidal amplitude, few constant winds, and irregular currents. Medieval galleys and galleasses had evolved out of the Byzantine dromons which were directly inspired by those of the Ancient Phoenician, Greek, and Roman navies. They were not totally independent of wind for their propulsion, as they had one or more short masts with triangular lateen sails. The sails were operated by a crew of sailors including carpenters and shipwrights and a master barber/surgeon. Galleys — with their comparatively shallow drafts — were designed for speed and mobility, not for their carrying capacity or seaworthiness in anything other than the months of summer. Galleys were always warships used for carrying armed forces, including from 50 to 200 soldiers on board, and for fighting and capturing the enemy.

In the days prior to the advent of guns on ships, tactics at sea were quite similar to those adopted by the cavalry, with the ships advancing in line abreast against the enemy. Occasionally Greek fire — an incendiary weapon — was used. Greek fire was probably invented by the Byzantines, and there were a number of closely guarded formulas. It was composed of a mixture of saltpeter, pounded sulphur, pitch, unrefined ammoniacal salt resin, and turpentine. It could be used as a liquid mixture and ejected from copper tubes so that it came out as a roaring flame, rather like a modern flamethrower. It could also be made into a mixture designed for a primitive hand grenade; it was poured into thin clay pots fitted with a fuse and thrown by hand or by means of a catapult. On highly inflammable wooden decks, or among tangled canvas and cords, Greek fire — which could not be put out by water — was indeed a deadly weapon. When conditions were favorable, blazing rafts were sometimes floated toward a trapped enemy. However, even if fire was an effective killer at a range, it was a clumsy weapon which could endanger the user almost as seriously as his enemy. A burning ship at sea was — and still is — one of the things most feared by sailors. There was no way to escape except by committing themselves to the sea and all its danger.

The *ram* was still the principal weapon of the war galley; it was a projecting device made of wood reinforced with metal, some 2 to 3 meters (eight to twelve feet) forward from the bow like the horn of a charging rhinoceros and could slice clean through an enemy ship. It was upon the men who manned the heavy oars that the galley depended for its speed in approach and for the run-in that preceded the action of ramming and boarding. Ramming could occur in two ways: either a direct beam-on attack with the objective of shattering the opponent's side or a glancing blow right down the side of the enemy, shattering his oars and leaving him stationary and helpless.

Venetian Galley (after Gueroult)

The final act was to close in on the opponent with grapnels and pour on board. Archers and crossbowmen would open fire hoping to clear the decks and facilitate the attack of the boarding party. Sea fighting was essentially land fighting afloat.

From the outside, the galley was a thing of beauty, with elegant lines from the gracefully decorated prow to the equally gilded and ornamented poop where the officers had their living quarters. But the inside of the galley was a hell. The power and speed of the galley varied with the size of the vessel and the number and disposition of the oarsmen. The human machinery that toiled below decks in circumstances of almost unbelievable hardship was made up of condemned criminals and captive Muslim slaves on Christian galleys (and Christians captives on Muslim galleys). These were supplemented by men who—to escape the jail that awaited debtors—had come to an arrangement with their creditors and served a necessary number of years until their debts was cleared; these men were paid and also enjoyed better living conditions than the slaves and the criminals. The expression "working like a galley slave" has passed into the language. On a large galley there could be some fifty oars and the oar men were chained six to a bench that was slightly more than one meter (four feet) wide and covered with sacking stuffed with wool.

The officer in charge stayed aft with the captain from whom he received his orders. There were subalterns, underofficers, some amidship and others at the prow. These were armed with whips with which they flogged the naked bodies of the slaves. When the captain gave the order to row, the officers gave the signal with a whistle and very soon all oars (each one weighing some 57 kilograms, about 125 pounds) rhythmically stroke the water as one. The stroke was a slow one, no more than 26 a minute at racing speed. The oarsmen were chained; they rose together from their seats. Placing a foot on the bench ahead to gain leverage, and they inserted their blades as far forward as possible; then they would all laboriously draw on the oar, falling back slowly into their seats as they did so. A gong or a drum provided encouragement and the beat. Only when there was a good breeze—and no enemy to ram—could the slave rowers at the galley benches take their ease. Sometimes they rowed for hours without the slightest rest or break. On these occasions the officers would go around and put pieces of bread soaked in wine into the mouths of the wretched rowers to prevent them from fainting, for which they redoubled their whip blows. If one of the rowers fell exhausted over his oar, he was flogged until he appeared to be dead and was thrown overboard without ceremony. It is little wonder that slave revolts aboard galleys were marked by unimaginable savagery. These would occur often during the action and boarding work. If it appeared that their own ship was being taken by the enemy, the slaves would rattle their chains and howl to be set free.

The use of slaves produced further problems when ships were in the harbor. The slaves could not permanently live aboard, so elaborate prison quarters had to be constructed to house them ashore. They also required guards and maximum security. Many a traveler, captive soldier, or pilgrim ended his days on the oar bench unless, or until, his ransom was forthcoming.

In the clash between Muslim crescent and Christian cross that lasted for centuries in the Mediterranean Sea, these hard conditions of life were to be known for generation upon generation. Whether Christian or Muslim, the fighting galley was an evil-smelling vessel, and conditions on board were fearful. The exception were the crews manning Venetian galleys; the oar men were volunteer free men who were well treated, and they formed a huge mass of well-armed soldiers when it came to boarding the enemy so that fewer permanent soldiers had to be carried. Venice was the most maritime-conscious nation in the Mediterranean for more than 500 years, and for most of this period the Venetians led the way in the small variations in design of the fighting galley.

Navigation

In the Middle Ages the oceans were considered hostile and mysterious; the relationship between man and sea was an uneasy one marked by anxiety and superstition. The development of ships from their earliest days was retarded by caution and traditionalism. Medieval navigation was slow, sometimes impossible in windless or stormy periods, and totally interrupted in the winter months from November to March (even longer in the ice-frozen seas of northern Europe). During that time, boats were brought ashore for refitting and repairing. The duration of a sea journey was very irregular depending upon weather, wind, and current. The average speed per hour was 8 to 10 kilometers (about 5 to 6 miles per house) with a maximum of 15 kilometers (about 9 miles) per hour if the wind was favorable. It took about four days to sail from Lübeck to Danzig several weeks from Italy to the Holy Lands with calls at Crete and Cyprus. Along the Atlantic shores, European sailing experience was almost entirely coastwise.

Navigation was in its infancy, and early sailors solved their problems of navigation by observing natural phenomena. Tides, currents, and changes of color of the sea could be indications of position. Flocks of eider ducks were a sure sign of land within 100 miles. Simple navigation close to the coastline was based on the three Ls of lookout, lead line, and log. The lead line had a hollow weight to sample the seabed; the log, flung over the side, helped the sailor estimate his speed through the sea. The simple cross-staff enabled the mariner to gauge the height of a celestial body — such as Polaris, the North Star — above the horizon and thus establish how far north or south he was; the lower the North Star was in the sky, the farther south was his ship. Experienced pilots were familiar with the sea around their harbors, had knowledge of the weather, and were expert in knowing what flow and safe anchorage might be expected. Charts did not exist, but the knowledge of capes and headlands, islands, depths, bays, and anchorages was mostly carried in the pilot's head. One navigated by using the particulars of the coastline such as islands, church towers and, watchtowers. Lighthouses existed, but there were very few of them, they were primitive with a short range, and they were lit only in bad weather. Coastwise navigation was not without danger, though. Fog and mist, sandbanks, reefs and rocks, sudden gales and winds, and strong tidal currents throwing the boat ashore had to be reckoned with to avoid fatal accidents. In addition there was always the danger of lurking pirates and that of criminal wreckers who intentionally drove ships into dangerous reefs by false light signal, then killed the sailors and plundered the stranded boats.

Nautical experiences and sailing art were transmitted by word-of-mouth from generation to generation. At the end of the 13th century, written charts, portulants and piloting books appeared in Spain and spread rapidly throughout Europe. The principal navigational instrument was the compass, which came into use in northern Europe about 1340. The astrolabe — a means of fixing the altitude of heavenly bodies — was invented by the Arabs around 700 A.D. On long journeys across deserts without landmarks, the problem of Arab travelers were akin to those of mariners out of sight of land. In the darkness of the desert with clear skies, the Arabs became aware of the shifting patterns of the heavenly bodies. Astronomy was thus developed by the people of the Near-East.

Until the 12th century, naval activities were not diversified. The same man was both owner and captain of his ship; the cargo he transported and traded was his; he recruited his own crew, over whom he had complete authority. With the advent of the Crusades, trading and traveling were intensified, ships increased in number and in size, and a specialization of the crew became necessary. Under the direction of the captain, able seamen supervised a crew composed of leading seamen, sailors, shipmates, and ship's boys. Other team members appeared such as shipwright, surgeon, accountant, and secretary. The naval business too was diversified. Fitters financed, equipped and exploited one or more ships;

Seal of the Hansa City of Lubeck, Germany, 1256, Displaying a Boat

charterers bought or hired ships for one or more voyages. Naval merchant companies were constituted which spread the risks, facilitated financing, and increased tonnages and thus profits.

Inland Navigation

Medieval navigation also included numerous small boats with a great variety of functions and names for shipping to harbors and ferrying cargo and passengers on local and regional rivers. In spite of sandbanks, watermills, bridges, and tolls, inland water transport was an important mean of communication especially for large and heavy cargo which was impossible to transport on bad roads. Inland boats were moved by wind, oars, or men or horses pulling from the bank. Inland transport was a flourishing business — not only on the great rivers such as the Seine, Rhône, Meuse, Rhine, and Danube, but on all smaller European rivers as well. The guilds of inland transporters were powerful and respected. The motto of the Parisian guild became that of the city

Hamburg, ca. 1497 (after Staatsarchiv der Freien und Hansestadt Hamburg)

itself *Fluctuat nec Mergitur* (beaten by the flow but never sinking). Navigation on rivers was much less risky than sea transport, but it was very slow because of natural conditions and was exposed to dangers. Every baron claimed the right to charge tolls to merchants passing through his land. If he wanted a lot of money in a hurry, he rarely had any objection to plundering the traders of all their goods. Ferrymen could also be victims of aggression, extortion, and ransom by thieves and river-pirates.

11

Crusaders in Palestine

Church and Violence

The traditions of the primitive Christian Church were wholly opposed to warfare of any kind, in sharp contrast to the *jihad*, the holy war which played so great a part in the history of Islam. "He that liveth by the sword, shall perish by the sword" had been the Church's teaching since time immemorial. After the adoption of Christianity in 313 by Emperor Constantine, practical and political considerations forced a change in this attitude.

Christ as Leader of the Crusade (after a 13th Century Apocalypse)

The Church of Rome continued to regard war with suspicion until Augustine wrote on the subject. The theologist and bishop of Hippone, Saint Augustine (354–430 A.D.), developed the idea that heretics and pagans could legitimately be converted by force, creating the concept of a "just war." After the 8th century "just" wars became politically possible, and the Carolingians kings fought wars of expansion — presented as religious wars — against the Saxons, Muslims, and pagans. This became the mission of the western warrior, and the idea of soldier of Christ against heathens became a sacred duty in the troubled times of the 9th and 10th century. The reward for those who fell in just wars was eternal life. The warrior came to be regarded as the defender of the faith, and his activities were blessed by the Church as long as he conformed with the Christian ideal. The Church had put forth several edicts (Peace and Truce of God), as previously discussed, and firmly encouraged knighthood to control and tame the warrior instinct. As an instrument of papal foreign policy, the Crusades were conducted against the Turks in Palestine, the Moors in Spain, and the pagans in northeast Europe. The Crusades had three main objectives. Religiously, they were intended to reconquer the Holy Sepulcher in Jerusalem, to keep it in Christian hands, but also to repulse the enemies of the Christian faith in Spain and to conquer territories and evangelize pagans in northeastern Europe. Socially, the Crusades proved a convenient outlet to divert the energy and aggressiveness of the most belligerent warriors, greedy adventurers, and boisterous knights by removing them from Europe and sending them to use their violence elsewhere in the service of the Church. Politically, the

Crusades represented the backlash of Christendom against Islamic conquest; the Byzantines wanted Western assistance in expanding their territories and stabilizing their frontiers; the papacy and the German emperor saw the expeditions as bringing some measure of unity to Christendom under their leadership.

The First Crusade

Pilgrimage was a penitential system created by the Church. The pilgrim atoned for his sins by the suffering and discomfort of a hard (sometimes dangerous) journey far from his home, and enjoyed the blessing of having visited a holy place such as Canterbury in southern England; Rocamadour, Saint-Denis, Tours, or Chartre in France; Rome in Italy; and Santiago de Compostella in Spain. The most prestigious place of pilgrimage was naturally the Holy Land of Palestine with Jerusalem. Pilgrims had traveled to Jerusalem to worship at the scenes of Christ's life and death for centuries, and they continued to do so after Palestine had been conquered by Muslims. The Arabs—though professing the faith of Islam—refrained from molesting the Christian pilgrims as the pilgrimages were an important source of income. A Christian community was allowed to stay in Jerusalem and maintain the Church of the Holy Sepulcher.

This situation of status-quo was seriously disrupted when the fanatical Seljuk Turks conquered Byzantine and Arab territories including Palestine in the 11th century. Therefore, Crusaders used the appellation "Turk" for all their Muslim enemies regardless of ethnic background. The "Turks," in turn, called the western invaders "Franks" without considering if they were English, German, Italian, or French. After the capture of Jerusalem in 1071, Christians pilgrims to the Holy Places were molested, ransomed, arrested, imprisoned, and even sold as slaves.

Reports of these abuses inspired Pope Gregory VII in his desire to lead a Christian army to the rescue of Jerusalem. The Byzantine emperor Alexis I Comnenus, who had ascended the throne in 1081, was determined to recover the lost provinces but found his resources unequal to the task. He requested the military help of the great lords and princes of the west. With a mixture of enticement and appeal, he excited their sense of outrage by describing in grisly detail the atrocities committed by the Turks and their contempt for the holiest shrines of Christianity and explained the threat they represented. He added that, besides the holy relics, Jerusalem was crammed with gold, treasures, and beautiful women. The French pope Urban II (1042–1099)—who had succeeded Gregory on the throne of Saint Peter in 1088—was deeply moved by the situation in the Holy Land, but he was also concerned about the depredations of Christian warriors in their own lands. He sought therefore to unify the quarrelling lords behind one great cause under his leadership and the authority of the Church. He was determined to carry out his predecessor's plan to provide military aid to the beleaguered Christians of the East, and he set in motion one of the most extraordinary events in the history of western Europe: the Crusades.

There were some advantages and privileges to going on crusade. Sinful knights and other people were offered a chance to redeem themselves. The Church gave expression to the revolutionary concept of the crusading indulgence. Those who fell in battle against the heathen would earn the salvation of their soul and a place in Paradise. In Saint Bernard's own word "killing for Christ" was not homicide; the extermination of injustice was desirable, and "to kill a pagan is to win glory for it gives glory to Christ." Crusaders had—in theory—temporary clerical status; they did not have to pay taxes or pay off any debts. The Church also promised to protect a Crusader's family and property against usurping claimants. Many Crusaders were motivated by religious zeal, but many knights did not undertake such a lengthy, costly, and dangerous expedition merely for the sake of faith. It was indeed no trivial matter for an established knight to go on crusade. To pay for the journey, equipment, horses, provisions, and staff to get him to the Holy Land, many a knight had to sell a part of his estate or borrow money by mortgaging his fief as a pledge. A crusade represented a splendid opportunity for landless younger sons and for wild and ruthless adventurers to make their fortunes and conquer new estates in the East. The papacy saw the Crusades as a way of harnessing the concept of knighthood to spiritual ends and of removing bellicose warriors from the west. Many knights saw the opportunity offered by the Crusades as a solution to earthly ills, with the promise of absolution and heavenly reward as well.

The First Crusade was preached by Pope Urban at the council of Clermont in France the end of November 1095. Urban set off on a tour of France to gather support for the Crusade. He was an evangelist preacher who raised the emotions of his listeners to a fever pitch, and the response was overwhelming. Sermons by bishops and itinerant preachers brought in immense crowds of the common people. Before long, huge numbers of enthusiast people "took the cross," the symbol of their holy pledge sewn onto cloaks and tunic, and shouted aloud "Dieu le veult!" (Deus li volt! That is God's will!). An unofficial and spontaneous crowd of peasants departed in early 1096. Undisciplined and ill-prepared, this "Crusade of the Poors" led by one Peter the Hermit, left behind it a track of pillage and disorder until it finally came to a disastrous end on the coast just across from Constantinople where they were massacred by the Turks.

In the meantime the noble leaders of the First Crusade proper were more cautious in preparing for the expedition. Five armies were raised and set off for the Holy Land in the summer of 1096 under the leadership of Count Raymond of Toulouse, Count Godfrey of Bouillon, Count Hugh of Vermandois (brother of the French king), Duke Robert of Normandy (brother of the king of England), and Buhemund of Otranto (leader of Normans settled in Sicily). The leader of the expedition was Urban's legate bishop Adhemar of Le Puy. They were inspired by religious devotion, desire to travel, and adventure and most probably by the hope of new lands and power. Their number is rather difficult to estimate, but it seems that there was a total of about 3,000 or 4,000 knights on horse and 31,000 soldiers on foot which included civilians.

The journey was particularly difficult, the Crusaders suffered burning heat and thirst, outbreaks of illness, and enemy ambushes. Following three different routes, the armies met in spring 1097 at Constantinople, and the real operations began. Nicaea was recaptured; Antioch was besieged and taken after a grueling seven-month siege. On the way Baldwin established the first Christian state at Edessa. Exhausted by illness, thirst, and starvation and weakened by the military operations, the Crusaders, however, managed to besiege and capture Jerusalem in July 1099.

Carried away by their success, they indulged a terrible frenzy of slaughter — a horrible holocaust that raged for three days killing almost the whole population, some 70,000 men, women, children, Jews, Muslims, and even Christians and Byzantines. The enthusiastic faith had turned to fanaticism and racial hatred, and an army dedicated to God's service proved as sinful as any other. The rabid ferocity of the sack showed how little the Church had succeeded in Christianizing atavistic instincts. The horrors and the massacre of Jerusalem were committed in a moment of folly and bloodthirstiness which was later to be repaid in full by the Muslims. Their effect upon the world of Islam was traumatic, and the memory of the massacre — even centuries later — prevented any attempts at some accommodation between cross and crescent. The religious intolerance of the Western Christians was far in excess of anything known in the East.

For centuries the Byzantines had traded with the Arabs, who, for their part, had usually shown a reasonable degree of religious tolerance toward Jews and Christians in the territories they occupied. The balance between ideal and reality was never achieved, and the Crusades were a mixture of religious enthusiasm, petty jealousy, bad organization, credulousness, racism, greed, and hatred.

The Kingdom of Outremer

The victorious army of the First Crusade might have been inspired by religious ideals, but it moved among political realities, and it proved impossible to reconcile faith and politics. The secular princes of the leadership set up Latin feudal territorial units, no different from their European counterparts, together forming what was then called the Frankish settlement of *Outremer* (overseas) with institutions closely modeled on those of their homelands. Outremer — extending for nearly 500 miles stretching from the Gulf of Aqaba to Edessa — included the kingdom of Jerusalem, the counties of Tripoli and Edessa, the principalities of Antioch and Galilee, the lordships of Transjordan and Sidon, and twelve lesser fiefs. All were divided into feudal domains, the holders of which owed the customary homage and feudal duties to their lords, counts, and king. It should be noted that the crusading barons had carved their principalities and counties first and then *elected* the king of Jerusalem from among themselves. Godfrey of Bouillon was elected "Advocate of the Holy Sepulcher" as he was too modest and pious to be king of Jerusalem. His successor, Baldwin of Edessa, was elected king of Jerusalem. The successive kings of Outremer had restricted power resulting in poor solidarity, organization, and unity. The position of the Latin states in Palestine was thus rather weak, these being only a beachhead sustained by the belief that God wished His children to occupy His personal fief and by the powerful Genoese, Pisan, and Venetian fleets controling the sea, eager for a very lucrative commerce. Only a few Crusaders stayed in the Holy Land, and many returned home after the successful campaign of 1099.

The Crusades lasted for almost 200 years, and during this long period, crusading armies and pilgrims came and went, but there were also Syrian-born Christians (called "Poulains") who were permanently established in Outremer. Many generations were born and died in the Holy Land and knew no other home. The problem for those settlers — the majority Frenchmen — was to maintain their domination. French was the language of administration, and the ruling classes remained French until the end. The Crusades to Palestine certainly belonged more to France than to any other European nation. The flourishing of French was a European phenomenon connected with the dominance of the French culture. English, German, or Spanish knights learned French because it was the language of chivalrous romance in the 13th century, and French writers claimed that France — at the time of Philippe Auguste and Saint Louis — was the center of Europe and the arbiter of good taste. Men of ambition were educated in Latin and French because these were the languages of lordship, which led to careers in the Church and advancement at royal or noble households.

The arrogant Poulains were surrounded by native Christian populations (Maronite, Melkite, Syrian, and Armenian), and they treated with contemptuous tolerance an overwhelming Muslim population of townspeople and peasants and made no serious attempt to convert them to Christianity. The Christians were largely outnumbered, and there was always the fear of an uprising. The permanent Crusaders themselves were disunited. Princes and barons, bishops, and clergy, knights and Italian merchants, all thought of their own interests. Gradually, a fragile balance was set, treaties were made with local native rulers, and the Poulains became used to living side by side with the Muslims (who had no choice than to cohabit with the invaders). A kind of status quo was agreed upon by both communities, who did not think it advisable to resume hostilities on a large scale.

The overall picture of the Crusades was characterized by countless skirmishes, raids, attacks on pilgrimage trains, and general hooliganism by the Crusaders. On the Muslim side, the fighting against the western invaders was in addition to constant tribal warfare and the struggle for supremacy by various Islamic chieftains. Treaties were frequently struck between Turks and Franks for a designated period and just as frequently broken when the pillaging urge became too strong or the right opportunity offered an easy victory. When one part of the Latin state was under arms, another area could be enjoying a peaceful interlude in which friendships were made between opponents.

The uneasy and fragile cohabitation between both communities was unfortunately broken in 1144, when the Emir Zangi captured the ill-guarded town of Edessa. In Europe this produced immediate alarm, and Pope Eugenius II called for a new expedition. The Second Crusade—preached by the most celebrated churchman of the time, Bernard of Clervaux—was at first enthusiastically supported by the German emperor Conrad III and King Louis VII of France. It was, however, a complete failure. Many Crusaders never reached the Holy Land, and the two rival monarchs laid a fruitless siege at Damascus, after which they quarreled and returned to Europe in 1148.

Saladin's Reconquest

During the thirty years that followed the fiasco of the Second Crusade, the situation in Palestine underwent a complete and ominous change. The Muslim world—at the time of the First Crusade—was in turmoil, weakened and disunited by internecine warfare, plots, counterplots,

and alliances to be broken; emirs appointed by rulers to govern towns frequently rebelled against their overlords. Had the Turks been united, the First Crusade might well have been repulsed. But in the 12th century the Muslim world was recovering.

The sultan of Egypt and Syria, Salah ad-Din Yusuf ibn Ayub, better known as Saladin I (1138–1193), devoted his untiring energy to uniting the Muslims, raising a formidable fighting force, and waging a *jihad* against the Christian invaders. Saladin was a remarkable man of great character and courage; he was a brave fighter and a cunning statesman but also a chivalrous and generous warrior who gained the admiration even of his Christian opponents. The Latin states were politically too disunited and militarily too weak to put up an effective resistance to the overwhelming Muslim forces. In 1187, Saladin inflicted a disastrous defeat upon a Christian force in the region of Tiberias.

The battle took place on July 3 and 4, 1187, on the hottest days of the year. After a grim trek through waterless desert, the Christian army pitched camp on a hill called the Horns of Hattin. Saladin encircled the hill while the Christians spent a terrible night without water. At dawn the Muslims set fire to the scrub. Flames and smoke swept up the slopes, maddening men and horses tortured by thirst. It was a terrible battle in the appalling heat. The Christian infantry was slaughtered and after many charges, the Christian cavalry was repulsed under a hail of arrows. King Guy's force — reduced to about 150 combatants— had to surrender. The Muslims captured the True Cross in its gold reliquary. Saladin was merciful, and most prisoners were spared.

The decisive defeat at Hattin marked the beginning of the end for the Christians. Saladin pursued his campaign unchecked. One by one the Latin strongholds at Acre, Jaffa, Beirut, and Ascalon fell to him. In September 1187, Saladin's army appeared before the walls of Jerusalem, and after a two-week siege, the Holy City had to surrender. In humane contrast with the Christian sack of 1099, there was no bloodbath; instead, Saladin demanded ransoms and granted the defenders a safe passage back to the nearest Christian territory. Saladin continued his conquest until a small strip of land in Lebanon — with Tripoli, Tortosa, Antioch, and Tyre as the only important towns— remained in Christian hands.

The Third and Fourth Crusades

The news of the fall of Jerusalem caused widespread consternation in Europe and a determination to retrieve the Holy Land. The new pope, Gregory VIII, proclaimed a new crusade to the East. The Third Crusade was supported by the most powerful monarchs of Europe: the German emperor Friedrich Barbarossa, King Philippe Auguste of France, and King Richard of England. It was intended to be a serious and decisive expedition. Unfortunately, Barbarossa died on the way in 1190 after bathing in a cold mountain stream, but his troops went on and managed to recapture Antioch. Meanwhile the Christians in the Holy Land had taken the offensive and reconquered the port of Acre. They were then surrounded by Saladin, and for eighteen months besiegers, besieged, and would-be-relievers fought fiercely until Philippe and Richard arrived and captured the port in 1191. Again discord broke out between the royal Crusaders. Philippe and Richard quarreled bitterly over precedence and standing. Since Richard, as duke of Normandy and Aquitaine, was the French king's vassal, Philippe considered that Richard should accept his leadership. Richard, as king of England, did not see any reason why he should not be the boss. Finally, Philippe abandoned the crusade and returned to France, where he proceeded to invade Richard's territory. Richard continued the crusade, and his skill won him two victories over Saladin at Arnif and Jaffa which gained him the name of "Lion Heart." Richard established a remarkable courtly understanding with Saladin resulting in a truce and negotiation. But Richard did not achieve his aim: to reconquer Jerusalem. However, he succeeded in preventing the complete expulsion of the Latins. The Christians retained a small coastal strip from Ascalon to Acre with the right of access to Jerusalem.

At the end of the 12th century, it looked like the time of the Crusades was over. The great hope of delivering the Holy Sepulchre from the victorious infidels seemed impossible. By that time the Catholic Church was in a difficult situation. In 1198, Pope Innocent III decided to promote the papacy again, using the traditional method of preaching a crusade in a renewed attempt to gain Palestine for Christendom. The Fourth Crusade was begun in 1199 by a group of enthusiastic French noblemen led by Boniface, marquess of Montferrat. Zealously supported by the papacy, the new generation of Crusaders were however mainly motivated by personal ambition, wealth, and power. As they had no money to pay the voyage to Palestine, they turned to Venice, and by 1201 a squalid bargain was made with hard, cunning, and greedy Venetian businessmen. The Crusaders agreed to conquer the rival (Christian!) city of Zara from the king of Hungary. In 1202, they discharged their debt by storming the town, so completing Venetian domination over the Adriatic Sea. Pope Innocent III was indignant about this disgraceful diversion of his crusade; he condemned the "Crusaders" outright, but the worst was yet to come.

Taking advantage of serious problems of succession and internal troubles in the Byzantine Empire in 1204, the Crusaders and the Venetians sacked the ill-defended city of Constantinople which had been weakened by poor rulers. This was one of the most miserable events in history. Many people were killed, houses looted, churches plundered, priceless treasures lost, manuscripts burned, paintings destroyed, statues melted down for weapons and armor, and four famous bronze horses were stolen and brought to Venice where they can still be seen today above the portico of Saint Mark's Cathedral. The Fourth Crusade was a scandalous and odious mistake which set an unbridgeable gulf between Eastern and Western Christendom. It also showed the decline of the papacy which had entirely lost control of the expedition.

Eight years after the sack of Constantinople, there occurred a strange and tragic episode in the sorry history of the Crusades. In 1212, for obscure reasons, bands of children gathered in France and western Germany and set out to march with the intention of recapturing Jerusalem. Most of them perished from hunger and disease, and the few survivors, who got no farther than Marseilles and other ports in the Mediterranean, were seized for local brothels or lured by unscrupulous merchants aboard their ships and sold as slaves in northern Africa. This Children's Crusade probably formed the historical basis for the tale of the Pied Piper of Hamelin.

The Last Crusades

The Crusades dragged on for another eighty years after the scandalous fourth expedition. Pope Honorius III decided to make one more effort to liberate Jerusalem. In 1217 he persuaded the king of Hungary and the duke of Austria to take an army to Egypt for a Fifth Crusade. After a lengthy siege, they captured Damietta in November 1219, but they achieved no further successes.

The strange Sixth Crusade was not blessed by the papacy. Its leader was the unusual and excommunicated German emperor Friedrich II, the grandson of Barbarossa. In 1229, Friedrich, proclaimed himself king of Jerusalem and negotiated the treaty of Jaffa with the sultan of Egypt granting free access for Christian pilgrims to visit Jerusalem, Jaffa, Bethlehem, and Nazareth.

The Seventh Crusade — preached by Pope Innocent IV in 1249 and led by King Louis IX of France — was remarkably similar to the Fifth. It was undertaken with the same aim (to destroy the power of the sultan of Egypt), pursued with the same ignorance, and came to the same disastrous conclusion. Louis IX was defeated at the battle of Mansurah, captured, and liberated after payment of a huge ransom. He returned to France just in time to defend his realm against the aggression of King Henry III of England. Meanwhile the military power of Egypt was steadily increasing and the Muslims had recaptured all of Palestine leaving only Acre in Christian hands.

The pious and stubborn Louis IX (later to be canonized as Saint Louis) resolved to go on another crusade in 1270.

The last expedition ever, the Eighth Crusade did not sail farther than Tunis (Tunisia) where the king of France and a part of his army died of plague. In 1289 Tripoli was taken by the Muslims; Tyre, Sidon, Beirut and a few minor places surrendered. Finally, in 1291, Acre, the last place held by the Christians, was captured, bringing a definitive and irreversible end to the Crusades. However, there was a final and vain attempt led by Pope Pius II in 1464. The long-lasting idea of Crusades to expel the infidel from the Holy Land had finally died. By and large the record in the history of the Crusades was politically disastrous, diplomatically inexcusable, and militarily incompetent. The Latin kingdom of Jerusalem had been founded in blood and ended in blood.

The Opposing Armies

Crusader Armies

The international armies of Crusaders were apparently united by the same religious fervor, but actually they carried with them all the frictions and rivalry which opposed them in their native lands. From the start until the end of the Crusades, the constant problems were the lack of discipline and unity, the bad organization, and the shortage of efficient fighting manpower, as the majority of the Crusaders returned home after their stay in Palestine. The resources in personnel of the occasional — and these of the settled Crusaders— were always far beyond those of the heathen. The Crusaders armies consisted of the three basic ingredients of feudalism: first, the barons and their retinues of tenants; second, the levies of free men forming the infantry, often city militia, who were neither well equipped nor well trained; and third, mercenaries, a professional body providing both cavalry and infantry who were of good quality but very expensive to maintain and sometimes unreliable. The costly use of mercenaries became necessary during the 12th century when the Muslims grew stronger while the Franks were unable to increase their fighting manpower. Moreover — owing to the structure of the kingdom of Outremer — the kings of Jerusalem enjoyed only a restricted power. They were in theory the upper-suzerains of the Holy Land, but in practice their vassals could lawfully refuse to help them militarily, could remain neutral, or might wage war and conclude peace as their own interests dictated. All this

Hauberk Made of Banded Mail, 12th Century

made the position of the feudal states of Outremer very weak.

The true numbers of the Crusaders' armies are very difficult to know as chronicles invariably exaggerated their size. The contemporary sources are highly influenced by the fantasy and the epic style of the writers. For

on foot and some 2,500 knights. These figures are vague estimates probably including great numbers of noncombatant personnel such as camps followers, pilgrims, wives, and children.

Weapons and Armor

The warriors of the First Crusade in 1099 were not radically different from William the Conqueror's soldiers of 1066. They were dressed and armed in the style so vividly illustrated in the Bayeux Tapestry: conical helmets with nasal; byrnies and quilted tunics; knee-length mail hauberks with wide elbow-length sleeves and mail coifs; large kite-shaped shields; spears, swords, and axes. This style of equipment was still being worn by foot soldiers and lesser knights as late as the Third Crusade in the 1190s.

After the Third Crusade it seemed that some changes occurred which were modified in accordance with the tastes and requirements and the climate. It is certain that the Crusades exercised a very powerful influence upon the many aspects of medieval warfare including equipment. The traditions, uses, and innovations that the Crusaders brought back with them from the East were rapidly adapted by them to the varying circumstances of their several homes. Among those changes were the sleeves of the hauberk which had been extended to form mittens protecting the hands, and round-topped helmets and surcoats were introduced. Possibly captured items were worn, and the Poulains' equipment led to a certain "orientalization." Some members of the Latin aristocracy and even occasional Crusaders might wear a burnous and wind an oriental turban or a keffiyeh around their heads and fight with curved scimitar. In return, Turkish warriors might wear Frankish helmets with nasals and captured coats of mail. Warriors of both sides could ride on a captured horse. Lesser soldiers such as poor knights, infantrymen, sergeants, and mercenaries wore *aketon, gambison,* and *pourpoint,* which were various forms of body armor made of buckram stuffed with cotton and quilted.

The Crusades lasted for two centuries, and weapons and armor underwent gradual changes. One must however bear in mind that developments in military equipment were not universal and immediate; arms and armor of old style and more recent types would have happily coexisted. About the middle of the 13th century, the chain mail hauberk with its quilted undergarment, the *haqueton,* was still widely worn, but primitive forms of plate armor were introduced. Innovations were reinforcement of the chain mail by secondary defenses. *Genouillères* (metal knee caps) were adopted as protection but also to ease the drag of chain mail upon the knee when flexing.

Crusader, 12th Century

the siege of Jerusalem in 1099, the armies probably totaled from 1,200 to 1,300 cavalrymen out of a total strength of 12,000 men. When the French king Philippe Auguste went on crusade in 1198, he disposed of a force including some 650 mounted men and 1,300 infantrymen. For the Fourth Crusade in 1204, the Venetians agreed to transport 20,000 infantrymen and some 4,500 mounted soldiers, so we may presume that this was the size of the force which sacked Constantinople. In 1248, when King Louis IX of France led the Seventh Crusade, he had 12,000 soldiers

Knight, Third Crusade

Ailettes

Various forms of metal leg plates also seemed to have been introduced to protect shins. The hauberk had long sleeves which were prolonged to cover the hand with mail gauntlets not divided for the fingers. The coif upon the head descended to the shoulders on either side and covered part of the surcoat. The loose surcoat tended to be shorter, reaching to the knees. Another innovation was the introduction of *tartschen*, *ailerons*, or *ailettes*. These were adjunct lozenge-shaped or square pieces of metal or stiff cuir-bouilli fastened vertically from the shoulders, designed to lessen the effect of a sweeping cut from a sword or battle-axe against slashing blows at the neck.

Ailettes presumably prefigured the passe-garde of the 15th century and the shoulder strap of present day. The ailettes could also display the owner's coat of arms.

By the close of the 13th century, a new species of armor made its appearance; known as banded mail, it was cheaper than chain mail. It consisted of rings or iron washers (about 1 inch in diameter) held together by pieces of leather and arranged like rolls of coins firmly fixed on a tunic. The helmet was the great barrel helm, though some preferred a light steel cap under a mail hood. Flat-topped helmets with a grille to protect the face were also introduced. About 1250 a transitional heaume appeared later to become the so-called *basinet*. This was generally round-topped or conical-topped and had a visor or *van-taille* fitted with two projecting studs adapted for raising at pleasure or for removal if not required. The movable vantaille greatly solved the breathing problems of the totally closed heaume. The shield was usually the smaller and triangular écu.

Muslim Armies

The armies of Islam which opposed the Crusaders were far from being homogeneous, and their leadership was disunited and often rival. There were the Abbasid caliphate of Baghdad, the Seljuks (Turkish invaders from Persia), the Fatimid dynasty from Egypt whose forces

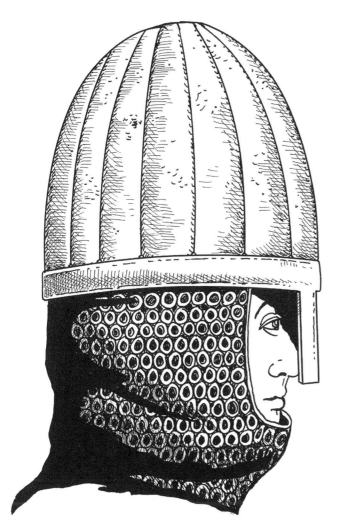

French Helmet with Nasal, 12th Century

were united to Syria by Saladin, as well as many other tribes more or less independent. The "Turkish" armies were actually a mixture of feudal troops and mercenaries of Turks, Syrians, Persians, Iranians, Egyptians, Arabs, and various eastern aliens converted to Islam such as Bedouins, Circassians, Armenians, and Kurds. Muslim armies also included Africans from Sudan and Libya who formed groups of foot soldiers or cavalrymen armed with bows and spears. Some of the most feared Muslim soldiers were the Mamelukes, who were purchased as slaves and, after converting to Islam and receiving heavy military training, were recruited in the armies. Each leader had his own elite troop of bodyguards which formed the core of his own army. Physicians, surgeons, doctors, and hospital equipment traveled with the army. The armies of Islam also included bands of musicians playing drums, oboes, flutes, and trumpets. These were used to give

Right: Byzantine Peltast, Early 12th Century. The figure is a Greek heavy infantrymen wearing a quilted and studded tunic, armed with a sword, a lance and a kite-shaped shield.

Turkoman Cavalryman. This auxiliary mounted man wears a fur-lined hat and a Turkish double-breasted coat over a mail tunic.

orders for maneuvers but were particularly effective at creating fear and chaos in the Christian ranks whose men and horses were unaccustomed to such noise.

The Muslims were also masters at quick communication. They organized networks of posting houses connecting cities and strongholds with relays of horses. They trained pigeons to carry messages with great speed from one point to another.

The Turks were superb horsemen. Their training included war games and polo. It was said that they spend more time on the saddle than on the ground. Polo was a popular game with the Muslim cavalry; as part of the military training it taught teamwork to the riders and tested the horses in maneuverability and speed. Rapid turns and sudden stops, excitement, and courage were part of the game but also a valuable asset in real combat situations. Turkish horsemen were able to attack suddenly and disappear with the coordination of a flock of birds.

Turkish Archer

The Turks did not — on the whole — risk their forces, but usually softened the Frankish ranks with continuous arrow fire before risking a charge. They were indeed deadly users of bows and arrows, using them while riding at full speed in the saddle, and this was a real achievement as the archer had several movements to synchronize: kicking his horse into a gallop, nocking the arrow, drawing the bow, aiming, and shooting. Even in retreat, they would turn half around and let loose a devastating rain of projectiles. The Turks were also well aware that the most vulnerable point of the western knight was the horse itself. They shot deliberately for the animal's vitals and

Arabian Horseman, 12th Century

thus broke the cohesion of the opposing battle plan. The composite Turkish bow was rather short and smoothly recurved; it was accurate at short range, but a barrage by massed archers could be effective up to 365 meters (400 yards). On the whole, the loosely dressed Saracen horsemen with mobility and their mounted bowmen had a marked advantage over the heavily armored Christians.

Muslim equestrian warfare showed a great deal more sense than the Christian variety, using stallions, mares and geldings according to the task undertaken. In the desert areas, Muslim armies on the march also rode on camels, leading their precious horses alongside to conserve their freshness, fire, and energy. Right before the battle, horses were warmed up with preliminary exercises to sharpen them up the coming fray. No wonder the Crusaders feared the massed and mobile Turkish mounted archery.

The Turk *sipahi* (cavalryman) was also experienced with other weapons. The *kilij* (a generic term for sword) included various forms of *saif,* a curved saber or scimitar, and the *nimcha,* a right saber with a knuckle

Mameluke Askari, Mid–13th Century. The depicted Mameluke wears a bayda (pointed helmet), a piece of mail protecting the face and shoulders, a lamellar cuirass beneath his robe, and felt or leather riding boots. He is armed with a heart-shaped shield, a sword, and a lance.

guard. The *nachakh* was a battle-axe; the *pesh kabz* was a dagger; the *khanjar* was a combat knife; and the *topuz* a metal mace. A weapon commonly used among nomadic

an armor composed of quilted caftan and a *zardiyyat*, a mail tunic rather similar to the Christian hauberk that was sometimes reinforced with plates hung from the shoulders on straps connected by buckles. Other types were noted with single- or double-ring mail, banded steel, jazerant, and double cordwain. Also worn was the lamellar armor consisting of small rectangular plates of iron or rawhide laced together with leather thongs in horizontal rows, the rows then being laced together vertically, overlapping each other upwards. The mail shirt often extended to protect to the thighs. Head and throat protection included a steel cap, helmet with nasal, coif, and vantail. Headgear also included the traditional oriental turban and keffiyeh to ward off the sun. To make sure of recognition, shields and helmets were often painted in gay colors.

Tactics

The main tactics employed by the Crusaders was the familiar charge on horse with bristling lances. A typical engagement would be made by the heavy knights, holding the lance in their right hand and the reins and shield in their left. At the battle of Ascalon in July 1099, the irresistible charge of the Christian knights shattered the enemy ranks and proved devastating, sweeping the Egyptian army before them into the sea, confirming the reputation of the Crusaders as unconquerable. Battles between Franks and Turks were often like the combat of bull and matador, and when the bull got home, the effect was shattering with victories won in the face of incredible odds. Not only were the Franks and their horses bigger and heavier than the Turks and their horses, but they were better at in-fighting and could deal out terrible punishment. The perennial problem for Outremers was to muster enough of these tank-like knights.

A heavy charge was powerful and decisive on bare, flat ground, but its success would depend on surprise, mass, weight, and—most important—on the willingness of the enemy to remain fixed while the charge was made. But the Turkish mounted men were quick to adapt. They would never wait to be charged; they would never stand still but formed and reformed their ranks in bewildering fashion. Unless they were superior in numbers, they did not commit themselves to a full-scale battle. They would open their ranks to let the Frankish knights pass through them and then attack the flanks, leaving their opponents

Ayyubid Soldier from Persia, 12th Century

Arab tribes was the *lasso*, which they wielded adroitly, snaring enemy rider, horse, or both in a single throw.

The protective equipment of the Muslim soldiers included a *kalkan* (a circular convex brass shield) and a *shishak* (helmet). Turkish soldiers often wore a *char-aina*,

no time to prepare defensive formations. The clumsy Western knights using the massive charge were not used to tactics that needed a light-moving, nimble horse that could respond quickly to a sudden change of course or a rapid stop. As Turkish armor was generally lighter than that of the Frankish knights, and as their horse breeds (Faras, Hedjin, Berdhun, Berber, and Turkmene) were usually of greater pace and agility, the Turkish riders were quick, effective, very mobile, and able to move rapidly in any direction. They performed equally well on the flat land, uphill, or down a steep slope either in attack or retreat. They avoided direct confrontations and pitched battles; they remained at a safe distance and turned around the Crusaders harassing them with arrows like a swarm of flies, attacking the rear and flank of armies, especially when they were on the march. They would employ a feign retreat, wearying and confusing their enemy. Often a small and apparently vulnerable group of horsemen would be the bait for a sustained ambush.

As ever in warfare, the exploitation of one tactic that proved successful was countered by a move from those who learned from their defeat. Muslims and Christians were both noted for their horsemanship, and it was inevitable that each would be influenced by the other. Furthermore, each side had spies and prisoners who could become renegades revealing information about strategy, tactics, and weaponry. To face the Turkish method of combat, the Crusaders learned to respect certain basic principles, such as never to split the formation and never separate foot soldiers from cavalrymen. They evolved close formations and tight-knit lines with shields forming screens. They learned to be more cautious and less impetuous and also paid more attention to the good working relationship between foot soldiers and cavalrymen.

There evolved, too, a new sort of western cavalryman. Known as

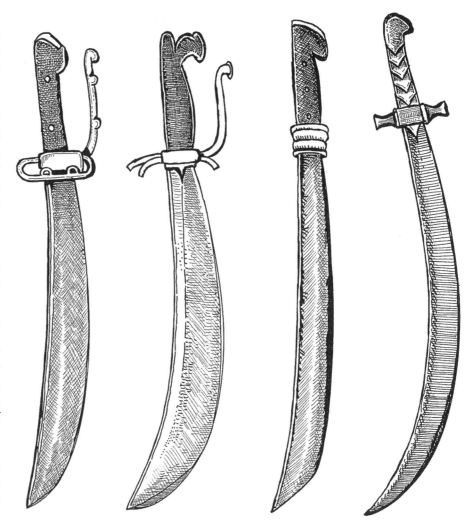

Turkish Swords. *Far left and left:* broad-bladed nimcha with knuckle guard; *middle:* saïf, a straight one-edged sabel; *right:* kilij or scimitar.

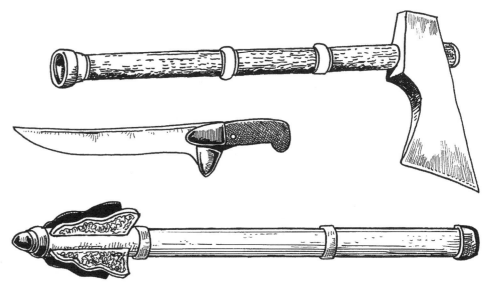

Muslim Weapons. *Top:* nachakh (axe); *middle:* pesh kabz (dagger); *bottom:* topuz (mace).

sergeant à cheval (mounted sergeant), this combatant was a copy of the Turkish *sipahi*, a lightly armored, well-armed, agile horseman who assisted the heavy-armored knight. The mounted sergeants—inferior in equipment and rank to knights—would be sent on speculative mission to reconnoiter and often to skirmish with the enemy using sword, bow, and crossbow. They would also be put in charge of spare horses that would be used by the knight. The sergeants were not always mounted; they were called upon service to serve in the field army in moment of emergency. Normally, their duties were to serve in their city's garrison, manning castles or guarding their lords' residence.

The Crusaders also hired *Turkopoles* drawn from the Latin states. These were local native-born or the offspring of mixed marriages between Franks and native Syrians. They formed a second line of horsemen, a light cavalry, warriors armed with bows often using the Turkish manner of combat for hit-and-run tactics, reconnaissance, and screening duties. Mercenaries formed an infantry force. Some men were armed with shield and spear and organized in box-like formations; their task was to repulse the charge of enemy cavalrymen by presenting a hedge of spear points and to provide a base of cover for their own horsemen enduring the Turks' barrage of arrows. They protected the precious horses from the enemy's projectiles until the right moment for the knights to charge. Others were armed with bow and crossbow to provide the missile factor. Mercenaries and Turkopoles were fighting for pay and were often less reliable under difficult conditions.

Because of the Turks' tactics of harassing Christian armies on the move, special attention was paid to the force on the march with scout, van, rear, and flank guards. These changes helped to cut down losses and resulted in a few victories, such as the battle of Arsurf fought in September 1191. Both the Hospitalers and Templars (military religious orders) provided military advisers to the Christian armies. But despite what they had learned, the heavily armored Christian knight on a clumsy heavy horse continued to lead the field.

Castles and Siege Warfare

Having battered their heads against Antioch, Nicea, and Jerusalem, the Crusaders quickly learned their lessons. There was a chronic shortage of manpower, and the only way to maintain some kind of domination was by holding the lands from fortified points. The Poulains started to build their own castles in order to hold what ground they had gained in a strange and distant land where they were surrounded by the constant fear of a local population's uprising and Turkish attacks. The castles built by the Crusaders in the 13th century were con-

structed to last forever. They were usually powerful concentric fortresses based on the Byzantine model with a regular double-crenelated walls and flanking towers. There were plenty of castles and strongholds, such as Saone, the Krak des Chevaliers, and Margat, for example. In the semi-arid, dry, and barren lands of the Middle East, castles and fortified points were also useful as logistical bases. To avoid dying of starvation and thirst, they always included a water supply, forage for the animals, and food and ammunition for the men. They offered well-supplied bases on which the army in the field could rely.

Other Minor Crusades

There were also minor crusades within Europe during the 12th century. The most important was directed against the so-called *Cathari* or *Albigensians*. Another was led against the Waldensian movement.

Crusade Against the Albigensians

Catharism had its origins in the East and appeared in Europe at the end of the 11th century. The so-called *Cathari* (meaning "pure" in Greek) or *Albigensians* (named after the town Albi in southern France) were followers of a strict non–Christian religion. Catharism was a complex and highly spiritual doctrine based on Greek Gnosticism (a confident belief in the power of pure spirit to attain direct communion with God) and Persian Manichaeanism (a dualist doctrine with a distinct and infrangible boundary between light and dark, between the good soul of the pure man created by God and the evil world around him created by Satan). Although there were great divergences of view among the various groups, the pure and perfect Catharism—strongly contrasting with the laxity of the Roman Catholic clergy—had a certain attraction for the nobility of Spain, northern Italy, and southern France in the early 12th century. The religious revivalist movement—with asceticism, radical purity, and the apostolic way of life as its dominating features mixed with beliefs taken from the Christian Gospel—spread quickly, particularly in the region of Toulouse and Albi, and was popular among all classes of society. With aristocratic protection, that of count of Toulouse Raymond VI, Cathar churches were established and Cathar bishops were appointed. Baptism and other sacraments were rejected; the Bible was "purified" of its unspiritual elements and offered to the believers in the vernacular tongues.

At first Pope Innocent II tried to convert the Albigensians, and he sent Cistercian monks as missionaries. The crisis came in 1208 when a papal legate was murdered near Saint-Gilles. This event made Innocent decide upon a military crusade against the Cathars. He called upon Philippe Auguste of France to provide the troops. Many barons of northern France were ready and glad to undertake such a holy war which would bring them a share of the wealth of the southern provinces. A large force — led by count Simon of Montfort — gathered in 1209, and the holy religious crusade soon degenerated into a savage war of conquest. The campaign opened by the frenzy storming of Béziers during which Arnold Amalric, the papal legate, ordered "Tuez les tous, Dieu reconnaitra les siens!" (Slay them all, God will know His own!). Toulouse, Albi, Carcassone, and Narbonne were also taken.

In addition, the Church created the tribunal of the Holy Inquisition. This — launched by Pope Innocent III in 1198 — was originally intended to be temporarily used to deal with the Cathars. But the tribunal became a regular and permanent institution established by Pope Gregory IX in 1229. The word *inquisition* itself is from the same root as *inquire* meaning "to ask and investigate." Its purpose was many-fold: officially, to save the soul of the heretic and to prevent him from corrupting others; in practice, its function was to seek out and punish those who deviated from the official Roman Catholic doctrine. Actually, the procedure was secret, and a simple denunciation was sufficient for a suspect to appear before the court. It was — in advance — a kind of Nazi Gestapo that used moral pressure, blackmail, and atrocious physical torture: People could be arrested, properties confiscated in the most arbitrary manner, and heretics condemned to be burned alive at the stake.

The Inquisition was in the hands of the Dominicans — a religious order of wandering friars dedicated to preaching and learning founded in 1216 by the Spanish evangelist Domenico de Guzmàn (ca. 1170–1221). The Inquisition formed the most odious, hysterical, and criminal method of religious intolerance. The Albigensian Crusade did not only serve a religious purpose. Behind the cover of combating heresy, there were important political issues at stake since the repression served the king of France by increasing his domains. Southern France had always been more Roman than Frankish and remained distinct in many ways from northern France.

The northern Crusaders won a decisive battle at Muret in 1213, and the capture of the fortress of Montségur in 1214 deprived the Cathars of their last stronghold. Overwhelmed by military ruthlessness and Inquisition terror, the power of the nobles who had supported the heresy was smashed. They were dispossessed of their lands; the armed resistance was brought to an end, and the Cathari heresy was eradicated. The fine civilization of southern France with its own customs, the distinctive Occitan culture with its own language — both inherited from the Roman time — were destroyed. The southern provinces were incorporated into the French realm by the treaty of Paris in 1229.

Waldensians

Another heresy was that of Pierre Valdo (1140–1217). Valdo — also named Valdes or Valdesius or Pierre de Vaux — was a prosperous and pious merchant of Lyon, France. Deeply moved by the words of Matthew (XIX: 21) he decided to distribute his money to the poor and adopt a life of poverty and celibacy as a wandering preacher supported by alms. He appealed — in vain — for official ecclesiastical recognition in 1179 and gathered a group of followers (known as the Vaudois, Poor Men of Lyon, or Waldensians) and began to preach his pure conception of the Bible. He proclaimed that the true spirit of Christ was not in episcopal palaces, decorated cathedrals, and opulent monasteries but in the open air, on the land, and in the hearts of those who received Him. The Waldensian movement — living and preaching the perfect pious life as taught by Jesus Christ — were disobedient enthusiasts who gradually enjoyed a large popular support. They became a threat to the Church as they attacked the very foundations of the Catholic doctrine. Consequently, Pierre Valdo was condemned by the pope in 1181 and excommuniated in 1184. Pope Innocent III instituted a crusade in 1209 against the Waldensians, and Valdo was captured and burned as an arch-heretic in 1217. The Waldensian movement ended in blood, tears, and persecution as Valdo's followers were repressed and crushed by the crusading force.

12

Templars and Hospitalers

Military Religious Orders

Out of the paradoxical wedding between Roman churchmen and Germanic warriors came a strange offspring: the military monk who wore the cross of Jesus on his surcoat while holding in his hand the hammer of the pagan god Thor and who unconsciously substituted Christ for Wodan and Paradise for Walhalla. It showed the syncretic genius of the Catholic Church to combine Christian humility and Germanic ferocity. The military orders were indeed composed of men who were both warriors and praying monks taking care of the pilgrims. Their dramatic history shows how religious, social, political, and economic motives could be intimately entangled. To combine monasticism and war was to take a departure from scriptural teaching, but the military orders were so badly needed that no one raised objections. Because the great majority of Crusaders returned home after their pilgrimage, the idea of a motivated and reliable armed force permanently stationed in the Holy Land was received with great enthusiasm in the Crusaders' world, and it provided the Roman Church with a corps of storm troopers.

The three main military orders (Templars, Hospitalers, and Teutonics) owed an enormous debt to the ardor, talent, and skill of Saint Bernard who made it possible for them to take up arms. Without the great Cistercian, the brethren would never have evolved into military orders. The highly mystic Bernard of Clervaux (1090–1153) was the abbot of Cîteaux (Burgundy, France) and one of the most influential churchman of the day. He lectured Christendom, dueled with the rationalist Abelard, and offered the assuaging cult of the Virgin Mary. He made fiery speeches in favor of the Second Crusade and was the chief instrument of revival of monasticism by spreading the new and strict Cistercian rule. This aimed at the purification of the Benedictine rule which had become wealthy, magnificent, and increasingly lax, as illustrated by the abbey of Cluny. The Cistercians—famous for their austerity, strictness, and piety—became a branch of Benedictism wishing to create a system that was midway between the centralization of Cluny and the mystic independent isolation of the Carthusian rule. Bernard was one of the important medieval reformers who revitalized the Catholic Church by winning popularity among the laity. In the military orders, Bernard's genius had transformed a Germanic warrior cult into a religious vocation just as pagan gods had been metamorphosed into saints and fertility rites into Christian festivals. Christ had ousted Wodan.

The monk-warriors lived under a monastic rule which included the usual injunctions of poverty, chastity, and obedience. This separated them from the dynastic concerns which preoccupied so many of their secular counterparts; they were prohibited from participating in the frivolous activities of knighthood, such as tournaments, hunting, social courtly life, or dancing. The military orders represented the mainstream of medieval knighthood, and they attracted many young knights in search of the ideal. Admission in the military orders was very selective, and postulants had to prove themselves high-born. The military orders rapidly became very wealthy through gifts of money and donation of land and properties—both in Palestine and in Europe—which were carefully administered. Therefore, the brethren were provided with excellent equipment, weapons, horses, supplies, and fortifications. They were almost a Church within the Church, as they were independent from the secular clergy; they were exempt from diocesan control and — most important — from any financial obligations toward the bishops.

The military orders were remarkably adaptable, turning their hands to many skills; they developed trading, navigation, banking, and diplomacy — taking full advantage of their exemption from customs dues. The monk-warriors were no intellectuals and produced very little literature; they were not completely illiterate though, some learned Arabic, and a few brethren wrote austere and didactic books, obviously considered suitable for their orders. The Templars produced several troubadours and trouveurs (poets) including one Grand Master, Robert de Sablé. The Hospitaler Guglielmo di San Stefano wrote a scholarly history of his order and treatises about Roman law. Such men were exceptions. If they lacked erudition, the brethren were the first organized professional armies of Western Europe since the legions of Rome had gone before the barbarians. They developed the military aspects to a high degree, particularly in training, tactics, and discipline; the construction of sophisticated fortresses; and the strategies of siege and naval warfare.

The Latin states of Palestine — hundreds of miles away from their support in the West — could only survive by their existence and commitment. The military orders invested large human resources and huge sums of money in the defense of the Holy Land. They were famous and dreaded by their enemies for their ferocity in combat. From their creation in the early 12th century until the fall of the Latin states in the late 13th century, their record of service was remarkable though somewhat marred by their rivalry. Because they lived permanently in Palestine, they often had a different perspective from that of the temporary Crusaders who appeared periodically in pursuit of short-term objectives. They entered into diplomatic negotiations with various Muslim leaders over the years. The Templars more particularly became involved in diplomacy and banking.

From the start there was, however, something drastically wrong with all Christian military orders. They were too concerned with the righteousness of their cause, too convinced that God would give them victory, and they had no clear plan for uniting their forces or dealing with their enemies through diplomacy. They were too prone to fight at the wrong moments and too scornful of peaceful pursuits. There was also rivalry between them. As early as the 1170s there had been bad blood between Templars and Hospitalers. It flared up with particular violence in 1197 over a trifling dispute over a small estate in Tripoli,

and the Christian brethren drew their swords. From 1256 to 1258 a state of war reigned between Templars and Hospitalers because of a conflict about the possession of the monastery of Saint-Sabas in the town of Acre. Harmony was fragile, and relations deteriorated continuously. Furthermore, the word *knight* had a certain fairytale flavor which obscured the fact that such a man was a specialized fighting machine. The brethren were vigorous young men, the products of a violent age and class, and it was probably very hard for them to observe chastity. Whether one thinks like Freud that religion is spiritualized sex or agrees with Jung that sexuality is necessary for a man's sanity, it seems that many warrior-monks did not achieve a happy balanced life based on prayer and humane activities. It is hardly surprising that there were many cases of mental and moral breakdown among the brethren.

After the capture of the last Christian bulwark, Acre, in May 1291, the military orders withdrew to their European estates; they had lost their raison d'être and met various fates.

Templars

By the time of the conquest of the Holy Land in 1099, a group of dedicated and pious men — known as the *Militia Christi* or *Pauvres Chevaliers du Christ* (Poor Knights of Christ) — had acted as guides and protectors to Christian pilgrims traveling through the unsafe roads. A French knight called Hugues de Payens had arrived in Syria in 1115 and formed the idea of formally incorporating the brothers as a religious military order. He was no mere adventurer but lord of Martigny in Burgundy (France) and a cousin of the count of Champagne. Hugues's group of Poor Knights were granted a house in Jerusalem situated near the Temple of Salomon and were known hence as the Knights of the Temple or, shortly, Templars. Bernard of Clairvaux embraced their cause with enthusiasm. In a written work entitled *De Laude Novae Militiae* (In Praise of the New Chivalry), he praised the noble austerity of the Templars in contrast with the luxury, vanity, greed, and violence of the secular knights.

The Templars were formally recognized as a military order by the Church at the council of Troyes in 1128. The Templars found themselves heroes almost overnight, and the order became rapidly prestigious and popular. New members were recruited, and donations poured in from the kings of Aragon and Castile, from the count of Flanders, and from many other princes. The order could soon support itself owing to gifts of money from protected pilgrims and the sick who had been cured and the wills of dying men granting their estates and donations of various rights in their fiefs to the order.

Two Templar Knights on One Horse Symbolizing the Poverty of the Order (after Matthew Paris). Actually the Order of the Temple was not poor at all and each knight had three horses.

The sober rule of the Templars was that of the abbey of Cîteaux, as reformed by Bernard with the three vows of chastity, poverty, and obedience. In 1139, Pope Innocent II granted them further privileges, including giving the order its own clergy and churches, and thus freeing them from the secular Church rulers, the bishops, and making them responsible only to the papacy. They were as a Church within the Church. Their discipline and rules were strict, their life was hard, and they were prepared to die in the service of Christ — a martyr road traveled by about 20,000 Templars in 200 years. In return a Templar's attitude toward his enemies became one of great fanaticism, forcing infidels to accept the faith at the point of the sword.

The hierarchy took many years to evolve, and gradually it was carefully defined. The *Magister Militum Templi* (Grand-Master of the Temple) was in overall charge, being both an abbot and a general, enjoying wide powers; he was elected for his lifetime by an elaborate combination of vote designed to ensure impartiality by a council, the Grand-Chapter, consisting of the following high officers and dignitaries. The *Sénéchal* was the Master's deputy. The *gonfalonier* carried the order's black-and-silver standard or *gonfalon*. The *maréchal* was the supreme military official in charge of knights, horses, arms, and armor. The *commander of the realm of Jerusalem* was the estate manager acting as both treasurer and head of the navy. The *commander of the city of Jerusalem* was

Templar Knight of Christ, about 1290 (after a Statue from the Cathedral of Strasburg)

Knight Templar, 12th Century   Knight Templar, ca. 1150

responsible for the welfare of pilgrims. The *drapier*, the keeper of the wardrobe, was in charge of clothing, a sort of quartermaster general. The *turkopolier* was in charge of the brother sergeants, men-at-arms, and mercenary Turkopoles. The fighting knights were young noblemen, and they were grouped in *escadron* (squadron) of twelve. Their number was swollen by *frères-sergents* (sergeant-brothers), who were mounted squires, subaltern officers, and assistants as well as *confratres,* fellow-knights, who served for only a short period (sometimes for years)

during which they accepted the rule of the order but did not have to take the monastic vows. The confratres could marry and have children, and they promised half their property to the order in the event of their death. The combatants were spiritually assisted by *chapelains* (chaplains), and the domestic tasks of the everyday life were performed by servants, peasants, and craftsmen from the common, the *frères laie* (lay-brothers). There were nine other commanders corresponding to the provinces (territorial possessions) of the order at Antioch, Tripoli,

Gongalonier, Knight Templar with Beau Séant Banner, ca. 1150

ter lands and estates with care and competence, to recruit and train new members, to hold religious services, to nurse elderly brethren, and to provide money, supplies, and equipment for the military activities in Palestine. The organization was thus equally well adapted for monastic and military needs. In war, the divisions of command in the field corresponded to the administrative ranks.

Military actions in Palestine included police works such as escorting pilgrim trains and funds to guard against Turkish raiders. However, because many criminals had been sent on crusade as penance for serious offenses and because they reverted to their unpleasant habits, the Templars' task consisted also in patrols and protection against highwaymen and robbers. The first large-scale offensive action in which 300 knights Templar took part was King Baldwin's expedition to Antioch in 1130. Ironically this was against rebellious barons within the kingdom. In 1147, with the arrival of the Second Crusade, the Templars saw real operations against the Turks. Between 1163 and 1168, the king of Jerusalem, Amaury I, launched a seriess of offensives toward Egypt, expeditions in which the Templars took part. At Montgirard in November 1177, owing to their cohesion and their tactics of massive charge, they defeated their enemies. The battle of Arsuf fought in September 1191 was one of the pitched battles won by the Christian knights. The Hospitalers initiated the charge, and the Templars led the van once they had erupted from the protective circle of infantrymen. Behind came the Angevins, Bretons, King Guy of Jerusalem, Normans, English, and Poitevins, with Hospitalers closing the rear. The combined weight of Frankish cavalry put the Turks to flight, a second charge completed the victory, but both sides had suffered high casualties.

The Templar army — always at the forefront of the war against Islam — was indeed a significant fighting machine. Each knight wore a *hauberk*, a long-sleeved, knee-length coat of chain furnished with a cap leaving only the face uncovered. Over this the monk-warrior wore the order's white cloak or surcoat. When not on armed service, the brother-knights wore the white hooded Cistercian cloister habit. The head was protected by several models of

France, England, Poitou, Aragon, Portugal, Apulia, and Hungary; these officers owed allegiance to the Grand Master. The provinces were divided into houses and preceptories headed by commanders' lieutenants and *frères casaliers* (farm managers) whose object was to adminis-

helmet that were often furnished with a nasal to protect the face, or it could have the form of a hat made of metal. It could also be a *heaume*, a closed conical helmet with a hole for breathing and slits for vision. Legs were covered by *chausses* made of mail, and feet were protected in heavy leather riding shoes reinforced with mail. Obviously the Templars adopted the military innovations, and the previously discussed improvements such as knee caps, ailettes, shin protection, and banded mail were introduced to the brethren's equipment. Each knight disposed of three horses equipped with full harnessing, trappings, and saddle. Weapons included a large double-edged sword, a lance made with an ash shaft and a conical sharp metal point, and a sharp combat dagger as well as two other knives for domestic purposes. Each fighting brother had an *écu*, a triangular wooden shield lined with leather and often reinforced with metal stripes and nails; or it could be a *rondache*, a circular wooden shield. Shields were often decorated with the red Templar cross. The same red cross was sown on the front and back of the white tunic, surcoat, and mantle. The sergeant-brothers wore a black surcoat and tunic with the red cross. Their hauberk was usually shorter than that of the knights and was short-sleeved, but the weapons were generally the same.

When campaigning, a team of knights and sergeant-brothers had various cooking gear including a pot, pan, drinking bowl, etc. Equipment, armor, dress, and weapons had to be properly used and carefully maintained by the men. They were not "given" to them; the knights had sworn the vow of poverty and were not allowed to own the slightest thing, even items or equipment they found or captured. The whole implement was the exclusive and collective property of the order. Nothing could be given away, abandoned, hired, traded, or sold. Any part of equipment broken, lost, damaged, or captured by the enemy had to be reported to the chapter which — after inquiry — possibly gave an order to the drapier and maréchal for replacement.

Admission to the order was very strict. Many questions were asked to see that there were no impediment to joining such as marriage, debt, chronic illness, illegitimate birth, or membership in another branch of the clergy. Repeated warnings were made about the hardships of life in the order, and the candidate could withdraw after hearing about these discomforts; therefore, only the best of the best were selected. The emphasis was entirely on duties, responsibilities, and hardships, never on prestige and rewards. Once selected, the candidate would donate all his property to the order, and this was a non-negligible source of profit. In a secret ceremony he would pronounced the triple vow of chastity, poverty, and obedience; he then swore to help in the conquest of the Holy

Land, never to desert the order or reveal its secrets, and never to suffer injustices done to a Christian. After this he was a Templar and was trained in a commanderie — sometimes for years. Within the organization every kind of talent could find a satisfying outlet: administrators, priests, treasurers, and, of course, warriors who were sent to combat in Palestine.

Brethren slept in dormitories in shirt and breeches; they said office together in their chapels and recited psalms and prayers several times a day. They attended the Ordinary Chapter — the council presided by a commander — to discuss and manage the everyday administrative issues. They ate in pairs to see that the other did not weaken himself by fasting. Meals were taken collectively and in silence while a chaplain recited psalms. Their food was balanced, healthy, and rather plentiful as the men were not only monks but also warriors needing all their physical strength in the service of God. Wine was served with every meal and meat three times a week. Their hair were shaven and beards were grown. Celibates, they shared to the full in the devotion to Christ and Our Lady. They were forbidden to look at or talk to women and girls. Emphasis was on silence, harmony, kind strictness, efficiency, and mutual respect. The brethren always addressed each other with *Beau Frère* (Fair Brother). Mutilated, disabled, and elderly brothers retired and were nursed in commanderies in Europe where they fulfilled tasks adapted to their handicap until the day they died. Brethren suffering from leprosy and other incurable deceases were isolated and nursed by a sister organization, the Order of Saint Lazarus.

Rules for the Templars were as detailed for conventual daily life as for battle. Discipline was scrupulously observed — the whole point was to make obeying monastic soldiers from boisterous secular young noblemen. Simple souls, the young brethren easily became unbalanced; prayer and mortification did not always eradicate those violent instincts which still lurked in a Wodan-haunted unconscious. Chivalrous glamour, personal whim, and pointless prowess were to be replaced by Christian humility, collective responsibility, and practical efficiency. Given the situation of permanent war in Palestine, it was of vital importance that knights, sergeants, squires, and Turkopoles be constantly in a state of readiness and able to take up arms at any moment. Jousting and tournaments as well as any other form of entertainment, such as games, gambling, hunting, and hawking, were forbidden, but the brethren were encouraged to train their horses and exercise individually and collectively with various weapons as long as nobody got hurt and no equipment was damaged. Total discipline — reflected in the fundamental vow of obedience — was thus of crucial importance. Punishment was harsh, ranging

Turkopole on Templar Service, 12th Century

monastery). For men trained for combat and action, the peace of a monastery imposed with the latter must have been punishment indeed. No knight was to talk without permission.

No knight was to do anything nor take any initiative without being ordered to do so by a superior. Even adjusting a stirrup required permission. When marching, the squadrons had to ride in an orderly manner and start and stop when ordered. For obvious security reason, scouts were sent to reconnoiter the terrain and no one was to leave the column without permission. The Christian heavily armored knights got rapidly tired and thirsty in a warm land like Palestine and their mounts even more so, but when watering their horses, the knights had to check if the well was not poisoned. When bivouacking during a campaign the knights had to set up their tents, take care of horses, search for firewood, collect forage for their horses and food for themselves from the quartermaster, cook and eat in silence, and go to bed after prayers. No one was to leave camp without permission. All this was done in order and discipline. In case of an alert, everybody had to be ready to face danger at any time, even during the night.

In combat, the knights Templar followed the black and silver "Beau Séant," the banner brandished by the gonfalonier and the pennon of their own squadron. They deployed when ordered to by the maréchal in the formation they had been assigned. Sometimes they had to wait hours in the sun and under a rain of arrows before being engaged. They charged generally in three waves; the first was an attempt to breach the opposite formation, the second to disorganize their ranks, and the third to reduce the dislocated enemy units. In the middle of the action, if a Templar lost his place in the formation, he had to rally the nearest Templar pennon or — might this be impossible — rally a pennon of the Hospitalers or any other Christian unit. In battle the knights neither gave nor asked for quarter. Of course they were expected to fight with courage. Even wounded or dismounted, no Templar knight might flee before the enemy nor retreat without an order. Cowardice was the supreme dishonor punished by the *perte de la maison*. Knights Templar were expected to fight until their last strength. Death, sword in hand for the glory of God, was the most praised fate. Of the twenty-one Grand Masters of the Temple, five died in battle, five of wounds, and one of starvation in a Turkish prison. Those captured by the enemy were not allowed to ask for ransom; they faced torture and death unless they were made slaves on a galley. According to the ethics of the order, captives were dishonored to abjure the Christian faith to save their lives. The attitude toward the enemy was one of unadulterated fanaticism; the Templars soon became a vital element in the defense of the Christian

from simple admonition, fasting, and sanctions for minor faults to *perte de l'habit* (loss of the dress, that was a humiliating temporary demotion to the status of servant) to *perte de la maison* (loss of the house, expulsion from the order and exile for life in a noncombatant Cistercian

Crusader states. At their height by the mid–12th century they numbered probably 20,000 knights and other personnel. They performed courageous service, but they were frequently reminded by popes and theologians that the Holy War for Christ was not an end in itself and that bloodshed was intrinsically evil.

As there was always a chronic shortage of manpower, the Templars came to rely upon fortification to protect the countries they controlled. In Palestine, they manned every town of any size. In addition, they maintained and garrisoned many fortified domains and huge castles. Before the disaster of 1187, these areas included Roche-Guillaume, Port-Bonnel, and Trepessac in the principality of Antioch; Tortose, Aryma, Bertrandimir, Chastel-Blanc, and Elteffaha in the county of Tripoli; a part of the walls of Jerusalem and Château-Rouge in the realm of Jerusalem; Gaza Castle and the fortress of Natron in the county of Jaffa; the fortress of Chaco and Chastel-Pèlerin in the county of Caesare; and the castles of La Fève, Saphet, Sephorie, and the Chastellet du Gué de Jacob in the principality of Galilee. In London the Templars had a large estate with a 12th century church, the Temple Church, which still exists today at the junction of Strand and Fleet Street. In the heart of Paris they had an enormous fortress, the Château du Temple, which was both a stronghold and a safe to protect their wealth.

Indeed, the Templars diversified their activities. They were so popular and respected that many people — including not only pilgrims but also noblemen and princes, even kings of France — entrusted them to keep their savings. The Templars offered security in an insecure world, and they were immune from the whims of secular and ecclesiastical princes alike. Their efficient organization and international network of properties and storehouses scattered throughout Western Europe, the Mediterranean, and Palestine were a convenient way for safe circulation and collection of funds to and from Europe and the Holy Land. Adding their own properties from gifts and donations and the profit made by their numerous estates, the Templars became immensely wealthy. The administrative branch of the order in Europe became a banking structure, trustworthy financier, convenient capital holder, and a flourishing commercial business as the administrator in the care of European possessions and — as money opens all doors — a political lobby, pressure group, and diplomat in international dealings. The Templars also developed a strong fleet of transport as they soon realized that it was cheaper to have their own ships than to rely upon hiring vessels from the Italian fleet of the merchants of Venice, Genoa, and Pisa. Originally the great network of Temple preceptories throughout Western Europe was to provide men and money for the war in Palestine. As the Crusades went from disaster to catastrophe, many of the western administrators began to regard funds spent on such a hopeless cause as a waste of money, a useless drain on their resources which would be better employed in consolidating the power of the order and increasing its standing in the West.

Over the years what had originally begun as a protective and charitable facility for pilgrims had grown to an international business which lent large sums of money to kings and governments — despite the official Church ban on usury. As early as 1148, the order had lent money to King Louis VII of France to finance the Second Crusade. In 1295, they lent important funds to finance Philippe IV's war against England. These activities were in total disaccord with the object for which the order had been founded. In later days the law and the vow regarding poverty fell into neglect, and the ambitious late Masters of the Order lived like princes in luxurious palaces with rich apparel. The Masters' political judgment was always poor; they were courageous military leaders and skilled administrators by no means diplomats or statesmen. They had long engaged in a bitter rivalry with the other great military order, the Hospitalers. The greatest fault made by the Templar leadership was to pursue self-interest much too far. Indeed, their wealth became the cause of much jealousy, and the size of the Templar estates throughout Europe gave rise to unfavorable comments.

After the fall of Acre in 1291, the last outpost of the Latin kingdom had fallen, and the Templars withdrew to their European estates. The order — perceived to be dangerous, too wealthy and corrupt — became unpopular. Their untouchable wealth and their many privileges made them a law unto themselves in the countries of Western Europe where they had lands — particularly in France. By 1304, there were rumors (probably false) about corruption, homosexuality, devil worship, and irreligious acts and blasphemies committed by the Templars during their secret rites of initiation. In 1307, king of France Philippe le Bel (who reigned from 1285 to 1314) thought of a way to unlock them. The reasons why Philippe sought to destroy the Templars remain unclear. He may have genuinely believed that they were corrupt, feared their power within his realm, or simply seen an opportunity to seize the order's wealth, being chronically short of money himself. Indeed the spoliation of the Templars was not Philippe's first criminal move; in July 1306 he had expelled the Jews from France and confiscated their properties. Anyway, the king and his chancellor, Guillaume de Nogaret, organized a cynical and squalid conspiracy. With forged evidence, they accused the Templars of various crimes and heresy. All Templars in France were arrested; some were tortured and confessed to the alleged

Knight Hospitaler with Pennon   **Hospitaler Priester**

crimes. In 1317, after ten years of disparaging and false accusations, the damage done to their reputation was irreversible, and Pope Clement V (himself a Frenchman elected with Philippe le Bel's support) reluctantly agreed to issue a papal bull suppressing the order in France, Germany, and England. The leadership of the Templars—including the Grand-Master Jacques de Moley—were burned alive at the stake after refusing to confess to the charges of heresy and blasphemy or for recanting confessions extracted under torture. The Templars' properties were officially handed over to the rival Hospitaler order,

but most of the wealth went into the French king's coffers. On the Iberian Peninsula the Templars were refounded and continued under new names: The *Order of Saint-Maria-of-Montesa* in Spain and *Order of Christ* in Portugal. The question of the guilt of the Templars has been a matter of fierce and passionate controversy for centuries, but modern opinion inclines to the idea that they were victims of a highly unjust manipulation from the pope and opportunistic persecution by the king of France. The Templars were part of the ideals of chivalry, and they continue to capture the imagination today. Their disturbing prestige, their supposed secrets, their alleged practices and hidden wealth, their mysteries, their tragic end, and the results of their cursing upon their tormentors gave rise to numerous creepy legends, fantastic tales, and extravagant beliefs.

The Hospitalers

The Hospitalers, as their name implies, were originally a charitable group of men who cared for the sick and weary Christian pilgrims but also for the local Arabs and Jews. As early as 1048 some merchants of Amalfi obtained from the Caliph of Egypt — then overlord of Palestine — permission to erect a convent and a small church in the neighborhood of the Holy Sepulcher. The convent was placed under the care of Benedictine monks, and in it pilgrims were given food, rest, care, shelter, and protection. Later on, two hospitals were created close to the convent, one for women dedicated to Saint Mary Magdalene and the other for men, dedicated to Saint John the Baptist. Within the convent and around the beds of the sick, it is commonly believed that the Order of the Hospitalers had its origin.

After the capture of Jerusalem in July 1099, the fraternal charity shown toward the Crusaders had developed into new vocations. In recognition of the valuable help given to pilgrims, the Community of the Hospital was endowed with riches and properties in foreign lands where they founded hostels in southern France and Italy on the route to the Holy Land. By that

Mounted Knight Hospitaler, Early 14th Century. The order's banner was adopted in 1130 and remained unchanged throughout the Hospitaler's history.

time a certain Brother Peter Gerard instituted the Community of the Hospital as a religious body bound by the three vows of poverty, obedience, and chastity. The brethren wore black mantles and after 1248 black robes with a white cross on the chest. When Gerald died in 1120, his successor, Raymond du Puy, introduced the eight-pointed cross — which symbolized the eight beatitudes (Christ's sayings in the Sermon on the Mount). In 1259

the order changed to a red surcoat with a white cross. The order's flag was a red cross on a white rectangular background.

As the Turks gradually recovered from their defeat of 1099 and became more aggressive, the peace and security of the pilgrims were threatened. Raymond du Puy — an organizer of genius — began building the power of the organization and proposed several modifications which

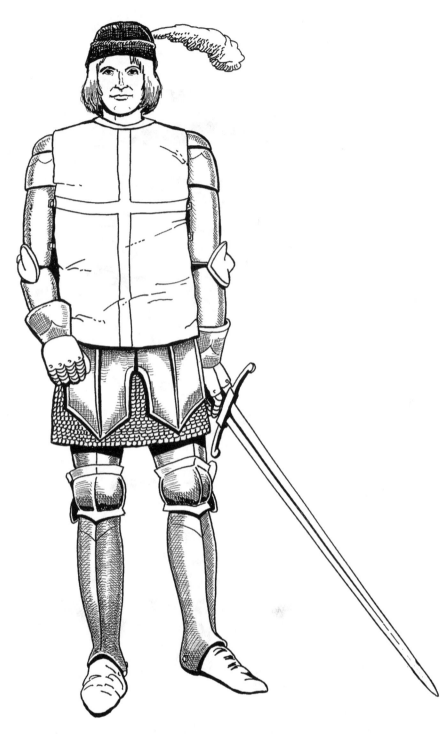

Knight Hospitaler, ca. 1480. By the time of the siege of Rhodes in 1480, the Hospitalers wore a mixture of mail and plate armor with a short red tabard bearing the cross of the order.

of Saint John. This was accepted and recognized by the Pope Pascal II in February 1113.

The order was militarized, but the Hospitalers combined the task of tending the sick with waging war on Islam. Fighting was only a secondary activity for the Hospitalers, and militarization was a long and slow process. Surgeons had mess with the fighting brethren, and much attention was given to the maintenance of the hospital. Until 1187, the hospital of Jerusalem had beds for about 1,000 patients where Christians—both Syrian-born Poulains and visitors—were nursed for ptomaine poisoning, plagues from insects, sand-fly fever, ophthalmia, desert sores, and endemic septicemia. The brethren's hospitals were influenced by Byzantine models, and they owed a lot to Arab medicine. They took the place of a field medical corps after a battle, besides wounds, there were always casualties with terrible bruises beneath their chain mail and those who suffered from shock or from heatstroke.

As they continued to take care of the pilgrims, the Hospitalers became even more popular and respected. As accommodation and nursing were hard to find, pilgrims and Crusaders had enough cause to be grateful, and thus the Hospitalers acquired wealth, houses, and lands through gifts and donations. The revenues of their possessions were spent in forwarding food, wine, clothes, and blankets for hospital use as well as weapons, armor, horses, and fortifications for military purposes. The papacy gave them many privileges such as having their own priests and churches, thus making them exempt from episcopal control.

The vows, admission, rules, discipline, structure, and the organization of the Hospitalers were rather similar to those of the Templars, and everything previously discussed about the Templars may be applied to the Hospitalers. They seemed, however, to have had a looser rule and possibly a better reputation; it was said that nursing—an important Hospitaler activity—made them more humane and influenced a softer attitude toward both friends and foe. Their spiritual life was probably influenced by the cult of Mary the Virgin and certainly deepened by their devotion to the sick and poor, for wherever they had estates, they also had hospitals and guest houses. Their twofold vocation, to nurse and to fight,

were unanimously adopted. The monks were incorporated as a military order and—as their hospital was dedicated to Saint John the Baptist—renamed *Ordo Equitum Hospitaliorum Sancti Johannis Hierosolymitani*, that is, the Order of the Knights of Saint John of the Hospital of Jerusalem, more commonly called Hospitalers, or Knights

gave them a significant role in the life of the Latin states of Outremer. Their service in Palestine was parallel to that of the Templars, and along with them, they became the most formidable military order in the Holy Land.

In 1136, King Fulk of Jerusalem gave them the castle of Beth Gibelin, a key position on the road from Gaza to Hebron. That was the first of their huge fortresses in Palestine. Hospitaler castles in the Holy Land included Belmont, Touban, Mont Ferrant, Forbelet, Castrum Rubrum, Turris Rubea, Qula, Recordane, Bordj es-Sabi, Bordj Arab, Coliath, Margat, Silifke, Ascalon, and Acre. The finest of the Hospitaler castles is undoubtedly the famous *Hosn el-Akrad* (Crak des Chevaliers). The Crak— standing on a naturally defensive hill dominating the Holm Gap — was taken over by the knights Hospitalers in the 1140s. After the earthquake of 1202, it was redesigned and rebuilt as an immensely strong fortress including a huge central core with a large keep surrounded by two powerful concentric enceintes. The castle was taken by Sultan Baybars in March 1271. Another famous Hospitaler castle was Belvoir — built north of Jerusalem in Galilee about 1168. It was a powerful concentric fortress based on the Byzantine model with a regular double crenelated walls and flanking towers. Well protected by their network of fortresses, the Hospitalers were always ready for war, and they took part in most expeditions against the infidels with undaunted valor.

Gradually the fortunes of the Order of Saint John changed. Internal dissension, quarrels among the Christian princes, rivalry with the Templars, unwise alliances, and ill-advised expeditions weakened the fraternity of the Hospitalers. After the capture of Jerusalem in 1187, the knights Hospitalers removed their headquarters to their castle Margat, and in 1191 the order retired to the port of Acre. After a hundred years of brave but hopeless fighting and many vicissitudes, the Hospitalers had suffered grievous setbacks and heavy losses in money and manpower, and many strongholds had to be abandoned. Neither the Hospitalers nor their rivals, the Templars came out well in the chaotic last period of the Crusades. After the fall of Acre in 1291, the Crusades and the dream of Outremer were over. The Hospitalers withdrew to Limassol in Cyprus, and in 1309 they invaded the island of Rhodes, where they established their headquarters and created an independent and sovereign military theocratic state.

Although defeated and weakened the order of Saint John was not demoralized; the brethren had not given up all hopes of regaining the lost Holy Land. The ranks of the order were strengthened by new volunteers, and the army was reconstructed. The knights of Saint John fortified the harbor and town, built a fortress for the Grand Master and a large hospital for the sick. They

developed a strong navy and continued the fight against the Muslims by naval operations. They began their role of Christian privateers, which later to made them the terror of the Turks in the Mediterranean.

The revival of the order stirred up all Europe, and the Hospitalers soon rose to fame again. By that time they reorganized their structure. From the start — although the official language was French and Frenchmen dominated the order — the recruitment of the knight monks of Saint John had always been largely international. Knights of different nationalities — called *langue* (tongue) — were grouped together in their *auberges* (inns or barracks) according to their origin, and here the members lived, trained, and held their meetings. Each langue was headed by an officer called a "bailiff." These officers represented their men in a council at the head of which presided the Grand Master who was elected for his lifetime — subject to papal confirmation. The langues included Provence, Auvergne, France, Italy, Aragon, England (abolished in 1560), Germany, and Castile — to which the langues of Leon and Portugal were added in 1462. Each langue had responsibility for the defense of a section of the town walls.

For more than two centuries, Rhodes was a strong Christian base in the eastern Mediterranean Sea; it was a thorn in the Muslims' side and the scourge of their shipping. The Turks — considering the military order too close to their quarters and knowing that as long as the knights had naval power, their territories could not be held completely — cast an envious eye on the island. Consequently the Turks hurled numerous raids and expeditions against the knights. In 1435 the army and the fleet of sultan Baybars attacked Rhodes, but the Knights succeeded in repulsing them. This resulted in rendering the name of the order more renowned all over Europe. After the fall of Constantinople in 1453, the Hospitalers on Rhodes were the last and only Christian outpost left in the East. In 1480 another Turk army — headed by Palaeologos Pasha — landed and, armed with massive guns, attempted to capture the city. Owing to the inspiring leadership of Grand Master Pierre d'Aubusson, this attack too was repulsed. The weakened knight Hospitalers were however submitted to another attack in 1522. The huge armies of Suleiman the Magnificent — commanded by his Grand Vizier, Pir Mahomet Pasha — were ultimately victorious after a terrible six-month siege. The knights, worn out by fatigue and much reduced in number, had to surrender in January 1523. Suleiman treated the defeated heroes liberally, giving them the honors of war. They were compelled to relinquish their hold on Rhodes but were allowed to leave the island. The Christian population of Rhodes was permitted to follow them with all their property and without any molestation.

The capture of Rhodes seemed to mark the end of the Hospitalers. The order had lost its might in the East, was homeless, and had scattered forces; its fame seemed to have passed away, and the hope of a recovery was remote. Astonishingly, the Order of the Knights of Saint John—like the phoenix—was quick once again to be reborn from its ashes. After various bargains with Pope Adrian VI and his successor, Clement VII, and with the king of Spain and emperor of Germany, Charles V donated them their next home in 1533. In return for the annual presentation of a falcon to his viceroy of Sicily, the Hospitalers were allowed to establish themselves in the town of Tripoli in Libya and on the islands of Malta, Gozo, and Comino. From then on the knight Hospitalers were also known under the name Knights of Malta.

Again the knights rebuilt their fleet of galleys and continued to fight the Muslims with naval operations. The superb leadership of the Grand Master Jean Parisot de La Vallette prevented the dislodging of the knights from Malta in 1565 in one of the most famous sieges in history. After the Great Siege of 1565, the knights' popularity was at its highest. They rebuilt their town (Valetta), established formidable fortifications, and continued as a theocratic sovereign state until June 1798 when the neutrality of the order was violated by the French. Malta was conquered by Napoléon Bonaparte on his way to Egypt, and the knights were expelled. By that time, there were talks with the government of the United States to house the Knights there, but that came to nothing.

After 1814, Malta was seized by the British, and the Knights never succeeded in reestablishing themselves on the Island—in spite of various promises made to them. Malta—together with Gibraltar, Egypt, and Aden—was an important harbor strategically situated on the way to British India. The knights set up their headquarter in Rome in 1834 and adopted new noncombatant status. Since 1961, the aristocratic Maltese knights are known as the Sovereign Military Hospitaler Order of Saint John of Jerusalem, of Rhodes, and of Malta. Still headquartered in Rome, the knights continue their humanitarian tasks in most parts of the world under several slightly different jurisdictions. Since 1964, Malta is an independent republic and a "must see" for fortification enthusiasts.

Other Minor Military Orders

The Order of the Saint Sepulcher of Jerusalem

Long before the Crusades, there was a small group of monks and canons (clergymen attached to a church) whose mission was to guard and defend Christ's tomb

Knight of the Saint Sepulcher

in Jerusalem. Formed of Augustine regular canons from the Order of Saint John, this community became the Order of the Saint Sepulcher, probably after the capture of Jerusalem in 1099. The brethren wore a white cloak with a red cross with four small crosses around it—

symbolizing Christ's five wounds. The small militia was intended to defend the city, but the brethren also took part at the battle of Ramlah in September 1101 where many of them were killed. In 1106 they fought with King Baldwin I, and in 1120 a contingent of them fought in Spain against the Moors. After the abandonment of the Holy Land in 1291, the order retreated to Perugia (Italy), and in 1254, King Louis IX of France entrusted them with the management of Sainte Chapelle in Paris. In 1336 the order was transferred to the convent of the Cordeliers brothers. Today the order is a small ecclesiastical association attached to the archbishop of Paris.

The Hospitalers of Saint Lazarus

The Order of Saint Lazarus probably had its origins in a leper hospital founded at Jerusalem before the conquest of 1099 and run by Greek and Armenians monks who devoted themselves to take care of all sick. As the years went by, the leper house also admitted Templar and Hospitaler knights who were infected with leprosy and all other forms of skin diseases. Early in the 12th century it was taken over by Frankish Hospitalers, and the brethren wore the black Hospitaler habit with a green cross. The order administrated a network of nursing houses in both Syria and Europe organized on a commandery framework similar to that of the Order of Saint John. The Lazar knights developed a force of military brethren, but they were never numerous and had only a handful of nonleper brethren for protection, though no doubt in time of crisis "unclean" knights also took up arms, as happened at the battles of Hattin in 1187 and Gaza in 1244 where some of them were killed. After the fall of Jerusalem in 1243, the order moved to Acre and was responsible for the defense of the northern suburb of Montmusard. After the abandonment of the Holy Land, they moved to Cyprus and ceased all military activities. They continued a shadowy existence in the castle of Boigny (France) and then moved to Paris, where they founded a hospital giving their name to a neighborhood and a railroad station in Paris. After many vicissitudes, the order was suppressed by the Vatican in 1603, but a dissident branch was created in France under the name Order of Our Lady of the Mount Carmel.

Knights of Saint Thomas of Canterbury at Acre

About 1198, William, chaplain to the dean of Saint Paul's, was deeply moved by the English crusaders' misery and began nursing sick and wounded pilgrims. Aided by King Richard, William built a small chapel, purchased a cemetery, and founded a hospital and a nursing frater-nity restricted to Englishmen. The brotherhood was named *Knights of Saint Thomas of Canterbury at Acre* after Thomas Becket, the archbishop of Canterbury who was murdered in 1170 because he tried to prevent King Henry II from gaining more control of Church affairs. In 1173 the pope had made Becket a saint, and his grave in Canterbury had become an important center of pilgrimage in England. The Order of Saint Thomas probably turned military by the time of the Fifth Crusade in the period 1217–1221. Their constitution was copied from the Templar rule. The habit was a white mantle bearing a red cross with a white scallop shell on it. The Order of Saint Thomas acquired lands and estates in Cyprus, Sicily, Naples, and later Greece; while in England, its headquarters was the Hospital of Saint Thomas Acon in London on the site of what is now Mercer's Hall. The Brethren of Saint Thomas were always a small brotherhood with little significance and little military power, most Englishmen preferring to join the Hospitalers of Saint John's langue d'Angleterre. After the disaster of 1291, the English order declined and ceased to exist after about 1360.

The Order of Saint James of Altopascio

This Italian order is often considered to be the oldest of all military orders. It was created in the year 952 by some Augustinian monks at Altopascio, near Lucca (Tuscany, Italy), as a hospitaler structure intended for the assistance to pilgrims on their way to Rome and Santiago de Compostella. Although never recognized or allowed by the pope, the brotherhood became a kind of armed police force providing escort and protection to pilgrims from 1056 onward. The order had a few hospitals in Italy, France, and England, but after about 1240 the order declined due to the waning of religious fervor and pilgrimage. From 1446 to 1537 the mastership of the order was in the hands of the Capponi family from Florence. In 1585 the declining order was absorbed by the knights of San Stefano of Tuscany and placed under the tutelage of the dukes of Tuscany. The order's emblem was a T-shaped Saint Anthony's tau cross worn on a red habit.

The Order of San Stefano of Tuscany

This Italian naval order was founded in 1561 by Grand Duke Cosimo de Medici of Tuscany to combat the pirates who infested the Mediterranean Sea. The members of the order followed the Benedictine rule, and the Duke of Tuscany was the Grand Master. The order had galleys which cooperated with those of the knights of Saint John from Malta in patrolling the sea. The Order of San Stefano fought with twelve galleys at the decisive battle of Lepanto in 1571 when the Turks finally lost control

Knight of Altopascio

of the western Mediterranean. The order's emblem was a gold-edged Maltese cross.

Secular Orders of Chivalry

A byproduct of the idea of knightly brotherhood was the development of various small private fraternities of knights which appeared in France at the end of the 14th century. These were apparently small orders of knighthood, with insignias, rules and chapters. Instead of being honorific institutions, however, they were practical. The French associations such as the *Pomme d'Or* in Auvergne, the *Saint George* in Rougemenont, and the *Tiercelet* in Poitou, for example, were a mixture between freemasonry, fighting companies, mutual protection associations, trade unions, veterans clubs, and commercial organizations, but with an element of chivalrous idealism as well. The members were expected to share the ethics of chivalry but also to help each other in any way they could, notably in lawsuits, and warn each other of any action likely to be taken against them.

Secular orders of knighthood became popular in the 15th and 16th centuries. Though they were inspired by the early medieval military orders, they had however little in common with the religious orders of the preceding period. They were much concerned with rewards and celebrations of worldly honor. They were formed for less idealistic reasons, but mainly as the reinforcement of the privileges and the exclusive status of the ruling class—the creation of useful alliances in the pursuit of diplomatic and political ends. These orders were many and varied. The most prestigious were created by kings or great lords, such as the Order of the Band founded in 1330 by King Alfonso XI of Castile, the Order of the Garter from 1348 by King Edward III of England, the Order of the Star founded in 1351 by King John of France, the Order of the Knot created in 1352 by King Louis of Naples, and the Order of the Golden Buckle founded in 1355 by Emperor Charles IV, to name but a few. In more recent centuries, prestigious orders of chivalry continued to be created. The Order of Saint Louis was founded by King Louis XIV of France as a reward and emulation for his senior officers. Napoleon's *Légion d'Honneur*—started in 1802—is another example. All orders, fraternities, and brotherhoods were usually exclusive to men. They had constitutions, regulations, and oaths laid down in statutes which defined the objectives of the associations and the rules governing eligibility for membership and conduct of members. Many associated themselves with a specific saint, and all held meetings to outline activities, celebrate achievements, and initiate new members. Members had specific duties to perform; all had ranks indicated by robes and special insignias. The secular orders of chivalry in the late Middle Ages, the Renaissance, and later represented a mundane version of early medieval chivalry, but practical aims in a contemporary context combined uneasily with respect for the traditional values of real—and obsolete—chivalry.

13

Reconquista in Spain

The second corner where cross and crescent met on the battlefield was Spain. The reconquest of the Iberian Peninsula was part of the same movement of Christian expansion as in Palestine but — being the only fully successful military operation of the Christian holy wars — assumed a special character. In the Iberian Peninsula, the Muslim conquerors were called Saracens or Moors, regardless of their ethnic origin that included Arabs, Berbers, Libyans, Egyptians, etc.

The Arab Occupation of Spain

The Moorish reconnaissance probe into Spain in 710 was investigated by an Arabian adventurer, Abu Abderahman Musa, who had subdued Tangier in 707; after a pillaging raid, the small force returned to North Africa with a report guaranteed to excite other raiders. In 711 a larger army under Tarik ibn Ziyad landed in southern Spain at a place then called Djebel Al Tarik (Tarik's mountain, whence Gibraltar). Tarik's force defeated the Visigoth king Roderick, subdued several cities, and began a rapid invasion of the peninsula. In 756 an Umayyad prince, Abd-al-Rahman, set up an emirate (principality) on Spain named Al-Andalus (whence the name of province of Andalusia) with Cordoba as its capital. Though the Abbasid caliphate in Baghdad was formally recognized, Al-Andalus was a virtually independent state. By that time a huge mosque was being built in Cordoba with a veritable forest of columns topped by double arches. In Spain the Arabs — and many Muslim Berbers (early inhabitants of North Africa) were never more than a ruling elite. Highly prosperous and rather tolerant in religion, Al-Andalus remained open to cultural influences from the whole Mediterranean. Its Arabic speaking merchants and scholars could and did travel the whole extended Islamic world and, at the same time, contact with the Catholic Latin north was not completely broken. However, this was to change when Spain became a front line in the struggle between Christians and Muslims. At the beginning of the 11th century, the Muslims held the Balearic Islands, Corsica, Sardinia, Sicily, the entire coast of northern Africa, and the southern two-thirds of Spain.

The Reconquista

Muslim conquest of the Iberian Peninsula had indeed never been complete. When the Saracens overran the country in the 8th century, the remnants of the Visigoths' army had withdrawn to the northwestern corner where they established the kingdom of Asturias. By the year 1000 Asturias was divided into two small states, León and Castile. To the east of these lands Charlemagne had established the march of Spain which developed into the independent kingdom of Navarre, the region of Aragon and the county of Barcelona. From these lands, the Christian cause was revived, and the Reconquista was launched. It was in Spain that a Christian version of the idea of religious *jihad* (holy war) first began to develop.

The Reconquista was a very long process that began before the First Crusade to Palestine, and it lasted for centuries. There were distinct stages in the reconquest of Spain by the Christians. As long as the Muslim power

Moorish Spearman

been very casual affairs with a minimum expenditure of effort in keeping with the custom of the age of chivalry. The tiny kingdom of Asturias was supplanted by new realms; León and Castile were independent, the county of Barcelona — soon to merge with Aragon — formed another state.

The Reconquista was halted for a time during the 12th century, partly because of rivalry between the Christian groups themselves. The various realms were rival, competing for power, and each waged its own war against the Moors. But in the 13th century the advance was resumed, and Muslim domination collapsed in the face of Christian offensives. After the victory of Navas de Tolosa in 1212, Cordoba was retaken in 1236, Valencia in 1238, Sevilla in 1248, Faro in Portugal in 1249, and Tarifa in 1291. Toward the end of the 13th century, the reconquest of the peninsula seemed virtually complete. All that remained in Muslim hands was the southern kingdom of Granada, which fell back to the Christian king only in January 1492.

The Reconquista was personified by famous heroes, such as Rodrigo Diaz del Vivar (1034–1099). Better known as El Cid (from the Arab *sid-y* meaning "my lord," a nickname given by his enemies who respected him), Rodrigo was one of the most complex and remarkable heroes of the Middle Ages. El Cid was famous for his just behavior, nobility, and magnanimity. Brave, heroic, loyal, a good husband and father, a redoubtable warrior and a man of honor, he was all that a medieval palatine might be expected to be. He was also a skillful politician, taking service indifferently with Christians and Muslims; after numerous feats of arms — and various bargains — he managed to make himself king of Valencia in 1094. El Cid became the idealized hero of countless legends and romances — not written down before the 14th century — chanted by wandering minstrels. For Spaniards he was the ideal of knightly virtue, patriotic duty, and Christian grace displayed in the holy struggle against the Moors.

In the 12th century, an army of Crusaders sailing toward the Mediterranean for the Second Crusade anchored at the mouth of River Douro. They were persuaded by the local people to stay to fight the infidels there. So, instead of Edessa, they stormed Lisbon in 1147, slaughtered the Muslim inhabitants, took over their lands, and supported the foundation of the independent realm of Portugal by the first king Afonso Henriques I.

remained united, the Christian states could do little than hold their own. A first period lasted — roughly speaking — from 720 to 1034, with small focal points of resistance beginning to emerge from Asturias to Catalonia with the River Douro as their frontier. It was a period of probing with small operations and setbacks but, nevertheless, an increasing pressure as Christians took advantage of the Muslims' internal problems.

Then in 1034 the quarrels among the Muslim chieftains came to the complete disruption of the caliphate of Cordoba. This gave the Christians their great opportunity to engage the process of liberation of the Iberian Peninsula. From 1034 onward the Christians launched various major offensives which cumulated in the capture of Toledo by King Alfonso VI in 1085. But Christian Spain was fragmented, and military campaigns seemed to have

The Reconquista was a complicated affair. There were Christian Spaniards; and Muslim Spaniards, both sides regarded Spain as their home with equally valid reasons after having lived there for centuries. Despite a veneer of Islam, many of the Spanish Muslims were originally of Gothic or Ibero-Roman stock and were separated from their northern Christian neighbors only by religious belief. The meeting and the influence of the two rich civilizations are still today an important feature of Spanish culture. There was such an important degree of integration and interaction between the two that modern Spain retains a powerful element of Orientalism within its cultural makeup.

The reconquest was a long series of wars intertwined with many periods of peace, truces, and continuous relationships. However, the increasing intervention of the Church in secular affairs rendered the reconquest a war of religion with mutual intolerance. It was a slow and cruel war, the emphasis became more and more on the fight and the slaughter of the infidels rather than on conversion. Not for nothing was the patron saint of Spain the apostle *Santiago Matamoros* (Saint James the Moor Slayer). The periods of combat saw both sides fanatically fighting for their faith with equal zeal as combatants on both sides were assured that they would go to their respective heaven if they died for their holy cause.

If the Reconquista was in many aspects a holy war, it was also a war of territorial domination, with each party trying to secure as much land as possible for economic reasons. Its main impetus came from the attempts of the sovereigns of the Christian kingdoms of Portugal, Navare, Castile, León, and Aragon. The French Gascons had strong political ties with the kingdoms beyond the Pyrenees and they too played their part in the expeditions, less inspired by the call to a sacred task than by ties of alliance and friendship, and the hope of booty from the wealthy Moorish realms. The crusading idea in Spain was largely local, royal, and unofficial. The popes on the whole did not give a lot of attention to it. The Reconsquista — if it had papal blessing — was a secondary front compared to the importance of Palestine. There was not a permanent state of

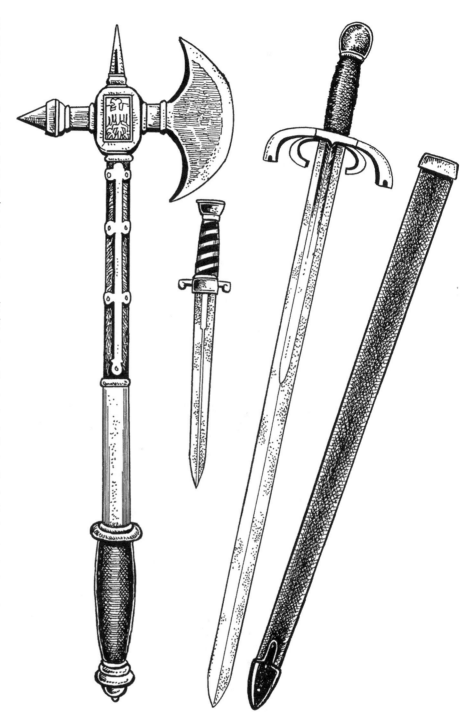

Spanish Weapons, 15th Century. *Left to right:* battle-axe, dagger, sword and scabbard.

war as Moors, Jews, and Christians managed to coexist rather peacefully for long periods of time.

Weapons and Tactics

Next to the great campaigns launched by the Christian monarchs, there was however a continuous *guerrilla*

Saracen Horsemen

their feudal retainers. The *hermangildas* were groups of volunteers with a semireligious character often later becoming military religious orders. The *milicia concejiles* were a militia of foot soldiers raised by the municipality and generally used to defend their own city walls. The *caballeria villana* were light nonnoble mounted warriors, usually raised among free settlers who had been granted lands in the newly conquered territories. The highly typical Spanish *hidalgo* (literally "son of something") was a poor and proud noble knight particularly common in Castile. There were also small groups of hired mercenaries who frequently included a certain number of Moorish renegades. The most famous of these gangs was that headed by El Cid which eventually numbered around 7,000 soldiers.

Spanish weapons and armor were the same as used throughout Europe: sword and lance, steel helmet, chain tunic, and shield. Tactics were based on the single, decisive mounted charge, the *cavalgada*, though there was a tendency to wear lighter equipment and ride agile Arab horses. Auxiliary light cavalrymen were armed with bullfighter's lances, javelins, and knives. Infantry consisted of spearmen, slingers, and archers carrying additional swords or axes. A rich man's arms would often be jeweled and damascened in the Saracen fashion, especially the superb swords from Toledo, while Andalusian mantles were worn and some Christian knights preferred to use Moorish curved scimitars.

Moorish light cavalry, the *jinetes,* wore mail shirts and spiked onion helmets; their armor was often gilded

(small war) on the never clearly defined front line. Border warfare consisted mainly of razzias (plundering raids) and skirmishes often degenerating into mere horse stealing and rustling. From this situation emerged a large part of the population bearing arms and permanent popular troops. There were small armies of noble landowners and

Moorish Horseman, 12th Century. This light cavalryman is armed with a kindjal (a straight sword) and an adarga (heart-shaped shield). He wears a soft head gear and a quilted tunic.

Spanish Christian Soldier, ca. 1300

or silvered. They charged with spears held overarm or hurled javelins. They also used hooked lances and lassos to pull opponents from the saddle. Their swords were light scimitars; their shields were often heart-shaped. Moorish horsemen frequently swamped Spanish cavalry by sheer numbers, preventing them from choosing suitable ground or assembling in their elaborate formations. The Moorish infantry comprised Berber footmen and a certain number of savage *gomeres*, Negroes

Right: Spanish Knights, 14th Century

sieges. The Christians virtually perfected the art of siege using massive hurling and assault machines. The Moors depended more on attrition tactics. Captured towns—either assaulted by force or taken by starvation—became bridgeheads, garrisoned during the winter, so that no ground had been lost when the advance was resumed the following spring. On both sides, warships (mainly galleys) were used for transport, for hit-and-run raids, or for blockade purpose.

The Iberian Military Orders

The Reconquista was a holy war in which military religious orders played an important role. The Spanish Reconquista—aiming to drive the Moors off the Iberian Peninsula—lasted for more than four hundred years. By many aspects it can be regarded as a Holy War and a Crusade. The Iberian military orders—like the orders created in Palestine—were a remarkable blend of Germanic warriors and Christian sacerdos. The Templars and the Hospitalers of Saint John of Jerusalem were at first encouraged to participate in the struggle against Islam in Spain. They were given castles, monasteries, estates, and territories. However, both Templars and Hospitalers were too busy in Palestine to involve themselves completely in Spain. Both orders were more interested in acquiring possessions outside the Holy Land which supported their endeavors there and provided revenue rather than becoming involved in what might be an extra drain on their resources. The rise of the native orders was rather late and was due mainly to the reluctance of Templars and Hospitalers to commit themselves fully to Spanish adventures. The atmosphere of the Spanish wars did not encourage the zeal with which the Templars and Hospitalers fought in Palestine. The contacts with the Moorish civilization were too frequent, and the mutual respect bred by familiarity too present. Both camps suffered from a proliferation of kingdoms and interminable quarrels among themselves. Consequently, the Spanish Christians realms had to create their own national military religious orders.

The Spanish military orders probably had a part of their origin in the *hermangildas* who were small temporary armed brotherhoods, self-defense groups, and bands of local farmers, rather like Boer commandos in the old Transvaal (South Africa). Gradually some of these groups became permanent and acquired a quasireligious character, and their members may have taken certain vows such as temporary celibacy and an oath to defend the border and to protect Christians. Their other root was undoubtedly from the military orders of Palestine. Between the former and the latter, there were many similarities,

Spanish Christian Knight, 13th Century

armed with broad-bladed stabbing spears and large hide shields. They were supported by archers and slingers who could discharge lethal clay bullets from a surprising distance. To impress or demoralize the enemy there was commonly a band with drums, trumpets, and cymbals, and the soldiers would bawl out shrill and savage war cries.

Both sides made a wide use of fortification; Castile itself being named after the *castillos* (castles) built along the border. Whoever held the fortresses had control over the lands, and both sides waged siege warfare. More than by pitched battles, the Reconquista was marked by many

particularly the severe Cistercian regular (however adapted to the special status of combatant), the hierarchy based on the three feudal classes (the noble fighting knights, the ecclesiastical chaplains, and the nonnoble working lay brothers), the Grand Master elected for his lifetime by a chapter of dignitaries, and the exclusiveness of male membership. Uniting fanatical faith and Christian charity to military courage and corps discipline, the Spanish *frayles* (knight-monks or brethren) provided a significant fighting force as the local monarchy held a tight rein on them. Some of these orders did not exist for long, some were as small as the garrison of a castle, their efficiency was sometimes questionable, and they sometimes suffered of internal rivalry. Nevertheless, they each formed a permanent, disciplined, and always available militia, a welcome additional force for the Spanish feudal armies.

The Order of Calatrava

The first military order to be founded in Spain was the Order of Calatrava. Its name came from the Moorish castle of *Qalat Rawah* (literally, the Castle of War) which was captured by the king of Castile, Alfonso VII, in 1147. The castle Calatrava was then entrusted by the king to the knights Templar as a frontier stronghold guarding the road to Toledo against the Moors. In 1157 the Templars abandoned the dangerous and untenable place, and offered it to King Sancho of Castile, who could not find anyone able to hold it against the Moors. In desperation, a Spanish nobleman, Diego Velasquez, who had become a Cistercian monk, persuaded his abbot, Ramon Sierra of Fitero, to move a community of monks and knights to the castle in 1158. When Ramon died in 1164, the untenable castle was still in Christian hands, and the region was cleared of Moorish raiders. The same year, the successful order was officially given canonical status affiliated to the Cistercian order by Pope Alexander III. In 1179 a commandery was founded at Alcaniz in Aragon, and this later became one of the order's greatest houses. In 1197 a new headquarters was established at Salvatierra, and the knights of Calatrava were sometimes called the Order of Salvatierra until that place was evacuated and the knights reverted to their original name.

Calatrava became one of the wealthiest and most powerful bodies in Spain, providing its standing army. The basic organization was completed within twenty years and included a *maestre* (master elected in the Ciscertian way) assisted by a *comendator mayor* (lieutenant), *freyles clerigos* (chaplains), and *caballeros freyles* (knights generally grouped by twelve). Their habit was a hooded white, later gray, tunic; the knight's skirt was shortened to facilitate riding. His armor was often

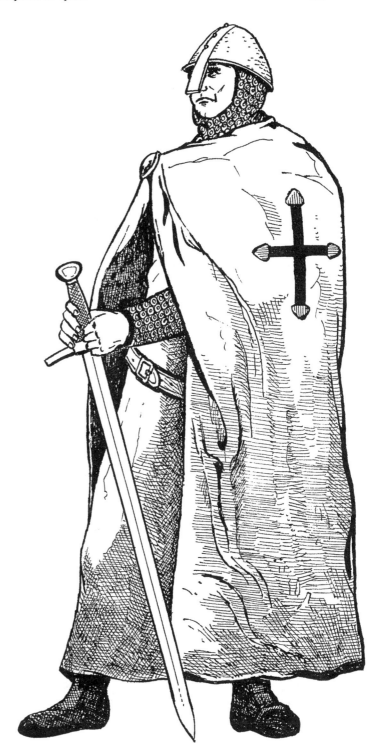

Knight of Calatrava

painted black. The insignia was a red cross with thick points. In 1397 Calatrava adopted a red cross fleur-de-lis which evolved into a curious and distinctive shape, the petals of the lily bending back until they touched the stem to form a Lombardic M — for Maria. The knights of Calatrava differed from the Templars and Hospitalers because they were obliged — after 1254 — to swear an oath

were affiliated with it, Alcantara and Aviz, and the three orders constituted the powerful Cistercian Iberian family. The order of Calatrava became a royal Spanish order in 1482. Even since then, the order has been purely honorific.

The Order of Alcantara

The monastic militia of Alcantara seemed to originate from a small *hermangilda* operating in the kingdom of León about 1170. Its origin could also have been a Cistercian community founded at San Julian del Pereiro in Portugal. The king of León, Alphonse X, gave the fortress of Alcantara to the brotherhood, who were formally recognized by Pope Lucius III in 1183. Such a small body seemed to have needed support from a powerful organization in order to survive, and soon Alcantara was affiliated with the larger order of Calatrava. Alcantara eventually became little more than a minor branch of Calatrava, and it was thus under the secular authority of the king of Castile. Like the other Spanish orders, Alcantara became a national honorific order taken over by the Spanish crown after 1494.

The Order of Saint Benedict of Aviz

The Order of Saint Benedict of Aviz (originally called Order of Santa Maria) was Portuguese. Its origin was a military *hermangilda* founded in 1162 operating in the plain of Alemtejo. In 1166 the militia adopted the Benedictine rule and was entrusted with the defense of the town of Evora (south of Lisbon). The brethren—known as the Brotherhood of Saint Mary of Evora—claimed to have been founded by the first king of Portugal's brother, Dom Pedro Henriques. For the same reason as Alcantara, the order was affiliated to the larger Calatrava. In 1187, the monk soldiers obtained the castle of Aviz from King Alfonso-Henriques II, thus their name. The order was officially recognized in 1204 and followed the Benedictine rule. Knights wore the black Benedictine surcoat with a green cross. In 1238 they became independent of Calatrava. After 1352 the order flourished and eventually provided Portugal with its ruling dynasty when the Grand Master of Saint Benedict was elected king of Portugal in 1384 under the name of João I. The dynasty of Aviz reigned over Portugal until 1578. Today the order still exists as an honorific association with the president of the Republic of Portugal as Grand Master.

The Order of Santiago

A small *hermangilda* was founded in 1170 by the king of León, Fernando II, for the defense of the city of Cáceres

Knight of Alcantara

of loyalty to the king of Castile thus acknowledging a secular lord, which did not enable them to resist pressures from the court of Castile. The king increasingly encroached on the order's freedom of action and often succeeded in getting his own candidate elected as Grand Master. The monastic militia of Calatrava absorbed the short-lived order of Montfrac in 1221 and was given some of the richness of the Templars in 1312. Two other orders

in Estramadura and for the protection and care of pilgrims traveling to the shrine of Saint James de Compostella. The secular knights of the military group were expelled from Cáceres by the Almohade Moors and established themselves at Uclès in Castile about 1174. The militia was officially upgraded to the military Order of Santiago by Pope Alexander III a year later and became the most famous Spanish military order. They wore a white habit with a red *espalda* (cross, the bottom arm of which resembled a sword blade) on the shoulder. Their motto was ferocious: *Rubet ensis sanguine Arabum* (May the sword be red with Arab blood). Santiago was unique among the military orders. After their militarization, the brethren continued to nurse pilgrims, the poor, and the sick.

Unlike the other Cistercian orders, Santiago's origin was a secular warrior fraternity, so they adopted the rule of the Augustinian canons. Although the brethren lived in community in their castles, they were not, strictly speaking, a monastic order, and the members were allowed to marry and have personal possessions—canceling two of the three basic vows. Gradually the order's prime role was military, and the knights rendered valuable service; they were prominent at the decisive battle of Navas de Tolosa in 1212. From 1254 onward, the king expected to have a say in elections of the master and arguments grew more and more frequent. By 1259, the connection with the royal court was evident, and Santiago insisted on noble birth for anyone wanting to become a knight.

Rapidly the order became a wealthy international structure possessing large domains in Portugal, Castile, and Aragon, and a few farms and estates in southern France, Italy, Palestine, Hungary, and England. The order's lands in the Iberian Peninsula were organized by the Grand Master Pedro Fernandez, who divided them in five regions or "realms" called Portugal, León, Castile, Aragon, and Gascony. The "realm" of Portugal became independent in 1316 and became known as the order of *Sao Tiago da Spada* (Saint James of the Sword). The knights of Santiago were skilled administrators. Their basic settlement consisted of *hacienda*, a tightly grouped village enclosed by defensive walls and garrison quarters where they tended herds of cattle and sheep. On the vast and lonely meseta where no peasant dared settle for fear of Moorish raiders, the monkish frontiersmen established a pattern of ranch-style farming which was to have considerable influence on the agricultural settlements both in Spain and the new American world. After 1485, the order's mastership was reserved for the Spanish crown. Today the order still possesses three monasteries: Santiado del Major in Madrid, Santa Fé in Toledo, and La Madre de Dios in Grenada.

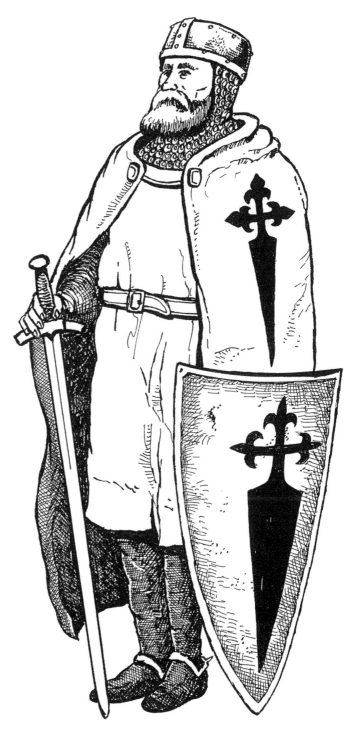

Knight of Santiago

The Order of Our Lady of Montjoie

The short-lived Order of Montjoie was founded in Palestine around 1175 by a knight originating from the Order of Santiago, Count Rodrigo Alvarez de Sarrià. Montjoie was a hill castle outside Jerusalem which took its name from the pilgrims' cries of joy when they saw the Heavenly City from its summit. The order was recognized by Pope Alexander III in 1180 and, besides ransoming captives, took an oath to fight the Saracens. Following the Cistercian rule, their habit was white with a red-and-white cross. In Palestine the order was granted the defense of several towers in the town of Ascalon by King Baldwin IV. A small detachment fought at the ill-fated battle of Hattin in 1187, after which the order retired to Aragon. The order was a vain attempt to purify Santiago. It was a protest against the loose rule, excessive wealth, poor discipline, admission of married men, elitism, and internal quarrels about elections of Masters. The new order was greatly favored by the king of Aragon, Alphonso II, who entrusted the monks with the defense of the southern part of his kingdom. The order did not prosper. It had difficulty attracting recruits because most Spaniards preferred joining the other great national orders. As king Alphonso rapidly became disappointed by the poor results obtained by the order, he decided to fuse them with the Knights Templars in 1196. A rump of the order then created the short-lived *Order of Montfrac* in Castile. This unsuccessful militia was absorbed by the Order of Calatrava in 1221.

The Order of Saint George of Alfama

The Order of Saint George of Alfama was founded in 1201 by King Pedro of Aragon for the defense of the coasts of Catalonia against the Moorish pirates. The order followed the Augustinian rule and sported a white habit. It seemed that that this order did not accomplish much, but they participated in the siege and capture of Valencia and were officially recognized in 1373. In 1400 The Order of Saint George of Alfama was absorbed by the Order of Saint Maria de Montesa.

The Order of Saint Maria of Montesa

The Aragonese Order of Saint Maria of Montesa was erected in 1317 with the Order of Saint Eulalia and on the ruins of the Templars, a decision taken by the king of Aragon, Jaime II. The knights of Montesa were the only legal successors to the Templars in Spain. They retained the white Templar mantle but exchanged the red cross for a black one. They took their name from their headquarters, a former Templar preceptory in Valencia after the dissolution of the Order of the Templars in 1312. Placed under the authority of the Cataline abbey of Santa Creus, the order fused with the Order of Saint George of Alfama in 1400. The order of Montesa ceased to exist after 1589.

The Order of Saint Maria of Spain

The short-lived Order of Saint Maria of Spain (also called the Order of the Star) was founded at Carthagena

Knight of Christ

in 1272 by the king of Castile, Alphonso X. Its main purpose was to be a naval militia intended to guard the Spanish coast, particularly the water off the Straight of Gibraltar. The order was defeated at the battle of Algesiras in 1279 and dissolved in 1281.

The Order of Christ

After the suppression of the Templars in 1312, the estates and the richness of the order were confiscated by the Portuguese crown. However, King Dinis I accepted only apparently the papal decision. Dinis was grateful for the role played by the knights Templar during the liberation of his kingdom. A new order was created in 1319 with the approval of Pope John XXII. The Order of Christ was under tutelage of the abbey of Alcoçaba and headquartered at Castro-Marino and later at Thomar. It was actually the continuation of the Templars in Portugal under another name. The knights had the same privileges as the Templars had enjoyed; they inherited their properties, and their wealth and prestige were even increased. The Knights of Christ wore a white cloak with a red cross with a twist in the middle. Long after the end of the Reconquista in Portugal, the knights of the Order of Christ pursued their activity. Under the leadership of their Grand Master and infante of Portugal, Henry the Navigator, they took part in the siege and capture of the Moorish stronghold of Ceuta in 1414. Later, supported by the Portuguese crown, successful adventurers of the order in their caravels with the Templars red cross on their sails led Portuguese discovery expeditions to Madeira (colonized after 1425), the Azore Islands (1445), and the unknown coasts of Africa, where they deployed missionary activities and established towns and trading posts. One of the members of the Order of Christ was Vasco da Gama (1469–1524), who was the first European sailor to reach the Indian continent via the Cape of Good Hope in 1499. In the 16th century, the order was in full decline; the brethren were allowed to marry and to have personal possessions. The order was reorganized in 1789 and 1918 to become a purely honorific association presided by the monarchs and later by the presidents of Portugal.

The Order of the
Very Holy Trinity

This community—created by Juan de Matha in 1098—was not a military order but a fraternity devoted to worship the Holy Trinity and to take care of the poor, sick, and wounded. However, the Trinitarians were closely related with the military aspect of the Crusades—not only in the Spanish Reconquista, but also in Palestine—as they devoted themselves to the liberation of Christian captives by negotiating ransoms and exchanges of prisoners. They had settlements in Spain, France, England, Germany, and Palestine.

The Christian Knights of
Saint Eulalia (Mercedarians)

There was another order devoted to the rescue of penniless Christian prisoners: the Christian Knights of Saint Eulalia also known as the Order of the Mercedarian Knights or Sacred Order of Our Lady of Mercy founded at Barcelona in 1235 by Provençe noblemen named Pere Nolasco (also known as Pierre de Nolasque, born about 1180) and Raymond of Peñafort. It is said that during the night of August 1–2, 1218, when in deep prayer, Pierre de Nolasque decided to found a religious hospitaler and military order. The king of Aragon, Jaime I, became interested in the militia and supported this development. In 1235 the institution was given the Augustinian rule and recognized by Pope Gregory IX. The knights wore a white robe bearing the royal arms of the house of Aragon surmounted by a cross. They participated in the reconquest of Majorca, Valencia, and Almeria. They also rescued Christian slaves and pilgrims by force and had the role of a military militia. They had several convents in Spain, Sicily, and southern France and one in Paris, but they were never very numerous, only able to field a small contingent of combatants. In 1317, the order lost a great part of its fighting function to be solely intended to negotiate ransoms and exchange prisoners from the Moorish prisons. Shortly after, the order was incorporated into the Order of Montesa.

The End of the Reconquista

The victory of Alfonso XI of Castile (1312–1349) on the River Salado in 1340 marked the end of the Moors' attempts to regain a foothold in Europe. By the second half of the 13th century, Moorish power in Spain was reduced to the kingdom of Granada in the south, which survived for more than another century owing to many wars opposing Castile, Portugal, Navarre, and Aragon. A fresh impulse was given to Spain by their Catholic majesties Ferdinand and Isabella, who married in 1469. They put an end to the civil wars, united the realm, and ousted the last Muslim bastion in the south. After a nine-month siege Granada was taken in 1492. The 700 years of Moorish occupation of Spain was over, leaving the Spanish military orders without purpose, and this rendered their decline inevitable. The Catholic kings of Spain had already seen the danger of rich and idle military orders brawling among themselves for want of better work. They did not intend to destroy the orders; they simply wanted to control them. As early as 1485, the kings declared their intention of reserving the mastership to the Crown. In 1487, the pope agreed, the kings of Spain were officially Masters of the orders and nominated themselves the *comendadores mayores*, royal lieutenants. Most of the orders became defunct and secularized; others just dissolved. The military orders remained a footnote to the pages of Spanish history, a splendid ghost, a symbol of the spirit of Spain during the centuries of the Reconquista: incredible gallantry, unspeakable ferocity, and high aims corrupted by petty ambitions and pride.

Ferdinand and Isabella made Spain the first world power. They instigated a strong outward surge, reaching to all corners of the world, toward North Africa, the Indian Ocean, and to a new continent that was suddenly revealed in 1492 — North America.

14

The Teutonic Knights

Creation and Structure

Crusading zeal was also directed against pagans in Europe. The conquest and evangelization of northeastern Europe was a complex issue. Crusades were pursued by religious military orders, among which the Teutonic knights played a central role. The Teutonic knights began as a charitable association formed by German merchants from Bremen and Lübeck to run a hospital for sick and wounded German pilgrims and knights during the siege of Acre in 1190. After the capture of Acre the fraternity took over a hospital in the town. An unknown German Crusader arranged that the group should be subjected to the rule of the Hospitalers of Saint John. They were recognized by the Church in 1191 by Pope Clement III and called the *Ordo Sanctae Maria Teutonicorum*, or Hospitaler of Saint Mary in Jerusalem, or *Orden der Ritter des Hospitals Sankt Marien des Deutschen Hauses zu Jerusalem*, shortly Teutonic Order. They gained full status from Pope Celestine III in 1196. The death of the Hohenstaufen emperor Heinrich VI in 1197 caused an important change as a number of German Crusaders decided to return home. To fill the gap, and given the crucial military situation, the German princes and bishops, together with King Amalric II of Jerusalem, decided to militarize the fraternity. They were incorporated as an independent military order in 1198 under the direction of the first Master, Heinrich Walpot von Bassenheim, and received privileges from popes Celestine III and Innocent III.

The structure of the Teutonics was similar to that of other military orders, but membership was exclusively reserved for German speakers. The brethren took the monastic vows of poverty, chastity, and obedience. The cult of the Virgin Mary seemed to have been very strong in the order as reflected by their greatest castle named in her honor — Marienburg (Mary's Castle). They followed strict rules, community life, and severe discipline. The hierarchy included the *Hochmeister* (grand master) who was elected for his lifetime by a chapter of bailiffs composed of the *Hofmeister* (councilor), *Großkomtur* (lieutenant), *Ordenmarschall* (marshal), *Spittler* (hospitaler), *Treßler* (treasurer), and *trapier* (quartermaster). The fighting brethren were divided into *Komturei* (groups of twelve knights) headed by a *Pfleger*. Just like the Templars and the Hospitalers, they were spiritually backed up by *Kaplanen* (chaplains). Their lowest ranks were *Laienbrüdern* (lay brothers) taking care of domestic and logistic tasks. Since 1205, they wore a white cloak or surcoat with a black Latin cross. In 1219 the king of Jerusalem granted the order the right to bear the cross of Jerusalem under the Teutonic's black cross, thus creating a silver edge. This black cross with white outline was later to become the German iron cross. The order had *Landkomtureien* or *Balleien* (houses with estates) each headed by a *Landmeister* in Palestine, Greece, Italy, and Germany, but these were small compared to the holdings of the Templars and Hospitalers. Later the territorial division included four main sections: Holy Land, Prussia, Livonia, and Germany.

The real founder of the Teutonic greatness was Hermann von Salza (born around 1170, mastership from 1210 to 1239). With statesmanship and foresight, von Salza succeeded in remaining on good terms with both the papacy and German emperor Friedrich, who encouraged the order's progress. The Teutonic knights obtained considerable advantages: they received rich gifts and were granted several castles in Palestine (notably Montfort and Thoron) and estates in the region of Tripoli and Antioch. They fought alongside the other orders, but they were always overshadowed by the Templars and the Hospitalers.

The German brethren were to find their true destiny in another crusade against the pagans in northeastern Europe. The order's first European operation started in Hungary in 1211 when King Andrew invited a contingent of Teutonic knights in Transylvania to convert the Cuman tribes to Christianity. But the knights' demands were so excessive that the Hungarian king soon realized that he had invited dangerous and ambitious guests; the knights were expelled from Hungary in 1225. By that time a new opportunity opened up when the Polish duke Conrad of Mazovia appealed to them to fight against the ferocious Prussian and Lithuanian tribesmen in 1226. The Grand Master, Hermann von Salza, proceeded carefully in order to avoid a repetition of the bad experience in Hungary. He agreed to fight in the Baltic states of northeastern Europe in exchange for the grant of the Burzenland and a territory in the region of Khelmo (Kulm). The order obtained from emperor Friedrich the legal right for settlement and also secured privileges from Pope Gregory IX. This might be regarded as a second foundation charter of the Teutonic Order. The knights then transferred their main center of activity from the Middle East to Eastern Europe. The order was—and that is one of the most remarkable things about it—very small in number by modern standards: in 1400 there were no more than 1,600 members.

Teutonic Knight, ca. 1200

Brethren of the Sword and Dobrzyn

The evangelization of the Baltic regions had begun in an attempt in 997 by the archbishop of Prague Adalbert and in 1008 by a Benedictine missionary named Bruno of Querfurt. These unsuccessful early missionaries were followed by an Augustine monk, Meinhart, in 1180, and by another monk named Berthold in 1195 who established a small Christian community. In 1199, Albrecht von Buxhövden and his brother Theodorik, both coming from Bremen, Germany, were helped by the German Church, Pope Innocent III, and the king of Danemark. They preached a crusade for the defense of the Church in Livonia. The Northeastern Crusade—known as *Drang nach Osten* (Push to the East)—was launched in earnest in 1230, though smaller campaigns had taken place before this. When the Teutonics arrived in the Baltic region, they combined with smaller preexisting local military orders.

The *Schwertbrudern* (Brethren of the Sword, also known as the Militia of Christ in Livonia) had been founded in 1201 in Riga by Albrecht von Buxödven, now archbishop of Riga. Recognized and officially created by

Pope Innocent III in 1210, the Brethren of the Sword wore a white habit marked with a red sword and a cross. The purpose was to defend and possibly expand the newly created Christian colony of Livonia. The Schwertbrudern proclaimed a holy war against the "Saracens of the north," and they made steady progress in Estonia, Kurland, and Lithuania, establishing castles, strongholds, colonies, and preceptories. However, in early 1237 their second Master, Wolquin Schenk, was killed, and the Brethren were severely defeated at Siaulia by the Lithuanians. The German Brethren of the Sword were absorbed by the Teutonic Order in May 1237.

In the meantime, in 1226, the bishops of Kujawia and Plock had organized a Polish military order, the Brotherhood of Dobrzyn (also known as the Knights of Christ in Prussia) for converting the pagan population of Moravia. The duke of Mazovia and Cujavia gave them a castle, villages, and estates in the region of Dobrzyn in 1230. The short-lived Polish Order of Dobrzyn was absorbed into the Teutonic Order in 1237. A third short-lived brotherhood was the Brethren of

Polish and Russian Warriors

Thymau. This order — derived from the Spanish military order of Calatrava — was founded in 1220 by Duke Sambor of Liubezow and incorporated into the Teutonics in 1235.

In 1233, led by landmeister Hermann Balk and using an army of volunteer soldiers recruited from central Germany, the Teutonics began the conquest of Prussia. During the next fifty years, the defenders of Christianity became conquerors; they advanced to the Niemen River and firmly established their control over Prussia. After the fall of Acre in 1291, the Holy Land was abandoned, the Teutonic knights were transferred to Venice, and the hochmeister Konrad-Siedfried von Feuchtwangen (mastership 1290–1297) established headquarters in Marienburg engaging the order totally, definitely, and permanently in the Baltic Crusade.

Schwertbruder, ca. 1270. The Brethren of the Sword wore a white surcoat. The cross and the sword on the shield were red.

Knight of Dobrzyn, 13th Century

Apogee and Decline of the Teutonic Order

Gradually, owing to a ruthless policy of conquest, harsh repression, and colonization, the German knights created their own empire. Although the Teutonics gave one-third of the conquered territory to the Church and granted a large degree of autonomy to the newly developing towns in the area, the order became the dominant power in Prussia. For 150 years, they were the rulers and the driving force of the *Drang nach Osten*. They colonized Prussia and the Baltic seashores, creating cities, villages, and settlements; and opening roads, waterways and markets to develop trade. The local population was deprived of rights, brutally exploited, and enslaved. The serfs were put to forced work draining marshes, building sea walls, claiming fallow lands, and clearing forests.

The Teutonics — who had previously been bound by a vow of poverty — were allowed in 1263 by the pope to engage directly in trading activities. They learned the value of commerce, maintained a Baltic fleet, adopted banking methods, enforced a uniform system of weights and measures, and minted their own coinage. They monopolized the lucrative Prussian grain trade and—cunningly—they closely collaborated with the *Hansa*, a league formed by German independent cities and Baltic free ports. This commercial association was a virtual maritime republic including about eighty major towns with depots and offices all over northern Europe. The merchants of the Hansa monopolized Baltic trade; they were so powerful that the league could defy kings, emperors, and popes. About fifteen Hansa towns were controlled by the knights, the most important being Danzig, Elbing, Königsberg, Braunsberg, Riga, and Dorpat. This allowed the order to get involved in maritime, commercial, and banking operations and, therefore, to play a significant political role in northern Europe.

The Teutonics invited German peasants to settle in the new conquered territories including Pomeralia, Samogitia, Memel, Courland, Dobrin, Livonia, Estonia, and a part of Lithuania as well as the islands of Gotland and Osel. Polish and German noblemen too were encouraged to come and were granted substantial estates, making them vassals of the order.

In 1238, the ambitious and powerful Teutonics allied with the Danes, allowing new conquests, notably the capture of Estonia. As they were insatiable, ambitious and aggressive, they intended to invade the orthodox Christian state of Russia, but they were decisively defeated by the grand duke of Novgorod, Prince Alexander Iaroslavitch Nevsky, in a pitched battle on frozen Lake Peipus in 1242—a battle immortalized by the famous anti–German film made by Serghei Eisenstein in 1938. The same year, 1242, saw a major uprising in Prussia which took thirty years to control.

In the 14th century the knights had recovered and had established a firm rule in Prussia. They concentrated then their efforts against the Lithuanians which had sub-

Teutonic Knight, 14th Century

mitted in 1386. Although the Grand Duke of Lithuania, Wladislaw II, converted to Christianity in 1387, he was still viewed with suspicion by the knights, and border disputes and hostilities remained between Poland, Lithuania, and Teutonic Prussia.

After the dissolution of the Temple in 1312, many Templars joined the Teutonics, and between 1300 and 1410 the prestige and power of the order was at its highest. It was also the time when the Teutonic Order had completely lost the moral and idealist purity of its origin. Wealth, greed, ambition, insatiability, decadence, arro-

Teutonic knight, Mid–15th Century

handed Teutonics. Poles, Bohemians, Hungarians, Czechs, Cossacks, and Lithuanians defeated the Teutonic knights at the Battle of Tannenberg (also called Grunwald) among the Masurian marshes on July 15, 1410. Tannenberg was the Teutonics Order's Hattin, a political humiliation, a military defeat marking the end of the Germanic advance in the Slavic world, and a spiritual disaster as it destructed the myth of the order's invincibility.

By then, the German Utopia — symbolized by the Teutonics — lacked efficient support from the German emperors and suffered from the decrease of crusading spirit. Consequently the order's power dwindled, its authority and financial position declined, and its territory was reduced to Prussia. The order was a reactionary institution with little ground for continued existence and unable to withstand the wars that Poland continued to wage. After Grunwald it seemed like the Teutonic knights had a feeling of fatalism making the order's days numbered. After two hopeless, bloody, and unsuccessful wars, the decadent and weakened Teutonics had become crusaders without a cause and were obliged to recognize themselves as vassals of Poland in 1446.

The decline and fall of the order became evident in 1525 when the Teutonics were torn apart by religious issues. Grand Master Albrecht von Brandenburg (mastership 1511–1525) converted to Lutheran Protestantism and was recognized secular duke of Prussia by the king of Poland. The once rich, proud, and powerful order was split up into two parts. A fraction remained Catholic, left Prussia, and was re-formed by Hochmeister Walter von Kronberg (mastership 1526–1543) and established itself at Mergentheim in Franconia (Germany) under the protection of Austria. So perished the *Ordo Sanctae Maria Teutonicorum*, that strange amalgam of military dictatorship, colonialism, and theocracy. It was then contemplated to merge the Teutonics with the Hospitaler knights of Malta in one sole military order, but this project came to nothing. As for the knights who followed Albrecht and became

gance, and political power were paradoxically the first signs of decline. The order's expansion and increasing power aroused the hostility of Poland, Lithuania, and Hungary, which saw the order as intruders and were jealous of its stable government and accumulating wealth. As the Baltic region became evangelized by force, the Teutonics found themselves as no more than a secular power struggling for political ends against their fellow Christians. The excuse of being on a crusade could no longer be used. The knights became involved in a quicksand of allegiances, treacheries, and double-dealings. A series of skirmishes punctuated these maneuvers, and eventually war broke out.

Wladislaw II succeeded in raising a huge army including anyone who had a grudge against the high-

protestant, some sadly departed to Germany: others stayed, married, and settled down. They formed the origin of the modern Prussian nobility — the Junkers — who were later to play a decisive part in the history of Germany. Prussia became a secular duchy in 1591, a powerful military kingdom in the 18th century, and the driving force of German unity in the late 19th century.

Weapons and Tactics

The conditions under which the Teutonics fought in northeastern Europe were very different from those in the Holy Land. In the dark, damp forests, swamps, and wildernesses, the knights were pitting themselves against savage pagan tribesmen who fought back with persistence and ferocity. The Prussian tribe was resistant to Christianity, and the war rapidly became cruel and merciless. The knights were outnumbered, and an armed militia was raised among the German settlers to reinforce them. These formed an infantry force including archers and spearmen for occupation duties and subaltern fighting roles. The Teutonics were also very popular throughout Europe, and their "holy" war attracted many non–German knights who came from everywhere to have their share of glory and booty on a parttime basis. Englishmen, Flemings, Austrians, Frenchmen, Bavarians, Dutchmen, Hungarians, Burgundians, Scots, Provençals, and Italians came as individuals to fight throughout the 13th and 14th centuries. Henry, Earl of Derby (later King Henry IV of England) came twice on campaign, taking with him a force of 150 men. In 1378, the Duke of Lorraine came to fight on the Teutonic side with a small force of 70 soldiers and knights. The Margrave of Meissen arrived in 1391 with a staggering 500 knights.

On the whole the military technology of the Christians was superior to that of Prussians. The Teutonic knights wore the classic 13th century closed helmet, various forms of gambeson, hauberk, and chain-mail armor as well as protection made of boiled leather. In the beginning of the 14th century plate armor was developed all over Europe. Chain mail was still worn, but it was reinforced by metal plates such ailettes, knee guards, and arm plates. The back of the upper arms from shoulder to elbow and the front of the lower arms from the bend of the elbow to the wrist were protected by plates of metal fastened by straps around the limbs. *Coudières* (elbow plates) and genouillères (knee plates) were being fixed over the chain mail to fulfill the office of reinforcement. The feet were covered by *solerets* consisting of lames of metal riveted together and kept in place by straps passing under each foot. The Teutonics' large white cloaks might have served as camouflage in the snow, though this was accidental, the white surcoat having been adopted in 1191 in Palestine. Their main weapons were large two-edged swords and long lances furnished with pennons as well as shields bearing the cross of the order.

The Prussians and Lithuanians — who are only known by chronicles and annals written by the Christians — were presented as savages worshiping the moon and the sun and practicing human sacrifice. They were denounced as ferocious, ugly, poor, and grubby primitives burning their dead, sinful polygamists, and heavy drinkers. This unfavorable portrait was probably used only as an excuse to convert, enslave, and eradicate them. "Who fights us, fights Jesus Christ!" claimed the Teutonic knights. The Prussian tribesmen developed a sort of guerilla warfare consisting of ambushes and raids on Christian settlements. They attacked in the snowy forests, riding over frozen lakes and rivers or charging out of blizzards like winter ghosts. They fought with savagery on horseback with swords and lances and on foot with battle-axes and bows, but they were not very well organized nor had they the sophisticated equipment necessary to besiege a well-defended stone-built castle. Therefore the Teutonics elaborated a network of towns strengthened with massive citadels, fortresses, strongholds, fortified monasteries, and defensive commanderies from which they could exploit and control the lands around and launch offensive operations after which they could safely retreat for winter quartering. The most impressive Teutonic castle was Marienburg (Malkborg in Polish), near Danzig (today Gdansk in Poland) built between 1309 and 1344. It was at the same time the order's headquarters, a functioning fortress, a large monastery, a hospital, and a magnificent guest house for visiting European nobles and their knights.

Many pockets of resistance remained however, and the regions controlled by the Teutonics were never completely safe. There were thus very few pitched battles but instead countless small operations, skirmishes, and razzias (plundering raids) which were not always won by the Christian knights. There were frequent and bloody revolts and terrible and harsh repression; at time the brethren saw themselves as a beleaguered force rather than as triumphant conquerors. During these numerous short-scale expeditions, atrocities were committed by both sides, particularly during the major rebellion in the period 1261–1283. It was a war of attrition in which no prisoners were taken, villages were looted and burned, fields laid waste, unarmed civilians were enslaved under harsh conditions, and even women and children were slaughtered with the blessing of the Church and good conscience to serve Christ. An expedition could last for months, and the knights endured all the hazards of ambush, wild animals, storm, cold, and starvation. They could lose their way and perish slowly in marshes and dense pine tree forests which hid sun and stars. Some brethren went mad from forest "blues."

Campaigning in Lithuania in the 14th century was—again—far from easy. The territory of the enemy was separated from that of the Teutonic knights in Prussia by a broad belt of trackless forests relieved only by normally impassable bog land. The severe climate of the area meant that there were usually only two periods in the year during which fighting could take place: the coldest months of winter, when the surface of the bogs was frozen, and a short month in summer, when a combination of sunshine and wind dried out the surface of the bogs. It was thus essential for the forces of both sides to be able to strike quickly, and a sudden summer rain or an unexpected thaw could mean disaster. Teutonic operations in winter were intended to imperil and depopulate the area. Raids would be conducted by soldiers and knights hacking their way through the forest or sometimes traveling in boats on the River Niemen. They bivouacked when they had penetrated within striking range of the enemy, and then rode out burning, looting, destroying, and killing in the countryside. Before the Lithuanians could mobilize against them, the knights retired with as much plunder as they could carry. In the summer, campaigns were launched which aimed at the permanent gain of enemy territory and the construction of strongholds from which further conquest would be undertaken. The Lithuanians were as stubborn as the Prussians had been, and the fortunes of war remained even. The Lithuanians were skilled riders and daring warriors, moving swiftly across the country, however wild; they were elusive in retreat and dangerous in victory. In peacetime they could not always be trusted, and both skillful and treacherous as diplomats, they outwitted the cleverest minds of the Teutonics on several occasions.

Teutonics and Nazism

In 1834, the Austrian emperor reestablished the Teutonic order in Vienna as an ecclesiastical institution for charitable, nursing, and pastoral activities; and this was approved in 1871 by Pope Pius IX. A new rule — adopted in November 1927 — emphasized the religious discipline.

The Teutonics' influence over German nationalists at the end of the 19th century and over the Nazi ideologists in the period 1919–1945 has frequently been mentioned. Their "Push to the East" can — to a certain extent — be considered as the forerunner of the Nazi's *Lebensraum* (living space). This concept was used by the Nazis for expansionism, especially eastward. Hitler rejected colonies abroad but asserted that security and vital space for Germany were to be conquered in eastern Europe (mainly in the rich plains of Poland, Ukraine, and Russia), if need be by force. Conceived by Hitler and his secretary Rudolf Hess and clearly exposed as early as 1925 in Hitler's book *Mein Kampf*, the theory of Lebensraum formed one of the main bases for the Nazi program of security and expansion. Lebensraum offered the opportunity to build the Nazi order, the empire of the *Herrenvolk* (master people) based upon the slave-labor of the *Untermenschen* (inferior races). Hitler's program was no detailed blueprint but a confused amalgam of various elements. The logical consequence of this policy was obviously war with Poland and Russia and territorial reshaping of Germany and Eastern Europe. The criminal Lebensraum policy — justified by the principle that "might is right" — included conquest, expulsion, enslavement, extermination, and annihilation of the resident population and its replacement by "Aryan," pure-blooded Germans. Hitler's determination to wage war and apply the Lebensraum policy were the cause of atrocities, crimes, and the largest-scale genocide mankind had ever seen.

 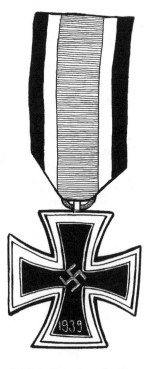

Teutonic Cross *(left)* and Iron Cross Second Class *(right)*. Based on the Teutonic cross, the Eisern Kreuz was created in 1813 by the king of Prussia, Friedrich-Wilhelm III, as a military medal. Forbidden by the Allies in 1918, the prestigious medal was reintroduced by Hitler in 1939.

The *Schutzstaffel* (protection squads or, in short, SS)—headed by Reichsführer Heinrich Himmler (1900–1945)—regarded themselves as an exclusive selected order, a community of racial "happy few" following a sort of rule like the ancient Spartans, the Teutonic knights, or the Jesuit order. The SS entertained the dream of Aryan Germanic world domination under the leadership of a new caste of aristocrats. Ancestor worship, Scandinavian mythology, German Aryan superiority, anti–Semitism and extreme racism, medieval Teutonic knighthood, belief in immortality, and the *Blut und Boden* (blood and soil) myths were elements of the new, confused Nazi faith glorifying the messiah and savior Adolf Hitler. For his SS "knights," the Reichsführer Himmler had restored the fortress of Wewelsburg in Westphalia which was intended to serve as a sanctuary and study center. Other medieval castles were turned for these purposes such as the Teutonic fortress Marienburg, the Teutonic castle Hermannsburg in Narwa in Estonia, or the SS "Order House" in Oldenburg (Lower Saxony). It would, however, be unjust to brand the Teutonic knights as medieval SS. Except for the *Drang nach Osten* policy, the fanaticism, the ruthless professionality and the selected character of both brotherhoods, the SS and the Teutonics had very little in common. In the first place, the Teutonics did not act according to racist prejudices; they were Catholic noblemen, not Aryan guttersnipes, and their bloodsheds and cruelty were for a questionable view of Christianity but not an attempt to build a Nazi hegemony. Denying the Christian character of the Teutonics, Himmler only misappropriated their achievements and their spirit based on honor, obedience, bravery, and loyalty. Indeed, after the *Anschluß* (annexation of Austria to Germany in 1938), the Teutonic order was assimilated by the Nazis to anti–German Free-Masonry. The order was forbidden, properties were confiscated, and many knights imprisoned in concentration camps where many of them died in atrocious conditions together with millions of Russians, Gypsies, and Jews.

After World War II, the *Ordo Sanctae Maria Teutonicorum* was reestablished in Vienna (Austria) in 1947 under the name of *Brüder des Deutschen Ordens Sankt Mariens zu Jerusalem*. Ever since then the knights—totaling about 600 members who have abandoned all military purposes—are priests and monks of a mundane honorific association who maintain a church and the archives of the order. Protected by the Vatican, they are divided in three "provinces": Austria, Italy, and Germany. A female branch of the order has reverted to the charitable hospitaling origin: assisting and nursing handicapped people and the elderly in hospitals and homes *ad majorem Dei gloriam* (to the greater glory of God).

PART III

THE LATE MIDDLE AGES (14TH–15TH CENTURIES)

15

Evolution of Armor and Weapons

The development of the crossbow and long bow resulted in the knights of the Late Middle Ages having to reconsider their equipment and tactics. Armor evolved to meet the knight's needs, but the lure of greater protection at the expense of mobility proved strong. Plate armor had been widely used in the Roman world, but after the barbarian invasions of the western empire, it had practically disappeared. The only survivors from ancient days of plate armor were shields. Much of our knowledge of the evolution of plate armor — of which few authentic specimens exist — is gained from the study of memorial brasses. These slabs of brass or latten, engraved with drawings of the deceased in his armor, as well as recumbent figures on tombs, are extremely valuable not only because they show the form of armor in great detail but also because they can be dated with accuracy. A great deal of nonsense has been written about the effect of wearing armor, and it is commonly believed that a fully armored man had to be lifted onto the saddle, and if pulled from his horse, he was at the mercy of his opponent. Most of this is quite untrue; in fact chain or mixed and plate armor was often lighter than the full equipment carried by soldiers of World War I (1914–1918). In a properly fitted armor the fully armored man could easily mount and dismount and fight equally well whether on horseback or on the ground. The only real discomfort suffered by a man in full armor came from the lack of ventilation. It was to this that Shakespeare alluded in *Henry IV Part 2*, when he described Majesty: "Like a rich armor worn in the heat of day / That scalds with safety."

Again, it must be understood that there was never any one style of armor that was at any time universally worn. Old equipment was always in part retained and only discarded by degrees. Each man did that which was pleasant in his own eyes and — most important — what he could afford. In an age which saw so many varieties, it may be difficult to distinguish essential characteristics, but a few salient features may be mentioned which were fairly persistent throughout. As has already been pointed out and described, the period of pure mail armor without any secondary or additional defense over the mail, except the closed heaume and shield, may be considered to have closed about the year 1250.

Mixed Armor, 1250–1410

For hundreds of years the basic form of body protection consisted of quilted byrnies and chain-mail hauberks. In one form or another these were good general forms of protection, but they could not withstand direct hits with a lance or an arrow. This gradually led to the adoption of additional protective elements. From about 1250 to about 1410, chain mail was mixed with plate armor, and during this period the warrior's bodily protection reached its most-complex point in that it was made up of a large number of individual pieces, often forming several layers which could be a burden and which complicated lacing to hold each element in its proper position. The length of time needed to don this equipment was underlined by the occasion when an army was taken by surprise. The period of mixed armor was a state of transition during which warriors sought to render themselves immune by every conceivable expedient,

Mixed Armor, Early 14th Century

adopting and augmenting those which proved efficacious and then discarding those which failed upon trial. The development of armor was not particularly paralleled by a similar development in the knight's aggressive weapons. The mounted man's usefulness in the field was dependant on the same skills in the 14th and 15th century as in the previous periods, and his weapons had scarcely changed. The lance might be of better wood, the sword was keener, but no great advances were made in this matter.

Chain Mail Reinforced, 1250–1325

In a first period, to about 1325, the main body defenses remained the hauberk of chain mail or banded mail, but additional plates of solid metal were placed over the mail at vital places. The first plates were provided for the knees, particularly vulnerable spots on a mounted man; knee guards (*genouillère* or *poleyn*) were therefore elaborated. Soon the arms were also protected with plates called *demi-brassard* (upper arm) and *vambrace* (lower arm). Gauntlets were introduced to protect the hands. Circular plates or roundles were fixed in front of both the shoulders (*epaulière*) and the elbows (*coudière* or *couter*) to guard the joint. The previously described *ailettes* (small shields fastened at right angles across the shoulders) began to fall in disuse. The *jambard* covered the front of the leg and continued in laminated work over the feet. With the leg and the foot covered, the shield became somewhat smaller, lighter, and often flat. The previously discussed closed *heaume* continued to be worn, some with a movable visor, some flat-topped, and some conical topped.

Cyclas Period, 1325–1335

In a second short period to about 1335, the long and flowing surcoat appeared to have been superseded by a garment called *cyclas*. This was laced at the sides and reached a little below the knee. The front of the cyclas was generally short and displayed the fringed border of the padded and quilted *haketon* worn under the mail hauberk. This padding served to protect the body from the pressure of the mail. Other defense included a *plastron* (a metal breastplate) and a *gambeson*, a body covering stuffed with wool, padded as a rule in vertical parallel lines of needlework and worn over the plastron and hauberk. Defenses of knees, legs, and feet remained the same, but a new helmet began to appear, known as *basinet*. This was comparatively light, close fitting, and somewhat globular in form; it was raised a little above the head and generally terminated in a point. A basinet was worn without any mail coif or hat beneath it; the neck was protected by a kind of tippet made of mail (*camail*) attached to the basinet. The shield assumed the "heater" form and spurs with *rowels* were beginning to be worn.

Studded and Splinter Armor, 1335–1360

The third period, to about 1360, was another era of transition. The surcoat — worn over the banded mail

Left and center: Armor of the Chain Mail Reinforced Period, 1250–1325. *Left:* Brass of Sir Robert de Septvans, Chartham Church, Kent, ca. 1306. *Center:* Brass of Sir Fitzralph, Pebmarsh Church, Essex, ca. 1320. *Right:* Armor of the Cyclas Period, 1325–1335. Brass of Sir John de Creke, Westley Waterless Church, Cambs, ca. 1325.

haubert and the breastplate — was sometimes shortened, and a loose skirt was worn open in front displaying the armorial of the bearer. The legs were protected by *gre-vières* and *jambarts*, and *chausses* of mail were also worn protecting nearly the whole length of the legs and covering the feet. A collar of mail or a plate (*gorget*) was worn to protect the neck. Helmets of the period were of varying shapes and models. The closed *heaume* of previous

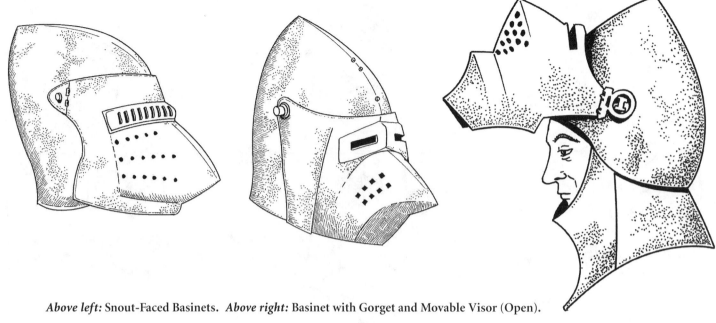

Above left: Snout-Faced Basinets. *Above right:* Basinet with Gorget and Movable Visor (Open).

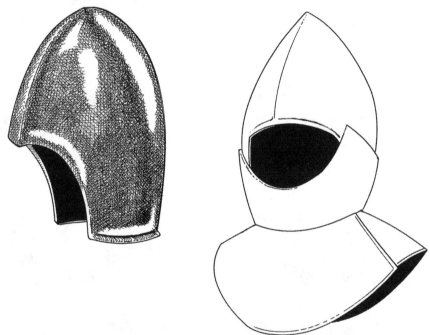

Left: Basinet. *Right:* Basinet with Gorget.

periods was still worn, though sometimes fitted with a movable visor, but new models gradually appeared. The globular *small basinet* left the face uncovered, but the *great basinet* was fitted with a movable visor known as a *ventail*; this was pierced for both sight and breathing and could be raised, lowered, or removed altogether at the pleasure of the wearer. The movable visor revolved upon pivots and could fulfill the duty of a gorget. It had various shapes and names throughout Europe. In Germany it was called *Hundsgugel* (dog's snout); in France, *bassinet en bec de passereau*; in England *hounskull* or *pig-faced basinet.* The shield was of the small heater-shaped variety.

Camail and Jupon Period, 1360–1410

In a fourth period, to about 1410, armor entered upon a time of a certain amount of uniformity in contrast to the preceding styles. This period was marked by the wars opposing France and England in which the decisive battle of Poitiers (1356) was fought. The various defenses underwent the fiery ordeal of actual use, and only those which emerged triumphantly from the struggle were retained. The arms and the lower limbs were entirely encased in curved plate. Feet were covered by laminated plate *solerets* (foot armor), pointed at the toe. The body was covered as usual by the quilted gambeson or haqueton and by a short hauberk constructed of banded mail

reaching to the middle of the thighs and apparently sleeveless. Under the hauberk a globular breastplate was sometimes placed, and over it was worn the sleeveless *jupon*, a species of surcoat which fitted tightly and reached from the neck to midway between the hips and the knees. The jupon could be made of some rich material, silk or velvet, and was often blazoned with the armorials of the wearer; its bottom was often escalloped or cut into some rich open-work patterns and, in some cases, quilted. The leather belt was sometimes richly decorated, and, on the

Armor of the Camail and Jupon Period, 1360–1410. *Left:* Brass of Sir John de Argentine, Horsheath Church, Cambridge, ca. 1360. *Center:* Brass of Sir John Wingfield, Letheringham Church, Suffolk, ca.1400. *Right:* Brass of Sir George Felbrigge, Playford Church, Suffolk, ca.1400.

left side, the long sword with crossguard, rich hilt, and (usually) octagonal pommel inside its ornate scabbard was suspended. Attached to the belt by a cord or strap hung a new weapon known as *miséricorde*, a dagger "of mercy" in its scabbard. The roundles at the shoulders and elbows tended to disappear, and in their places were introduced laminated *épaulières* and elbow guards. *Goussets* of mail were worn at the joints where the plates were necessarily open to allow for the movement of the armpit.

After 1380 the basinet was reduced in weight, and a flowing scarf (called *contoise* or *mantling*) was worn attached to the crest of the helmet; this was made of rich material, ended in tassels, had its edges jagged or escalloped, and hung down behind on the shoulders. Heaumes, and basinets with visors, were still worn, but new helmets were introduced such as the *cabasset* and the *berruyer*, which was a light helmet generally worn by soldiers on foot. The last years of that period formed a transitional time during which the mail camail was retained with an increasing use of armored plates.

Full-Plate Armor, 1410–1600

Full-plate armor, the sheath of jointed metal units that covered a knight from head to toe, was developed in the 15th century. The construction of a workable metal skin for a man was a challenge that fired the imaginations of craftsmen. The armor became a complete panoply of plates with designs in steel that attained a perfection that has not since been surpassed. It was a plain fighting metal suit designed to give the maximum protection without impeding the free movement of the limbs.

Full plate armor was usually closely tailored to the body, and the armorer needed a sculptor's understanding of human anatomy; he had to know the play of every muscle, the hinging of every joint both human and in metal. The contours followed those of the figure; it was never lifeless, and it had equilibrium with a certain vibrant grace and a good posture. The fit of the metal suit was most important, and those that still exist display a surprising range of sizes. There are harnesses made for men six feet tall and some that were fashioned for noble children who were destined to be knights. But on the whole, the study of existing armor shows that the average Late Middle Ages knight was a brawny, muscular man whose body reflected his activities and way of life; he had broad shoulders, strong arms, and slender legs because he did little walking but went to exercise and battle on horseback. Full-plate armor was — of course — never worn continually but only for the occasions of exercise, parade, tournament, or war.

It was probably no easier to put on than mixed armor, but its construction was simpler and stronger. The smooth, polished, convex surfaces caused arrows or bolts striking it at any angle other than ninety degrees to glance off, and metal suits were generally strong enough to withstand most missiles unless delivered at point-blank range.

There can be no doubt that a fully armored knight was well protected during battle. He was only vulnerable if he was knocked down to the ground when his restricted mobility and the sheer weight of the harness might prevent his being able to rise again and make him an easy target for the nimbler foot soldier. Accounts of battles record the horrible sight of infantrymen sitting astride fallen knights and driving daggers into the slits in their visors or between the vulnerable joints of their armor. For this reason it was important for armored mounted men to fight together and to rescue any knight who had been cut off from his companions or been knocked down.

Full-plate armor weighted about the same as a complete chain mail hauberk (about 50 pounds or 23 kilograms) but — if properly made to fit its wearer perfectly — it was more comfortable because the weight was distributed evenly over the body instead of being suspended entirely from the shoulders. It was made-to-measure, therefore extremely expensive, and only a few wealthy knights, kings, and

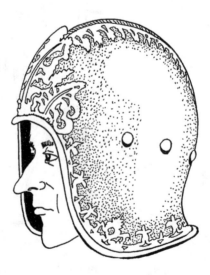

Barbutes. *Left:* **barbute with hinged nasal, mid–15th century;** *right:* **decorated Venetian barbuta, late 15th century.**

princes could afford it. Consequently older equipment was still worn during this period.

Surcoatless Period, 1410–1430

In a short period from 1410 to about 1430, the jupon had disappeared and plates were worn without textile covering at all. The breastplate was the main protection of the body; it was often globose in order to ward off the heaviest of blows. Roundles resembling small shields were added in front to the upper part of the breastplate for the protection of the shoulder joints. These separate plates whose purpose was to guard the armpit when the arm was raised were sometimes termed *besagew*. Below the waist, connected with the bottom of the breastplate, the body was protected by a series of narrow overlapping lames of steel attached to a lining of leather called *taces* or *tassets*.

The arms were covered by *brassards*, often formed of lames of plate riveted together and the *coudières* (elbow joints) were generally guarded with fanlike plates in some cases of very large proportions. The metal gauntlets had larger cuffs and were more elaborated and articulated with leather holding overlapping metacarpal plates shaped to the fingers—some with a knuckle guard embossed to form low spikes—to ensure the free movement of the wearer. Some gauntlets represented the human hand with fingernails engraved upon them. With the hands in this kind of gauntlet, a heavy sword could be manipulated without difficulty. Legs were covered with *cuissards* (thigh plates), *genouillères* (knee joints), and *grevières* (lower leg plates), and the feet were protected by pointed *solerets*.

The helmet was still the *basinet*, which—though still pointed at its apex—tended to be more globular than in earlier periods and gradually developed into the *barbute* type, particularly in Italy. It was connected with a *gorget*, a concave collar around the neck.

Armor of the Surcoatless Period, 1410–1430. *Left:* Brass of an anonymous knight, South Kelsey Church, Lines, ca. 1410. *Right:* Brass of Sir Thomas Swynborne, Little Horkesley Church, Essex, ca.1412.

Scabbards and belts preserved their general characters without significant modification, but swords tended to have a straight, plain, and larger cross guard, and the

Far left: Decorated Blade of a Pole-Axe. This pole-axe belonged to King Edward IV of England (1442–1483). *Right:* European Swords, 14th–15th Centuries. *Left:* Italian one-and-a-half-hand; *center:* French sword; *right:* one-and-a-half-hand.

pommel could have the form of a pear. The long cutting sword of previous periods continued to be used, but gradually the advent of pure plate armor rendered it rather ineffective. Once an opponent was totally protected by angled, rounded, or fluted metal surfaces, the only sword that could be of any real use was one designed for the thrust — to slide up and over a metal expanse and find the weak point between one metal area and another. This larger, sharply pointed type of sword, the typical knight's sword of the 15th century, was usually referred to as a *one-hand-and-a-half,* as its hilt could be used with one or both hands as the occasion demanded.

Another weapon became popular, the pole-axe, a long-handled axe with a sharp blade on one side and a flat, ridged hammer-head on the other. The range of blows was extended by the provision of a spike on top. With pointed swords and pole-axes knights could batter and jab at each other to find the weak point in the armor. Daggers too were generally sharper to be used between the joints of the armored carapace. The ballock-knife (also known as kidney dagger) was used in northern Europe notably in Britain and Holland. The French *poignard à oreilles* (ear dagger) had two disk-shaped features splayed from the top of the grip.

Tabard Period, 1430–1500

In this period, from 1430 to about 1450, armor continued to improve in its defense power. New and supplementary pieces of armor were introduced designed to reinforce body armor, the head, and the limbs. All of them tended toward increasing extravagances of form, dimensions, and adornment. The breastplate was made of one plate, but it was generally reinforced by another overlapping piece, called a *demi-placcate,* springing upward from the waist; the upper part, as a rule, was molded into a graceful system of cusps. The taces (thigh guards) were sometimes escalloped or made of small plates named *tuiles* suspended by straps to cover the thighs in addition to the *cuissards* (thigh plates). The tuiles appeared in variety of forms— square, hexagonal, lozenge-shaped, serrated, etc. Another form to protect hips and belly was a skirtlike layer of plates known as *fauld* or *tonne.* Plates of various sizes and forms were added to the gauntlets, to the elbow (*gardes-de-bras*), and in front of the shoulders (*placates* and *pauldrons*). The shoulders—notably in Italian armor which favored a simple and large, rounded surface— were covered with large plate defenses; these pauldrons extended around the shoulders to cover the back like a pair of wings.

Over the armor a new variety of surcoat was worn — the most distinguishing feature of the period—known as *tabard;* this was either very short, reaching to the waist, or somewhat longer, reaching to mid-thigh. It had sleeves generally reaching to the elbow. The tabard served as a protection against sun and rain and also as a means of personal adornment as its front displayed the armorials of the wearer. It was of silk or other material and some-

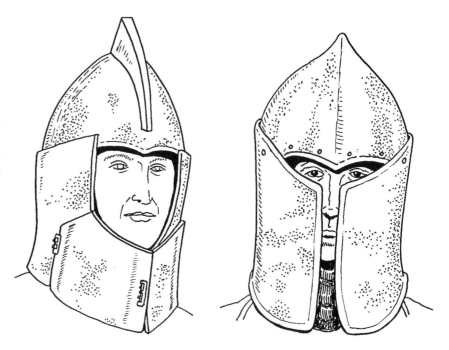

Italian Helmets. *Left:* basinet with crest and hinged cheek and chin pieces, ca. 1440; *right*: Venetian salade or Corinthian helmet, late 15th century.

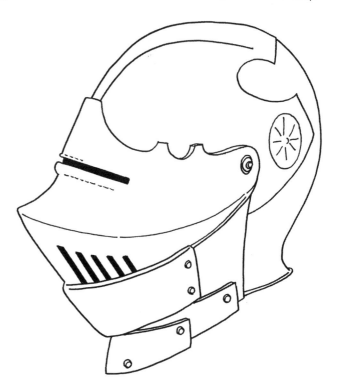

Armet, Closed Helmet, ca. 1500

times padded so as to hang stiffly. The protection of the legs did not undergo major transformations, but the pointed *solerets* (feet protection) became of extravagant length.

A popular new helmet was the *barbut* also called *Venetian salade.* This was a distinctive Italian helmet with

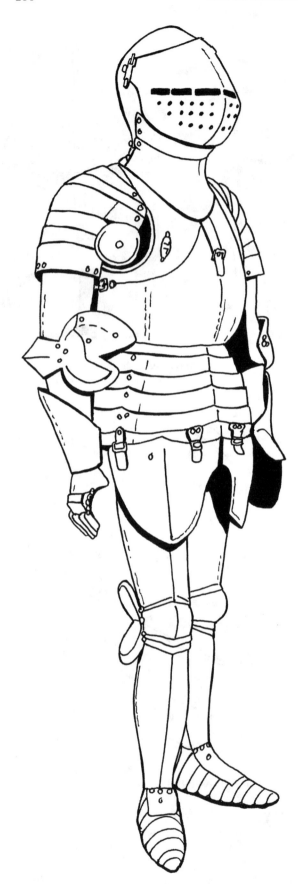

Italian Armor, ca. 1451

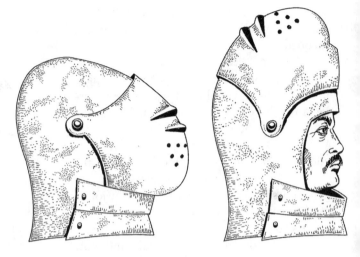

Bicoquet, 15th Century (Closed and Open)

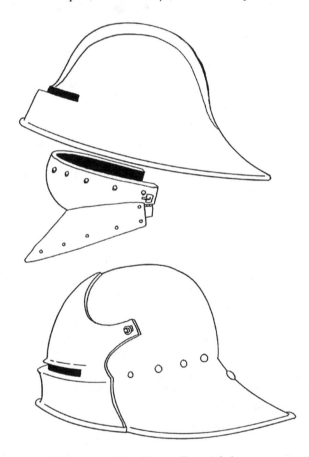

German Sallet or Salade. *Top:* sallet with bevor, ca. 1440; *bottom:* salade with movable visor which could be raised or lowered at pleasure, ca. 1470.

a T-shaped face opening inspired by the ancient close-fitting Greek Corinthian helmet. There were many other types such as the *armet* or *heaumet.* The armet — originating probably from Italy — was light and close-fitting to the skull. It had a movable visor with slits for vision and perforation for breathing. It existed in numerous variations such as the *bicoquet*.

In the 1460s German armor manufacturers developed the so-called "Gothic armor"—a name given in the 19th century by historians because of the general resemblance of this type of armor to the spired, pinnacled and fretted form of the "Gothic" architecture. The spiky Gothic armor was characterized by slender, elongated form emphasized by ripple-like fluting. Laminations at all the joints were multiplied to increase the flexibility, and the edges of the plates were pierced with design based on the fleur-de-lis. The effect was often heightened by edges of gild brass. The most common form of helmet associated with Gothic armor was the *sallet* or *salade* (from the German *Schalle*, meaning shell), a close-fitting cap, extended so as to cover the sides of the face and the back of the neck. The sallet could be fitted with a separable and movable visor with a horizontal eye slot and it was constantly enriched with varied ornamentation. The bowl was forged from a single piece of steel so that the thickest part of the metal was in the front covering the forehead. Additional strength was afforded by a central ridge which ran

Two Sorts of "Gothic" Armor. *Left:* a cap-à-pie suit of Gothic armor, ca.1470;. *right:* Gothic armor, ca. middle of the 15th century. The figure wears a visorless sallet and is equipped with a pole-axe, the shaft being partially sheathed in iron.

along the top and an articulated piece tail piece protecting the back of the neck. The chin was often protected by a plate known as the *bevor* or *mentonnière*. The sallet formed the headpiece of knights, men-at-arms and archers all over Europe in the 15th century. A rather similar helmet was the Italian *celata*, with its roundish form and outwards at the back of the neck. German "Gothic" armor reached its apogee in the 1480s.

Italian Plate Armor, 15th century

Evolution of Armor after 1500

In the early 16th century, armor became more massive and cumbersome, heavier, and smoother and rounder in style. The civilian fashion began to prevail for adorning it with elaborate enrichments. Indeed, plate armor lent itself to decorative ornamentation indicating wealth and status. The armor of princes, nobles, and wealthy knights continually increased in fashioned splendor while at the same time the military character continued to degenerate. The plain surface of the metal became covered with rich artistic designs, some of them being of exquisite beauty and marvelous workmanship. Aqua fortis was freely used for etching in combination with hand engraving, while damascening in gold and silver was also resorted to, the resulting suit presenting the absolute perfection of ornamentation. Plumes of flowing colored feathers were attached to helmets. Fluted, laminated, and puffed suits were made with elaborate decorations. Gorgets and goussets reinforced the globose breastplate. Very large and roundish *pauldrons* were worn, laminated skirts of small overlapping steel plates called *lamboys* took the places of taces and tuiles. The light armet and other derivations of closed helmets with movable visors were in general use. The pointed solerets were replaced by broad sabatons, cut off square or rounded at the toes.

In England, King Henry VIII established the Royal Armories at Greenwich about 1515. There developed an English style known as "Greenwich armor" which had discernible Italian and German influences but which had the characteristic English simplicity and solidity.

The so-called "Maximilian armor" developed in the 1530s. The term has been coined by modern collectors, and there is no evidence that the German emperor Maximilian (1459–1519) was responsible for its introduction. The fluted Maximilian armor prevailed throughout the 16th century for use both at war and joust. It reached a high degree of excellence but was rapidly obsolete with the introduction of firearms. It showed the Gothic trend, but it may be said that it was a fusion of the German and Italian styles. To the Italian rounder, blunter forms was brought the decorative fluting of the German Gothic, with the difference that the lines of fluting were more vertical than parallel. They also served to strengthen the metal in the same way as those on corrugated iron. Applied brass borders were replaced by pronounced turned edges with the appearance of rope. The long, pointed Gothic sabaton was discarded, and

Left: Plate Armor, 15th Century. *Right:* French "Harnois Blanc," Second Half of the 15th Century

one imitating contemporary civilian shoes with broad. round toes, so-called "bear-paw" sabatons, were substituted. The helmet was of the *armet* type or a closed model with a skull something like a short-tailed sallet and with both a visor and a bevor pivoted from the same ponts on either side. The *bourguignotte* (also called *burgonet*) was introduced during the war in Burgundy. This was roundish in form, fitted with a crest, and had two movable cheek plates and a chin piece for the protection of the face.

Other types of armor were designed for parade purposes rather than for protection in battle. Some were made to imitate the elaborate, extravagant, slashed and puffed civilian costume prevalent in the early Renaissance. Metal parts were thinner and lighter than before. The high degree of sophistication and decoration went together with grotesque and bad taste. Some armor was fitted with a *brayette*, a rather obscene codpiece, a protuberant metal case in the form of a large penis. Some helmets of the Late Middle Ages became grotesque with a menacing appearance. The visored fronts could bear a likeness to an animal's head or bird's beak decorated with etched flutes, winged monsters, and scrolls. It was then evident that the successive changes which occurred in warfare tended to the gradual disuse of all armor. The invention and use of gunpowder was the death knell of chivalry in the full sense of its meaning. Armor had become insufficient as a guard against firearms and mail-clad knights and heavily armored men-at-arms who had played their part through many centuries were now to disappear.

16

The Hundred Years' War (1340–1453)

The 14th century was a period of crisis, an age of rapid change, much of it change for the worst. There were wars, rebellions, famine, and schism in the Church causing intellectual, social, economic, and political problems. If many of the tensions, problems, and wars of the 14th century may be blamed on individual rulers, society also had to endure one of the greatest natural calamities, an unprecedented bubonic plague called the "Black Death." The great plague which started at the end of the 1340s and lasted for years represented a turning point in history. The Black Death — brought from the East — killed a third, possibly half, of the European population. In Lubeck (Germany), for example, the plague is said to have killed 90,000 of the 100,000 inhabitants. In Vienna (Austria) between 500 and 700 died each day. In the populated Limoges (France) only five people survived. Many Italian cities lost three-quarters of their population. Everywhere the doctors went through the streets wearing face masks and pointed hats and carrying their smoke bottles. Mass graves were dug and bodies buried. Madness was rife. Evil rumors spread, saying that the Jews had poisoned the wells and that their black magic art were to blame for the pestilence, and so a terrible wave of anti–Semite persecution flared up around Europe. Witches, heretics, and strangers were suspected of misdeeds, hunted, and killed. Hosts of flagellants traveled the highways and tried to avoid God's thorn by indulging in ascetism, penance, and self-inflicted torment. Others delivered themselves up to the full life, held wild orgies,

indulged in free love, and reveled in intemperance and hedonism. When people died by the thousands in the streets, the princely castles and royal palaces resounded with joyful, luxurious, and noisy feasts. Even within the Church — the so-called protector of morale and religion — the most disparities were evident. Monks and nuns died caring for the sick while the high clergy, bishops, and popes amassed money in their coffers and held brilliant feasts. Because of this, the late medieval period has often been called an age of disintegration, the gloomy twilight of a waning civilization. But this very much of a simplification. The late medieval period was an age of extreme complexity because it was an age of transition, and the people of the 14th and 15th centuries showed creative vigor in many fields.

Causes

There were many disagreements between England and France and enough causes to provoke a conflict. First, there was the question of the succession to the throne of France. The king of France, Charles IV, had no son when he died in 1328, and the vacant throne was disputed by two pretenders, Philippe de Valois and Edward III, king of England. Edward III's mother, Isabelle, was the sister of the deceased French king; he was therefore the grandson of Philippe III the Fair. The second pretender, Philippe, was Charles de Valois's son who himself was the brother of King Philippe III. The French prelates, dignitaries, and *légistes* (lawyers) chose Philippe probably because they were unanimous to reject France being ruled by a foreigner — even worse an Englishman! — a first manifestation of French nationalism. Edward — though deeply displeased to be rejected — eventually gave his approval and rendered homage to the new king of France, Philippe de Valois, who was crowned in 1328 as Philippe VI, the first king of the Valois dynasty replacing the direct Capetians who had ruled France since Hugh Capet in 987.

For a while Edward III accepted this situation but, in October 1337, however, he openly challenged Philippe and declared his own intention to uphold his rights to the crown of France. French jurists invoked then the ancient — probably forged for the occasion — *Salic Law*, whereby women were not allowed to transfer their rights to their husbands. Edward was rejected for the second time, and war became inevitable. One reason for Edward to embark upon war with France was his imperialist policy that war was still the king's s business, and Edward loved it. The other main cause of conflict was purely economic. France dominated the rich northern province of Flanders whose main economy was based on the import of English wool and the export of cloth, a situation which was very inconvenient for both the English stock breeders and the Flemish weavers and merchants. Furthermore, the English crown still dominated large parts of France, notably the rich southwestern provinces of Aquitaine and Guyenne, with wines from Bordeaux and salt from the Atlantic coasts — a situation intolerable to the French king.

The struggle between England and France designated as the Hundred Years' War is an inaccurate name for the long contest which began in 1337, as it lasted more than a century. It was however not really one single war but several series of campaigns broken by civil wars, sieges, skirmishes, ambushes, local wars, and occasional periods of peace and interludes of truce. In the course of these operations, all the inherent violence of a feudal society, which the Church had never more than half tamed, flared out in a savagely destructive way. The French civilian population suffered the most. The pillage of towns and burning of village were common practices that were intended to pay the fighting troops and to enrich their leaders. Politically, destruction perpetrated by the English was also designed to demoralize the population and persuade them that their French masters were broken reeds of protectors. Knights were expected to uphold the standards of chivalry in *chevauchée* (guerilla) warfare, but it is an open question as to how far they could restrain themselves and their men. Neither the Black Prince in 1335 nor his father were able to prevent devastation and large-scale pillage.

In the history of warfare the Hundred Years' War

Edward, the Black Prince, 1330–1376. The Black Prince was son of King Edward III and Prince of Wales. He is seen here with jupon armor. The Prince's surcoat displays the fleur-de-lis of France and the three lions of England.

marked a period of transition. The conflict grew out of a classical feudal dispute, and the leading participants did not always behave toward each other according to the approved code of knightly honor. Feudal levies proved inadequate for the operations, and both sides relied heavily on mercenaries. The great battles were not won by the armored mounted knights but by soldiers on foot armed with bows. By the end of the conflict, firearms made their appearance and gradually changed the art of warfare. The war was deeply intertwined in the general politics of Western Europe, and it inspired a mood of nationalism both in France and England.

Genoese Crossbow Man

Opposing Forces

The French Army

The French army of 1337 differed little from the force of the 12th and 13th centuries. Its basic element was the levy of heavily armed noble knights who followed their suzerains to battle. Their armor was somewhat heavier than in the past. The visored helmets were usual, pieces of plate metal protecting exposed spots, and the horses were protected with armor as well. As this equipment was very costly, only the richer lords possessed it, and many other knights served in lighter armor; these were, as a rule, called "mounted sergeants," a corps created during the Crusades. The essential difference between the heavy cavalry of the Hundred Years' War and the traditional feudal levy of the past centuries was that it was paid for its service, but because each great lord received the money to pay the vassals who followed him, the discipline of the French army was poor. In addition to the horsemen, there was the militia from the main towns armed with spike weapons. When the cavalry was patient enough to allow the footmen to arrive on the battlefield—something which rarely happened—these troops were reasonably useful in combat. The only troops in the French army equipped with missile weapons were crossbowmen who were generally foreign mercenaries. The Genoese were especially hired for their skill with this weapon and were frequently used, but because such mercenaries were very expensive, their numbers were usually small.

The English Army

The English army was mainly composed of infantrymen. When King Edward I was planning the conquest of Wales, he realized he needed soldiers on foot to follow the Welsh infantry into their mountains. For this purpose he levied large numbers of men from the western shires and paid them for their service. Later when he conquered Scotland, he used the same kind of army. Thus there was built up in England a troop who had military experience and who were willing to fight for pay.

At the beginning, almost all of these soldiers were armed with spike weapons, but as time went on many of them adopted a new and highly effective weapon — the long bow. The long bow was apparently invented by the southern Welsh. During the Welsh wars, it was taken over by some of the English infantry, and soon each shire was well supplied with archers who were adept in its use. From about the middle of the 13th century, all able-bodied Englishmen from the age of 15 were compelled to train in archery practice on Sundays. By 1250 Edward I had wisely ensured that the long bow was part of the standard equipment of his army. Some six feet long, the long bow was made of yew, hickory, ash, or elm. It had a linen or hemp string, its arrow was slightly less than a meter (about three feet) long, fledged or feathered, and pointed with a small sharp head that would deliver the greatest possible impact on the smallest possible area. The long bow had a good range (about 182 meters or 200 yards) and a striking power that could pierce chain mail. Its great advantage was its high rate of fire; a good bowman could shoot ten or twelve arrows a minute as against the two bolts of the most expert crossbowman. In consequence of the rapidity of fire, the English archer invariably beat down the attack of Continental crossbowmen, and the English delivered such a missile fire that the enemy ranks were disorganized before the knights started their dreaded charge. Moreover — owing to the vertical position of the bow — they could stand close together in compact ranks, The long bow was possibly as long as a man; it had a pull of about 48 kilograms (100 pounds) and, to string it, the bowman usually bent it between his legs. That was actually the main drawback of the long bow; archers had to start their training in early youth and keep in constant practice; long bow men were products of the countryside. To fire the bow, the string was drawn back to the ear; because of the great pull, the knack was to put the weight of the body *into* the bow with the left arm. English archers

English Longbow Man, ca. 1346

wore iron head pieces and sometimes breastplates or mail shirts, but generally their principal defense was their thickly quilted tunic. The long bow was to be a decisive trump in the English victories of Crécy, Poitiers, and Agincourt.

Edward I had little enthusiasm for the clumsy undisciplined feudal levy of heavily armored horsemen. As a rule he relied on paid companies. An experienced and able soldier, usually a knight, was paid to raise a company and hire a few other knights and squires to serve as officers; then he send men out to recruit archers and pikemen. Such a company totaled some hundred soldiers and consisted of a few mounted men and a fair-size body of infantrymen. The great English earls and barons were expected to serve without pay, and each of them brought with him some horsemen supplying a small troop of cavalry. In addition the king recruited Frenchmen from his province of Gascony, which supplied him with a fair number of crossbowmen and a few cavalrymen.

The English had to learn a new tactic. Bowmen were usually placed between the horsemen so that they would be protected; then the archers would shoot a rain of arrows. It also became customary for the archers and infantrymen to bear a stake sharpened at both ends which the front ranks drove firmly into the ground with the second and uppermost point sloping from them, while the rear ranks filled up the intermediate spaces with theirs; this primitive form of field fortification helped to defy the charge of the enemy heavy cavalry. When the enemy formation wavered and gaps appeared in its ranks, the cavalry would charge. It also happened that the English cavalrymen dismounted and fought with the infantry. This they did for various reasons: partly because of the vulnerability of their horses, and partly out of consideration of pure gallantry — a dismounted knight could not flee to save himself but had to stand and fight. So long as they stood and fought the French enjoyed some successes. But when they attacked on foot, their invulnerability to arrows was outweighed by their ponderousness of movement and restriction of vision. This enabled the English to notch further victories at Poitiers in 1356 and, most notably, at Agincourt in 1415 where the English killed probably 5,000 French knights and took 1,000 prisoners, for the loss of a few hundred men of their own. These two tactical devices, one defensive and one offensive, were to be the English army's chief reliance throughout the Hundred Years' War.

Another tactic developed by the English was the so-called *chevauchée* (cavalcade). Initiated in 1355 in southern France by Edward the Black Prince — son of Edward II of England and a paragon of chivalrous virtue — a chevauchée was a quick mounted raid on the territory of opponents. The object of the chevauchée was systematic,

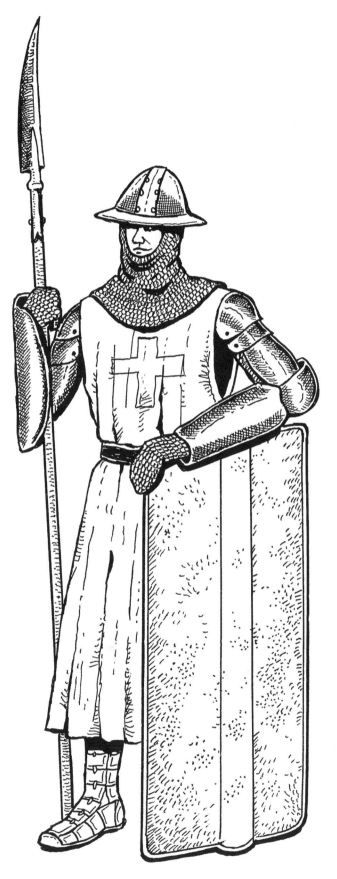

French Infantryman, ca. 1300

cold-blooded destruction of the enemy's wealth and resources, which meant pillaging and killing peasants and looting and burning villages and towns. The devastation was accompanied by small sieges, skirmishes, and local fighting. The combatants escaped lightly, and it was the noncombatant civilians who suffered most from the fire and sword of this quick-moving army ravaging the countryside. These campaigns were as valid and as important as battles and sieges, as they were economically interesting. They also reduced the morale of the French as the thousands of homeless, hungry, and angry people were a further drain on the resources of the French king. This kind of terror activity was totally unchivalrous, but it was viewed as part of the necessary strategy required to reduce the opposition.

First Part of the War, 1337–1388

Sluys, Crécy, Calais, and Poitiers

The war began by a series of military disasters for the French. The battle of Sluys (L'Ecluse off the coast of Brugge in Belgium), in June 1340, was one of the few naval battles of the Middle Ages. On June 8, 1340, the French had gathered about 200 vessels under command of Admiral Quieret to invade England. The English fleet included some 150 ships commanded by experienced sea leaders like Morley and Crabble. The encounter took place at the mouth of River Zwin. The battle began at 11:00 in the morning and lasted for about eight hours. The English were reinforced by Flemish boats coming from Brugge. The French were defeated and lost some 170 ships and almost 18,000 men including the navy leadership. Their fleet being destroyed, the French pretensions to exercise any control over the sea were wiped out; the invasion had to be postponed. Instead it was the English who had command of the sea, and, therefore, they could set foot in France where and when they wanted. France became from then onward the main battlefield.

On land things went equally wrong. In the spring of 1346 Edward landed in Normandy at the head of a powerful army and routed the French cavalry at the calamitous battle of Crécy on August 26, 1346. The battle of Crécy was remarkable for the role played by the English infantry among which were the archers armed with long bows against the French army, which had many times their number. The superior rate of fire of longbows told against the slower crossbows of the Genoese mercenaries in French service. The retreating crossbowmen were actually ridden down by the French knights in their eagerness to grip with the English, but the knights charged only to be mown down by a storm of arrows. According to reliable authorities more than 1,500 French knights were killed for about 100 English casualties. It was one of the first occasions on which the mounted feudal knights had been worsted by foot soldiers.

The battle of Crécy demoted the orthodox knights from being the main asset of an army to being almost a liability, relying instead on dismounted cavalry to with-

English Knight, ca. 1356

stand charges and on archers to act as an offensive force. The lance as a weapon of war had become obsolete. The efficiency and thus the progress of the new tactics were so rapid that the last major medieval cavalry battle was fought at Tannenberg in July 1410 when the Teutonic Knights were defeated only sixty-four years after Crécy, and no cavalry victory of any size is recorded after Crécy itself. Crécy was also remarkable as being the first battle where primitive artillery was used.

After Crécy, the king of England turned north and laid siege to Calais. This crucially important harbor — only 38 kilometers (about 23 miles) from Dover — had to surrender in August 1347 after a siege of eleven months. It is on this occasion that the six burghers, dressed in sackcloth with halters around their necks to signify penitence, prayed for mercy to Edward III. They were pardoned by Edward's wife. The capture of Calais was an important move as it provided the English with a very good port close to their country. Calais remained occupied by the English until 1558 when the port town was retaken by Duke François de Guise.

After the loss of Calais, the situation in France was becoming increasingly desperate as the military disasters were worsened by the Black Plague which caused great loss of life. Philippe VI died in 1350; his son Jean II (nicknamed Le Bon as he was devoted to the notion of chivalry) succeeded him. Edward III had not abandoned his hopes of becoming king of France. His son, the Prince of Wales, nicknamed the "Black Prince," landed in Aquitaine and adopted a cruel form of warfare — the previously discussed *chevauchée.* The Black Prince's terror expeditions in the period 1355–1357 were intended to be no more than an armed raid for the purpose of economic warfare and to break the morale of the French population. The English prince made such an effective nuisance of himself that a drastic response became necessary. Jean Le Bon moved south to stop him. The two armies met near Poitiers in September 1356. The battle of Poitiers was another disaster. Once again the French knights were defeated by the English archers, and Jean II Le Bon was captured and released after payment of a huge ransom.

The war, devastation, pillage, and military defeats resulted in serious social troubles. In Paris, the provost of the merchants, Etienne Marcel, supported by a large fraction of the population, entered into rebellion, took temporary control of the capital, and set up a virtual dictatorship over Paris— so unbearable that he was killed by the burghers. Jean Le Bon's son (called the "Dauphin") fled from Paris. In the meantime, in the countryside— exasperated by the excesses of both English and French men-of-war — peasants rebelled against the authorities. These bloody rebellions known as *Jacqueries* (from the nickname "Jacques" given to the peasantry) were

suppressed with savagery by the French royal troops. In a background of military disasters, civil war and open rebellion, the French were forced to accept a disastrous peace. On May 8, 1360, a treaty was signed at Brétigny, near Calais.

Jean II le Bon died in 1364, and the Dauphin became

French Knight, Reign of King Jean II the Good, 1319–1364

king of France as Charles V le Sage ("the Wise," who reigned from 1364 to 1380). The reign of Charles V began in the most auspicious manner. The companies of mercenaries who roamed the country looting as they went were removed to Spain by his constable Bertrand Du Guesclin. Charles V restored the economic situation of his kingdom that lay in ruins and devastation. The new king realized good financial reforms, allowing regular funds to pay soldiers. He reorganized the army and gradually resumed hostilities against the English. His constable, Bertrand Du Guesclin, waging a type of attrition warfare and guerilla tactics, achieved significant successes. Du Guesclin liberated large parts of France and — reassured by the royal successes — many towns occupied by the English rebelled and drove them out. By the late 1370s it seemed like the war had came to an end.

Grandes Compagnies

The Hundreds Years' War saw the activities of mercenaries reach an appealing peak on the soil of France. The war produced the greatest concentration yet seen of mercenary companies on both sides, both of noble and base-born soldiers of fortune. In the interval of fighting they simply lived off the countryside. They desolated whatever country that was the scene of their operation, and their presence was the sure signal for ruin and devastation.

From the middle of the 14th century until the middle of the 15th, these *routiers*, *Grandes Compagnies*, or *écorcheurs* — scorchers as they were called with horrible descriptiveness — roamed France at will, collectively or individually pillaging, raping, and burning. These free companies of soldiers of fortune were headed by a captain — a nobleman or a respected man-of-arms well versed in the art of war, who took it upon himself to collect volunteers from among the most lawless of men, such as brigands, robbers, bold serfs who had escaped from serfdom, ruined nobles, and any other adventurous men. They suspended their criminal activities only during the increasingly brief and irregular periods of war when they were rerecruited into the service of an authority in a position to provide regular pay.

The treaty of Brétigny in 1360 created a temporary lull in the war, and the vast international band of mercenaries was suddenly laid off. Since much of northern and eastern France had already been so devastated by war that there was nothing left to plunder, a large "Great Company" moved southward, looting as it went. A French army, under the leadership of Jacques de Bourbon, was raised to crush them and met them in battle at Brignais in 1362. The Great Company — composed principally of Germans and Hungarians and led by an experienced warlord, Montreal d'Albarno — had grown so strong and warlike, that the French army was defeated.

The company then moved on toward the rich and powerful city of Avignon, home of Pope Innocent VI, where they laid siege and obtained a huge ransom. The Company scattered but reappeared in northern Italy as the "White Company" under the leadership of an English warrior, John Hawkwood (known in Italy as Giovanni Acuto). Here they became part of a tradition of mercenary forces, the *Condottieri*, in the employment of factious Italian cities. Other gangs roamed France, and in desperation French authorities mounted campaigns abroad. Bertrand du Guesclin is known to have led one of those "Great Companies" to Spain where they were engaged to fight the Moors, simply to get them out of the way.

Second Part of the War, 1415–1453

Charles VI, the Mad King

When Charles V died in September 1380, his son Charles VI was only twelve years old. France was then governed by the king's uncles who were primarily concerned with their own interests. Charles resumed control and was determined to bring about certain reforms. Suddenly for some unexplained reason the king became mad, the precarious royal power was shaken, and the uncles took control once again. They were soon at loggerheads among themselves, and the rivalry became particularly intense. The struggle reached such a violent pitch that France was divided into two rival camps. On the one hand there was the *Bourguignons* (with the duke of Burgundy) and the *Armagnacs* (named so after their leader the high constable Bernard of Armagnac).

The Bourguignons took control of Paris, and this was the moment the king of England, Henry V, chose to resume his plans for the conquest of France. The battle of Agincourt in October 1415 was another disaster for the French heavy cavalry who faced the English archers' fire power under adverse conditions. This showed that the French had learned nothing of their previous defeats at Crécy and Poitiers. Agincourt was a remarkable English victory against large odds which enabled Henry to reconquer Normandy and ravage the Ile de France.

The short reign of Charles VI had been a disaster, and the years that followed were among the darkest of the whole of the history of France. The northern part of the country was occupied and ruled by the English. The new king of France, Charles VII (who reigned from 1422 to 1461), was in exile from his capital and ruled over a small territory around the city of Bourges. Fortunately, Charles VII was gradually shaken out of his torpor.

Jeanne d'Arc

A simple peasant girl from Lorraine, Jeanne d'Arc, had heard voices from heaven ordering her to drive the English out of France. With a small escort she set out to meet the king and disclosed to him that he was truly a son of France. Jeanne was given some troops and liberated the town of Orléans in May 1429 which the English were besieging. She won the battle of Patay and took the king to Reims where he was solemnly crowned. Jeanne was to continue her heroic struggle until her capture near Compiegne. After a shameful ecclesiastical trial conducted by Archbishop Cauchon of Beauvais, a man wholly committed to the English cause, Jeanne was delivered to her enemies and burned at the stake as a witch at Rouen (Normandy) in May 1431.

The story of Jeanne d'Arc — though having all the appearances of a heroic tale — is historically true. Only the importance of Jeanne d'Arc to the liberation of France might be an interesting point of discussion. A few historians in France and elsewhere stress that she died in 1431 and that France was totally liberated only in 1453. Furthermore, they claim that her role has been greatly overestimated — particularly in the 19th century — for nationalistic reasons. Probably her main remarkable feat of glory was to shake Charles VII from his apathy and to give the French hope in a very dark hour. Jeanne d'Arc — one of the most symbolic personifications of French Catholic nationalism — was canonized in 1920.

Charles VII's Permanent Army

During this period of the blossoming of nationalist feelings — exemplified in Jeanne d'Arc — and military successes, the French — at last — learned to change their military tactics. A new and modern army was created which proved more formidable than any feudal army, and with which they forced the English to the defensive which ultimately led to total victory. The French had suffered a lot of mercenaries who had proved unmanageable, very expensive, and danger-

The Battle of Auray, 1385. *Left:* **the English John of Montford;** *on the ground:* **the French Charles de Blois.**

ous in peace time and unreliable in time of war as they had no scruples about serving the highest bidders. Therefore, during the second period of the Hundred Year's War, some sort of a permanent army was established.

Charles VII was able to obtain the right to levy a special tax, the *taille des gens de guerre* (tallage of men-of-war). By the end of the 15th century, the taille had become a permanent tax for which the authority of the estates was no longer required—placing thus royal finances on a regular basis. The original grant was made by the estates to Charles VII in 1439. In 1444, the king issued ordinances whereby a number of mercenary bands pullulating about his realm were taken into the royal service on a permanent basis and used to forcibly disband the rest. There was no question here of feudal obligation but one of wage. Each captain was a military contractor who recruited, equipped, trained, led, and paid his own men in return for a royal lump sum. The units formed were called *compagnies d'ordonnance* (companies of regulation) and the men-at-arms became truly soldiers who were paid by a wage. All officers were appointed by the crown and thus became truly officers, that is, office holders. All, both officers and soldiers, were paid by the authority, were submitted to a kind of discipline, and had to reside in certain garrison towns designated by the authority. This rudimentary permanent army was a fully stipendiary force, though not yet a national one. Frenchmen but also many Germans, Scots, Walloons, Swiss, and Italians were part of this comradeship in arms. The bond of loyalty to their employer was the assurance of cash payment—punctually and in full—not patriotism, which was a notion unknown to people of Middle Ages.

While making military reforms, Charles VII made new alliance: He achieved a reconciliation with the duke of Burgundy, and by 1450 he was ready to resume the struggle against England. Many French towns had already risen in opposition to the English. With some outstanding military leader such as Richemont making a wide use of firearms, Charles VII defeated the English in Auray in 1385, Rouen in 1418, and Orléans in 1429. Normandy was reconquered in 1449 and Aquitaine and Guyenne in 1451. Finally the battle of Châtillon in 1453 was won owing to the French artillery. This marked the end of the Hundred Years War. The English, divided by the Two Roses civil war, were driven off France keeping only Calais which stayed in their hands until 1588.

Aftermath

The long contest between France and England affected developments in both English and French societies.

In France Jeanne d'Arc has been seen as an emotional expression of nationalism and even the first manifestation of a collective patriotism paving the way for the notion of citizenship and national pride. National sentiment is often voiced under stress, when the national group is threatened by a powerful and victorious neighbor or torn by civil war. The enemy is then clearly identified, and nationalists have the tendency to associate and charac-

French Couleuvrinier, End of the Hundred Years' War. The man is armed with a couleuvrine—a culverine, a primitive portable firearm.

terized him in abusive terms while their own people are defined with extravagant and tendentious panegyric. The force of patriotism has always been associated with feelings rather than facts, with prejudice fed by fear, and with a sense of identity sharpened by an unfavorable comparison with aliens and foreigners.

In England, the hostility encouraged the growth of a distinctive culture, and the English people became more aware of their own identity. Edward III had actually forbidden the speaking of French in his armies. It was a way of making his men aware of their Englishness. English replaced French as the rulers' language and was at last accepted as a literary language. This was illustrated by the works of writers such as William Langland and more particularly Geoffrey Chaucer (1340–1400), the "father of English literature." The anti–French cultural reaction was particularly evident in architecture as the French exuberant flamboyant Gothic style was never adopted in England; instead, the English evolved the more restrained and elegant perpendicular style as can be seen at the King's College Chapel, Cambridge, with its fan-vaulted roof, large areas of glass, and delicate stone work.

Relationships between France and Great Britain were marked by rivalry since the conquest of England by the French Normans in 1066. The struggles of the French Capetians against the English Angevine Plantagenêts as well as the Hundred Year's War brought both lands into a state of profound hostility, and these were not the last confrontations between the two countries. Until today, Louis XIV and particularly Napoléon are still hated in Great Britain, and the French have not forgotten (some have not forgiven) the burning of Jeanne d'Arc. The French would always try to support the enemies of Britain, and they helped the rebellion of the North American colonies resulting in the creation and independence of the United States of America in July 1776. In return, the English did the same, and whoever could harm France might count on Britain's support.

There was a quasi permanent state of war in the 17th and 18th century for colonial issues between the "Frog Eaters" and the "Perfide Albion." Mutual resentment, rivalry and mistrust reigned until 1904 when both lands signed the *Entente Cordiale* allowing them (with the decisive help of the USA) to achieve the victory of 1918 against Germany. But during World War II, there were difficult moments between the two Allies. Such expression as "filer à l'anglaise" (in English "to take the French leave") illustrated the climate at the time of Dunkirk in May–June 1940. Relationships between De Gaulle and Churchill

French Franc-Archer, Period of Charles VII

were always strained. The destruction of the French fleet by British ships at Mers-El-Kebir (in July 1940), the war in Syria (in June–July 1941), the Anglo-American landing in North Africa (in November 1942) were other crucial and extreme tensions which the Nazi Germans tried to exploit —fortunately in vain — to force Marshall Pétain's puppet government to declare war on Great Britain and the USA.

17

European Mercenaries

Decay of Feudalism

During the 12th century, both lords and vassals found it to their advantages to decrease the old emphasis on personal service. The vassals—absorbed in their work as landlords, administrators, and judges—wanted time to look after their affairs and succeeded in establishing rules limiting the number of days of service and reducing service in distant expeditions outside certain boundaries. As for the lords, they accepted the limitations because ordinary vassals were not necessarily good soldiers and they did not always have the time or inclination to spend on military training. As fiefs became hereditary, there was no assurance that heirs would have the physical and moral qualities required to make an effective armed horseman-of-war. What kings and powerful lords wanted was a force of well-trained warriors who would serve anywhere at any time; what they needed were professional soldiers not vassals. If the lords took money instead of service, the interests of both sides were served. The vassal could buy himself off and thus avoided inconvenient, dangerous, and onerous duties, and the lord acquired funds with which he could pay permanent soldiers for long campaigns. Increasingly, vassals were excused from service in return for a fixed sum. This was called *scutage* or shield-money in England and *army-aid* in France.

The money intended to meet the expenses of a war was at first rather infrequent, but gradually it turned in effect into a general taxation on the whole population. That was the sign of the decay of feudalism. Since the overlords no longer expected personal service but money, it mattered little to them who held the fief. They received the same payments whether the holder were a man, a woman, an old friend, or a stranger. This tendency helped the development of bureaucratic administration in the form of clerks, lawyers, laymen, and revenue collectors. These administrators came either from the low gentry—country gentleman and poor knights with spare time and no money—or from the bourgeoisie, an urban social group which had scarcely existed before the 12th century. Though the power of kings and great dukes increased in the 12th and 13th centuries, they made no attempt to totally wipe out the rights of justice which vassals had earlier acquired. The aristocracy continued to have power in civil and military offices as well as in high positions in the Church. As long as the superior could hear appeals or intervene directly in important cases, he was quite content to leave the tedious work of settling village quarrels and larcenies to local lords.

Physical training—such as riding and fencing—continued to be important but it was no longer enough. A certain degree of literacy and education and knowledge of law was now demanded to hold positions in government. The number of gentlemen who could read and write Latin with a certain ease increased in the 12th and 13th centuries. Young aristocrats who wanted social success had to know about literature, music, and art. Life at the court of a duke, a prelate, or a king was itself an education in manners and tastes, in politics and administration. This developed in the 14th and 15th centuries in the ideal aristocrat who had been trained in the physical skills needed for combat, the social manners required for sophisticated court life, and the intellectual capacities demanded for leadership.

By the end of the 12th century, the vassal-lord relationship had ceased to be important either as a means of raising an army or as a way of getting the work of government done. The tendency toward fragmentation of political power had been reversed, and large political units were being built in many parts of Europe. Feudalism was becoming a matter of empty formalities; there was a growing concentration of power in the hands of the ruler, and — in short — the sovereign state was emerging. Here again, this process was slow and multiformed, and it took at least two centuries for this concept to be fully realized as many of the conditions which had made feudalism possible persisted, such as poor communication, agricultural population, and respect for aristocratic leadership.

Gradually a new way of recruiting soldiers emerged — and this became more evident in the 14th and 15th centuries. When a ruler wanted to raise an armed force, he usually commissioned knights or men of noble rank to recruit warriors for him. Each captain raised his own gang or company and was paid according to its size. The captain and his men asked for cash and booty not land of fief. When the war or the expedition was over, the company was supposed to be disbanded, but if it had proved to be a good fighting unit, the captain was inclined to hold it together. The men were *his* not that of the lord who had hired them, and he could always try to find another employer. Before that happened — that is, when the captain was between contracts — the company of a soldier who had no territory of its own to live off became a gang of brigands who simply turned to "soft" targets; they plundered weakly defended areas, ransomed merchants, looted peasants, or attacked small towns. Before the state was to create its permanent standing armies, the time of the mercenaries and illegal armed bands had broken out.

The development of armed retainers into knights was explained by the military aspect of feudalism. The feudal arrangements of vassals and knights serving in the post were a convenient way of raising an important element of an army — the mounted elite — but they were not the only way of raising an armed force. Light-armed cavalry and infantry also had some value even in the period when the heavily-armed feudal knight reached the peak of his military efficiency. Rulers of any importance did not depend entirely upon the service of mounted knights for their military expeditions, and not all significant battles were ever decided simply by the clash between knights of two opposing sides charging each other. As soon as a large number of vassals held fiefs, they began to strive to reduce the amount of military service which they owed, and this already had serious effects by 1100.

Even at its peak, the feudal system never furnished enough soldiers for major military operations, and after 1100 it became increasingly useless as a way of providing any armed service at all. As we have seen in previous chapters, rulers were continuously forced to require military service of foot soldiers. These were usually recruited among free men — most of whom were not knights — especially for defense duties in the castles, siege warfare, and even in pitched battles. Various types of infantrymen, archers, crossbowmen and light-cavalrymen were recruited. Some were peasants who were either drafted or volunteered for an expedition and who were rewarded by a share of the booty of war. Others were professional mercenaries who were paid wages for a single campaign.

There had been — as we have seen above — some stipend element in military service throughout the Middle Ages. For prolonged and distant campaigns mercenaries had always been employed even in the time when feudal obligation included the holding of land against military service. Since the 12th century there had always been a class of soldiers who had nothing to occupy their time except to fight for pay. Mercenaries were of course not all of knightly origin, but a surprisingly large number were. The number of available fiefs had drastically shrunk; the safety valve of the Crusades was closed. Therefore, according to the system of primogeniture in inheritance of land, younger brothers and landless knights had to seek their fortunes, and many turned mercenary or became soldiers-of-fortune.

The later Middle Ages saw the development of a larger military class than the available wars could support. Hence, if no wars were available, it is not surprising that the military class tended to manufacture their own wars. The existence of these free-lance soldiers — prepared to put their swords at the disposal of the highest bidder — at first enhanced the power of the princes, so long as they had money to pay for them. Duke William of Normandy shipped mercenaries across the Channel to conquer England in 1066. The great Spanish adventurer El Cid had once fought on behalf of the Moors. During the Hundred Year' War the kings of England and France were able to maintain armies in the field throughout a whole campaign by virtually placing their military forces on a stipend basis. By the 14th century it was no longer possible for kings to levy armies or nobles to keep their retinues of knights by calling on feudal duties alone. They had to employ professional mercenaries to wage war.

Even the service given by a knight to his lord was frequently rewarded with pay, stipulated in a contract. The money came from various taxes and from scutage, payment in lieu of military service from vassals whose services were no longer required. Funds also came from the proceeds of trade, from dues or loans advanced by rich merchants, or from privileges granted to the urban economically productive classes. Bankers and financiers began to figure largely in the capacity of the prince to make war, and a famous Latin adage illustrated this fact clearly: *pecunia nervus belli*, money rules warfare. The recruiting of soldiers became a classless, international, and a fruitful — if precarious — trade.

In England a sort of compromise was reached in what became known as the indenture system. An indenture was a contract agreed upon between a king and a lord, or between a lord and a knight, defining the terms of service and the payment for it. It differed from the mercenary's contract because it attempted to define the employment of the knight in terms of loyalty and lifelong service — in peace and war — to one lord. The contract, when drawn up and signed, was cut in two, with a jagged edge (hence the term *indenture*), to prevent forgery. The indenture — a hybrid between properly rewarded service and a purely professional contract — was of course difficult to observe.

Life for mercenaries was hard. Pay was erratic, when money ran out, mercenaries were left without employment, and — having no estates to live off — they roamed at will and lived on racketeering, looting, and pillaging. Roaming at large in the country, preying on the civilian communities, fully armed and experienced soldiers, they were a terrifying social menace. Each man had to provide his own weapons and equipment; the utterly indigent were thus excluded. But once enrolled, the prospects before a tough, ruthless, ambitious, and unscrupulous young man of moving upward on the social ladder were very fair, that is, at least if he survived diseases and battle, was not hung for robbery, was not robbed by his colleagues, did not squander his money on women, and did not drink or gamble his fortune away. Not many of these soldiers of fortune attained great wealth and power, as often happens, *multi sunt vocati, pauci vero electi*, there were many candidates but only a few of them went in at the top.

Urban Militia

In their heyday in the 11th and 12th centuries, knights and aristocratic rulers had been in an almost unchallenged position. Only the clergy held comparable power as a class and had some hand in government. The 13th century brought other changes besides the growth of the royal power. A new economic social group emerged in the cities: the trading bourgeoisie. The development of European cities began at the end of the 11th century with the gradual reappearance of a money economy, the increase in trade and commerce, and the revival of specialized craftsmanship. The growth of towns had gradually a profound effect on all western Europe; they first appeared in Italy, and during the Crusades, Venice, Genoa, and Pisa revived Mediterranean commerce. Encouraged by the authorities, towns developed in Flanders, France, England, and Germany.

Many towns became prosperous, and the townsmen gradually managed to free themselves from feudal ties and interferences. They obtained a charter, a document to guarantee their rights, privileges, and freedom. Inside their walls citizens were able to create new social and economic organizations free from feudal rule, thus starting the development of a middle class and a capitalist economy. Some wealthy cities became quasi-independent republics headed by an oligarchy of mercantile families, banking dynasties, and rich merchants. The townsmen were extremely proud of their political, economic, and military successes. Throughout Europe appeared a splendid architecture with cathedrals, town halls, public palaces, and private residences.

Among the urban privileges stipulated by the charter of freedom, there was the right of a free city to raise troops. The urban militia was an armed force composed of physically able volunteers recruited among the inhabitants. Militiamen were not paid and, therefore, were recruited among the richest men of the town, the only ones who had spare time to train and enough money to finance weapons and military equipment. Militiamen were usually well-motivated because they defended their family and property; they fought for a simple cause and for concrete interests: customs, privileges, and liberty. The municipal militia's main purpose was to defend the town; the city walls were divided into sectors manned by neighboring militiamen who were grouped in companies under the command of a captain. In time of trouble, the militia was on alert, gatehouse control was reinforced, and persons, boats, and vehicles were searched. The municipality might also raise the entire male population — between the ages of 14 and 60 — in case of siege or for an expedition into enemy territory.

The towns struggled to increase their commercial and political power. They attacked rural villagers and even noble landowners in their vicinity to force them to submit to the communal authority. Larger cities attempted to bring under their rule smaller neighboring towns. The great communes waged ceaseless war on one another as each sought to extend its territory. They could also ally together, forming a political alliance and uniting their military forces to resist powerful threatening princes or even kings and emperors. Venice, for example, originated from a small community of poor fishermen to a powerful empire including the whole Adriatic Sea with possessions all over the Eastern Mediterranean.

Urban troops might be led into battle by a sacred war chariot, the precious palladium of the city. At Florence there was the famous Carrocio, drawn by two steers decked out with red hangings. Parma had its Blancardo decorated with pictures of the Madonna and the town's saints on a white ground. In wartime, the militia could be reinforced by a royal contingent or allied units, but the municipality often felt reluctant to introduce foreign troops within its walls for financial reasons and in fear of losing a part of its independence. In peacetime, the militia served as a police force for keeping public order, arresting criminals and thieves, guarding the accesses, and walking night-watch. It played also a significant political role by securing the established order and, possibly, repressing popular rebellion or internal rival parties against the ruling class.

Medieval municipal armed forces obtained several military resounding victories. In 1176, Italian militias defeated the German emperor Friedrich Barbarossa in Legnano, a disaster which stupefied the entire feudal world. The so-called battle of the "Golden Spurs" fought on July 11, 1302, near Kortrijk (Courtrai in south Belgium) illustrated the revival of infantry and the efficiency of the well-motivated urban militias. The elite of the French chivalry, under command of Robert d'Artois, were defeated by the Flemish urban militia from Brugge and Yper. The French knights underestimated their lower-class opponents and recklessly thrust aside their own infantry so as to charge, as they thought, to victory. The Flemings dug a ditch into which most of the knights in the front fell headlong, bringing the knights behind them down also. The vicious slicing blades of the Flemish pole weapons then killed the cavalry of France as it flailed helplessly on the ground. The casualties at this battle were heavy, according to some estimates up to 40 per cent of the French cavalry — the cream of their knights — were killed. After the battle the spurs of about five hundred dead knights were collected and displayed in Our Lady Church in Courtrai. In 1315, the Swiss won the battle of Morgarten over the German emperor Leopold of Austria, marking freedom for the Helvetic confederation.

However, the military value of urban militias on the whole was various. After all, they were composed of dilettante civilians, men who were more at ease in their shops, behind their desks, or in their workshops than on the battlefield. The use of levied militia presented serious disciplinary problems, and — if they were easier to manage —

Urban Militia Foot Soldier with Holy Water Sprinkler, ca. 1300

they were not as well trained as professionals. Besides, the busy populations of the thriving cities could not spare essential productive manpower for the conduct of war. Moreover, many rich bourgeois found the condition of soldier unworthy of their rank; they considered fighting too dangerous for themselves and their sons. They had better things to do — such as devoting their energy to business and internal politics — than training, patrolling at night,

Italian Infantryman with Bardiche, ca. 1320

Italian Mercenary, End of 15th Century

and wasting their precious time on guard on the windy city walls. Instead, rich citizens obtained exemptions and, as time went on, gladly accepted paying taxes to allow the municipality to recruit professional soldiers to do the fighting for them. To meet the demand of war there grew up in the 14th century a class of mercenaries. In the Late Middle Ages and during the Renaissance, urban militias proper were usually deprived of active military service. They were relegated to auxiliary police forces or fire brigades; they became mundane associations or shooting clubs, marching with colorful uniforms, drums, and flags in parades and at feasts.

Italian Condottieri

In Italy the fragmentation of the feudal structure and the precocious development of a rich urban economy produced clients in the form of wealthy city-states who were prepared to pay well for the hire of mercenary military skills. Rival commercial interests and aristocratic factions created an endemic intercity warfare, and no authority could conceal the fact that in the north Italian plain the sole arbitrator of legitimacy was brutal force. Local noblemen and bands of foreign knights—brought south by the German emperors or washed up by the receding

Italian Daggers, ca. 1500. *Left:* stiletto; *right:* cinque-dea ("five fingers") dagger.

Italian Condottiere with Milanese Armor, ca. 1450

tides of the Crusades—were prepared to put their swords at the service of anyone who could pay them. After 1360 when the first part of the Hundred Year' War was over in France their ranks were filled with *Grandes Compagnies* and other Routiers left unemployed.

Italy swarmed with bands of professional soldiers, and by the end of the 14th century, the legal-minded Italians institutionalized the system of *condottieri*. Con-

dottieri means simply "contractors," being so called after the *condotta* which was the contract of service specifying with great detail the *ordinamenti*, the conditions of employment stipulating the exact size of the force to be provided, how it would be led and equipped and armed, the length of time and the place it was to serve, and the sum of money the force was to be paid. Though the condottieri were generally known for changing sides if someone made them a better offer, many of them became notorious for the concern of their professional reputation and enjoyed much respect for their fidelity to their word.

These groups came in all shapes and sizes, from small gangs headed by petty leaders to larger forces commanded by nobles like the Gonzagas, the Estes, or the Colonnas who took their rewards in lands and fiefs. Some condottieri established themselves—as did Federico of Montefelto at Urbino—as independent princes with whom any contract was virtually a treaty between sovereign powers. Others either became politically dominant in the states which employed them—as did the Visconti in Milan—or became commanders and trainers of the citizen levies. The most famous of these mercenaries turned princes was Francesco Sforza who, as a result of his marriage to the illegitimate daughter of Filippo Maria, the last of the Visconti dukes, finally succeeded in winning control of Milan and assumed the much-coveted title of duke in 1450. Today, the Colleoni Monument in Venice—made in the 1480s by Andrea del Verrochio—commemorates one of the most notable condottiere of the age, Bartolomeo Colleoni (1400–1475). Occasionally a condottiere became pope; that was the case of Baldassare Cossa who was elected pope (or, better said, anti-pope) during the Great Schism under the name of John XXIII (pontificate from 1410 to 1415). Cossa was a mercenary of very disreputable life who was a haughty, intolerant, and violent Holy Father in a period of religious turmoil and crisis within the Catholic Church.

The forces provided by the condottieri were predominantly mounted. The basic unit was a lance or barbue consisting of a small group headed by armored knights with a train of attendants including squires and pages. About five barbues made up a post headed by a corporal. Two posts formed an *enseign* commanded by a *decurion*, and two enseigns formed a banner under the orders of a *bannerrerio*. This armed force provided by the condotta often included a various number of *fanti* (foot soldiers) armed with pole weapons including various forms such as the halberd, pike, corsesque, partisan, spontoon, glaive, and runka which have been previously described. There were also crossbowmen both mounted and on foot.

During the 14th century the Italian armorers had been making steady progress toward quality and fame, particularly those from Milan. Italian armor was characterized by the use of large pieces of plate, particularly large *pauldrons* covering the shoulders and large elbow and knee guard plates. Each plate was carefully shaped for the body's movement. Helmets included various forms such the *sallet*, *burgonet*, and the *barbut*. A distinctive short sword was used by the Italian: Known as *cinquedea* ("five fingers"), it had a flat, double-edged triangular blade; this was often enriched with etchings and gilded decoration. By the end of the 15th century, foot soldiers were armed with arquebuses, and artillery and gunmen increased in number.

The troop raised by the condotta was self-administrating and included musicians, writers, and officers for maintaining discipline and internal justice. The conduct of war—especially in the hands of experts like Andrea Braccio and Francesco Sforza—became a subtle affair of feints and surprises, of forces held in reserve until the last moment, and of cunning maneuvers and shocks. Strategy became something of an art form, and tactics on the battlefield was characterized by the caution of professionals who had heavily invested in their own force. Condottieri were often reluctant to squander their expensive-to-replace men by a single rash decision. Battles were sometimes bloodless, and the results were often less decisive than the employers—who had paid good money—had demanded and expected. It was not cowardice however but business. Living off the enemy's country and avoiding bloody battles, thus preserving their capital and prolonging campaigns, were ways of staying longer in service until the money ran out. However satisfactory the condottierri were to their employers, they were a plague to the ordinary people—both citizens and peasants—in war-ravaged northern Italy. Many chronicles recorded the devastation and ruin that were left after an army of such men had passed through. The activities of the condottierri would seem to be incompatible with the spirit of knighthood, but surprisingly, young knights were often advised to travel to Italy to seek experience in warfare. Certainly the sophistication and indecisiveness of the condottieri made a poor showing when—at the end of the 15th century—Swiss pikemen, French gens d'armes, and Spanish *tercios* converged into Italy, bringing a new bloodiness to the battlefields of the peninsula.

Hussites

Johannes Huss (1369–1415), a professor at the university of Prague, vehemently denounced the inordinate wealth and temporal power of Church leaders, the abuses of the monastic life, and the scandalous sale of indulgences. Huss's critics and doctrine formed the premises of the Reformation as Martin Luther—the founder of Protestantism—took up some of his ideas. At the Council of Constance called by the pope in 1414, Huss was condemned and burned alive at the stake as a heretic. This

and who also saw in the movement a chance to express their Bohemian nationalism, continued to trouble the Church and the German empire for twenty years. The talented patriot Johann Ziska—and after his death in 1424, his successor, the priest Prokop the Shaven—led a Czech army composed of peasants, free men, burghers, and laborers against the German feudal knights. The Czech people's army held five imperial and papal anti–Hussite crusading armies at bay. The Hussite army, in their turn, took the offensive and broke out in plundering masses through Palatinate and Franconia, burning monasteries, looting churches, plundering villages, and sacking towns as they went. Eventually they burned and murdered their way through Saxony, Thuringia, Brandenburg, Silesia, and Austria.

The military successes achieved by the Hussite popular army were due to pioneering in warfare. Ziska and Prokop organized *Wagenburgen* (wooden armored wagons) mounted into circular formations. The wagons—simple peasant carts—were covered by thick wooden boards reinforced with metal bars, presenting a formidable defense against which their enemy, protected only by conventional armor, flung itself with self-destructive futility. The wagons were bristling with armaments, notably a high number of firearms and light cannons named *snakes* with appropriately lethal bite. The wagons formed an armored barricade behind which the infantry was well protected. It was a safe sanctuary from which they could make sudden sorties using various arms, such as long-poled weapons and swords, and to which they would retreat as quickly. The mobility of the wagon train was one of its greatest assets. It amounted to a moveable fortress that could be set up on any prominent position ready for action on very short notice.

It was not until the rebels split up into opposing religious sects quarreling more and more about religious issues that they could be overcome. The king of Hungaria, emperor of Germany, and king of Bohemia, Sigismund of Luxemburg (1368–1437) defeated the popular radical wing of the movement in open battle in 1434. The Hussite threat was eradicated by force in Europe, but

Hussit Foot Soldier with Guisarme

released all kinds of religious and social passions and gave rise to the Hussite rebellion in Bohemia.

The religious problem rapidly took the form of a war of liberation as the Czechs had enough of the German disorder and confusion. Huss's followers, who believed in the supremacy of the Scriptures over the immoral pope

the descendants of the radical Hussites, the Moravian Brethren — who wanted to set up Christ's millennium upon earth — played a not-negligible religious role in Germany and in Northern America in the 18th and 19th centuries.

Swiss Infantry

There were other interesting developments in weapons and tactics in the 15th century during the wars opposing the Duke of Burgundy and the Swiss. Northern Switzerland — controlling the strategically important passes in the Alps between Italy and Germany — was originally a part of the duchy of Swabia and attracted the ambitions of the German emperor of the Hapsburg dynasty. In 1291 three *cantons* (Swiss federal states) around Lake Lucerne rebelled to obtain privileges, swore a *rütli* (oath), and formed a league to resist the German oppressors. These were Uri, Unterwald, and Schwyzt (the latter giving Switzerland its name). In 1315, in a narrow pass near Mortgarten, the Swiss rebels ambushed the proud German knights sent by the duke of Austria, Leopold II. The crushing defeat inflicted proved again that mobile foot soldiers armed with pole weapons could overcome mounted armored horsemen. The rebels were joined up between 1332 and 1353 with the cantons of Lucerne, Zurich, Glaris, Zug, and Berne. Together they formed the Helvetic Confederation and again defeated the Hapsburg forces in 1386 at Sempach, killing Duke Leopold III.

The Swiss mountaineers, peasants, and burghers, helped by their favorable geographical position, showed

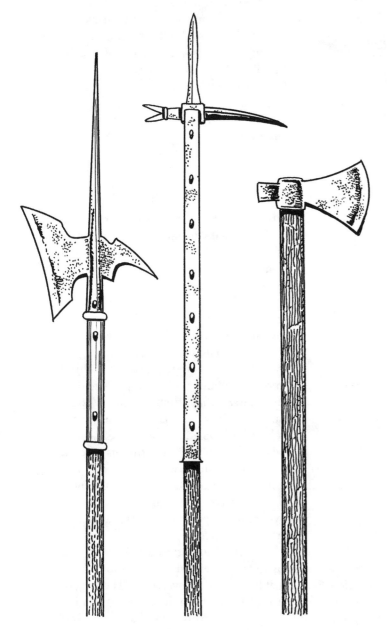

Swiss Pole Weapons. *Left:* halberd; *middle:* Luzern hammer; *right:* pole-axe.

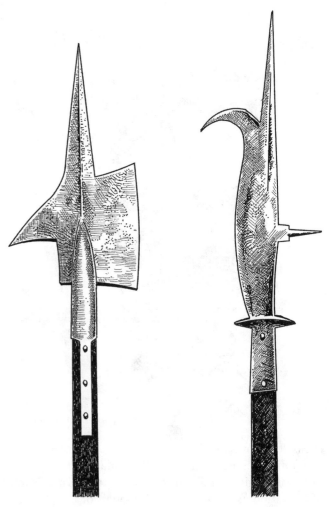

Pole Weapons Used by the Swiss. *Left:* sempach halberd; *right:* guisarme.

how the people of a country thrown into disorder by its ruling classes and lacking any central power could set about establishing their own rule of freedom and law. In the 15th century, the confederation — increased by the cantons of Friburg, Wallis, Solothern, Bale, Appenzel, Grisons, and Schaffhausen — took the offensive and began to expand its territory at the expense of the Hapsburgs, the counts of Savoy, and various petty Alpian lords. The Swiss defeated the duke of Burgundy, Charles le Témé-raire (the "Rash" 1433–1477), at Grandson and Morat (1476) and Nancy (1477).

The original weapon of the Swiss mountaineers was not the pike which made them famous but the halberd with which they slaughtered the Austrian knights, hacking though their armor not only when they trapped them in the defiles at Morgarten in 1315 but in the open field at Laupen in 1339 and Sempach in 1386. These events bear out the view that the revival of infantry of non-noble soldiers was due far more to moral and social factors than to any technical change. The halberd was a dreadful weapon, quite easy to handle, and admirably adapted for hand-to-hand combat against a mounted man. Its pole was about 2.5 meters (8 feet) long, and its metal head combined a spike to thrust, a heavy axe to cut, and a sharp hook to unseat a horseman. Another typical Swiss pole weapon was the so-called *Luzern hammer*, composed of a heavy war hammer fixed to the end of a strong shaft intended to smash the armor of a mounted soldier.

Later, the Swiss made their reputation with the pike, a weapon that they adopted in time for victories over the Burgundian knights of Duke Charles le Téméraire. The Swiss were essentially spearmen who fought on foot in massive formation reviving the ancient Greek/Macedonian phalanx equipped with long pikes at the time of Alexander the Great (356–323 B.C.). This was based on a principle easy to understand: The simplest weapon with which a man on foot can be armed against cavalry is a spear. If the spear is long enough, the ranks are dense enough, and the morale of the men is high enough, such a formation of pikemen can be almost invincible. The Swiss pike was between 5 and 6 meters (18–21 feet) long with a sturdy shaft of ash and a long sharp steel head. It was heavy and cumbersome, and its full effect was not achieved as an individual weapon but in mass formation. Each pikeman — firmly grasping his long weapon — stood as close as possible to his comrades and developing a dense phalanx, usually comprising a battalion of men 30–40 across and almost 100 deep. The ranks of the formation were staggered so that a highly dangerous picket line of razor-sharp blades was presented

Swiss Infantryman, ca. 1315

which horsemen were unable to penetrate. As the vulnerability of the horse became apparent, the result was that the traditional charge of massed heavy cavalrymen began to be abandoned. Like a Roman legion, the Swiss phalanx was highly disciplined and could maneuver rapidly. When standing against an enemy cavalry charge, they held the end of their pike against their foot and leaned into the length of the weapon to withstand the shock of impact without being pushed over. The Swiss developed precise drill and learned not only to stand on the defensive like a huge hedgehog but how to move as well. They wore little armor; they found shields to be serious impediments to the formation of their compact columns and close lines and consequently abandoned them. The Swiss peasant/pikemen were therefore able to attack quickly maintaining all the while the even closeness of their ranks. They were well drilled so that they could march and charge in solid formations which could completely rout the horsemen; their phalanxes several thousand strong trundling forward annihilated anyone unwise enough to remain in their path.

The Swiss became the most valuable soldiers of Europe, other European armies adopted the long pike, and their tactics—in slightly modified form—remained an integral part of warfare and proved a useful weapon until the 17th century. In the paintings of the period, dense with the rich pattern of infantry and cavalry marching seemingly in every direction or struggling in combat, pikemen are always to be seen, like tall ears of wheat or barley, the multiple fences of the pikes rising high above the heads of the combatants.

Once they had assured the independence of their own cantons and restored peace, the Swiss were prepared to rent out their skilled battalions to whomever could pay them well enough, a natural-enough way of supporting a population becoming too great for its own sparse pastoral economy. The Swiss had achieved such astonishing military successes that they became the most famous and most sought-after mercenary spearmen of all European armies—though increasingly, as the 16th century went

Swiss Pikemen, ca. 1480

on, this tended to be in French service. Swiss regiments—as part of the French army—fought later at the battle of Malpaquet (1709), Denain (1712), Fontenoy (1745), Rossbach (1757), and Berezina (1812). Even today the Pope's Vatican guard is composed of Catholic Swiss volunteers armed with halberds and wearing cuirass, Spanish-styled morion and 16th century colorful dress. Hired military service became a Swiss social institution and a nationalized industry. The negotiation of all contracts was in the hands of the canton authorities, as was the selection of troops. They were highly specialized and produced their great pike phalanxes including men armed with swords and halberts for close-quarter fighting. Later these were accompanied with arquebuses and guns to protect their flanks, but basically they showed no inclination to diversify their techniques.

The dense pikemen formation had certain disadvantages: The squares were easy targets for missiles; they were not suited to operate on rough ground and useless for siege warfare. Thus as firearms became increasingly important, the Swiss pike phalanx became left behind like dinosaurs unable to adapt. At the battle of Marignano (1515) they were smashed by the artillery of François I of France, after which a perpetual peace was signed with France. Infantry fighting in the end of the 15th century and during the 16th century became an international trade and was to be shaped by professionals: the German *lansquenets* and the Spanish *tercios*.

German Landsknechten

The Swiss' method of fighting was copied by their mountaineer neighbors in southern Germany and Austria, equally impoverished and no less bellicose. During

Landsknecht Drummer

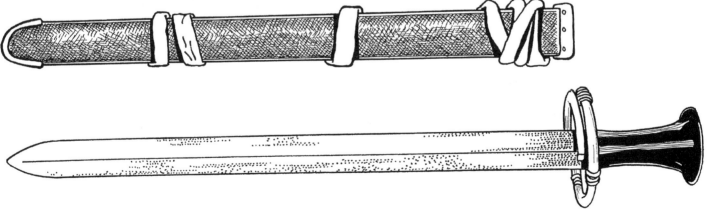

Lansquenet's Katzbalger. The typical lansquenet's sword could be as long as 3 feet.

Lansquenet Doppelsöldner   Feldweibel (Sergeant Landsknecht)

the wars in Burgundy, the Netherlands, Germany, Bavaria, and Bohemia at the end of the 15th century, soldiers were badly needed. German formations were raised, known as *Landsknechten* or *lansquenets* (from the German terms *Land*, meaning "country" and *Knecht*, meaning "servant"); this term appeared for the first time about 1470. One difference from the Swiss was that the lansquenets were drawn from a broader social spectrum. Southern German and Austrian nobility did not have scruples about not only raising and organizing them but also serving on foot

in their ranks. Thereafter "to trail a pike" became a perfectly acceptable form of military activity for the German nobly born. The lansquenets became the great rivals of the Swiss. But — as they regarded warfare as pure business — they diversified their activities and adapted themselves more easily to the rapidly changing requirements of war. Soon they accepted within their ranks experienced troops of all classes and from all nations, from Germany of course but also from Spain, France, Wallony, Flanders, Italy, and even Switzerland. Consequently, the proportion of nobility declined as the forces grew in size and attracted the adventurous and the desperate from every social class.

The organization of the lansquenets—due to competent warriors such as Georg von Frundsberg (1473–1528) and Götz von Berlichingen (1481–1562)—was quite modern. The *Rotte* (squad) was the smallest unit counting about ten *Söldner* (soldiers) commanded by a *Feldweibel* or *Oberste Feldweibel* (a kind of corporal or sergeant). Twenty squads formed a 400-men-strong *Fähnlein* (battalion) commanded by officers called *Hauptmann* (captain) and *Lecotenent* (lieutenant). About ten of these units constituted a regiment totaling some 4,000 men commanded by a *Feldobrist* (colonel) assisted by a staff including various officers with various functions such as *herold* (herald), *Dolmetscher* (translator), *Kaplan* (chaplain), *Schreiber* (writer), and *Feldartz* (doctor) as well as *Quartiermeister, Fourier,* and *Proviantmeister* who were quartermasters in charge of logistics. The feldobrist was generally protected by eight personal body guards called *Trabanten* or *Leibwache*. The Feldobrist could sometimes have command over more than one regiment and in this case he had the rank of *Obersten Feldhauptmann* (general). The *Profoß* (provost)—assisted by *Stockmeister* and *Aufseher* (supervisors)—was charged with maintaining discipline. Representatives called *Weibel* and *Gemeinweibel* were elected every month by the soldiers; they were charged with having contact with the senior officers. Each regiment and Fähnlein had a *Fähnrich* carrying the *Standarte* (banner or flag) and musicians, *Pfeifer* (fife player), and *Trommler* (drummerboy).

The lansquenets were mercenaries hired by whomever could afford them, but they were particularly related to the German emperor Maximilian I of Austria (1459–1519) and his follower king of Spain and emperor of Germany Charles V (1500–1558). Maximilian had a huge interest in all aspects of the military. He was a pioneer in the development of artillery and organized the so-called imperial *Kreisen* (circles) which were to be used until 1805; in case of danger, each members of the German Empire—vassals, bishoprics, principalities and free cities—had to provide armed

Lansquenets Armed with Pole Weapons

Pikemen Fighting

contingents in proportion to their importance. In addition, Landsknechten were widely hired for the purpose of combat.

The lansquenets were well-disciplined but ferocious. There were many tales celebrating their courage and ironic sayings about them. One said that they could not go to Heaven because they were too evil but were not accepted either in Hell because they frightened the Devil himself. They made a tremendous impact on the battlefields of Europe, notably in the Italian wars at the battles of Ravenna (1512), Creazzo and Novara (1513), Marignano (1515), and Bicocca and Pavia (1523).

They made their reputation with various weapons. The long pike was used in Swiss-like tight formation. They also used various pole weapons such as the halberd, partisan, and others; daggers; and remarkably impressive huge and heavy swords. Named *espadon, flamberge, zweihänder* (two-hand), *Schweizerdegen* (Swiss sword) or *anderthalb hand* (one-hand-and-a-half), this large two-handed sword was almost as high as a man. It was fitted with a strong blade, a broad guard, and a long grip in

order to be held with both hands. In battle the Zweihänder sword was swung by a vigorous volunteer who marched right to the enemy pike formation, violently twirling his huge weapon aiming to cut the sharp pike ends. If the man was not killed, his action could create a breach in the opposing phalanx, inside which his comrades would charge. The audacious and athletic volunteer was a *Doppelsöldner*, a soldier paid a double wage — when he survived — for his courage and the risk taken. The impressive, cumbersome, and heavy two-hand sword became obsolete about the beginning of the 16th century, but it remained in the military arsenal as a parade weapon. The lansquenets had various sorts of other swords including a very popular type known as *Katzbalger* with an S-shaped cross guard. There was also a typical Swiss and German dagger — often referred to as Holbein dagger — with a broad and double-edged blade. Certain Nazi daggers of World War II (1939–1945) were copied from it.

The landsknechten wore no uniforms but did wear various exuberant colorful dress in the gaudy fashion of

Lansquenet Formation of Pikemen

the time, including tight-fitting pants and large slashed sleeves. Officers often wore the — previously described — Maximilian armor. Headgear included various sorts of helmets, but large hats with colorful plumes were popular and widely worn by all ranks. They often put black wax on their armor and incidentally on hands and faces, thus the nickname of "black devils"; they also let their beards and moustaches grow which increased their ferocious look.

As firearms became more important on the battlefield, the lansquenets also recruited men armed with arquebuses and developed a team of artillery gunners. Until the advent of more refined firearms pronounced their doom, the lansquenets proved a formidable fighting machine. In tight ranks, relying on close combat, they were however vulnerable to accurate fire from greater range. Like the English longbow men, brilliant in their time, the gaudy lansquenets were dreaded troops that had to give way to more efficient devices of progress. The lansquenets were seen as one of Germany's greatest military achievements, and not surprisingly they served as model to establish the tradition of the German armies. During World War II, two elite Waffen SS armored units carried the names of their legendary ancestors: the Tenth SS Panzer Division Georg von Frundsberg and the Seventeenth SS Panzer Grenadier Division Götz von Berlichingen.

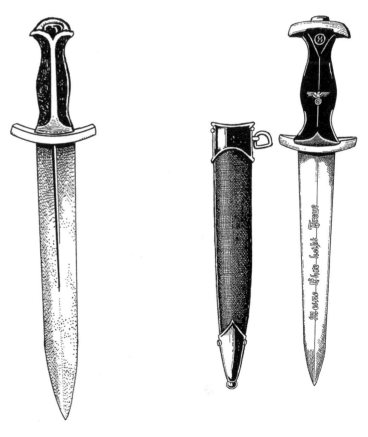

German and Swiss Daggers. *Left:* Swiss "Holbein" dagger; *right:* SS dagger, 1933.

Spanish Tercios

Spanish Soldier with Halberd, Early 16th Century

In Spain, heavy cavalry had never been a major component of the Christian armies in a dry country lacking forage and in the slow campaigns of the Reconquista. The Spanish kings found no problem in recruiting the poor but proud Castilian nobility to serve on foot in their wars. The novel *Don Quixote de La Mancha* published in 1605 and 1615 by the Spanish soldier and writer Miguel de Cerventes (1547–1616) was intended to satirize the excesses of romance literature and, particularly, the striving for individual glory through ever more extravagant feats of arms: Don Quixote illustrates very well the difference between the old-fashioned poetic dream of chivalry characterized by the *hidalgo* (poor but proud noble knight) and the concrete reality.

In 1494, the Spanish army was totally reorganized in a modern pattern. Based on the experience of the Swiss and lansquenet model, and created by the brilliant man-of-war Gonzalvo di Cordoba, new formations appeared called *tercios*. Soldiers were professional volunteers paid by the Spanish crown. The smallest unit was a squad of 25 men; 10 squads formed a company of 250 soldiers; and 10 companies constituted a regiment totaling 2,500 men. Each unit was provided with modern services such as logistics and transport, military justice, and sanitary service including doctor, surgeon, pharmacist, and barbers. The remarkable efficiency of the tercios was based on a well-balance synthesis between fire power provided by men armed with arquebuses and shock provided by pikemen. The great difference between the dense Swiss square of pikemen and the Spanish tercio was a greater flexibility enabling a better individual use of the weapons, greater mobility giving a superior maneuverability on the field, and better combination of units required in a peculiar situation.

The tercio included various kinds of soldiers. The arquebusiers were no longer equipped with armor, and that gave them a good mobility and facilitated the operation of their cumbersome and heavy weapons, the matchlock arquebus. They had a sword, a powder flask, and a bullet bag. The pikemen wore back and breastplates with tassets, gorget, and gauntlets as well as distinctive helmets such as the *cabasset* and the popular combed *morion* with its curved brim and roped edge. There were armored man on foot equipped with swords and round shields (bucklers) for close-range fighting. In combat, handgun men opened the battle being in the van, their task was disorganizing and harassing the enemy before the main encounter or assault took place. Then they slipped behind the formations of pikemen to reload and eventually came back to the front to deliver another deadly volley. The pikemen did the real business of

Formation of Spanish Pikemen, End of 15th Century

fighting; they stood steady to receive cavalry charges, checking horses at the end of their long pikes, hauling off the riders with the hooks of their halberds, marching forward to the tap of drum, hacking their way through all opposition, and finishing off the retreating enemy with their swords. The tercio also included a lightly armored cavalry for scouting, mobile firepower, skirmish, and escort.

The presence of logistics services, regular pay and fairly good morale coming from the feeling of serving God, the Catholic Church, king, fatherland, and personal honor made the Spanish army a dreaded fighting machine which dominated the 16th and the beginning of the 17th century. A great fraternity mixed with paternalism seemed to have reigned between officers and the rank-and-file, but — as the Spanish armies served mainly abroad — the men were often cut off from their roots and ties with the fatherland. Increasingly they developed a narrow arrogant esprit de corps and a dangerous self-confidence of being invincible. The battle of Rocroi — won in May 1643 by Louis de Bourbon, Duke of Enghien — marked the end of the supremacy of the Spanish tercios.

18

Firearms

Gunpowder

It was not the French chivalry nor Jeanne d'Arc who finally brought the Hundred Years' War to a close and bundled the English back to their island. It was actually a small professional group who enjoyed no social status whatever and were barely accorded the humble status of soldiers: the gunners. Some form of combustible material had long been in use in warfare both by the Byzantine armies and the Muslims. Loosely called "Greek fire," this substance was made of a petroleum-based compound with sulfur and quicklime which, terrifyingly, burned also under water. Greek fire was normally used in the form of fireballs and primitive grenades propelled by catapult in siege or naval warfare. To reverse the process and use combustion itself as a propellant of a missile was a more difficult and dangerous affair.

The invention of gunpowder has been credited to the Chinese. There is no certainty of this, but experiments were made there at an early date, and results were variable and often unstable. The Arabs may also have known about gunpowder, but how it came to Europe is totally unknown. It is logical to think that the substance was brought to Europe through the channel of Arab merchants who traded with both the West and the Far East.

The first report of its manufacture was the English Franciscan friar, Roger Bacon (1214–1294), in the middle of 13th century. Bacon was a theologian and a man of experimental science or "black art." It is not known how Bacon came to the formula of black powder, but he was working also on incendiary substances. Bacon did not actually invent gunpowder but gave the formula for the correct mixture (75 percent saltpeter, 15 percent charcoal and 10 percent sulfur), in a coded anagram in his book *De Mirabili Potestate Artis et Naturae* (On the Marvelous Power of Art and Nature), a treatise on contemporary scientific beliefs written in 1242. The use of a secret anagram too remained an unanswered question debated between historians. It may be explained by the politics of the time. Since the second Council of the Lateran in 1139, an anathema was laid to any person who made fiery composition for military purpose. Had Bacon expressed or alluded to black powder (a secret we may assume known to a few alchemists), he would have flouted this decree and probably hazarded his life. There is also the persistent story of a mysterious German monk named Berthold Schwartz who is often credited to have invented gunpowder about 1380. Despite the alleged story, a portrait of him (made in 1643), and a statue to his memory in his hometown of Freiburg-in-Brisgau, it is possible that Schwartz was only a legend.

The explosion of gunpowder produces a tremendously strong thrust with a loud noise and heavy smoke composed of hot toxic gas. Powder gave a source of energy thousands times stronger than that of human muscular force; its use as an explosive charge to provide the power to fire missiles was the most influential innovation in the history of warfare. To this day the gun remains one of the most effective machines of war in a variety of shapes and sizes. The introduction of firearms was, however, not a sudden revolution but a long development that lasted for nearly two centuries.

Early Artillery Pieces

The origins of gunpowder are hidden away, and who made the first firearm using black powder as propellant remains equally forever unknown. The first positive record of such a weapon is not until at least sixty years after Bacon's publication. Cannons seemed to be known in Europe at the beginning of the 14th century. As early as 1326, permission was granted by the city council of Florence (Italy) for the delivery of *canones de metallo* for the defense of the town. The first known illustration of a gun occurred in about 1327 in an illuminated manuscript, *De Nobilitatibus, Sapientiis et*

The Earliest Illustration of a Gun (after *De Nobilitatibus, Sapientiis et Prudentiis Regum*, by Walter of Milemete, Christ Church Library, Oxford, ca. 1327)

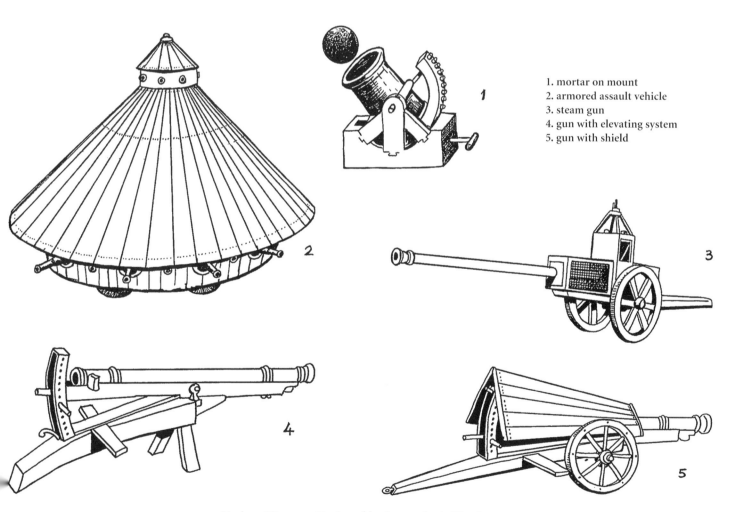

1. mortar on mount
2. armored assault vehicle
3. steam gun
4. gun with elevating system
5. gun with shield

Various Weapons Designed by Leonardo da Vinci

Bombard. The bombard was manufactured as a beer barrel, with forged iron staves kept in place by hoops.

Prudentiis Regum, written by Walter of Milemete in honor of King Edward III. In this illustration a knight, wearing chain mail, a long surcoat and ailettes, is shown putting a red iron to the touch hole of a pot-bellied, vase-shaped cannon from whose mouth an arrow — a projectile most familiar in those year — is about to be fired. This gun was mounted on what appears to be no more than a four-legged table.

In 1338 there was a cannon used at Cambray from which arbalest quarrels were discharged. In the following year, at the siege of Le Quesnoy, similar pieces were present and in use. In 1342, at the siege of Algesiras, guns were used. In 1346 the king of England, Edward III, seemed to have possessed several guns which were used at Crécy and during the siege of Calais. Contemporary historians made mention of this novelty in warfare in a manner which proved them to have been regarded simply as a curiosity of no great value or importance. Probably the main efficiency of those early guns were the terrible noise they made coupled with the smoke and

flame they produced which had a terrifying effect on horses and men. Even the overwhelming terror which cannons might have made on their first appearance on the battlefield seemed to have been tales of later ages. In any case the noise on a typical medieval battlefield was so great that a few bangs and smoke were not going to make much difference, and it is probable that the first men using guns were regarded as a lot of daft so-and-so's.

As soon as the first guns appeared, inventive unknown minds turned their attention to the novelty of the new machine and produced them in a proliferation of shapes and sizes, all with different purposes. Some of these never got further than the drawing board. Illustrations from Leonardo da Vinci, for example, still exist today showing extraordinary imaginative designs: organ guns intended to spray shots, mortars to shower a veritable hailstorm of small stones striking the enemy with terror, wooden battle tanks, and even a parachute.

The first experiments were infernal machines. They had a low rate of fire and were cumbersome, ineffective, unreliable, and dangerous for the gunners themselves as they could explode — much to the delight of the enemy. Their projectiles — mostly balls of stone used as an economy and convenience — were too light and were thrown with too little force to do much harm to the stone castle walls or to the enemy force. Early carriages for guns consisted merely of a great beam of timber that was hollowed out so the piece could lie snugly along the length. As cannons lacked movable mounts, they were of little use in the field except when an army on the defensive wanted to forbid the enemy the use of some narrow passage. There was a wide variety of guns with many calibers and names such as *veuglaire, vasii, pot-de-fer, serpentine, crapaudine, basilisk, saker, falconet, flanker, perrier, culverine* and many others. The so-called *bombards* appeared in the 1380s. These primitive heavy guns were for firing stones and were made of staves of wood or iron laid lengthwise in a circular formation to form the barrel; the staves were forced together by rings of brass or iron. It was not a satisfactory method as the gases from the explosion of the propelling gunpowder charge tended to escape through the cracks. The mounting was a kind of timber-framed bed which greatly limited the possibility of aiming. Not fitted with wheel, bombards were transported on wagons resulting in poor maneuverability.

War chariots had been used in warfare since the ancient Egyptians, and a logical move was to mount light guns on a cart. One of these war machines consisted of a two-wheeled shield, pushed forward by soldiers, with pikes protruding through its face and loopholes provided for primitive firing tubes. Another variation was the organ gun. The *ribaudequin*, for example, was a bundle of several guns with their barrels laid in a row, sometimes as many as ten side by side, mounted on the same wheeled carriage. Each gun had its own touch hole, and one gun could be fired at a time or several together for a startling volley. The *shrimp* was a gun cart giving some cover to the gunners owing to a conical nose fitted with pikes and gun openings in the side of the cone. Orgel guns were intended to kill or wound grouped troops, and — in theory and under especially favorable conditions — they could have a tremendous effect on a dense phalanx of pikemen. But the danger was always as great for the gunners as it was for the enemy. The artilleryman might explode the whole contraption in a self-destructive conflagration. Furthermore, early guns took so long to move, load, and fire that they were of little use on the battlefield. The noise and smoke they made created a certain amount of confusion and consternation, but there is little evidence that they did anyone much harm.

There were also references to small portable cannons and handguns carried by individual soldiers — the ancestors to the musket — appearing in the 1370s. The smaller firearms were not much more effective than the large ones. It seems very doubtful however that they could compete in effectiveness with the crossbow or the long bow as a missile weapon. They were very slow firing, magnificently inaccurate, unreliable, cumbersome, and highly dangerous for the user. The technical development of firearms was still in its infancy.

Cannons and Handguns

By the 15th century, artillery formed a regular part of the military equipment of the armies of Western Europe. From that time on the more-exotic products had disappeared and the two fire weapons which between them were to dominate the conduct of war for another five hundred years were emerging in clearly recognizable form: the cannon and the handgun.

Cannons

As time went by and the design of firearms improved, the brass hats of the period began to take notice. Several major innovations in artillery warfare occurred during the 15th century.

Black powder was greatly improved. In the early days of artillery, gunpowder was weak stuff with a low grade of purity and uncertainty of action; the substance, if ground and mixed before use, gradually sifted all the grains back into three layers of saltpeter, charcoal, and sulfur. Early artillerymen preferred thus to transport the three dry ingredients separately and mix them on arrival in the siege or in the battlefield — not an easy task on a wet day, and positively hazardous and highly dangerous in combat conditions. Invented about 1425, corned powder involved mixing saltpeter, charcoal, and sulfur into a soggy paste, then sieving and drying it so that each individual small granule contained the same and correct proportion of ingredients. The process obviated the need for mixing in the field; it also resulted in more efficient combustion, thus improving safety, power, range, and accuracy.

Bronze (copper alloyed with tin) castings began to take the place of iron. Gun manufacturing demanded among other things an expertise in metal casting which was developed in the West — ironically enough — to serve that most peaceful of purposes, bell founding. From bell to cannon was an all-too-easy step. The development of foundries allowed cannons to be cast in once piece in cast iron and bronze; in spite of its expense, casting was the best method to produce practical and resilient weapons with lighter weight and higher muzzle velocity.

The combination of reliable propellant energy and strongly built barrels resulted in an important improve-

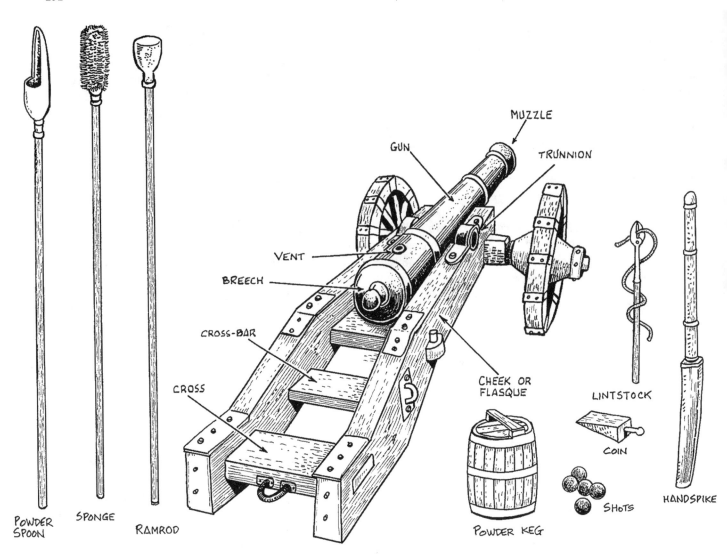

MUZZLE

GUN

TRUNNION

VENT

BREECH

CROSS-BAR

CROSS

CHEEK OR FLASQUE

LINTSTOCK

COIN

SHOTS

HANDSPIKE

POWDER KEG

POWDER SPOON

SPONGE

RAMROD

Various Parts of a Gun and Accessories

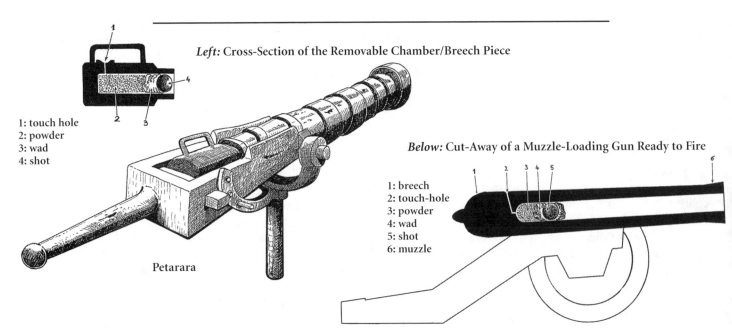

Left: Cross-Section of the Removable Chamber/Breech Piece

1: touch hole
2: powder
3: wad
4: shot

Petarara

Below: Cut-Away of a Muzzle-Loading Gun Ready to Fire

1: breech
2: touch-hole
3: powder
4: wad
5: shot
6: muzzle

Transport of a Gun. The introduction of the limber — forming a detachable wheeled cart at the back of the gun carriage — made the transport of artillery easier.

ment to the projectile. Stone balls were gradually replaced by solid round metal shot. The solid iron shot — introduced at the beginning of the 15th century — could destroy medieval crenelation, ram castle gates, and collapse towers and masonry walls. It broke through roofs, made its way through several stories, and crushed to pieces all it fell upon. One well-aimed projectile could cut down a splendid armored knight and his horse. At the battle of Ravenna in 1512, one Spanish cannonball was said to have knocked down a row of almost forty soldiers. The all-metal shot could also be heated in a furnace to red-hot before firing to become a highly dangerous incendiary projectile which — it was hoped — would set fire to enemy fortifications or ships or if possible explode the enemy's gunpowder store. It was a tricky operation to fire such a dangerous device because fire could be set to the propelling charge by accident. Therefore, a thick wet wadding was placed between the red-hot shot and the powder, and the projectile had to be fired almost immediately; the red-hot ball was put into the barrel by tongs.

Another important improvement was the introduction of trunnions. These pieces of metal were pivots on either side of the barrel, cast at the same time as the piece. They were set slightly forward of the point of balance so that, when unsupported, the breech of the gun came down and the muzzle was raised. The use of trunnions made it a great deal easier to elevate or lower the gun to adjust its range, aim better, and improve accuracy. Trunnions were placed at the point where the gun received almost the entire impulse of the recoil (the strong backward movement occurring when shooting), and they conveyed the force to the trail of the carriage. Trunnions also made possible the development of simple, mobile, and reliable carriages. The gun was firmly fixed on a strong timbered two-wheel mounting composed of two *flasques* or trails — lateral pieces held together by crossbars — which issued from the flanks of the gun and descended in its rear to the ground and were curved with a greater or lesser curvature. The cross was fitted with a hook to trail the gun.

Breech loading — the modern method of loading a gun — was known in the Late Middle Ages. The *petarara* for example was a small gun introduced in the 15th century. A trough was left at the rear of the gun into which was wedged a mug-shaped cylinder (chamber) with a handle, complete with propellant charge and shot. When the gun had been fired the cylinder was taken out and replaced by another that had already been prepared with powder and projectile. By this means a fairly rapid rate of fire could be maintained; if enough cylinders were available, from twelve to fifteen 15 rounds could be fired in an hour. The drawback was however that — due to the primitive metallurgic technology — the chamber often fit too loose and gases tended to escape, thus wasting a large part of the energy; and there was also the problem of overheating after several shots. Breech loading was revived in the second half of the 19th century. Until then the main method to load a gun was muzzle loading.

The successive steps of loading the gun were carefully carried out on gun commander's order. First, the propelling gunpowder (carried in kegs) was poured into the barrel with a long-shafted spoon and pushed down with a ramrod; next, a gunner drove the cannonball in the bore with a wooden rammer. The projectile was often wrapped in a wad (old cloths, paper, mud, grass, or hay) to avoid gas dispersion and to keep the round shot from rolling out. When the piece was loaded it had to be aimed; this happened horizontally by manually moving the gun to the right or to the left with heavy hand spikes (iron-shod wooden levers) and vertically by adjusting one or more coins (wooden wedges) under the breech. Aiming was done by direct sight or with the help of primitive instruments (quadrants), but accuracy was poor, especially in the case of a moving target. Inflammation of the propelling charge was done with a lintstock (a staff holding a burning match), brought close to the ignition vent or touch hole pierced in the upper side of the gun. Flashing through the vent, fire ignited the gunpowder charge which exploded and expelled the shot with flames, awful loud noise, and violence so that the gun brusquely moved

German 22-Kilogram (48-Pound) Gun, about 1500. Until the 19th century, the caliber of guns was indicated by the weight of the projectile that the pieces fired.

backward; this sudden movement, the recoil, made re-aiming necessary. Firing also produced toxic bad-smelling clouds of smoke which soon hung thickly over batteries and obscured gunners' views on windless days. Right after every shot the barrel had to be scraped with a spiral (a sort of large corkscrew fixed on a staff) to remove fouling and swabbed out with a wet sponge attached on a wooden staff in order to extinguish all burning residues of wad. After several shots the gun began to get overheated; the barrel had to be cooled down with water or with wet sheepskins. This was sometimes not enough, and the crew had to stop firing for hours, otherwise the gun could crack and could even explode with disastrous consequences for them.

On the battlefield — in good conditions — a few artillery discharges at the beginning shattered the ranks of the archers and the mounted knights and enabled foot soldiers to close in for hand-to-hand fighting on equal terms. At the battle of Marignano in 1515, the French army combined artillery and small arms and decimated the hitherto invincible Swiss pikemen who left 7,000 dead on the field. English military dominance which characterized European warfare at the end of the 14th century had fifty years later completely disappeared, and the archers of Crécy and Agincourt were looked on as a historical curiosity. However, firearms were however slow to take effect on the battlefield, and this was particularly true of artillery. The wide variety of calibers complicated the task of supplying and carrying ammunition. The great guns were indeed to have profound and lasting effect, but — originally at least — their effectiveness was slight compared with their heavy cost, the difficulty to transport and deploy them on the battlefield, their low rate of fire, and their vulnerability once they had delivered their deadly volley. Artillery was still of little value in the field except under unusual circumstances. If an army was operating on the defensive, cannons could make the ground directly in front of them untenable, but they could be moved only with great difficulty. Occasionally, cannons could be used against an army drawn up in defensive position, as at Formigny. But in a battle where the troops had freedom of movement, troops could easily get out of the way of the enemy guns. Their immobility, inaccuracy, short range, and low rate of fire meant that for maximum efficiency cannons had to be placed in front of the army or in the interstices between the formations. If they could fire on time, they might indeed inflict horrible loss in enemy tight formations, but the chance that they rapidly were overrun and captured was great because loading took quite a long time. This happened at the battle of Novarra in 1513 when the Swiss mercenaries managed to capture all the French guns in one daring attack.

Heavy specialized artillery moved in what was called a *train*, a ponderous collection of all the equipment necessary for its operation. The train would not be permanently attached to any particular army but was kept at a central location, typically a fortified arsenal in a fortress, to ensure its safety. Once summoned, the train was made ready and began its slow journey to the appointed battlefield or siege site. The eighteen guns proudly deployed by the Duke of Milan in 1472 required no less than 522 pairs of oxen and 227 carts to draw them and their train. Oxen were often replaced by horses, but the whole apparatus remained ineffably ponderous. In 1497, even though 100 workmen and a team of oxen accompanied the heavy Mons Meg cannon to Edinburgh (Scotland), she broke down just outside the city, and it took three days to repair the carriage. A single medium gun needed a team of several horses to draw it, with a further team to pull ammunition and equipment carts, and the artillery train moved at a snail's pace. The effects of these lumbering convoys on the movement of armies over the unpaved roads of Europe may be well imagined. War in the autumn and winter was out of the question. As a rule, heavy guns could only be brought to their target when water transport was available.

Man-of-Arms Firing a Handgun

Small Arms

Small arms were quick to develop. They were cheaper to produce than heavy artillery pieces. The first handguns were actually cannons in reduction, consisting of a simple iron tube with a touch hole. After early attempts proved that the tube became too hot to hold once a round or two had been fired, the tube was fixed with a wooden handle, called a *tiller*, secured by iron straps or slotted into the end of the breech. Early designs were clumsy and needed to be supported on the ground. The loading procedure was similar to that of a big gun: pouring propellant charge in the muzzle, placing a bullet, ramming both down home, and putting igniting powder in the touch hole. The firing operation often required two soldiers; one man held and aimed the gun and the other applied a slow burning match to the touch hole. The slow match consisted of a string of woven hemp that was soaked in saltpeter in order to make it burn more slowly. Early handguns had various names such as *clopi*, *scopet, baston-de-feu, petro-nel, fire stick, culverine, bom-bardelli,* and others. Despite their clumsiness and al-though they could not sustain a high rate of fire, handguns proved their worth rapidly. Their killing power against armored horsemen became gradually decisive — so long as the soldier operat-ing the gun could achieve a hit, which was never certain of course.

Significant develop-ments in handguns were made in the 1470s. In Ger-many particularly, good, serviceable handguns were introduced. The clumsy hand cannon became a much more useful and manageable ob-ject. The arquebus, "hooked-gun" (from the German *Hackenbüschse*), was fitted with a hook under the tube to hold it when fired from a rampart or from a similar support. The reduction of size and weight, the shoulder butt, and the matchlock enabled the arquebus to become carried, loaded, and fired by one single man. The matchlock was a method of igniting the powder leaving

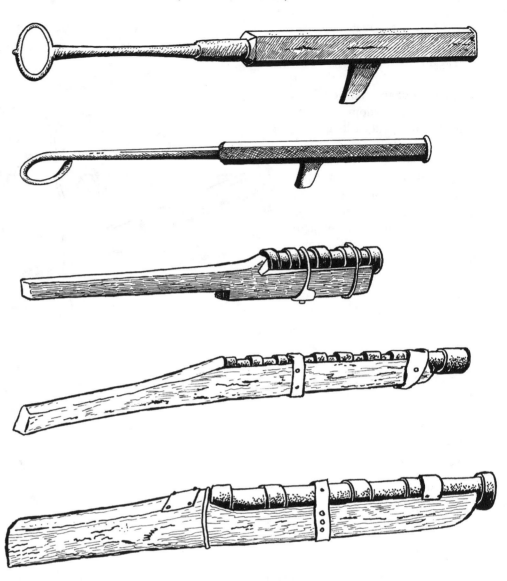

Various Forms of Primitive Handguns

the operator with his hands free to hold, aim, and fire. It consisted of a serpentine, an S-shaped piece of metal, fixed to the side of the gun. The slow-burning match was held in one end of the serpentine and brought down onto the touch hole when the lower end of the S — the trig-ger — was pulled up. The matchlock arquebus weighed up to 11 kilograms (25 pounds) and probably fired a 28 gram (one ounce) bullet about a range of 91 meters (100 yards). At close range, the projectile could penetrate con-ventional armor worn by knights with little difficulty. Some arquebuses were beautifully decorated with inlaid figures, carving, and ornaments.

Older weapons such as the shields, lances, pole weapons, bows, and crossbows did not suddenly disap-pear though, and they remained in use for many years. But gradually small firearms moved from auxiliary harassing role to one where they were central and deci-

sive weapons used on the battlefield and in siege warfare by both the attackers and defenders. The battle of Cerig-nola in 1503 set a pattern to be frequently repeated. The Spaniards allowed their enemies, both French cavalry and Swiss pikemen, to batter in vain against their fortified positions while the arquebuses picked them off until they were too weakened to stand up to the Spanish counter-attack. Early in the 16th century various mechanisms were invented for firing the handgun, each of which added to its reliability, accuracy, and effectiveness, and the arque-bus gave way to the long powerful matchlock musket. The number of musketeers was gradually increased while the number of pikemen decreased. This was the begin-ning of an ineluctable process, and in the early 18th century the pike disappeared as weapon of war to make way for the bayonet fixed at the end of the infantryman's musket.

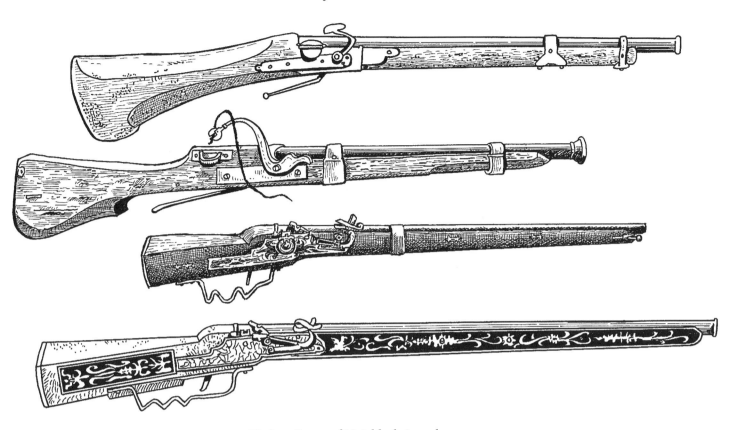

Various Forms of Matchlock Arquebuses

Gunners

Traditionalist knights were not interested in learning the skills of firearms. When the new weapons became more than a noisy and smoky curiosity, they complained as bitterly about firearms as their ancestors had done about the introduction of the crossbow: not simply because the new weapons were inhumane in their effect but because they degraded the vision they had of war, putting as they did the noble mounted men-at-arms at the mercy of the vile and base-born. There was another reason for knights to oppose to firearms: profit. Indeed the new weapons proved rapidly more lethal than conventional weapons of the time, and a dead enemy was only worth the price of his armor and possessions when a live prisoner was a potential source of ransom money. But those who complained about the presence of these weapons in their opponents' armies regarded it as an unanswerable argument for providing them in their own forces. Cannons and handguns were integrated into the revived French forces of the 15th century and used effectively against an English army where a combination of military nostalgia and political confusion held back any comparable innovations. Rapidly though, all European armies followed the French example, and cannons and handguns were gradually introduced into warfare.

At first artillery and handgun men were ill-regarded as newcomers who disturbed the well-defined chivalrous warfare. That a base-born man armed with a firearm could kill a noble horseman from a safe distance, that knights were defrauded from ransoming each other, and that a nobleman's castle could be shot to a heap of smoking ruins by cannons were intolerable thoughts for traditionalist medieval knights. Knights hated gunners, who were regarded as evil men using devilish and unfair weapons, and did not hesitate to slaughter any of them. Tradition also played a role, many leaders were reluctant to use the new weapons. Even Duke Charles the Bold of Burgundy, who fully appreciated the importance of missiles in battle, still trusted in the 1470s to archers rather than to gunners. Gradually as the new weapons had proved their worth on the battlefield and in siege warfare, artillerymen were regarded as a cut above the rank-and-file soldier. Artillery crews became elite units as they had to be courageous, cool, calm and collected, well drilled, and well disciplined. Everyone can imagine the chance taken by transporting and manipulating dangerous stuffs as gunpowder as well as putting in action primitive and not always reliable guns. Tragic accidents were common; already dangerous when at exercise, the predicament was even worse when in the middle of the stress of a battle. In 1460 James II of Scotland died when he stood too close to a gun whose staves exploded when it fired. The master gunner was progressively a most important figure who was responsible for the transport, the siting of the batteries, and the firing plans. Throughout the early history of artillery there was usually only a very small contingent of competent powder manufacturers and skilled gunners. Gunners were, however, not considered soldiers; their status was that of specialist, professional civilians fulfilling a temporary military function. In Britain it was not until 1716 that the Royal Artillery was put on a proper footing. In France, it is only in the late 17th century — during the reign of Louis XIV — that artillery was fully militarized.

Influence of Firearms on Siege Warfare

It was at siege warfare that cannons proved the most efficient. Everything previously discussed about surprise, treachery, and attrition as well as negotiation, surrender, and fate of a conquered fortress by force can still be applied to siege warfare with firearms. The new weapons had only an influence on the purely military aspect of siege warfare. Medieval stone castles with their high dungeons, projecting towers, relatively thin vertical walls, and impressive gatehouses were built to resist escalade and to command the surroundings of the fortress. With the appearance of firearms, castles offered a prime and massive target and became pathetically vulnerable to battering cannonballs. Siege guns were gradually developed. They tended to be heavier than their counterparts used in field action and had sturdier carriages and larger bores. Monster cannons were designed and — being unique — were given names, some of which are still intact today. Their dimensions, firepower, and capabilities were formidable and must have had a terrifying effect on the defenders against which they were engaged. *Krimhild*, a heavy piece built in Nuremberg (Germany) about 1388 had a range of 1,000 paces and could penetrate a wall almost 2 meters (6 feet) thick. *Dulle Griet* (Mad Margaret) was built about 1410 and can still be seen in the Belgian town of Ghent. It is over 4 meters (16 feet) long, weighs about 13.6 metric tons (15 tons), and has a bore of about 76 centimeters (30 inches). *Mons Meg*, another monster now at Edinburgh, Scotland, was built in Flanders about 1470; it is about 4 meters (13 feet) long and weighs 4.5 metric tons (5 tons), its bore is almost 50 centimeters (20 inches) and could fire — with the right charge — a stone shot of more than 300 pounds over a range of 1,400 yards. *Katherine*, a

Right: **Lansquenet with Arquebus**

Tyrolean cannon cast in 1487 was 12 feet long. The *Dardanelles Gun*— now at the tower of London — was built for sultan Mahomet in the 15th century. For ease of transport the gun was made in two pieces which were screwed together; it took nonetheless 140 oxen and 200 men to haul this monster into position. It is cast in bronze and weighs over 16 metric tons (18 tons), is 3.6 meters (17 feet) long with a bore of 25 inches. It could fire a shot of nearly 800 pounds. At the siege of Constantinople in 1453, Mahomet is reported to have had twelve of such similar monsters which hurled each about seven shots a day at the city defense.

Siege Fortifications

Professional artillerymen acquired great skills in handling fire weapons as much in defense as in offense. The same weapons could be used for more roles of course. When attackers began to employ guns against fortresses, nothing could prevent the defenders from keeping attackers at a distance by using firearms. As these weapons became more valuable in the 15th century, they were quite useful when shot from a well-protected combat emplacement behind the walls of a fortress. When fortresses began to be armed with cannons and handguns, besieging troops were confronted with devastating fire while approaching with classical siege methods. To achieve maximum destructive efficiency, the batteries of the besiegers had to be sited at short or point-blank ranges, being themselves in the range of enemy fire and thus exposed to casualties. As siege artillery could be countered by defensive firearms, field or siege fortifications were devised. To protect themselves from the fire of the defenders, to shield both men and guns, the besieging forces used gabions (cylindrical earth-filled wicker baskets used as a temporary parapet), fascines (large cylindrical bundles of brushwood), and earthworks. Soldiers took to the spade and established sunken trenches, saps, and concealed batteries to protect men and weapons behind earth screens and entrenchments. It was the beginning of the tedious, dangerous, and murderously unhealthy trench warfare which was to be the staple fare of the European soldier until 1918, and even during World War II as position warfare was still then widely used. The traditional siege machines of the ancient times and Middle Ages were progressively replaced by artillery pieces. However, the transition was slow, and many sieges saw the use of old and new technology at the same time. Worthy of mention, prince and stadhouder Maurits of Nassau still employed — as late at 1592 — wooden assault towers at the siege of Steenwijk (Netherlands), probably the last recorded use of this kind of obsolete machine.

Breach

The purpose of siege artillery was generally two-fold: first, to kill the defenders on their walls (or to hinder their movement); second, to knock down the walls to create a breach. For the making of a breach, the attacker would group his cumbersome guns in battery in order to fire the heaviest and most numerous possible projectiles against the enemy's defenses. Guns were placed behind screens of earth and rested on solid wooden platforms to avoid sinking in loose ground. Firing was not carried out on a random basis but to a preconceived plan. The idea was that the guns concentrated their fire on one or perhaps two areas of the defenses. The continual bombardment would eventually cause those defenses to crumble into heap of stones into which the assault was launched. The breach offered the besiegers a gap through which they could access the interior of the position, but the defenders were also well aware of this prospect. Since the site of the breach was fixed, the garrison knew the point of the intended forthcoming assault and could locally reinforce the area. The fallen rubble often provided a slope for the attackers to clamber up, but the defenders would sweep the breach with their own firearms, making the area very unhealthy. Given the time and opportunity, the defenders would strengthen the breach with improved defenses and, unless they moved relatively swiftly, the besiegers might well find the breach shored up. A greater number of breaches could be made of course, but the attacker needed an increasingly large train of artillery to achieve this. The option was then available to the attacker to launch feint assaults, leaving the defenders guessing as to which breach would actually be attacked. Until they were sure — and even then they could be mistaken — the defenders needed to guard all the attacking points, and they were not able to quite so easily concentrate their force to repel the main attack.

Mines

Gunpowder also helped to destroy high walls and towers by using mines. This old method was adapted to the devastating power of black powder. Such an undertaking was slow but sure, and it was less expensive in men. A party of specialized miners would pick away at the base of a wall and dig an underground tunnel. There, kegs of gunpowder would be placed, a match would be lit, the party would quickly withdraw to safety, the charge would exploded under the fortification, and a section of the wall would tumble down to the ground creating a breach that could be assaulted. As ever in underground mine warfare, the besieged could counteract — once the enemy tunnel had been detected and discovered — by

Siege with Firearms

digging a counter-mine gallery where countercharges were exploded. Tunneling and mining were indeed the most frightening aspect of siege warfare. The first uses of explosive mines were recorded at the siege of Orense in 1468, Malaga and Sarzanello in 1487, and Naples in 1503. Mines were ever since an integral and important part of siege warfare, still being used during the World War I trench warfare of 1915–1918. It is interesting to note that the meaning of the word *mine* has been extended from the underground tunnel to the explosive device itself. Another use of black powder was the so-called *pétard* (detonator), an exploding device used mainly to destroy "soft targets" such as doors and gates. This item — in the form of a church bell — was essentially an early type of demolition mine. Some brave volunteering soul would secure the pétard to a door, light its fuse, and — quickly as he could — retreat to safety. After a very short time the

fuse flashed to the charge, the bomb exploded, and the gate was smashed to pieces.

Assault

When the breach had been made — either by demolition battery or mining — it had to be assaulted by force. As always through the history of siege warfare, the assault was the most hazardous part of the enterprise. It was often done by volunteers motivated by the promise of glory, promotion, or loot. Their task was to secure a foothold in the smoking ruins of the breach and hold it until the main force came up. The initial assaulting party had — realistically — only a very slim chance of surviving. Some did and lived to collect whatever reward was offered, but by far the greater number of unknown and unnamed soldiers fell as the assault went in. Given sufficient time, the defenders could even mine the breach and blow the device as the assaulting party went in. Fighting in the breach was grim indeed. The higher morale initially went to the attackers as they surged in to take on the undoubtedly stunned defenders, but gradually one side or the other took the upper hand. The defenders called on more men from the garrison, while the assault columns of the attacking force attempted to pile into the breach. Frenzied individual combat took place with the combatants on both sides fiercely engaged in a life-and-death struggle. The determination of the defenders was matched by both the zeal and the raw aggression of their attackers. There was no half-way in the breach as both parties knew that to lose was fatal.

The Siege of Constantinople

The demolition of the walls of Constantinople by the Turkish artillery in April through May 1453 symbolized in this as in so many other respects the end of a long era in the history of western warfare. Situated on a triangular promontory, between the Sea of Marmara and the bay called the Golden Horn, the defenses of Constantinople were formidable. Built by the emperor Theodose II between 408 and 450, the fortifications of the capital of the Eastern Orthodox Byzantine Empire included on the landward side three 5-mile-long concentric walls. First there was a wide ditch of 18 meters broad and 6.5 meters deep, dominated by a first crenellated wall 5.5 meters high and reinforced by buttresses. About 15 meters behind this, a second crenellated wall was built with a height of about 8 meters, 2 meters thick and square flanking towers. Behind this there was a third wall with a height of 12 meters, a thickness of 4.5 meters, flanked by 96 towers which were 20 meters high and arranged so as to shelter hurling machines. On the seaward side natural defenses combined with artificial ones to present an inaccessible face. A huge chain stretched across the mouth of the Golden Horn which itself provided a defense from that side. In 1453, the garrison included some 10,000 soldiers placed under the skilled and experienced Genoese commander Giovanni Giustiniani and Basileus (Emperor) Constantine XI. The garrison had at its disposition a great quantity of supplies. The attacking force, led by the enlightened and ruthless 23-year-old sultan, Mohamet II, was well over 200,000 men. The Turks had a fleet of about 300 ships with which to blockade the city from the sea. They had a vast siege train including catapults, trebuchets, assault towers and, most important of all, a number of monster siege cannons.

After a two-week bombardment such as no city had ever before experienced, the Turks launched a first large assault on the landward defenses on April 18, 1453. This was repelled with a concentrated fire of small firearms and a barrage of catapult and gun missiles. Negotiations were undertaken, but the basileus made it known to Mohamet that there would be no surrender. A further setback to the Turkish force occurred when Genoese vessels succeeded in beating aside the massed Turkish fleet that was blockading the Bosphorus. Infuriated at being snubbed a second time, Mahomet determined on the astounding project of seizing the Golden Horn by dragging some 80 ships 10 miles overland. A timber roller track was laid, greased with the fat of sheep and oxen and the galleys were hauled by bulls and slaves. With the town totally surrounded, Mohamet offered the emperor new proposals for surrender, but once more these were refused.

The Turks renewed their offensive. Breaches were made by cannons, gates and walls were attacked, but all assaults were fiercely rebuffed. A huge assault tower was built, and it was destroyed by explosives thrown by the defenders. Attempts at undermining were repulsed by countermines and by hand-to-hand fighting in the cramped subterranean passages. Every failure caused the sultan greater anger and concern as his supplies had not anticipated a long siege. On May 29, a wide-scale desperate attack was launched against the 4,000 surviving Byzantines who were not only weakened by the siege but divided by religious quarrels opposing Catholics and members of the Orthodox Church. A ill-defended gate was discovered and stormed by a group of Janissaries. The Turks could outflank the weakening defenders, and bitter fighting went on for another day. When Giustiniani himself was severely wounded and the Basileus Constantine XI was killed, the defenders' morale and strength collapsed. The Turks entered the city indulging in an orgy of killing, looting, and destruction. Allah had conquered; Mahomet had won his coveted prize, and the Western world was shocked by the loss.

The Siege of Beauvais

The operation of Beauvais in northern France illustrates very well how a small garrison could successfully resist the armies of one of the most powerful rulers of Western Europe. At the end of June 1472, the duke of Burgundy, Charles the Bold (1433–1477), laid siege to Beauvais. The walled city counted fifty crossbowmen, thirty archers, and an additional force of civic guards armed with arquebus and a few artillery pieces. Charles the Bold's army totaled some 80,000 soldiers, while other sources give 50,000 or 40,000 men. Anyway, whatever the real number of attackers, it seemed that the small garrison should be no match to such a force. The operation began by a summons to open at once the gates of the town

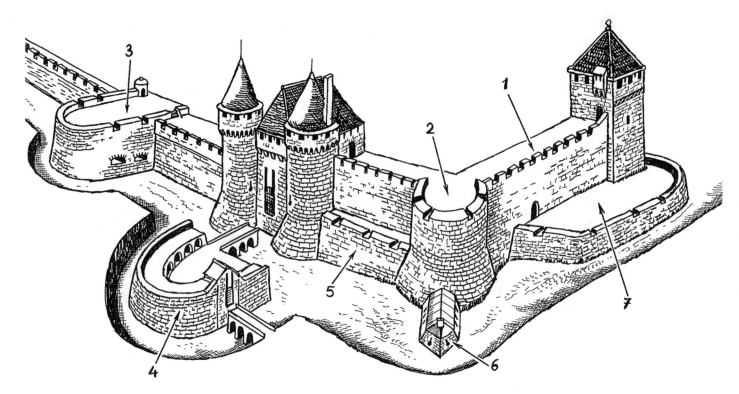

Transitional Fortification Adapted to Firearms (15th Century). 1. low, thick ramparted wall; 2. Medieval tower lowered to the level of the wall; 3. low artillery tower fitted with artillery casemate; 4. detached barbican placed in the ditch to protect the gatehouse; 5. fausse-braie, a low artillery emplacement; 6. moineau or caponier, a projecting casemated work for the close-range defense of the moat; 7. bulwark, a low artillery platform.

for the duke. This was politely refused, and the Burgundarians attacked the west side of the city resulting in the capture of a part of the suburb. To the east side another force assaulted a gatehouse. The citizens, helped by their wives and daughters, defended themselves fiercely against their enemies — who were scaling the walls — by pelting them with arrows, spears, boulders, and flaming projectiles. To support and lift the morale of the defenders, the coffer containing the sacred relics of Saint Angadresma was carried to the scene of combat. Jeanne Layné, later popularly named Jeanne Hachette as she fought with a battle-axe, was especially noteworthy among the defenders. By the end of June 27, the Duke of Burgundy received his artillery train, and Beauvais was submitted to a heavy bombardment by colubrines, serpentines, and heavy bombards. Meanwhile a Burgundian mine was discovered under the gate of Bresle, and a countermine blew it with disastrous effectiveness as more than six hundred attackers were killed at a time. By that time the besiegers had already suffered some three thousand casualties. The stubborn duke resumed his attack and a breach was made in a wall, but the defenders had built a temporary barricade by taking the paving stones from their streets to fill the gap. An assault on this improvised barricade was then repulsed. Charles the Bold then concentrated his powerful artillery on bombarding the houses of the citizens for

fifteen consecutive nights and days. As the morale of the city did not collapse, he launched a last attack on July 9th. This assault too was repelled and turned into a disastrous defeat when a successful sortie from the besieged caused serious losses in the Burgundian ranks. On July 11th Charles made a proclamation to his troops stating that the army was called elsewhere to accomplish more pressing matter than the capture of the insignificant town, but everyone knew this was only an excuse to conceal his discomfort. On the 22nd July 1472, the defeated and humiliated Burgundian duke's army struck camp. The citizens of Beauvais had won not only their own battle but that of all France as Duke Charles the Bold intended to invade the realm. As a chronicler noted, Burgundy *oncques puis ne prospéra* (from then on would prosper no more). Charles was indeed defeated again, and again by civilians, the Swiss, at Granson and Morat in 1476. The ambitious duke — who had dreamed to create his own kingdom between France and Germany — was killed in 1477 at the siege of Nancy in Lorraine.

Influence of Firearms on Fortifications

The impact of siege artillery had a profound change on the way fortifications were conceived and built. For

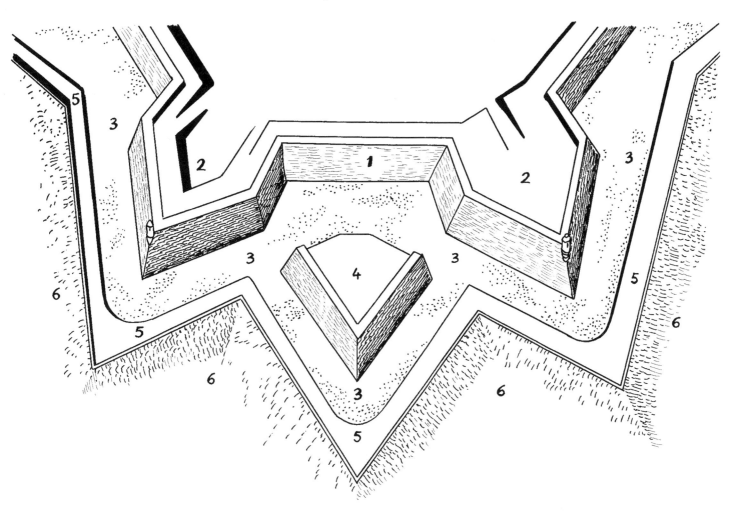

Bastioned Fortification of the 16th Century. 1. low and thick ramparted wall; **2.** pentagonal bastion; **3.** deep moat (possibly filled with water); **4.** ravelin or demi-lune; **5.** covered way; **6.** glacis.

centuries fortifications had adapted themselves to the prevailing means of attack; it was time for them to do so again. At first the defenders improvised and installed the defensive artillery to fire through apertures designed for bows and crossbows. Then they abandoned the vulnerable advantage of height and visibility for the more-practical one of defense in depth using low artillery towers and various artillery placements made of a mass of earth held by masonry, named *bulwarks*, with cunning arcs of fire and flanking disposition. But these improvisations—since they remained within the framework of the traditional vertical defenses—could only delay the deadly onset of an artillery barrage; they could not avert it.

Experiments—at first improvised ad hoc by the Italian cities in the first decade of the 15th century—led to a star-shaped configuration, angled defense giving birth to artillery fortresses based on a new design. The so-called *fronte bastionato* (bastioned front) was characterized by being horizontal and thicker and supporting interlocking fields of fire and defense in the depth. The new method of fortification gave a fortress not only the necessary solidity to withstand artillery bombardment but also the ability to bring as much fire power as possible to bear on the attackers. It consisted of the arrangement of mutually supporting *bastions* (low pentagonal artillery towers) projecting from the walls, so positioned as to give fire from the flank and rear against any assault on the wall or one another. The walls themselves were lowered and embedded with a thick mass of earth to present the smallest possible target to besieger fire and to deflect the shot of the attackers. Instead of building up for defense, the reaction was to dig down for a low profile. A deep moat surrounded the fortress, itself covered by fire from the bastions and often protected by additional outworks named *ravelins* or *demi-lunes*, acting as geometric fortified islands. On the outer side of the ditch, the *counter-scarp*, there was a broad lane protected by a breastwork, the covered way and, beyond that, there was a smooth and bare *glacis* over which any approach was exposed to concentrated fire from all the defense works.

Ships about the End of the 16th Century

The bastioned fortification had the great merits of being flexible and adaptable to suit varying conditions—important characteristics which led to its adoption all over Europe during the next fifty years. Its main drawback was the colossal expense involved which had as result that fortification became the monopoly of the state. Building modern bastioned fortifications could only be undertaken in anticipation of a threat, not in response to one. There emerged gradually a new arm in the European armies: military engineering. Originating as local civic defenses, the new method developed into a system of continuous frontiers which Sébastien le Prestre de Vauban (1633–1707) was to establish in France and Menno van Coehoorn (1641–1704) in the Netherlands at the end of the 17th century.

Naval Warfare with Firearms

The use of firearms also had an important impact on naval warfare. As early as the 14th century light guns were used to defend merchant ships as a useful addition to crossbowmen and archers. The use of large guns was slow to make its appearance on board because of their weight, size, recoil, and unpredictable performance. Gradually larger guns were placed in the existing castles at each end of the vessel. From the 15th century onward, the use of still powerful cannons and small arms was to be central in the development of naval warfare. Cast in bronze in a single piece and capable of bearing far higher charges of explosives and firing a heavier caliber of shot, cannons could not only kill men but bring down masts and rigging, smash through decks, and even sink ships. So firepower began to replace shock in sea battles. Large cannons were too heavy though to be placed in the castles. They were gradually mounted broadside, and both castles were lowered and, in the end, disappeared. With guns mounted along flush decks, even merchantmen could more than hold their own against war galleys whose guns could only be mounted in prow and stern. So, gradually, the distinction between warship and merchantman almost disappeared. All ships put to sea could both carry cargo and fight, making war, discovery, and trade almost interchangeable words.

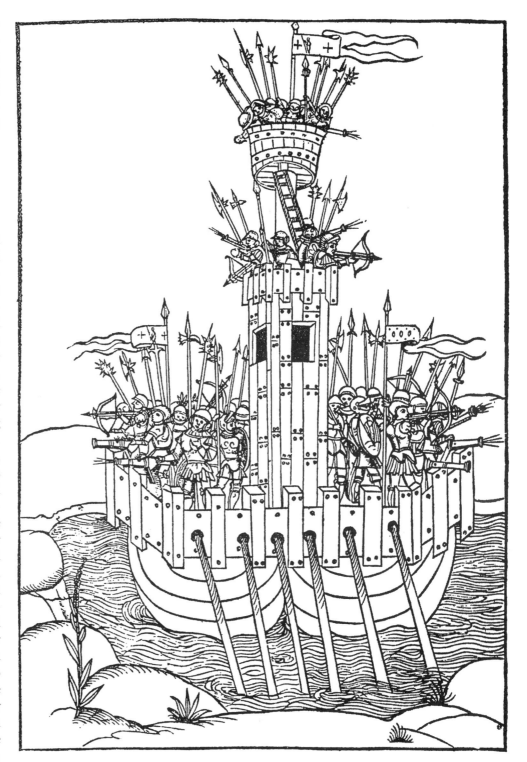

Warship (after an Illustration from Del'Arte Militario by Valturio about 1483). Clearly shown are crossbows, various pole weapons, and primitive handguns.

A major breakthrough was the invention of new kinds of vessel. Northern and Mediterranean naval construction methods met in the waters off Spain. From the parentage of both maritime cultures sprang, about 1430, vessels built around a complete skeleton with ribs and

Wheel-Lock Pistols, 16th Century

braces fitting the planks without any overlap. The added strength conferred by this technique made possible a more complex rig including three and sometimes four masts carrying a variety of sails. The *carrack* was the prototype galleon. The square rig of its sails was suitable for running before the oceanic trade winds. The lateen remained on the third — mizzen — mast to aid steerage in light wind. The high stern, which provided living quarters, protected the ship from being "pooped" by following seas. This three-mastered, decked, square-rigger, ocean-going ship was the immediate forerunner of the world-conquering Portuguese and Spanish caravel. The *karvel*, or *caravel*, was the most seaworthy ship of the day. She was an elegant, fast, well-armed, ocean-going, freight carrier. She had a center rudder and three masts. Rigged with several sails both square and lateen, she was easy to handle and required only a small crew. The planks were flush against each other presenting a smooth hull surface to the sea. These ocean-going ships enabled Spaniards and Portuguese to sail on exploring trips into unknown waters to new continents and to traffic with unknown people. After 1500, new and modern ships appeared which could sail for thousands of miles, cross the oceans,

hover off an enemy coast, blockade, strike at targets ashore, maneuver freely, and engage an enemy in the open sea, and naval warfare extended to parts of the Americas, Africa and Asia. Henceforth the major European powers had to create and maintain expensive navies. The fighting ship had grown up and was not to change fundamentally for another 400 years.

Evolution of the Cavalry

The introduction of firearms did not create a sudden revolution in warfare. The process was slow, more that of a difficult evolution than a sudden change. Many traditional weapons remained in use as gunpowder, cannons, and handguns were — at first — unreliable and always very expensive to produce, slow to transport, and difficult to put in use. Firearms were produced in peacetime, and since people in the Late Middle Ages had only rudimentary ideas of economics, science, and fiscal administration, only a few kings, powerful dukes, and wealthy high prelates had the financial resources to build, purchase, transport, maintain, and use such expensive

Infantrymen, 16th Century

equipment in any numbers to make an appreciable impression during war. Conflicts with firearms became an economic business involving qualified personnel backed up by traders, financiers, and bankers as well as the creation of comprehensive industrial structures. Consequently, firearms and the establishment of permanent armies contributed to the decline of the mounted warrior and private wars and were major elements in restoring the central power of the state.

The supremacy of cavalry in the Early and High Middle Ages had been as much moral as social and technical. Developed because of its mobility, endowed with a total and economic dominance, and blessed by the Church, cavalry had for centuries a virtual monopoly of military activity. Foot soldiers were regarded as despised auxiliaries. But the arrogant and traditional chivalry had shown its limitations and proved ineffective when facing archers, crossbowmen, and gunners on numerous occasions. It was clear, therefore, that the future of warfare was to lie with foot soldiers of another kind. A revival of non-noble infantry in the 14th and 15th centuries took place

reflecting an aspiration for freedom and social emancipation marked by revolts and rebellions.

So by the end of the 15th century, heavy battalions of pikemen were a necessary part of any serious armed force. Increasingly there were being attached to them contingents of foot soldiers armed with handguns, arquebuses, and muskets. The Swiss tactic improved by the German lansquenets and the Spanish tercios—combining pikemen and musketeers—was to dominate all open battlefields during the 16th and 17th centuries and was only replaced by the introduction of the flint gun with bayonet at the beginning of the 18th century. The chivalry, noblesse and wealth always associated with the horses began to undergo a subtle metamorphosis with the appearance of gunpowder. Medieval archers and horsemen could now be defeated by foot soldiers armed with pikes and fire weapons. However armored and magnificent a rider might appear, however expensive or beautiful the horses, knights were no match for an ordinary infantryman armed with a handgun. The powerful charge of mounted men—properly timed—was still possible though, and the cavalry did not disappear altogether, but it had to adapt itself. The old chivalry of the feudal time in which every knight charged for himself and was concerned as much with personal honor as with victory had seen its day. Middle Ages chivalry was gradually replaced by a modern cavalry. The new cavalry of the 16th and 17th century was more disciplined and, combined with infantry and artillery, was at the will of a general. It could now provide not only an efficient mobile firepower but fulfill more diversified roles.

At first cavalrymen were armed with cumbersome arquebuses, but soldiers on horseback met with tremendous difficulty using them because the operation required both hands. One significant improvement was the creation of a new portable weapon. The pistol holds its name from the city of Pistoia in Tuscany (Italy) where the weapon—a small harquebus—was first built in the 15th century. The wheel-lock pistol made it possible to ride with a firearm already primed and loaded. The wheel-lock pistol worked by friction, rather like a cigarette lighter. A spark was produced to fire the priming powder when a

Cavalryman, 16th Century

piece of iron pyrite struck down against a steel wheel with a milled edge. The pyrite was held in the cock, and the wheel was made to revolve by means of a spring wound up by a handle at the side of the weapon. The trigger actuated the spring. The great advantage of the wheel-lock was its reliability and the fact that it could be fitted to a compact gun. It was, however, a very expensive weapon,

and it had a short range. Reserved for cavalrymen, the wheel-lock pistol allowed a new tactic known as *caracole* to develop. Successive ranks of horsemen rode up to the enemy line, fired at close range, and rapidly withdrew to reload while another wave came along. When the enemy ranks were weakened, the cavalry could charge with sword in a disciplined mass.

The modern lightly armored cavalry could also be used as scouts. Time and effort spent on reconnaissance were (and still are) never wasted, as intelligence gathering is a vital process in the conduct of war. Reconnaissance may be performed by fighting for information or by stealth, which is the more usual way. The reconnaissance units of any army require considerable specialized skills, insightm and above all daring as they have the most dangerous task to do: They form the point of the advance; they must probe forward until they encounter enemy forces, penetrate enemy deployment, and remain unseen in order to observe and obtain tactical intelligence. If they are located and attacked, they have to quickly evade. Gathered information such as an enemy's strength, identification, intention, position, speed, direction, and so on are then transmitted to headquarters who, according to their reports, send other units forward. Cavalrymen could also be used in small formations, making swift and deadly raids deep into enemy territories. They could also be very useful as a mobile armed escort for convoys of supply, columns of infantry, and artillery trains.

19

Conclusion

The French horsemen who took part in the Italian Wars between 1494 and 1529 certainly saw themselves in the same light as the knights in the tales of the literature of courtesy. Throughout Europe, knights tried to revive such anachronisms as tournaments, jousts, duels, and single combat, and they dressed themselves more for conspicuous display than for the grim business of war. Elegant anachronism was to remain a characteristic of European noble horsemen for many centuries yet. By the 15th century the knight with all his equipment and servitors was thus proving both inefficient on the battlefield and expensive to sustain. During the 14th century, the increased effectiveness of the crossbow and longbow led the knights to increase the thickness and weight of their armor. By the time of Agincourt, a fully armed cavalryman was completely encased in heavy plate armor, and his horse was similarly equipped. As a result the knight was helpless on foot and when mounted could only move with ponderous dignity over the most favorable ground. In short, heavy cavalry became useful only for charges under ideal conditions. By the end of the 14th century, most troops were using lighter armor to increase their mobility. Officers and knights continued to wear the massive plate armor. As seen before, armor and weapons became impossibly ornamented. The armored knight on his armored horse became a military mastodon all covered with iron plates. Size, weight, and design of armor became in some cases grotesque. By the end of the 15th century, tournaments were more and more costly, designed as purely ceremonial occasions with ostentatious and lavish pomp. Knights would charge either into single combat (joust) or in a form of a simulated battle

German Tilting Armor, ca. 1485. The armor includes a heavy heaume, a small targe (shield), and a faucre, a hook to hold the heavy tilting lance.

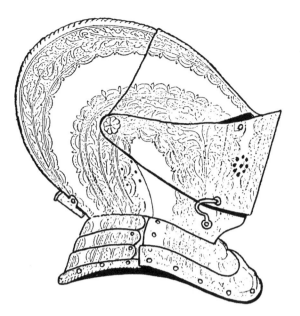

Helmets, Early 16th Century

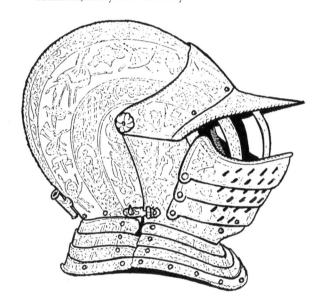

(tournament). Armor of incredible complexity was specially designed for the joust. They were often real works of art displaying the virtuosity of the armorers.

Safety measures were taken to prevent the serious injuries of previous times. The heavy heaume *à tête de crapeau* (toad's head or frog-mouthed) was a head protection developed especially for the tournament and the joust; it was completely closed and was secured to the breast- and back-plate. The eye slit was placed so high that the wearer could only see when leaning forward in the correct position for couching his lance. When the

Left: King Henry VIII's Armored Suite, ca. 1520. This armor — preserved in the Tower of London — was designed for the king for fighting on foot in the lists. It is a very elaborate piece of workmanship including no less than two hundred separate pieces. It weights nearly one hundred pounds. Henry was born in 1491 and reigned from 1509 until his death in 1547.

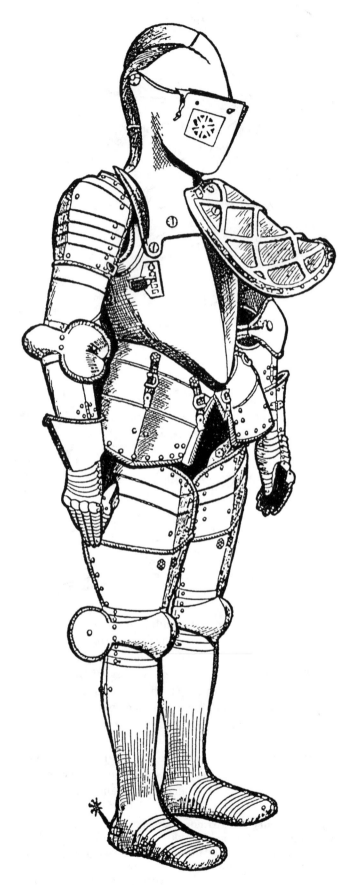

Tilting Armor, ca. 1580

jouster straightened up for the impact, his eyes were completely protected, and his opponent's lance was deflected to one side. The frog-mouthed helmet was richly decorated with an extravagant and in some cases even grotesque crest. Joust armor often incorporated a small shield named *targe*. A *faucre*, a lance rest in the shape of a hook, was fixed to the upper part of the breastplate on the right side. The lances were particularly long and heavy, they were fitted with a large circular deflecting plate intended to protect both arm and hand. Lances were made to shatter easily and saddles were designed to enable the rider to slide off the back of his horse.

Weighed down increasingly with armor, the days of the heavy knight on the battlefield were fast becoming numbered. Armor had served its purpose so long as sword and lance, javelin and bolt were the usual weapons of war. But when it was discovered that against the deadly lead of cannons and firearms armor was of no avail, it was gradually discarded as too cumbersome. As the times were changing, the armored knights armed with their lances were greatly obsolete; the almost impersonal armored machines could no longer perpetuate their true raison d'être but were still in search of glory in physical feats. Like the great dinosaurs that had ruled the world before their huge development rendered their extinction inevitable, the armored knight heralded the end of a military mastodon.

The disappearance of the formidable fighting armored knight brought to an end a style of warfare and an attitude of life. However as the usefulness of chivalry diminished, so its pretension grew. The social status was more jealously hedged around by a heraldic lore which concentrated all the more on questions of status as it had less to do with military function. New knightly orders were founded in conscious imitation of the great orders of the 12th century. The Knights of the Garter, instituted by the English king Edward III about 1348, and the Knight of the Golden Fleece, founded in 1429 by the Duke of Burgundy, Phillip the Good, were the decadent if decorative successors of the knights Templars, Teutonics, and Saint John of Jerusalem.

Naively, some knights continued to think doggedly, of the reconquest of Jerusalem — even as the advancing Ottoman Turks were prizing loose the last strongholds of the crusaders in the eastern Mediterranean Sea and beginning to threaten their bases in the West. The reconquest of Jerusalem was indeed one of the misty objectives of Charles VIII of France (reign 1484–1498) when he invaded Italy in 1494. But if the French knights and *gens d'armes* who invaded Italy in 1494 were feudal in their ideology, there was nothing feudal about their economic base. Like infantrymen and the gunners, they now served purely for pay. When eventually Charles VIII of France set out for

German Emperor Maximilian I (after a Drawing by Hans Burgkmair in 1508). Nicknamed *der letzte Ritter* (the last knight), Maximilian (1459–1519) is depicted here with the so-called Maximilian armor, a style of body protection used principally for tilting, display, and pageant purposes. Following the lines of the civil dress, it was a sign of the decadence of armor for use in the battlefield, the turning point which eventually led to the abolition of full armor for warfare.

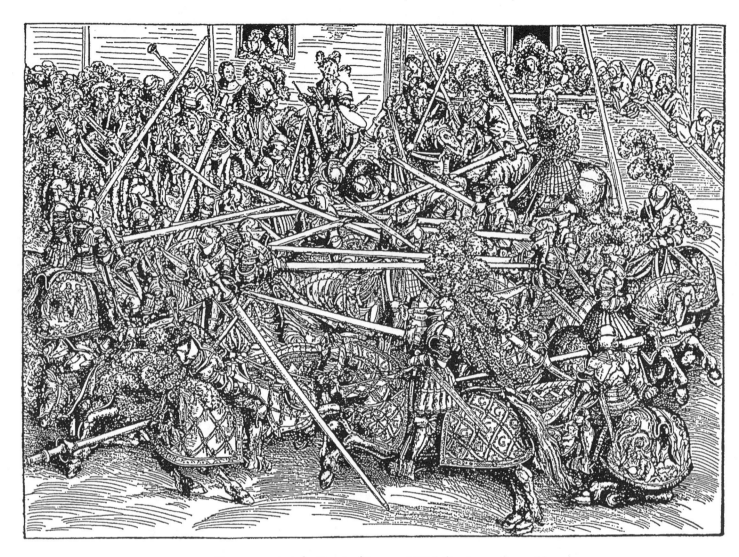

Tournament at the Court of Saxony, 1509 (after Lucas Cranach)

Italy in 1494 in quest of glory, he did so with the finest army Europe had yet seen. His modern forces—all drawing wages from a well-stocked treasury—were constituted of the three ground arms deployed in various mutually supporting tactical combinations: Swiss and other mercenary pikemen making the core of the infantry, a proud and noble cavalry, and a train of modern mobile bronze artillery which was to lay every castle it attacked in ruins. Charles VIII's artillery included 140 heavy cannons and 126 light guns served by 200 artillery masters and 300 gunners. The French army was not fundamentally different in composition from that which Napoléon was to lead to the same battlefields three hundred years later. The system of permanent armies was continued by King of France François I (1494–1547), who raised infantry legions in his wars against Charles V of Spain.

Few soldiers at the end of the 15th century were conscious of a new era dawning in warfare, and although the noble horsemen themselves would have indignantly denied it, the wars of the knights were over. The use of artillery in siege and naval warfare as well as on the battlefield, the deployment of comparatively disciplined infantrymen armed with long-shafted weapons and an increasing number of firearms, and the princes' sufficient control of their resources to maintain fully permanent professional armies composed of both nationals and foreign mercenaries, all these changes influenced the art of war for prolonged campaigns as well as the art of government by strengthening the power of rulers who learned to use the new techniques more effectively. Cautious professional military competence took the place of the quest for glory in the planning and conduct of war. Courage, endurance, and on occasion self-sacrifice were still demanded; there was no market for cowards or blunderers in the business of war. But professional soldiers did not get themselves and those they commanded killed if there was some other way to gain their object. The change—gradual but profound—was reflected in writings about war. The Italian diplomat and writer Niccolo Machiavelli (1469–1527) in his treaty *The Prince*, published in 1531, developed the modern notion of *raison d'état* (reason of state). He asserted that a prince "should hold to what is right when he can, but must know how to do evil when he must" and that "war is just when it is necessary." No higher authority could judge that necessity, and states alone could judge of their own interests. The view *Salus principis suprema lex* (the prince's salvation is the only rule) was gradually endorsed by all leading European jurists: Bodin in France, Gentili in Italy, Victoria in Spain, and later — reconciled with older concepts of Christian unity — by the great Dutch thinker Hugo Grotius in his treaty *De Jure Belli ac Pacis* (published in 1625). In Robert Barret's military treatise of 1598, *The Theory and Practice of Modern Warfare*, innovation and change resulting from the introduction of firearms were fully understood and recognized.

By the end of the 15th century, Europe was still medieval in many ways, but there were signs that a new era was beginning. However, there was no sudden break in the threads of history but simply an accelerated pace of change. There had been a rise, an apogee, and a decline of medieval civilization, but the borders between historical periods are never clear cut. There is obviously no one particularly year which can be designated as the end of the Middle Ages. The 14th and 15th centuries were a period of transition during which things that had been steadily growing bloomed to produce the time of great discoveries, the Renaissance, and the beginning of a new and different world, the modern time.

Bibliography

Ailleret, Charles. *Histoire de l'Armement.* Paris: Presses Universitaires de France, 1948.

Bainville, Jacques. *Histoire de France.* Paris: Editions Plon, 1933.

Banniard, Michel. *Le Haut Moyen Age Occidental.* Paris: Presses Universitaires de France, 1980.

Barton, Stephanie. *De Vikingen.* Helmond: Uitgeverij Kok, 1988.

Bordonove, Georges. *Les Lances de Jérusalem.* Paris: Editions Pygmalion, 1994.

_____. *La Vie Quotidienne des Templiers au XIIIe Siècle.* Paris: Hachette, 1975.

Carpentier J., and Lebrun F. *Histoire de France.* Paris: Editions du Seuil, 1987.

Chedeville, André. *La France au Moyen Age.* Paris: Presses Universitaires de France, 1969.

Corvisier, André. *Dictionnaire d'Art et d'Histoire Militaires.* Paris: Presses Universitaires de France, 1988.

Demurger, Alain. *Brève Histoire des Ordres Religieux Militaires.* Gavaudun: Editions Fragile, 1997.

_____. *Vie et Mort de l'Ordre du Temple.* Paris: Editions Seuil, 1989.

Destrée, A. *Histoire des Techniques.* Brusselles: Editions Meddens, 1980.

D'Haucourt, Geneviève. *La Vie au Moyen Age.* Paris: Presses Universitaires de France, 1987.

Dollinger, Philippe. *La Hanse.* Paris: Editions Montaigne, 1964.

Dubois, Jacques. *Les Ordres Monastiques.* Paris: Presses Universitaires de France, 1993.

Dudley, Donald. *Roman Society.* Harmondsworth: Penguin Books, 1975.

Du Puy de Clinchamps, Philippe. *La Chevalerie.* Paris: Presses Universitaires de France, 1961.

Eyre, A.G. *An Outline History of England.* Harlow: Langman Pub., 1971.

Faure, Paul. *La Renaissance.* Paris: Presses Universitaires de France, 1949.

Flori, Jean. *La Chevalerie en France au Moyen Age.* Paris: Presses Universitaires de France, 1995.

Fouquet-Lapar, Philippe. *Histoire de l'Armée Française.* Paris: Presses Universitaires de France, 1986.

Funcken, Liliane, and Fred Funcken. *Le Costume et les Armes des Soldats de Tous les Temps.* Paris: Editions Casterman, 1966.

Gautier, Léon. *La Chevalerie.* Paris: Editions Arthaud, 1959.

Genicot, Léopold, and Houssiau, Pierre. *Le Moyen Age.* Paris: Presses Universitaires de France, 1959.

Griess, Thomas E. *Ancient and Medieval Warfare.* Wayne: Avery Pub. Group, 1984.

Grousset, René. *L'Epopée des Croisades.* Paris: Poche Editions Plon, 1939.

Harmand, Jacques. *La Guerre Antique.* Paris: Presses Universitaires de France, 1973.

Heer, Friedrich. *The medieval World.* London: Cardinal Pub., 1974.

Jacquart, Jean. *François Ier.* Paris: Editions Fayard, 1981.

Jansen, H.P.H. *Middeleeuwse Geschiedenis der Nederlanden.* Utrecht: Uitgeverij Prisma, 1965.

Jusserand, Nicole. *La France Médiévale.* Paris: Editions Gallimart, 1997.

Laporte, Michel. *Lexique des Rois de France.* Paris: Editions Fontaine du Roi, 1989.

Laspina, Mgr. S. *Outline of Maltese History.* Valetta: Aquilina, 1971.

Lepage, Jean-Denis. *Castles and Fortified Cities of Medieval Europe.* Jefferson, N.C.: McFarland, 2002.

Lot, Ferdinand. *La Fin du Monde Antique et le Début du Moyen Age.* Paris: Presses Universitaires de France, 1927.

Martin, Paul. *Armes et Armures.* Fribourg: Editions Office du Livre, 1967.

Maurois, André. *Histoire d'Angleterre.* Paris: Editions Fayard, 1937.

McDowal, David. *An Illustrated History of Britain.* Harlow: Langman, 1989.

Miller, Douglas. *Die Landsknechte.* Bonn: Wehr & Wissen Verlag, 1976.

Miquel, Pierre. *Histoire de la France.* Paris: Editions Marabout Histoire Fayard, 1976.

Morrisson, Cécile. *Les Croisades.* Paris: Presses Universitaires de France, 1969.

Newark, Tim. *Celtic Warriors.* London: Blandford Press, 1986.

Pernoud, Régine. *Les Templiers.* Paris: Presses Universitaires de France, 1974.

Reid, William. *Les Armes.* Fribourg: Editions Hatier, 1984.

Seward, Desmond. *The Monks of War.* Bungay: Chaucer Press Ltd, 1972.

Simmons Sue. *The Military Horse.* London: Cavendish Books, 1984.

Sloot, R.B.F. v.d. *Middeleeuws Wapentuig.* Bussum: Van Dishoek Uitgeverij, 1964.

Suret-Canale, Jean. *Panorama de l'Histoire Mondiale.* Paris: Editions J.P. Gisserot, 1996.

Thiriet, Freddy. *Histoire de Venise.* Paris: Presses Universitaires de France, 1969.

Toomaspoeg, Kristjan. *Histoire des Chevaliers Teutoniques.* Paris: Editions Flammarion, 2001.

Vercauteren, F. *L'Europe, Histoire et Culture.* Bruxelles: Editions Meddens, 1972.

Vlamynck, Maria. *Het Beleg van Niewpoort.* Antwerp: Mercurius Uitgeverij, 1977.

Volkman, Jean-Charles. *Chronologie de l'Histoire.* Paris: Editions J.P Gisserot, 1999.

Voogd, Christophe de. *Histoire des Pays-Bas.* Paris: Editions Hatier, 1992.

Wenzler, Claude. *The Kings of France.* Rennes: Editions Ouest-France, 1995.

Index